Belize & Guatemala

Fodor's Travel Publications, Inc.
New York • Toronto • London • Sydney • Auckland
http://www.fodors.com/

Fodor's Belize & Guatemala

Editor: Andrea E. Lehman

Editorial Contributors: Patricia Alisau, Robert Andrews, Jacob Bernstein, Bob Blake, Judy Blumenberg, David Brown, David Dudenhoefer, Audra Epstein, John Mitchem, Richard Nidever, Kate Pennebaker, Heidi Sarna, Helayne Schiff, Mary Ellen Schultz, M.T. Schwartzman, Dinah Spritzer, Simon Worrall

Creative Director: Fabrizio La Rocca

Associate Art Director: Guido Caroti

Photo Researcher: Jolie Novak

Cartographer: David Lindroth

Cover Photograph: Peter Guttman

Text Design: Between the Covers

Copyright

First Edition

ISBN 0–679–03309–2

Special Sales

Fodor's Travel Publications are available at special discounts for bulk purchases for sales promotions or premiums. Special editions, including personalized covers, excerpts of existing guides, and corporate imprints, can be created in large quantities for special needs. For more information contact your local bookseller or write to Special Marketing, Fodor's Travel Publications, 201 East 50th Street, New York, NY 10022. Inquiries from Canada should be directed to your local Canadian bookstore or sent to Random House of Canada, Ltd., Marketing Department, 1265 Aerowood Drive, Mississauga, Ontario L4W 1B9. Inquiries from the United Kingdom should be sent to Fodor's Travel Publications, 20 Vauxhall Bridge Road, London, England SW1V 2SA.

PRINTED IN THE UNITED STATES OF AMERICA

10 9 8 7 6 5 4 3 2 1

CONTENTS

Maps

ON THE ROAD WITH FODOR'S

WE'RE ALWAYS THRILLED to get letters from readers, especially one like this:

It took us an hour to decide what book to buy and we now know we picked the best one. Your book was wonderful, easy to follow, very accurate, and good on pointing out eating places, informal as well as formal. When we saw other people using your book, we would look at each other and smile.

Our editors and writers are deeply committed to making every Fodor's guide "the best one"—not only accurate but always charming, brimming with sound recommendations and solid ideas, right on the mark in describing restaurants and hotels, and full of fascinating facts that make you view what you've traveled to see in a rich new light.

About Our Writers

Our success in achieving our goals—and in helping to make your trip the best of all possible vacations—is a credit to the hard work of our extraordinary writers.

Brooklyn-born but Mexico City–based, **Patricia Alisau** cherishes her trips to Guatemala as much to delve into the soul of the people as to add to her collection of jade, which she says is charged with the essence of the Maya past. Spanish is her second language and trekking to pyramids her first love. She never tires of visiting Tikal. Her material has appeared in the *New York Times, Vogue, Time, Business Mexico,* and *Mexico City News,* among others.

David Dudenhoefer is a freelance hack who has spent the better part of the past decade in Central America. Based in San José, Costa Rica, he travels regularly within the isthmus, writing about everything from surfing to presidential summits. He is the author of *The Panama Traveler,* and is a regular Fodor's contributor. His favorite kind of writing, however, is graffiti and shopping lists, which he composes from the balmy calm of his San José home.

The husband-and-wife dream team of **Simon Worrall** and **Kate Pennebaker** worked long and hard to come up with the chapter on Belize. Simon Worrall is a British-born journalist whose long list of publishers includes, among others, *The Times* of London Sunday magazine, *The Observer, Geo, Islands,* and *Men's Journal.* Kate Pennebaker is a photographer, film-maker, and diver. Together they hiked through the jungle, swam with dolphins, and rode horseback trails. They had to separate for the diving, however, as only Kate is certified. The solution? When she surfaced, Simon was on hand with a tape recorder, waiting to debrief her.

New This Year

This year we've reformatted our guides to make them easier to use. Each chapter of *Belize & Guatemala* begins with brand-new recommended itineraries to help you decide what to see in the time you have; a section called When to Tour points out the optimal time of day, day of the week, and season for your journey. You may also notice our fresh graphics, new in 1996. More readable and more helpful than ever? We think so—and we hope you do, too.

Also check out Fodor's Web site (http://www.fodors.com/), where you'll find travel information on major destinations around the world and an ever-changing array of travel-savvy interactive features.

How to Use This Book

Organization

Up front is the **Gold Guide.** Its first section, **Important Contacts A to Z,** gives addresses and telephone numbers of organizations and companies that offer destination-related services and detailed information and publications. **Smart Travel Tips A to Z,** the Gold Guide's second section, gives specific information on how to accomplish what you need to in Belize and Guatemala as well as tips on savvy traveling. Both sections are in alphabetical order by topic.

Both Belize and Guatemala have their own chapter. Each country chapter is divided by geographical area; within each area, towns are covered in logical geographical order, and attractive stretches of road and minor points of interest between them are indicated by the designation *En Route*. Throughout, Off the Beaten Path sights appear after the places from which they are most easily accessible. And within town sections, all restaurants and lodgings are grouped together.

To help you decide what to visit in the time you have, chapters begin with recommended itineraries; you can mix and match those from each chapter to create a complete vacation. The A to Z section that ends each chapter covers getting there, getting around, and helpful contacts and resources.

At the end of the book you'll find Portraits, wonderful essays about natural resources in Central America and Maya ruins in Belize, followed by suggestions for pretrip reading, both fiction and nonfiction.

Icons and Symbols

★ Our special recommendations
✕ Restaurant
🏠 Lodging establishment
✕🏠 Lodging establishment whose restaurant warrants a detour
⚠ Camping facilities
☻ Rubber duckie (good for kids)
☞ Sends you to another section of the guide for more info
✉ Address
☎ Telephone number
FAX Fax number
☉ Opening and closing times
💲 Admission prices (those we give apply only to adults; substantially reduced fees are almost always available for children, students, and senior citizens)

Numbers in black and white circles—②and ❷, for example—that appear on the maps, in the margins, and within the tours correspond to one another.

The restaurants and lodgings we list are the cream of the crop in each price range. Price charts appear in the Pleasures and Pastimes section that follows each chapter introduction.

Hotel Facilities

We always list the facilities that are available—but we don't specify whether they cost extra: When pricing accommodations, always ask what's included.

Assume that hotels operate on the **European Plan** (EP, with no meals) unless we note that they use the **Full American Plan** (FAP, with all meals), the **Modified American Plan** (MAP, with breakfast and dinner daily), the **Continental Plan** (CP, with a Continental breakfast daily), or are **all-inclusive** (all meals and most activities).

Restaurant Reservations and Dress Codes

Reservations are always a good idea; we note only when they're essential or when they are not accepted. Book as far ahead as you can, and reconfirm when you get to town. Unless otherwise noted, the restaurants listed are open daily for lunch and dinner. We mention dress only when men are required to wear a jacket or a jacket and tie. Look for an overview of local habits in the Pleasures and Pastimes section that follows each chapter introduction.

Credit Cards

The following abbreviations are used: **AE**, American Express; **D**, Discover; **DC**, Diners Club; **MC**, MasterCard; and **V**, Visa.

Don't Forget to Write

You can use this book in the confidence that all prices and opening times are based on information supplied to us at press time; Fodor's cannot accept responsibility for any errors. Time inevitably brings changes, so always confirm information when it matters—especially if you're making a detour to visit a specific place. In addition, when making reservations be sure to mention if you have a disability or are traveling with children, if you prefer a private bath or a certain type of bed, or if you have specific dietary needs or any other concerns.

Were the restaurants we recommended as described? Did our hotel picks exceed your expectations? Did you find a museum we recommended a waste of time? If you have complaints, we'll look into them and revise our entries when the facts warrant it. If you've discovered a special place that we haven't included, we'll pass the information along to our correspondents and have them check it out. So send your feedback, positive *and* negative, to the Belize and Guatemala Editor at 201 East 50th Street, New York, New York 10022—and have a wonderful trip!

Karen Cure

Karen Cure
Editorial Director

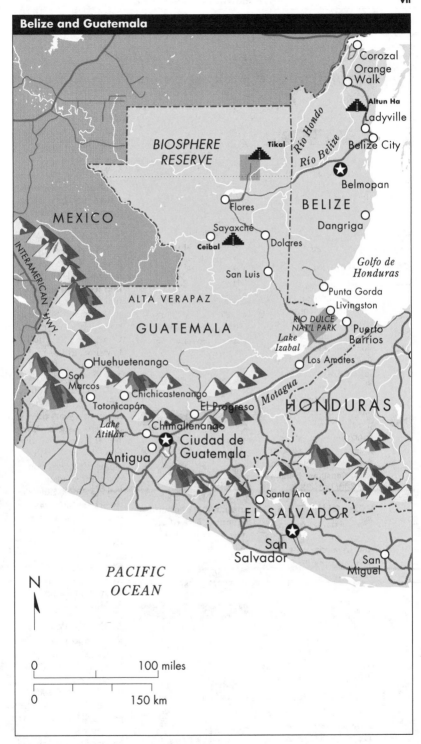

Belize and Guatemala

MEXICO

BIOSPHERE RESERVE

INTERAMERICAN HWY.

ALTA VERAPAZ

GUATEMALA

Huehuetenango

San Marcos

Totonicapán

Chichicastenango

Lake Atitlán

Chimaltenango

Antigua

Ciudad de Guatemala

El Progreso

Tikal

Río Hondo

Río Belize

Flores

Sayaxché

Ceibal

Dolores

San Luis

Corozal

Orange Walk

Altun Ha

Ladyville

Belize City

BELIZE

Belmopan

Dangriga

Golfo de Honduras

Punta Gorda

Livingston

RÍO DULCE NAT'L PARK

Lake Izabal

Puerto Barrios

Los Amates

Motagua

HONDURAS

Santa Ana

EL SALVADOR

San Salvador

San Miguel

N

PACIFIC OCEAN

0   100 miles

0   150 km

IMPORTANT CONTACTS A TO Z

An Alphabetical Listing of Publications, Organizations, & Companies that Will Help You Before, During, & After Your Trip

A

AIR TRAVEL

For information on airports, airlines, and flying times, *see* Arriving and Departing *in* Belize A to Z (Chapter 3) and *in* Guatemala A to Z (Chapter 4).

COMPLAINTS

To register complaints about charter and scheduled airlines, contact the U.S. Department of Transportation's **Aviation Consumer Protection Division** (✉ C-75, Washington, DC 20590, ☎ 202/366–2220). Complaints about lost baggage or ticketing problems and safety concerns may also be logged with the **Federal Aviation Administration (FAA) Consumer Hotline** (☎ 800/322–7873).

CONSOLIDATORS

For the names of reputable air-ticket consolidators, contact the **United States Air Consolidators Association** (✉ 925 L St., Suite 220, Sacramento, CA 95814, ☎ 916/441–4166, FAX 916/441–3520). For discount air-ticketing agencies, *see* Discounts & Deals, *below.*

PUBLICATIONS

For general information about charter carriers, ask for the Department of Transportation's free brochure **"Plane Talk: Public Charter Flights"** (✉ Aviation Consumer Protection Division, C-75, Washington, DC 20590, ☎ 202/366–2220). The Department of Transportation also publishes a 58-page booklet, **"Fly Rights,"** available from the Consumer Information Center (✉ Supt. of Documents, Dept. 136C, Pueblo, CO 81009; $1.75).

For other tips, consult the Consumers Union's monthly **"Consumer Reports Travel Letter"** (✉ Box 53629, Boulder, CO 80322, ☎ 800/234–1970; $39 1st year).

B

BETTER BUSINESS BUREAU

For local contacts in the hometown of a tour operator you may be considering, consult the **Council of Better Business Bureaus** (✉ 4200 Wilson Blvd., Suite 800, Arlington, VA 22203, ☎ 703/276–0100, FAX 703/525–8277).

C

CAR RENTAL

For information on agencies, *see* Car Rentals *under* Contacts and Resources *in* the last section of individual country chapters.

RENTAL WHOLESALERS

Contact **Auto Europe** (☎ 207/828–2525 or 800/223–5555).

CHILDREN & TRAVEL

FLYING

Look into **"Flying with Baby"** (✉ Third Street Press, Box 261250, Littleton, CO 80163, ☎ 303/595–5959; $4.95 includes shipping), cowritten by a flight attendant. **"Kids and Teens in Flight,"** free from the U.S. Department of Transportation's Aviation Consumer Protection Division (✉ C-75, Washington, DC 20590, ☎ 202/366–2220), offers tips on children flying alone. Every two years the February issue of *Family Travel Times* (☞ Know-How, *below*) details children's services on three dozen airlines. **"Flying Alone, Handy Advice for Kids Traveling Solo"** is available free from the American Automobile Association (AAA); send legal-size SASE: (✉ Flying Alone, Mail Stop 800, 1000 AAA Dr., Heathrow, FL 32746).

KNOW-HOW

Family Travel Times, published quarterly by Travel with Your Children (✉ 40 5th Ave., New York, NY 10011, ☎ 212/477–5524; $40 per year), covers destinations, types of vacations, and modes of travel.

TOUR OPERATORS

Contact **Rascals in Paradise** (✉ 650 5th

St., Suite 505, San Francisco, CA 94107, ☎ 415/978–9800 or 800/872–7225).

If you're outdoorsy, look into the family adventure tours, ranches, and lodges of **American Wilderness Experience** (✉ Box 1486, Boulder, CO 80306, ☎ 303/444–2622 or 800/444–0099), the **American Museum of Natural History** (✉ 79th St. and Central Park West, New York, NY 10024, ☎ 212/769–5700 or 800/462–8687), and **Wildland Adventures** (✉ 3516 N.E. 155th St., Seattle, WA 98155, ☎ 206/365–0686 or 800/345–4453).

CUSTOMS

IN THE U.S.

The **U.S. Customs Service** (✉ Box 7407, Washington, DC 20044, ☎ 202/927–6724) can answer questions on duty-free limits and publishes a helpful brochure, **"Know Before You Go."** For information on registering foreign-made articles, call 202/927–0540 or write U.S. Customs Service (✉ Resource Management, 1301 Constitution Ave. NW, Washington, DC 20229).

COMPLAINTS➤ Note the inspector's badge number and write to the commissioner's office (✉ 1301 Constitution Ave. NW, Washington, DC 20229).

IN CANADA

Contact **Revenue Canada** (✉ 2265 St. Laurent Blvd. S, Ottawa, Ontario K1G 4K3, ☎ 613/993–0534) for a copy of the free brochure **"I Declare/**

Je Déclare" and for details on duty-free limits. For recorded information (within Canada only), call 800/461–9999.

IN THE U.K.

HM Customs and Excise (✉ Dorset House, Stamford St., London SE1 9NG, ☎ 0171/202–4227) can answer questions about U.K. customs regulations and publishes a free pamphlet, **"A Guide for Travellers,"** detailing standard procedures and import rules.

D

DISABILITIES & ACCESSIBILITY

COMPLAINTS

To register complaints under the provisions of the Americans with Disabilities Act, contact the U.S. Department of Justice's **Disability Rights Section** (✉ Box 66738, Washington, DC 20035, ☎ 202/514–0301 or 800/514–0301, FAX 202/307–1198, TTY 202/514–0383 or 800/514–0383). For airline-related problems, contact the U.S. Department of Transportation's **Aviation Consumer Protection Division** (☞ Air Travel, *above*). For complaints about surface transportation, contact the Department of Transportation's **Civil Rights Office** (✉ 400 7th St. SW, Room 10215, Washington, DC 20590, ☎ 202/366–4648).

ORGANIZATIONS

TRAVELERS WITH HEARING IMPAIRMENTS➤ The **American Academy of Otolaryngology** (✉ 1 Prince St., Alexandria, VA 22314, ☎ 703/836–4444, FAX 703/

683–5100, TTY 703/519–1585) publishes a brochure, **"Travel Tips for Hearing Impaired People."**

TRAVELERS WITH MOBILITY PROBLEMS➤ **Mobility International USA** (✉ Box 10767, Eugene, OR 97440, ☎ and TTY 541/343–1284, FAX 541/343–6812), the U.S. branch of a Belgium-based organization (☞ *below*) with affiliates in 30 countries; **MossRehab Hospital Travel Information Service** (☎ 215/456–9600, TTY 215/456–9602), a telephone information resource for travelers with physical disabilities; the **Society for the Advancement of Travel for the Handicapped** (✉ 347 5th Ave., Suite 610, New York, NY 10016, ☎ 212/447–7284, FAX 212/725–8253; membership $45); and **Travelin' Talk** (✉ Box 3534, Clarksville, TN 37043, ☎ 615/552–6670, FAX 615/552–1182), which provides local contacts worldwide for travelers with disabilities.

TRAVELERS WITH VISION IMPAIRMENTS➤ Contact the **American Council of the Blind** (✉ 1155 15th St. NW, Suite 720, Washington, DC 20005, ☎ 202/467–5081, FAX 202/467–5085) for a list of travelers' resources or the **American Foundation for the Blind** (✉ 11 Penn Plaza, Suite 300, New York, NY 10001, ☎ 212/502–7600 or 800/232–5463, TTY 212/502–7662), which provides general advice and publishes *Access to Art* ($19.95), a directory of museums that accommodate travelers with vision impairments.

THE GOLD GUIDE / IMPORTANT CONTACTS

IN THE U.K.

Contact the **Royal Association for Disability and Rehabilitation** (✉ 12 City Forum, 250 City Rd., London EC1V 8AF, ☎ 0171/250–3222) or **Mobility International** (✉ rue de Manchester 25, B-1080 Brussels, Belgium, ☎ 00–322–410–6297, FAX 00–322–410–6874), a travel-information clearinghouse for people with disabilities.

LOCAL INFORMATION

For information on facilities in Belize, contact the **Central American Information Center** (✉ Box 50211, San Diego, CA 92105, ☎ 619/262–6489). In Guatemala, contact **INGUAT** (✉ 7 Avenida 1–17, Zona 4, ☎ 331–1339 or 331–1333).

PUBLICATIONS

Several publications for travelers with disabilities are available from the **Consumer Information Center** (✉ Box 100, Pueblo, CO 81009, ☎ 719/948–3334). Call or write for its free catalog. The Society for the Advancement of Travel for the Handicapped (☞ Organizations, *above*) publishes the quarterly magazine *Access to Travel* ($13 for 1-year subscription).

The 500-page *Travelin' Talk Directory* (✉ Box 3534, Clarksville, TN 37043, ☎ 615/552–6670, FAX 615/552–1182; $35) lists people and organizations who help travelers with disabilities. For travel agents worldwide, consult the *Directory of Travel Agencies for the Disabled* (✉ Twin Peaks Press, Box 129, Van-

couver, WA 98666, ☎ 360/694–2462 or 800/637–2256, FAX 360/696–3210; $19.95 plus $3 shipping).

TRAVEL AGENCIES & TOUR OPERATORS

The Americans with Disabilities Act requires that all travel firms serve the needs of all travelers. That said, you should note that some agencies and operators specialize in making arrangements for travelers with disabilities, among them **Access Adventures** (✉ 206 Chestnut Ridge Rd., Rochester, NY 14624, ☎ 716/889–9096), run by a former physical-rehab counselor.

TRAVELERS WITH MOBIL-ITY PROBLEMS➤ Contact **Hinsdale Travel Service** (✉ 201 E. Ogden Ave., Suite 100, Hinsdale, IL 60521, ☎ 708/325–1335), a travel agency that benefits from the advice of wheelchair traveler Janice Perkins, and **Wheelchair Journeys** (✉ 16979 Redmond Way, Redmond, WA 98052, ☎ 206/885–2210 or 800/313–4751), which can handle arrangements worldwide.

TRAVELERS WITH DEVEL-OPMENTAL DISABILITIES➤ Contact the nonprofit **New Directions** (✉ 5276 Hollister Ave., Suite 207, Santa Barbara, CA 93111, ☎ 805/967–2841).

TRAVEL GEAR

The **Magellan's** catalog (☎ 800/962–4943, FAX 805/568–5406) includes a section devoted to products for travelers with disabilities.

AIRFARES

For the lowest airfares to Belize and Guatemala, call 800/FLY–4–LESS.

CLUBS

Contact **Entertainment Travel Editions** (✉ Box 1068, Trumbull, CT 06611, ☎ 800/445–4137; $28–$53, depending on destination), **Great American Traveler** (✉ Box 27965, Salt Lake City, UT 84127, ☎ 800/548–2812; $49.95 per year), **Moment's Notice Discount Travel Club** (✉ 7301 New Utrecht Ave., Brooklyn, NY 11204, ☎ 718/234–6295; $25 per year, single or family), **Privilege Card** (✉ 3391 Peachtree Rd. NE, Suite 110, Atlanta, GA 30326, ☎ 404/262–0222 or 800/236–9732; $74.95 per year), **Travelers Advantage** (✉ CUC Travel Service, 49 Music Sq. W, Nashville, TN 37203, ☎ 800/548–1116 or 800/648–4037; $49 per year, single or family), or **Worldwide Discount Travel Club** (✉ 1674 Meridian Ave., Miami Beach, FL 33139, ☎ 305/534–2082; $50 per year for family, $40 single).

STUDENTS

Members of Hostelling International–American Youth Hostels (☞ Students, *below*) are eligible for discounts on car rentals, admissions to attractions, and other selected travel expenses.

PUBLICATIONS

Consult *The Frugal Globetrotter,* by Bruce Northam (✉ Fulcrum

Publishing, 350 Indiana St., Suite 350, Golden, CO 80401, ☎ 800/992-2908; $16.95 plus $4 shipping). For publications that tell how to find the lowest prices on plane tickets, *see* Air Travel, *above*.

G

GAY & LESBIAN TRAVEL

ORGANIZATIONS

The **International Gay Travel Association** (✉ Box 4974, Key West, FL 33041, ☎ 800/448-8550, FAX 305/296-6633), a consortium of more than 1,000 travel companies, can supply names of gay-friendly travel agents, tour operators, and accommodations.

PUBLICATIONS

The 16-page monthly newsletter **"Out & About"** (✉ 8 W. 19th St., Suite 401, New York, NY 10011, ☎ 212/645-6922 or 800/929-2268, FAX 800/929-2215; $49 for 10 issues and quarterly calendar) covers gay-friendly hotels, cruise lines, and airlines.

TOUR OPERATORS

Toto Tours (✉ 1326 W. Albion Ave., Suite 3W, Chicago, IL 60626, ☎ 312/274-8686 or 800/565-1241, FAX 312/274-8695) offers group tours to worldwide destinations.

TRAVEL AGENCIES

The largest agencies serving gay travelers are **Advance Travel** (✉ 10700 Northwest Fwy., Suite 160, Houston, TX 77092, ☎ 713/682-2002 or 800/292-0500), **Club Travel** (✉ 8739 Santa Monica Blvd., W. Hollywood, CA 90069, ☎ 310/358-2200 or 800/429-8747), **Islanders/Kennedy Travel** (✉ 183 W. 10th St., New York, NY 10014, ☎ 212/242-3222 or 800/988-1181), **Now Voyager** (✉ 4406 18th St., San Francisco, CA 94114, ☎ 415/626-1169 or 800/255-6951), and **Yellowbrick Road** (✉ 1500 W. Balmoral Ave., Chicago, IL 60640, ☎ 312/561-1800 or 800/642-2488). **Skylink Women's Travel** (✉ 2460 W. 3rd St., Suite 215, Santa Rosa, CA 95401, ☎ 707/570-0105 or 800/225-5759) serves lesbian travelers.

H

HEALTH

FINDING A DOCTOR

For its members, the **International Association for Medical Assistance to Travellers** (✉ IAMAT; 417 Center St., Lewiston, NY 14092, ☎ 716/754-4883; 40 Regal Rd., Guelph, Ontario N1K 1B5, ☎ 519/836-0102; 1287 St. Clair Ave. W, Toronto, Ontario M6E 1B8, ☎ 416/652-0137; 57 Voirets, 1212 Grand-Lancy, Geneva, Switzerland, no phone; membership free) publishes a worldwide directory of English-speaking physicians meeting IAMAT standards.

MEDICAL ASSISTANCE COMPANIES

The following companies are concerned primarily with emergency medical assistance, although they may provide some insurance as part of their coverage. For a list of full-service travel insurance companies, *see* Insurance, *below*.

Contact **International SOS Assistance** (✉ Box 11568, Philadelphia, PA 19116, ☎ 215/244-1500 or 800/523-8930; Box 466, Pl. Bonaventure, Montréal, Québec H5A 1C1, ☎ 514/874-7674 or 800/363-0263; 7 Old Lodge Pl., St. Margarets, Twickenham TW1 1RQ, England, ☎ 0181/744-0033), **Medex Assistance Corporation** (✉ Box 5375, Timonium, MD 21094-5375, ☎ 410/453-6300 or 800/537-2029), **Traveler's Emergency Network** (✉ 1133 15th St. NW, Suite 400, Washington DC, 20005, ☎ 202/828-5894 or 800/275-4836, FAX 202/828-5896), **TravMed** (✉ Box 5375, Timonium, MD 21094, ☎ 410/453-6380 or 800/732-5309), or **Worldwide Assistance Services** (✉ 1133 15th St. NW, Suite 400, Washington, DC 20005, ☎ 202/331-1609 or 800/821-2828, FAX 202/828-5896).

PUBLICATIONS

The Safe Travel Book (✉ Jossey-Bass Publishers, Inc., 350 Sansome St., San Francisco, CA 94104 ☎ 800/956-7739, FAX 800/605-2665; $12.95 plus $5 shipping), by Peter Savage.

WARNINGS

The hot line of the **National Centers for Disease Control** (✉ CDC, National Center for Infectious Diseases, Division of Quarantine, Traveler's Health Section, 1600 Clifton Rd.,

M/S E-03, Atlanta, GA 30333, ☎ 404/332–4559, FAX 404/332–4565) provides information on health risks abroad and vaccination requirements and recommendations. You can call for a menu of recorded information or use the fax-back service to get printed matter.

I
INSURANCE

IN THE U.S.

Travel insurance covering baggage, health, and trip cancellation or interruptions is available from **Access America** (✉ 6600 W. Broad St., Richmond, VA 23230, ☎ 804/285–3300 or 800/334–7525), **Carefree Travel Insurance** (✉ Box 9366, 100 Garden City Plaza, Garden City, NY 11530, ☎ 516/294–0220 or 800/323–3149), **Near Travel Services** (✉ Box 1339, Calumet City, IL 60409, ☎ 708/868–6700 or 800/654–6700), **Tele-Trip** (✉ Mutual of Omaha Plaza, Box 31716, Omaha, NE 68131, ☎ 800/228–9792), **Travel Guard International** (✉ 1145 Clark St., Stevens Point, WI 54481, ☎ 715/345–0505 or 800/826–1300), **Travel Insured International** (✉ Box 280568, East Hartford, CT 06128, ☎ 203/528–7663 or 800/243–3174), and **Wallach & Company** (✉ 107 W. Federal St., Box 480, Middleburg, VA 22117, ☎ 540/687–3166 or 800/237–6615).

IN CANADA

Contact **Mutual of Omaha** (✉ Travel Division, 500 University Ave., Toronto,

Ontario M5G 1V8, ☎ 416/598-4083 or 800/465–0267).

IN THE U.K.

The **Association of British Insurers** (✉ 51 Gresham St., London EC2V 7HQ, ☎ 0171/600–3333) gives advice by phone and publishes the free pamphlet **"Holiday Insurance and Motoring Abroad,"** which sets out typical policy provisions and costs.

L
LODGING

APARTMENT & VILLA RENTAL

Among the companies to contact are **Property Rentals International** (✉ 1008 Mansfield Crossing Rd., Richmond, VA 23236, ☎ 804/378–6054 or 800/220–3332, FAX 804/379–2073), **Rent-a-Home International** (✉ 7200 34th Ave. NW, Seattle, WA 98117, ☎ 206/789–9377 or 800/488–7368, FAX 206/789–9379), **Vacation Home Rentals Worldwide** (✉ 235 Kensington Ave., Norwood, NJ 07648, ☎ 201/767–9393 or 800/633–3284, FAX 201/767–5510), and **Villas International** (✉ 605 Market St., Suite 510, San Francisco, CA 94105, ☎ 415/281–0910 or 800/221–2260, FAX 415/281–0919). Members of the travel club **Hideaways International** (✉ 767 Islington St., Portsmouth, NH 03801, ☎ 603/430–4433 or 800/843–4433, FAX 603/430–4444; $99 per year) receive two annual guides plus quarterly newsletters and arrange rentals among themselves.

M
MAIL

SENDING MAIL

FROM BELIZE➤ Belizean mail service is excellent, and the stamps, mostly of wildlife, are beautiful. An airmail letter takes about a week to the States. Parcels have to be standard, wrapped in brown paper, and, if you are in Belize City, sent from a **special post office** (✉ Church St., next to BTL offices), open Monday–Thursday 8–noon and 1–4:30, Friday 8–noon and 1–4.

FROM GUATEMALA➤ Letters to the U.S. take one–two weeks, slightly longer to Canada and the U.K. Postage is inexpensive; a letter to the States costs 30 centavos, and it's 1 quetzal to the U.K. For packages, it's safer to use a major shipping service like **UPS** (✉ 4 Calle 6–56, Zona 9, Guatemala City, ☎ 331–2421) or a smaller service like **Quick Shopping** (✉ 6a Calle Poniente 27, Antigua, ☎ 332–0697). Avoid express-mail services common in the capital. If you have to send something fast, use **DHL** (✉ 7 Avenida 2–42, Zona 9, Guatemala City, ☎ 332–3023), which is expensive but efficient.

RECEIVING MAIL

IN BELIZE➤ You can receive mail sent Poste Restante at the **main post office** (✉ Front St., at northern edge of swing bridge, Belize City, ☎ 027/2201), where it will be kept for at least a month (you will need a passport or other ID to pick it up). The post office is open Monday–Thursday 8–5 and Friday 8–4:30. **American Express** (✉ Belize Global Travel, 41 Albert St., Belize City, ☎ 027/ 7363) handles mail for cardholders free of charge.

IN GUATEMALA➤ Travelers can receive mail addressed to Poste Restante Guatemala at the **main post office** (✉ Correos Central, 12 Calle between 7 and 8 avenidas, Zona 1, Guatemala City, no phone). American Express cardholders or traveler's-check holders can use the **American Express office** (✉ Avenida La Reforma 9–00, Zona 9, Guatemala City, ☎ 331– 1311); you must show your card or check when you pick up your mail.

MONEY

ATMS

For specific foreign **Cirrus** locations, call 800/424–7787; for foreign **Plus** locations, consult the Plus directory at your local bank.

CURRENCY EXCHANGE

If your bank doesn't exchange currency, contact **Thomas Cook Currency Services** (☎ 800/287–7362 for locations). **Ruesch International** (☎ 800/ 424–2923 for locations) can also provide you with foreign banknotes before you leave home and publishes many useful brochures, including a **"Foreign Currency Guide"** and **"Foreign Exchange Tips."**

WIRING FUNDS

Funds can be wired via **MoneyGram℠** (for locations and information in the U.S. and Canada, ☎ 800/926– 9400) or **Western Union** (for agent locations or to send money using MasterCard or Visa, ☎ 800/325–6000; in Canada, 800/321– 2923; in the U.K., 0800/833833; or visit the Western Union office at the nearest major post office).

P

PACKING

For strategies on packing light, get a copy of **The Packing Book** (✉ Ten Speed Press, Box 7123, Berkeley, CA 94707, ☎ 510/559– 1600 or 800/841–2665, FAX 510/524–4588; $7.95 plus $3.50 shipping), by Judith Gilford.

PASSPORTS & VISAS

IN THE U.S.

For fees, documentation requirements, and other information, call the State Department's **Office of Passport Services** information line (☎ 202/647– 0518). Application forms for both first-time and renewal passports are available at the 13 U.S. Passport Agency offices and at some post offices and courthouses. Passports are usually mailed within four weeks, five weeks or more in spring and summer.

For more information, contact the **Belize Embassy** (✉ 2535 Massachusetts Ave. NW, Washington, DC 20008, ☎ 202/332– 9636, FAX 202/332–

6880). To obtain a visa, valid for one year, contact the **Guatemalan Embassy** (✉ 2220 R St. NW, Washington, DC 20008, ☎ 202/745– 4952) or the nearest consulate, located in New York, Miami, Houston, San Diego, and Los Angeles.

IN CANADA

For fees, documentation requirements, and other information, call the Ministry of Foreign Affairs and International Trade's **Passport Office** (☎ 819/994–3500 or 800/567–6868). Passport application forms are available at 28 regional passport offices, as well as post offices and travel agencies. Whether for a first or a renewal passport, you must apply in person. Children under 16 may be included on a parent's passport but must have their own to travel alone. Passports are valid for five years and are usually mailed within two to three weeks of application.

IN THE U.K.

For fees, documentation requirements, and to request an emergency passport, call the **London Passport Office** (☎ 0990/210410). Applications for new and renewal passports are available from main post offices and at the passport offices in Belfast, Glasgow, Liverpool, London, Newport, and Peterborough. You may apply in person at all passport offices or by mail to all except the London office. Children under 16 may travel on an accompanying parent's passport. All passports

THE GOLD GUIDE / IMPORTANT CONTACTS

are valid for 10 years. Allow a month for processing.

For visa forms, contact the **Guatemalan Embassy** (⊠ 13 Fawcett St., London SW 10 9HN, ☎ 0171/351–3042).

IN GUATEMALA

If you want to extend or replace a lost tourist card or visa, contact the **Immigration Office** (⊠ 41 Calle 17–36, Zona 8, Guatemala City, ☎ 371–4670).

PHOTO HELP

The **Kodak Information Center** (☎ 800/242–2424) answers consumer questions about film and photography. The *Kodak Guide to Shooting Great Travel Pictures* (available in bookstores; or contact Fodor's Travel Publications, ☎ 800/533–6478; $16.50 plus $4 shipping) explains how to take expert photos.

S
SAFETY

"Trouble-Free Travel," from AAA, is a booklet of tips for protecting yourself and your belongings when away from home. Send a legal-size SASE to Trouble-Free Travel (⊠ Mail Stop 75, 1000 AAA Dr., Heathrow, FL 32746).

SENIOR CITIZENS

EDUCATIONAL TRAVEL

Interhostel (⊠ University of New Hampshire, 6 Garrison Ave., Durham, NH 03824, ☎ 603/862–1147 or 800/733–9753), for travelers 50 and older, has two- to three-week trips; most last two weeks and cost

$2,000–$3,500, including airfare.

ORGANIZATIONS

Contact the **American Association of Retired Persons** (⊠ AARP, 601 E St. NW, Washington, DC 20049, ☎ 202/434–2277; annual dues $8 per person or couple). Its Purchase Privilege Program secures discounts on lodging, car rentals, and sightseeing.

Additional sources for discounts on lodgings, car rentals, and other travel expenses, as well as helpful magazines and newsletters, are the **National Council of Senior Citizens** (⊠ 1331 F St. NW, Washington, DC 20004, ☎ 202/347–8800; annual membership $12) and Sears's **Mature Outlook** (⊠ Box 10448, Des Moines, IA 50306, ☎ 800/336–6330; annual membership $14.95).

STUDENTS

HOSTELING

In the U.S., contact **Hostelling International– American Youth Hostels** (⊠ 733 15th St. NW, Suite 840, Washington, DC 20005, ☎ 202/783–6161, FAX 202/783–6171); in Canada, **Hostelling International– Canada** (⊠ 205 Catherine St., Suite 400, Ottawa, Ontario K2P 1C3, ☎ 613/237–7884); and in the U.K., the **Youth Hostel Association of England and Wales** (⊠ Trevelyan House, 8 St. Stephen's Hill, St. Albans, Hertfordshire AL1 2DY, ☎ 01727/855215 or 01727/845047). Membership (in the U.S., $25; in Canada, C$26.75; in

the U.K., £9.30) gives you access to 5,000 hostels in 77 countries that charge $5–$40 per person per night.

ORGANIZATIONS

A major contact is the **Council on International Educational Exchange** (⊠ Mail orders only: CIEE, 205 E. 42nd St., 16th Floor, New York, NY 10017, ☎ 212/822–2600, info@ciee. org). The **Educational Travel Centre** (⊠ 438 N. Frances St., Madison, WI 53703, ☎ 608/256–5551 or 800/747–5551, FAX 608/256–2042) offers rail passes and low-cost airline tickets, mostly for flights that depart from Chicago.

In Canada, also contact **Travel Cuts** (⊠ 187 College St., Toronto, Ontario M5T 1P7, ☎ 416/979–2406 or 800/667–2887).

PUBLICATIONS

Check out the *Berkeley Guide to Central America* (available in bookstores; or contact Fodor's Travel Publications, ☎ 800/533–6478; $18.95 plus $4 shipping).

T
TOUR OPERATORS

Among the companies that sell tours and packages to Belize and Guatemala, the following are nationally known, have a proven reputation, and offer plenty of options.

GROUP TOURS

SUPER-DELUXE➤ **Abercrombie & Kent** (⊠ 1520 Kensington Rd., Oak Brook, IL 60521-2141, ☎ 708/954–

2944 or 800/323–7308, FAX 708/954–3324) and **Travcoa** (✉ Box 2630, 2350 S.E. Bristol St., Newport Beach, CA 92660, ☎ 714/476–2800 or 800/992–2003, FAX 714/476–2538).

DELUXE➣ **Globus** (✉ 5301 S. Federal Circle, Littleton, CO 80123-2980, ☎ 303/797–2800 or 800/221–0090, FAX 303/795–0962).

FIRST-CLASS➣ **Brendan Tours** (✉ 15137 Califa St., Van Nuys, CA 91411, ☎ 818/785–9696 or 800/421–8446, FAX 818/902–9876) and **Maupintour** (✉ Box 807, 1515 St. Andrews Dr., Lawrence, KS 66047, ☎ 913/843–1211 or 800/255–4266, FAX 913/843–8351).

PACKAGES

Independent vacation packages are available from major tour operators and airlines. Contact **Adventure Vacations** (✉ 10612 Beaver Dam Rd., Hunt Valley, MD 21030-2205, ☎ 410/785–3500 or 800/638–9040, FAX 410/584–2771), **Armadillo Tours International** (✉ 4301 Westbank Dr., No. B360, Austin, TX 78746, ☎ 512/328–7800 or 800/284–5678), **Avanti Destinations** (✉ 851 S.W. 6th Ave., Portland, OR 97204, ☎ 503/295–1100 or 800/422–5053), **4th Dimension Tours** (✉ 7101 S.W. 99th Ave., No. 105, Miami, FL 33173, ☎ 305/279–0014 or 800/877–1525, FAX 305/273–9777), **Ladatco Tours** (✉ 2220 Coral Way, Miami, FL 33145, ☎ 305/854–8433 or 800/327–6162), **Mar-**

nella Tours (✉ 33 Walt Whitman Rd., Huntington Station, NY 11746, ☎ 516/271–6969 or 800/937–6999), **M.I.L.A.** (✉ 100 S. Greenleaf Ave., Gurnee, IL 60031-3378, ☎ 847/249–2111 or 800/367–7378, FAX 847/249–2772,), and **Sun Holidays** (✉ 26 6th St., No. 603, Stamford, CT 06905, ☎ 203/323–1166 or 800/243–2057). **Gogo Tours**, based in Ramsey, New Jersey, sells packages only through travel agents.

Regional operators specialize in packages for travelers in their local area and often feature nonstop flights. Arrangements may include charter or scheduled air. Contact **Friendly Holidays** (✉ 1983 Marcus Ave., Lake Success, NY 11042, ☎ 800/344–5687).

THEME TRIPS

ADVENTURE➣ Lengthy overland adventures are offered by **Adventure Center** (✉ 1311 63rd St., No. 200, Emeryville, CA 94608, ☎ 510/654–1879 or 800/227–8747, FAX 510/654–4200). **Himalayan Travel** (✉ 112 Prospect St., Stamford, CT 06901, ☎ 203/359–3711 or 800/225–2380, FAX 203/359–3669) operates a range of adventure tours. **Mountain Travel-Sobek** (✉ 6420 Fairmount Ave., El Cerrito, CA 94530, ☎ 510/527–8100 or 800/227–2384, FAX 510/525–7710,) has tours focused on Maya culture and Guatemalan festivals. Wildlife safaris are the focus of **Safari-centre** (✉ 3201 N. Sepulveda Blvd., Man-

hattan Beach, CA 90266, ☎ 310/546–4411 or 800/223–6046, FAX 310/546–3188). Exploration of Maya culture and ruins is combined with a river and camping expedition in tours operated by **Wilderness Travel** (✉ 801 Allston Way, Berkeley, CA 94710, ☎ 510/548–0420 or 800/368–2794, FAX 510/548–0347).

ART AND ARCHAEOLOGY➣ Contact the **Archaeological Conservancy** (✉ 5301 Central Ave. NE, No. 1218, Albuquerque, NM 87108-1517, ☎ 505/266–1540), a nonprofit educational organization, and **Far Horizons Archaeological & Cultural Trips** (✉ Box 91900, Albuquerque, NM 87199-1900, ☎ 505/343–9400 or 800/552–4575, FAX 505/343–8076).

FISHING➣ **Anglers Travel** (✉ 3100 Mill St., No. 206, Reno, NV 89502, ☎ 702/324–0580 or 800/624–8429, FAX 702/324–0583), **Cutting Loose Expeditions** (✉ Box 447, Winter Park, FL 32790-0447, ☎ 407/629–4700 or 800/533–4746), **Fishing International** (✉ Box 2132, Santa Rosa, CA 95405, ☎ 800/950–4242), and **Rod & Reel Adventures** (✉ 3507 Tully Rd., No. B6, Modesto, CA 95356-1052, ☎ 209/524–7775 or 800/356–6982, FAX 209/524–1220).

HEALTH➣ Contact **Spa-Finders** (✉ 91 5th Ave., No. 301, New York, NY 10003-3039, ☎ 212/924–6800 or 800/255–7727).

THE GOLD GUIDE / IMPORTANT CONTACTS

HORSEBACK RIDING➤ Contact **FITS Equestrian** (✉ 685 Lateen Rd., Solvang, CA 93463, ☎ 805/688–9494 or 800/ 666–3487, FAX 805/ 688–2943).

LEARNING➤ **Earthwatch** (✉ Box 403, 680 Mount Auburn St., Watertown, MA 02272, ☎ 617/926–8200 or 800/776–0188, FAX 617/ 926–8532) recruits volunteers to serve in its EarthCorps as short-term assistants to scientists on research expeditions. Contact **Nature Expeditions International** (✉ Box 11496, Eugene, OR 97440, ☎ 503/484– 6529 or 800/869–0639, FAX 503/484–6531), **Oceanic Society Expeditions** (✉ Fort Mason Center, Bldg. E, San Francisco, CA 94123-1394, ☎ 415/441– 1106 or 800/326–7491, FAX 415/474–3395), **Questers** (✉ 381 Park Ave. S, New York, NY 10016, ☎ 212/251– 0444 or 800/468–8668, FAX 212/251–0890), and **Smithsonian Study Tours and Seminars** (✉ 1100 Jefferson Dr. SW, Room 3045, MRC 702, Washington, DC 20560, ☎ 202/357–4700, FAX 202/633–9250).

SCUBA DIVING➤ Contact **Go Diving** (✉ 5610 Rowland Rd. No. 100, Minnetonka, MN 55343, ☎ 612/931– 9101 or 800/328–5285, FAX 612/931–0209), **Rothschild Dive Safaris** (✉ 900 West End Ave., No. 1B, New York, NY 10025-3525, ☎ 212/ 662–4858 or 800/359– 0747, FAX 212/749– 6172,) **See & Sea Travel Service** (✉ 50 Francisco St., No. 205, San Fran-

cisco, CA 94133, ☎ 415/434–3400 or 800/ 348–9778, FAX 415/ 434–3409), and **Tropical Adventures** (111 2nd Ave. N, Seattle, WA 98109, ☎ 206/441– 3483 or 800/247–3483, FAX 206/441–5431).

WALKING➤ **Backroads** (✉ 1516 5th St., Berkeley, CA 94710-1740, ☎ 510/527–1555 or 800/ 462–2848, FAX 510/ 527–1444) and **Butterfield & Robinson** (✉ 70 Bond St., Toronto, Ontario, Canada M5B 1X3, ☎ 416/864–1354 or 800/678–1147, FAX 416/864–0541) explore ancient Maya ruins as well as Belize's natural history.

YACHT CHARTERS➤ Contact **Ocean Voyages** (✉ 1709 Bridgeway, Sausalito, CA 94965, ☎ 415/332– 4681, FAX 415/332– 7460) for adventures at sea.

ORGANIZATIONS

The **National Tour Association** (✉ NTA, 546 E. Main St., Lexington, KY 40508, ☎ 606/ 226–4444 or 800/755– 8687) and the **United States Tour Operators Association** (✉ USTOA, 211 E. 51st St., Suite 12B, New York, NY 10022, ☎ 212/750– 7371) can provide lists of members and information on booking tours.

PUBLICATIONS

Contact the USTOA (☞ Organizations, *above*) for its **"Smart Traveler's Planning Kit."** Pamphlets in the kit include the "Worldwide Tour and Vacation Package Finder," "How to Select a Tour

or Vacation Package," and information on USTOA's consumer protection plan. Also get copy of the Better Business Bureau's **"Tips on Travel Packages"** (✉ Publication 24-195, 4200 Wilson Blvd., Arlington, VA 22203; $2).

For names of reputable agencies in your area, contact the **American Society of Travel Agents** (✉ ASTA, 1101 King St., Suite 200, Alexandria, VA 22314, ☎ 703/739–2782), the **Association of Canadian Travel Agents** (✉ Suite 201, 1729 Bank St., Ottawa, Ontario K1V 7Z5, ☎ 613/521–0474, FAX 613/521–0805), or the **Association of British Travel Agents** (✉ 55–57 Newman St., London W1P 4AH, ☎ 0171/ 637–2444, FAX 0171/ 637–0713).

For travel apparel, appliances, personal-care items, and other travel necessities, get a free catalog from **Magellan's** (☎ 800/ 962–4943, FAX 805/ 568–5406), **Orvis Travel** (☎ 800/541–3541, FAX 703/343–7053), or **TravelSmith** (☎ 800/ 950–1600, FAX 415/ 455–0554).

ELECTRICAL CONVERTERS

Send a self-addressed, stamped envelope to the **Franzus Company** (✉ Customer Service, Dept. B50, Murtha Industrial Park, Box 142, Beacon Falls, CT 06403, ☎ 203/723–6664) for a copy of the free brochure **"Foreign**

Electricity Is No Deep, Dark Secret."

U

U.S. GOVERNMENT TRAVEL BRIEFINGS

The U.S. Department of State's American Citizens Services office (⊠ Room 4811, Washington, DC 20520; enclose SASE) issues **Consular Information Sheets** on all foreign countries. These cover issues such as crime, security, political climate, and health risks as well as listing embassy locations, entry requirements, currency regulations, and providing other useful information. (Travel warnings that counsel travelers to avoid a country entirely are issued in extreme cases.) For the latest information, stop in at any U.S. passport office, consulate, or embassy; call the interactive hot line (☎ 202/647–5225, FAX 202/647–3000); or, with your PC's modem, tap into the department's computer bulletin board (☎ 202/647–9225).

V

VISITOR INFORMATION

IN THE U.S.

For information on Belize, contact the **Belize Tourist Board** (⊠ 421 7th Ave., Suite 701, New York, NY 10001, ☎ 212/563–6011, FAX 212/563–6033). For information on Guatemala, contact **INGUAT** (⊠ 299 Alhambra Circle, Suite 510, Coral Gables, FL 33134, ☎ 800/742–4529, FAX 305/442–1013).

IN CANADA

For information on Belize, contact the **Belize Tourist Board** (☞ *above*). For information on Guatemala, contact **SACA** (⊠ 72 McGill St., Toronto, Ontario M5B 1H2, ☎ 416/348–8597).

IN THE U.K.

For information on Belize, contact the **Belize High Commission** (⊠ 10 Harcourt House, 19A Cavendish Sq., London W1M 9AD, ☎ 071/499–9725). For Guatemalan information, see the **Guatemalan Embassy** (⊠ 13 Fawcett St., London SW 10 9HN, ☎ 0171/351–3042).

W

WEATHER

For current conditions and forecasts, plus the local time and helpful travel tips, call the **Weather Channel Connection** (☎ 900/932–8437; 95¢ per minute) from a Touch-Tone phone.

The *International Traveler's Weather Guide* (⊠ Weather Press, Box 660606, Sacramento, CA 95866, ☎ 916/974–0201 or 800/972–0201; $10.95 includes shipping), written by two meteorologists, provides month-by-month information on temperature, humidity, and precipitation in more than 175 cities worldwide.

THE GOLD GUIDE / IMPORTANT CONTACTS

SMART TRAVEL TIPS A TO Z

Basic Information on Traveling in Belize and Guatemala & Savvy Tips to Make Your Trip a Breeze

A

AIR TRAVEL

If time is an issue, **always look for nonstop flights,** which require no change of plane. If possible, **avoid connecting flights,** which stop at least once and can involve a change of plane, even though the flight number remains the same; if the first leg is late, the second waits.

For better service, **fly smaller or regional carriers,** which often have higher passenger satisfaction ratings. Sometimes they have such in-flight amenities as leather seats or greater legroom and they often have better food.

CUTTING COSTS

The Sunday travel section of most newspapers is a good place to look for deals.

MAJOR AIRLINES➤ The least-expensive airfares from the major airlines are priced for round-trip travel and are subject to restrictions. Usually, you must **book in advance and buy the ticket within 24 hours** to get cheaper fares, and you may have to **stay over a Saturday night.** The lowest fare is subject to availability, and only a small percentage of the plane's total seats is sold at that price. It's smart to **call a number of airlines, and when you are** quoted a good price, **book it on the spot**—the same fare may not be available on the same flight the next day. Airlines generally allow you to change your return date for a $25 to $50 fee. If you don't use your ticket, you can apply the cost toward the purchase of a new ticket, again for a small charge. However, most low-fare tickets are nonrefundable. To get the lowest airfare, **check different routings.** If your destination has more than one gateway, **compare prices to different airports.**

FROM THE U.K.➤ To save money on flights, **look into an APEX or Super-Pex ticket.** APEX tickets must be booked in advance and have certain restrictions. Super-PEX tickets can be purchased right at the airport.

CONSOLIDATORS➤ Consolidators buy tickets for scheduled flights at reduced rates from the airlines, then sell them at prices below the lowest available from the airlines directly—usually without advance restrictions. Sometimes you can even get your money back if you need to return the ticket. Carefully read the fine print detailing penalties for changes and cancellations. If you doubt the reliability of a consolidator, **confirm your** reservation with the airline.

ALOFT

AIRLINE FOOD➤ If you hate airline food, **ask for special meals when booking.** These can be vegetarian, low-cholesterol, or kosher, for example; commonly prepared to order in smaller quantities than standard fare, they can be tastier.

SMOKING➤ Smoking is not allowed on flights of six hours or less within the continental United States. Smoking is also prohibited on flights within Canada. For U.S. flights longer than six hours or international flights, **contact your carrier regarding their smoking policy.** Some carriers have prohibited smoking throughout their system; others allow smoking only on certain routes or even certain departures of that route.

B

BUSINESS HOURS

Belize is a very laid-back place, so **be prepared to be flexible.** Shops tend to open according to the whim of the owner but are generally open 8–noon and 3–8. Some shops and businesses work a half day on Wednesday and Saturday. On Friday, many shops close early for the weekend, and on Sunday, Belize takes it very easy. Few shops are open, flights are very limited, and almost all restaurants are closed, except those in the major hotels. Banks are open Monday–Thursday 8–1 and Friday 8–1 and 3–6.

In Guatemala, most banks are open 9–3:30, although the branch offices of the major banks stay open until 8. Museums have variable hours. Most shops are open 10–7, with a lunch break 1–3.

C

CAMERAS, CAMCORDERS, & COMPUTERS

IN TRANSIT

Always **keep your film, tape, or disks out of the sun;** never put these on the dashboard of a car. Carry an extra supply of batteries, and **be prepared to turn on your camera, camcorder, or laptop computer for security personnel** to prove that it's real.

X RAYS

Always **ask for hand inspection at security.** Such requests are virtually always honored at U.S. airports, and are usually accommodated abroad. Photographic film becomes clouded after successive exposure to airport X ray machines. Videotape and computer disks are not damaged by X rays, but **keep your tapes and disks away from metal detectors.**

CUSTOMS

Before departing, **register your foreign-made camera or laptop with U.S. Customs.** If your equipment is U.S.-made, call the consulate of the country you'll be visiting to find out whether it should be registered with local customs upon arrival.

CAR RENTAL

Renting cars is not common among Central American travelers. The reasons are clear: In capital cities, traffic is bad and car theft is rampant **(look for guarded parking lots or hotels with lots);** in rural areas, roads are often unpaved, muddy, and dotted with potholes; and often the cost of gas is steep. However, for obvious reasons, a car can be a wonderful asset to your trip. You don't have to worry about unreliable bus schedules, you have a lot more control over your itinerary and the pace of your trip, and you can head off to explore on a whim.

In order to reach areas that are off the beaten path, particularly during the rainy season, **rent a four-wheel-drive (doble-tracción) vehicle.** They can cost roughly twice as much as an economy car and should be booked well in advance. A four-wheel-drive vehicle (Land Rover is an excellent choice) is crucial in Belize, where paved roads are at a minimum. However, Belize is a particularly expensive spot to rent a car—prices are generally $20 more per day than in Guatemala.

CUTTING COSTS

To get the best deal, **book through a travel agent who is willing to shop around.** Ask your agent to **look for fly-drive packages,** which also save you money, and **ask if local taxes are included** in the rental or fly-drive price. These can be as high as 20% in some destinations. Don't forget to find out about required deposits, cancellation penalties, drop-off charges, and the cost of any required insurance coverage.

Also **ask your travel agent about a company's customer-service record.** How has it responded to late plane arrivals and vehicle mishaps? Are there often lines at the rental counter, and—if you're traveling during a holiday period—does a confirmed reservation guarantee you a car?

Always **find out what equipment is standard** at your destination before specifying what you want; automatic transmission and air-conditioning are usually optional—and very expensive.

INSURANCE

When driving a rented car, you are generally responsible for any damage to or loss of the rental vehicle, as well as any property damage or personal injury that you cause. Before you rent, **see what coverage you already have** under the terms of your personal auto insurance policy and credit cards.

If you do not have auto insurance or an umbrella insurance policy that covers damage to third parties, purchasing CDW or LDW is highly recommended.

THE GOLD GUIDE / SMART TRAVEL TIPS

LICENSE REQUIREMENTS

Most rental companies will accept your driver's license, but some require an International Driver's Permit, available from the American or Canadian Automobile Association or, in the United Kingdom, from the AA or RAC. Be sure to check with the agency before you arrive.

SURCHARGES

Before you pick up a car in one city and leave it in another, **ask about drop-off charges or one-way service fees,** which can be substantial. Note, too, that some rental agencies charge extra if you return the car before the time specified on your contract. To avoid a hefty refueling fee, **fill the tank just before you turn in the car**—but be aware that gas stations near the rental outlet may overcharge.

CHILDREN & TRAVEL

When traveling with children, **plan ahead** and **involve your youngsters** as you outline your trip. When packing, **include a supply of things to keep them busy** en route (☞ Children & Travel *in* Important Contacts A to Z). On sightseeing days, try to **schedule activities of special interest to your children,** like a trip to a zoo or a playground. If you **plan your itinerary around seasonal festivals,** you'll never lack for things to do. In addition, **check local newspapers for special events** mounted by public libraries, museums, and parks.

BABY-SITTING

For recommended local sitters, **check with your hotel desk.**

DRIVING

If you are renting a car, don't forget to **arrange for a car seat when you reserve.** Sometimes they're free.

FLYING

As a general rule, infants under two not occupying a seat fly at greatly reduced fares and occasionally for free. If your children are two or older **ask about special children's fares.** Age limits for these fares vary among carriers. Rules also vary regarding unaccompanied minors, so again, check with your airline.

BAGGAGE➢ In general, the adult baggage allowance applies to children paying half or more of the adult fare. If you are traveling with an infant, **ask about carry-on allowances** before departure. In general, for infants charged 10% of the adult fare you are allowed one carry-on bag and a collapsible stroller, which may have to be checked; you may be limited to less if the flight is full.

SAFETY SEATS➢ According to the FAA, it's a good idea to **use safety seats aloft** for children weighing less than 40 pounds. Airline policies vary. U.S. carriers allow FAA-approved models but usually require that you buy a ticket, even if your child would otherwise ride free, since the seats must be strapped into regular seats. However, some U.S. and foreign-flag airlines may require you to hold your baby during takeoff and landing—defeating the seat's purpose. Other foreign carriers may not allow infant seats at all, or may charge a child rather than an infant fare for their use.

FACILITIES➢ When making your reservation, **request for children's meals or freestanding bassinets** if you need them; the latter are available only to those seated at the bulkhead, where there's enough legroom. If you don't need a bassinet, **think twice before requesting bulkhead seats**—the only storage space for in-flight necessities is in inconveniently distant overhead bins.

GAMES

Milton Bradley and Parker Brothers have travel versions of some of their most popular games, including Yahtzee, Trouble, Sorry, and Monopoly. Prices run $5 to $8. Look for them in the travel section of your local toy store.

LODGING

Most hotels allow children under a certain age to stay in their parents' room at no extra charge; others charge them as extra adults. Be sure to **ask about the cutoff age.**

CUSTOMS & DUTIES

To speed your clearance through customs, **keep receipts for all your purchases abroad** and **be ready to show the inspector what you've bought.** If you feel that you've been incorrectly or unfairly charged a duty, you can **appeal assessments in dispute.** First ask to see a supervisor. If you are still unsatisfied, **write to the port director** at your point of entry, sending your customs receipt and any other appropriate documentation. The address will be listed on your receipt. If you still don't get satisfaction, you can take your case to customs headquarters in Washington.

ON ARRIVAL

IN BELIZE➤ Duty-free allowances for visitors entering Belize include 3 liters of liquor and one carton of cigarettes. All electronic and electrical appliances, cameras, jewelry, or other items of value must be declared at the point of entry. Visitors are allowed to bring in the equivalent of $250 in foreign currency per day of their stay. Any amount above that should be declared.

IN GUATEMALA➤ Tourists may enter Guatemala duty-free with a camera, up to six rolls of film, any clothes and devices needed while traveling, 500 milligrams of tobacco, 3 liters of alcoholic beverages, 2 bottles of perfume, and 2 kilograms of candy. Unless you bring in a lot of merchandise, customs officers probably won't even check your luggage.

ON DEPARTURE

FROM BELIZE➤ To take home fresh seafood of any kind, you must first obtain a permit from the Fisheries Department; there is a 20-

pound limit.

FROM GUATEMALA➤ No fruits or vegetables may be brought out.

IN THE U.S.

You may bring home $400 worth of foreign goods duty-free if you've been out of the country for at least 48 hours and haven't already used the $400 allowance, or any part of it, in the past 30 days.

Travelers 21 or older may bring back 1 liter of alcohol duty-free, provided the beverage laws of the state through which they reenter the United States allow it. In addition, regardless of their age, they are allowed 100 non-Cuban cigars and 200 cigarettes. Antiques, which the U.S. Customs Service defines as objects more than 100 years old, are duty-free. Original works of art done entirely by hand are also duty-free. These include, but are not limited to, paintings, drawings, and sculptures.

Duty-free, travelers may mail packages valued at up to $200 to themselves and up to $100 to others, with a limit of one parcel per addressee per day (and no alcohol or tobacco products or perfume valued at more than $5); on the outside, the package must be labeled as being either for personal use or an unsolicited gift, and a list of its contents and their retail value must be attached. Mailed items do not affect your duty-free allowance on your return.

IN CANADA

If you've been out of Canada for at least seven days, you may bring in C$500 worth of goods duty-free. If you've been away for fewer than seven days but for more than 48 hours, the duty-free allowance drops to C$200; if your trip lasts between 24 and 48 hours, the allowance is C$50. You cannot pool allowances with family members. Goods claimed under the C$500 exemption may follow you by mail; those claimed under the lesser exemptions must accompany you.

Alcohol and tobacco products may be included in the seven-day and 48-hour exemptions but not in the 24-hour exemption. If you meet the age requirements of the province or territory through which you reenter Canada, you may bring in, duty-free, 1.14 liters (40 imperial ounces) of wine or liquor *or* 24 12-ounce cans or bottles of beer or ale. If you are 16 or older, you may bring in, duty-free, 200 cigarettes, 50 cigars or cigarillos, and 400 tobacco sticks or 400 grams of manufactured tobacco. Alcohol and tobacco must accompany you on your return.

An unlimited number of gifts with a value of up to C$60 each may be mailed to Canada duty-free. These do not affect your duty-free allowance on your return. Label the package "Unsolicited Gift—Value Under $60." Alcohol and tobacco are excluded.

IN THE U.K.

From countries outside the EU, including Belize and Guatemala, you may import, duty-free, 200 cigarettes, 100 cigarillos, 50 cigars, or 250 grams of tobacco; 1 liter of spirits or 2 liters of fortified or sparkling wine or liqueurs; 2 liters of still table wine; 60 milliliters of perfume; 250 milliliters of toilet water; plus £136 worth of other goods, including gifts and souvenirs.

D

DISABILITIES & ACCESSIBILITY

When making plans to travel to Central America, **remember that accessibility is extremely limited.** Outside major cities, roads are unpaved, making wheelchair travel difficult. Exploring most of Central America's attractions involves walking down cobblestone streets and, sometimes, steep trails and muddy paths. Buses are not equipped to carry wheelchairs, so wheelchair users should hire a van to get about. However, there is a growing awareness of the needs of people with disabilities, and the friendly, helpful attitude of people helps somewhat to make up for the lack of provisions.

When discussing accessibility with an operator or reservationist, **ask hard questions.** Are there any stairs, inside *or* out? Are there grab bars next to the toilet *and* in the shower/tub? How wide is the doorway to the room? To the bathroom? For the most extensive facilities, meeting the latest legal specifications, **opt for newer accommodations,** which more often have been designed with access in mind. Older properties or ships must usually be retrofitted and may offer more limited facilities as a result. Be sure to **discuss your needs before booking.**

DISCOUNTS & DEALS

You shouldn't have to pay for a discount. In fact, you may already be eligible for all kinds of savings. Here are some time-honored strategies for getting the best deal.

LOOK IN YOUR WALLET

When you **use your credit card to make travel purchases,** you may get free travel-accident insurance, collision damage insurance, medical or legal assistance, depending on the card and bank that issued it. Visa and MasterCard provide one or more of these services, so **get a copy of your card's travel benefits.** If you are a member of the AAA or an oil-company-sponsored road-assistance plan, always **ask hotel or car-rental reservationists for auto-club discounts.** Some clubs offer additional discounts on tours, cruises, or admission to attractions. And don't forget that auto-club membership entitles you to free maps and trip-planning services.

SENIORS CITIZENS & STUDENTS

As a senior-citizen traveler, you may be eligible for special rates, but you should mention your senior-citizen status up front. If you're a student or under 26, you can also get discounts, especially if you have an official ID card (☞ Senior-Citizen Discounts *and* Students on the Road, *below*).

DIAL FOR DOLLARS

To save money, **look into "1-800" discount reservations services,** which often have lower rates. These services use their buying power to get a better price on hotels, airline tickets, and sometimes even car rentals. When booking a room, always **call the hotel's local toll-free number** (if one is available) rather than the central reservations number—you'll often get a better price. Ask the reservationist about special packages or corporate rates, which are usually available even if you're not traveling on business.

JOIN A CLUB?

Discount clubs can be a legitimate source of savings, but you must use the participating hotels and visit the participating attractions in order to realize any benefits. Remember, too, that you have to pay a fee to join, so **determine if you'll save enough to warrant your membership fee.** Before booking with a club, **make sure the hotel or other supplier isn't offering a better deal.**

GET A GUARANTEE

When shopping for the best deal on hotels and car rentals, **look for guaranteed exchange** rates, which protect you against a falling dollar. With your rate locked in, you won't pay more even if the price goes up in the local currency.

H
HEALTH

SHOTS & MEDICATIONS

In Belize and Guatemala, the major health risk is posed by the contamination of drinking water, fresh fruit, and vegetables by fecal matter, which causes the intestinal ailment known as Montezuma's Revenge or traveler's diarrhea. To avoid this, watch what you eat. Stay away from ice, un-cooked food, and unpasteurized milk and milk products, and drink only bottled water or water that has been boiled for at least 20 minutes. Mild cases may respond to Imod-ium (known generically as loperamide) or Pepto-Bismol (not as strong), both of which can be purchased over the counter; paregoric, another antidiarrheal agent, may require a doctor's prescription in Belize and Guatemala. Drink plenty of purified water or tea—chamomile is a good folk remedy for diar-rhea. In severe cases, rehydrate yourself with a salt-sugar solution (½ teaspoon salt and 4 tablespoons sugar per quart of water).

According to the CDC there is a limited risk of malaria, hepatitis A and B, dengue fever, typhoid fever, and rabies in Central America, partic-

ularly in Guatemala. Travelers in most urban or easily accessible areas need not worry. However, if you plan to visit remote regions or stay for more than six weeks, check with the CDC's International Travelers Hotline (☞ Health *in* Important Contacts A to Z). In areas with malaria and dengue, both of which are carried by mosquitoes, use mosquito nets, wear clothing that covers the body, apply repellent containing DEET, and use a spray against flying insects in living and sleeping areas. Also consider taking anti-malarial pills. No vac-cine exists against dengue. Rabies is al-ways a concern when you get bitten by a stray dog or other wild animal. Scrub the wound under clean, running water with soap or iodine—failing that, some local rum—and get an antirabies shot immediately.

Children traveling to Central America should have current inocula-tions against measles, mumps, rubella, and polio.

I
INSURANCE

Travel insurance can protect your monetary investment, replace your luggage and its contents, or provide for medical coverage should you fall ill during your trip. Most tour operators, travel agents, and insurance agents sell specialized health-and-accident, flight, trip-cancellation, and luggage insurance as well as comprehen-

sive policies with some or all of these cover-ages. Comprehensive policies may also reim-burse you for delays due to weather—an important consideration if you're traveling during the winter months. Some health-insurance policies do not cover preexisting conditions, but waivers may be available in specific cases. Coverage is sold by the companies listed in Important Contacts A to Z; these companies act as the policy's administrators. The actual insurance is usually underwritten by a well-known name, such as The Travelers or Continental Insurance.

Before you make any purchase, review your existing health and homeowner's policies to find out whether they cover expenses incurred while traveling.

BAGGAGE

Airline liability for baggage is limited to $1,250 per person on domestic flights. On international flights, it amounts to $9.07 per pound or $20 per kilogram for checked baggage (roughly $640 per 70-pound bag) and $400 per passenger for unchecked baggage. Insurance for losses exceeding the terms of your airline ticket can be bought directly from the airline at check-in for about $10 per $1,000 of coverage; note that it excludes a rather extensive list of items, shown on your airline ticket.

COMPREHENSIVE

Comprehensive insur-ance policies include all the coverages described above plus some that may not be available in more specific policies. If you have purchased an expensive vacation, especially one that involves travel abroad, comprehensive insurance is a must; **look for policies that include trip delay insurance,** which will protect you in the event that weather problems cause you to miss your flight, tour, or cruise. A few insurers will also sell you a waiver for preexisting medical conditions. Some of the companies that offer both these features are Access America, Carefree Travel, Travel Guard, and Travel Insured International (☞ Insurance *in* Important Contacts A to Z).

FLIGHT

You should **think twice before buying flight insurance.** Often purchased as a last-minute impulse at the airport, it pays a lump sum when a plane crashes, either to a beneficiary if the insured dies or sometimes to a surviving passenger who loses his or her eyesight or a limb. Supplementing the airlines' coverage described in the limits-of-liability paragraphs on your ticket, it's expensive and basically unnecessary. Charging an airline ticket to a major credit card often automatically provides you with coverage that may also extend to travel by bus, train, and ship.

HEALTH

Medicare generally does not cover health care costs outside the United States; nor do many

privately issued policies. If your own health insurance policy does not cover you outside the United States, **consider buying supplemental medical coverage.** It can reimburse you for $1,000–$150,000 worth of medical and/or dental expenses incurred as a result of an accident or illness during a trip. These policies also may include a personal-accident, or death-and-dismemberment, provision, which pays a lump sum ranging from $15,000 to $500,000 to your beneficiaries if you die or to you if you lose one or more limbs or your eyesight, and a medical-assistance provision, which may either reimburse you for the cost of referrals, evacuation, or repatriation and other services, or automatically enroll you as a member of a particular medical-assistance company. (☞ Health *in* Important Contacts A to Z.)

U.K. TRAVELERS

You can buy an annual travel insurance policy valid for most vacations during the year in which it's purchased. If you are pregnant or have a preexisting medical condition, make sure you're covered before buying such a policy.

TRIP

Without insurance, you will lose all or most of your money if you cancel your trip regardless of the reason. Especially if your airline ticket, cruise, or package tour is nonrefundable and cannot be changed, it's essential

that you **buy trip-cancellation-and-interruption insurance.** When considering how much coverage you need, look for a policy that will cover the cost of your trip plus the nondiscounted price of a one-way airline ticket should you need to return home early. Read the fine print carefully, especially sections that define "family member" and "preexisting medical conditions." Also **consider default or bankruptcy insurance,** which protects you against a supplier's failure to deliver. Be aware, however, that if you buy such a policy from a travel agency, tour operator, airline, or cruise line, it may not cover default by the firm in question.

L

LODGING

APARTMENT & VILLA RENTAL

If you want a home base that's roomy enough for a family and comes with cooking facilities, **consider taking a furnished rental.** This can also save you money, but not always—some rentals are luxury properties (economical only when your party is large). Home-exchange directories list rentals—often second homes owned by prospective house swappers—and some services search for a house or apartment for you (even a castle if that's your fancy) and handle the paperwork. Some send an illustrated catalog; others send photographs only of specific properties, sometimes at a charge;

up-front registration fees may apply.

M

MAIL

When sending mail to Central America, be sure to **include the district in the address,** especially to remote areas like Belize's Cayo and Orange Walk.

MEDICAL ASSISTANCE

No one plans to get sick while traveling, but it happens, so **consider signing up with a medical assistance company.** These outfits provide referrals, emergency evacuation or repatriation, 24-hour telephone hot lines for medical consultation, cash for emergencies, and other personal and legal assistance. They also dispatch medical personnel and arrange for the relay of medical records.

If you haven't signed up and have an emergency, **first contact your hotel, local tourist office, or, of course, your tour leader.** They can point you in the right direction. Sanitary conditions in local clinics might not be good enough, especially in Guatemala and in areas far from civilization.

MONEY

ATMS

CASH ADVANCES➤ Before leaving home, **make sure that your credit cards have been programmed for ATM use** in Belize or Guatemala. Note that Discover is accepted mostly in the United States. Local bank cards often do not work

overseas either; **ask your bank about a Visa debit card,** which works like a bank card but can be used at any ATM displaying a Visa logo.

TRANSACTION FEES➤ Although fees charged for ATM transactions may be higher abroad than at home, Cirrus and Plus exchange rates are excellent, because they are based on wholesale rates offered only by major banks.

CURRENCY

The monetary unit in Belize is the dollar (BZ$). For many years now it has been tied to the U.S. dollar at a rate of BZ$2 per dollar. Most tourist prices are quoted in U.S. dollars, but smaller restaurants and hotels tend to work in BZ$. Major credit cards are accepted at most of the larger hotels and a few restaurants. In the rest of Belize, **be prepared with cash.**

The quetzal, named after Guatemala's national bird, is divided into 100 centavos. There are 1-, 5-, 10-, and 25-centavo coins. Bills come in denominations of ½, 1, 5, 10, 20, 50, and 100 quetzals. In spring 1996, the quetzal was worth about 16¢— 6 quetzals to a U.S. dollar. Unless otherwise stated, prices are quoted in U.S. dollar amounts.

EXCHANGING CURRENCY➤ For the most favorable rates, **change money at banks.** You won't do as well at exchange booths in airports or rail and bus stations, in hotels, in restaurants, or in stores, although you may find their hours more convenient. To

avoid lines at airport exchange booths, **get a small amount of the local currency before you leave home.**

In Belize, money changers at the border give a standard 2:1 rate for U.S. dollars. The best place to get pesos is in Corozal, where the exchange rate is quite good.

In Guatemala, cash can be changed on the street in the area around the central post office for slightly more than the official rate, but it's illegal and you run the risk of being shortchanged.

TAXES

In Belize, there is a government hotel tax of 6% and an airport departure tax of $10, plus $1.25 security tax, when you leave the country. As of 1996, there is a 12% value-added tax (VAT) on consumer goods.

Guatemalan stores, restaurants, and hotels charge a 10% VAT, while most hotels and some tourist restaurants charge an additional 10% tourist tax. When departing from Guatemala by air, tourists must pay a $10 (60-quetzal) exit tax.

TIPPING

As there is a government service charge of 10% in Belizean restaurants and bars, tipping is not necessary. Elsewhere, Belizeans tend not to look for tips, though it's nice to **tip hotel staff.** It is not customary to tip taxi drivers.

In Guatemala, gratuities are not included in

SMART TRAVEL TIPS / THE GOLD GUIDE

restaurant bills, and it is customary to **tip 10%**. Bellhops and maids expect tips only in the expensive hotels. Guards who show you around ruins and locals who help you find hotels or give you little tours should also be tipped. Indians will often charge a quetzal to let you take their photo, which may seem absurd, but these folks are poor.

TRAVELER'S CHECKS

Whether or not to buy traveler's checks depends on where you are headed; **take cash to rural areas and small towns, traveler's checks to cities.** The most widely recognized checks are issued by American Express, Citicorp, Thomas Cook, and Visa. These are sold by major commercial banks for 1%–3% of the checks' face value—it pays to **shop around.** Both American Express and Thomas Cook issue checks that can be countersigned and used by either you or your traveling companion. So you won't be left with excess foreign currency, **buy a few checks in small denominations** to cash toward the end of your trip. Before leaving home, **contact your issuer for information on where to cash your checks** without a incurring a transaction fee. Record the numbers of all your checks, and keep this listing in a separate place, crossing off the numbers of checks you have cashed.

WHAT IT WILL COST

There are two ways of looking at the prices in

Belize: Either it is one of the cheapest countries in the Caribbean, or it is one of the most expensive countries in Central America. A good hotel room for two will cost you upwards of $100; a budget one, as little as $6. A meal in one of the more expensive restaurants will cost $25–$35 for one, but you can eat lobster and salad in a small seafood restaurant for as little as $10. Prices are highest in Belize City and Ambergris Caye.

Guatemala can be remarkably inexpensive, especially in the highlands, but prices for first-class hotels approach those in developed countries. Trips into remote parts of the jungle or specialty travel like river rafting and deep-sea fishing are also relatively expensive. Sample costs are: a cup of coffee, 4 quetzals; bottle of beer, 8 quetzals; ½-kilometer taxi ride, 25 quetzals.

WIRING MONEY

For a fee of 3%–10%, depending on the amount of the transaction, you can **have money sent to you from home through Money-Gram℠ or Western Union** (☞ Money *in* Important Contacts A to Z). The transferred funds and the service fee can be charged to a MasterCard or Visa account.

P
PACKING FOR BELIZE & GUATEMALA

Pack light because baggage carts are scarce

at airports and luggage restrictions are tight. Your best bet is to **bring casual, comfortable, hand-washable clothing.** T-shirts and shorts are acceptable near the beach and in heavily touristed areas. Loose-fitting long-sleeved shirts and pants are good to have in the smaller towns (where immodest attire is frowned upon) and to protect your skin from the ferocious sun and mosquitoes. **Bring a large hat** to block the sun from your face and neck. If you're heading into the mountains—the Guatemalan highlands, for example—**tote a light sweater and a jacket** because the nights and early mornings can be chilly. Sturdy sneakers or hiking boots are essential if you plan to do a lot of sightseeing and hiking. Sandals or other footwear that lets your feet breathe are good for strolling about town.

Without a doubt, **bring insect repellent, sunscreen, sunglasses, and an umbrella to Belize and Guatemala.** Other handy items—especially if you will be traveling on your own or camping—include toilet paper, facial tissues, a plastic water bottle, and a flashlight (for occasional power outages or use at campsites). Snorkelers should consider bringing their own equipment unless traveling light is a priority; shoes with rubber soles for rocky underwater surfaces are also advised.

Bring an extra pair of eyeglasses or contact

lenses in your carry-on luggage, and if you have a health problem, **pack enough medication** to last the trip or have your doctor write you a prescription using the drug's generic name, because brand names vary from country to country (you'll then need a duplicate prescription from a local doctor). It's important that you **don't put prescription drugs or valuables in luggage to be checked,** for it could go astray. To avoid problems with customs officials, carry medications in the original packaging. Also, don't forget the addresses of offices that handle refunds of lost traveler's checks.

ELECTRICITY

To use your U.S.-purchased electric-powered equipment, **bring a converter and an adapter.** The electrical current in Belize and Guatemala is 220 volts, 50 cycles alternating current (AC); some wall outlets in Belize take continental-type plugs, with two round prongs. Outlets in Guatemala take U.S.-style plugs and run at 110V.

If your appliances are dual-voltage, you'll need only an adapter. Hotels sometimes have 110-volt outlets for low-wattage appliances near the sink, marked FOR SHAVERS ONLY; don't use them for high-wattage appliances like blow-dryers. If your laptop computer is older, carry a converter; new laptops operate equally well on 110 and 220 volts, so you need only an adapter.

LUGGAGE

Airline baggage allowances depend on the airline, the route, and the class of your ticket; ask in advance. In general, on domestic flights and on international flights between the United States and foreign destinations, you are entitled to check two bags. A third piece may be brought on board, but it must fit easily under the seat in front of you or in the overhead compartment. In the United States, the FAA gives airlines broad latitude regarding carry-on allowances, and they tend to tailor them to different aircraft and operational conditions. Charges for excess, oversize, or overweight pieces vary.

If you are flying between two foreign destinations, note that baggage allowances may be determined not by piece but by weight—generally 88 pounds (40 kilograms) in first class, 66 pounds (30 kilograms) in business class, and 44 pounds (20 kilograms) in economy. If your flight between two cities abroad *connects* with your transatlantic or transpacific flight, the piece method still applies.

SAFEGUARDING YOUR LUGGAGE➤ Before leaving home, **itemize your bags' contents** and their worth, and label them with your name, address, and phone number. (If you use your home address, cover it so that potential thieves can't see it readily.) Inside each bag, **pack a copy of your itinerary.** At check-in, **make sure that each bag is correctly tagged** with the destination airport's three-letter code. If your bags arrive damaged—or fail to arrive at all—file a written report with the airline before leaving the airport.

If you don't already have one, **get a passport.** (For addresses of passport offices, consulates, and embassies, *see* Passports & Visas *in* Important Contacts A to Z.) It is advisable that you **leave one photocopy of your passport's data page** with someone at home and keep another with you, separated from your passport, while traveling. If you lose your passport, promptly call the nearest embassy or consulate and the local police; having the data page information can speed replacement.

FOR BELIZE

To enter Belize, no visas are required for U.S., Canadian, and British citizens and citizens of other EU countries, but you must have a passport. Canadian citizens also need a return ticket to enter Belize. Technically, visitors are permitted to stay in the country for only 30 days. If you're young and you arrive by road from Mexico, you may be asked to prove you have enough money to cover your stay.

FOR GUATEMALA

British, U.S., and Canadian citizens need a valid passport and a

THE GOLD GUIDE / SMART TRAVEL TIPS

visa or tourist card to enter Guatemala. The best way to travel is with a tourist card, which allows you to stay longer. You can **purchase a tourist card** for $5 from airlines serving Guatemala when you depart your country (the easiest way), through Guatemalan consulates, and from immigration officials at the airport in Guatemala. A multiple-entry visa is needed if you arrive by land and can be obtained from the Guatemalan consulate in your country.

S

SENIOR-CITIZEN DISCOUNTS

To qualify for age-related discounts, **mention your senior-citizen status up front** when booking hotel reservations, not when checking out, and before you're seated in restaurants, not when paying the bill. Note that discounts may be limited to certain menus, days, or hours. When renting a car, **ask about promotional car-rental discounts**—they can net even lower costs than your senior-citizen discount.

STUDENTS ON THE ROAD

Central America is a fantastic place for students and youths on a budget. In Guatemala you can live well on $15 a day. Belize is more expensive; expect to shell out $35–$45 a day. There are no youth hostels as such, but Guatemala and Belize are packed with cheap lodging possibilities.

Any option near the bus station is usually a good bet moneywise. One of the cheapest ways to spend the night is camping. As long as you have your own tent, it's easy to set up camp anywhere. (If it looks like you're near someone's home, it's always a good idea to inquire first.) Central America is a popular travel destination for adventurous backpackers, so you'll have no problem hooking up with other like-minded travelers in any major city or along the popular travel routes. To get good tips and advice on traveling within a budget, **look for informational bulletin boards and chat with other backpackers.** Guatemala City has a major university with a thriving student population.

To save money, **look into deals available through student-oriented travel agencies.** To qualify, you'll need to have a bona fide student ID card. Members of international student groups are also eligible (☞ Students *in* Important Contacts A to Z).

T

TELEPHONES

The country code for Belize is 501; for Guatemala, 502. Omit the "0" from Belize's area codes when dialling from outside the country. Before you go, **find out the local access codes** for your destinations by calling AT&T USADirect (☎ 800/874–4000), MCI Call USA (☎ 800/444–4444), or Sprint Express (☎ 800/793–1153).

LOCAL AND IN-COUNTRY CALLS

IN BELIZE➤ Belize has a good nationwide telephone system. Pay phones are on the street in the main centers. Local calls cost BZ25¢; calls to other districts, BZ$1. When you are in the same area as the area code you are calling, do not dial the area code.

IN GUATEMALA➤ Pay phones take 10-centavo coins, but they are difficult to find even in the capital and major cities and are virtually nonexistent in most of the country. Though more expensive, it's easier to **make local calls from your hotel.** Guatel is the government phone company, and any decent-size town has a Guatel office, most of which are open daily 7 AM–midnight. You usually have to wait to **submit your number to the cashier,** and then wait again to be called and directed to a booth.

As of April 5, 1996, Guatemala converted every telephone number in the country to seven digits. Now, to make a local call or a call between the capital city and the country's interior, **dial seven digits only.** The "0" and "2" used previously to phone outside a calling area have disappeared, and all telephone numbers in this book have been updated.

INTERNATIONAL CALLS

The long-distance services of AT&T, MCI, and Sprint make calling home relatively convenient, but in many hotels you may find it impossible to dial the access number. The hotel operator may also refuse to make the connection. Instead, the hotel will charge you a premium rate—as much as 400% more than a calling card—for calls placed from your hotel room. To avoid such price gouging, **travel with more than one company's long-distance calling card**—a hotel may block Sprint but not MCI. If the hotel operator claims that you cannot use any phone card, ask to be connected to an international operator, who will help you to access your phone card. You can also dial the international operator yourself. If none of this works, try calling your phone company collect in the United States. If collect calls are also blocked, call from a pay phone in the hotel lobby.

IN BELIZE➤ You can **place international calls from a Belize Telecommunications Limited (BTL) office,** located in most towns, including Belize City (✉ 1 Church St., ☎ 023/2868). Offices are open Monday–Saturday 8 AM–9 PM, Sunday 8–6. To reach an AT&T Direct operator, dial 55; for Sprint International, dial *4. MCI has no service from Belize.

IN GUATEMALA➤ Direct phones to AT&T operators in the U.S. are in the airport and at the Guatel office in Guatemala City's Zona 1. At any other phone, dial 190 for an AT&T operator, 189 for MCI, 195 for Sprint International, 198

for a Canadian operator, 121 for all other countries *or* for Guatemalan operator assistance (Spanish), and 124 for information (Spanish). Phone calls can be made and faxes sent inexpensively in Antigua at the Villa San Francisco (✉ 1a Avenida Sur 15), in Panajachel at the Grapevine (✉ Calle Santander), and in Quezaltenango at the Tecun Saloon (✉ Pasaje Enriquez, off the central park).

TOUR OPERATORS

A package or tour to Belize or Guatemala can make your vacation less expensive and more hassle-free. Firms that sell tours and packages reserve airline seats, hotel rooms, and rental cars in bulk and pass some of the savings on to you. In addition, the best operators have local representatives available to help you at your destination.

A GOOD DEAL?

The more your package or tour includes, the better you can predict the ultimate cost of your vacation. Make sure you know exactly what is covered, and **beware of hidden costs.** Are taxes, tips, and service charges included? Transfers and baggage handling? Entertainment and excursions? These can add up.

Most packages and tours are rated deluxe, first-class superior, first class, tourist, or budget. The key difference is usually accommodations. Remember, tourist class in the United States might be a comfortable chain

hotel, but in Central America you might share a bath and do without hot water. If the package or tour you are considering is priced lower than in your wildest dreams, **be skeptical. Also, make sure your travel agent knows the accommodations** and other services. Ask about the hotel's location, room size, beds, and whether it has a pool, room service, or programs for children, if you care about these. Has your agent been there in person or sent others you can contact?

BUYER BEWARE

Each year a number of consumers are stranded or lose their money when operators—even very large ones with excellent reputations—go out of business. To avoid becoming one of them, take the time to **check out the operator**—find out how long the company has been in business and ask several agents about its reputation. Next, **don't book unless the firm has a consumer-protection program.** Members of the USTOA and the NTA are required to set aside funds for the sole purpose of covering your payments and travel arrangements in case of default. Nonmember operators may instead carry insurance; look for the details in the operator's brochure—and for the name of an underwriter with a solid reputation. Note: When it comes to tour operators, **don't trust escrow accounts.** Although there are laws governing those of charter-flight operators, no governmental body prevents tour operators from raiding the till.

Next, **contact your local Better Business Bureau and the attorney general's offices** in both your own state and the operator's; have any complaints been filed? Finally, **pay with a major credit card.** Then you can cancel payment, provided that you can document your complaint. Always **consider trip-cancellation insurance** (☞ Insurance, *above*).

BIG VS. SMALL➤ Operators that handle several hundred thousand travelers per year can use their purchasing power to give you a good price. Their high volume may also indicate financial stability. But some small companies provide more personalized service; because they tend to specialize, they may also be more knowledgeable about a given area.

USING AN AGENT

Travel agents are excellent resources. In fact, large operators accept bookings made only through travel agents. But it's good to **collect brochures from several agencies** because some agents' suggestions may be skewed by promotional relationships with tour and package firms that reward them for volume sales. If you have a special interest, **find an agent with expertise in that area;** ASTA can provide leads in the United States. (Don't rely solely on your agent, though; agents may be unaware of small-niche operators, and some special-

interest travel companies only sell direct.)

SINGLE TRAVELERS

Prices are usually quoted per person, based on two sharing a room. If traveling solo, you may be required to pay the full double-occupancy rate. Some operators eliminate this surcharge if you agree to be matched up with a roommate of the same sex, even if one is not found by departure time.

TRAVEL GEAR

Travel catalogs specialize in useful items that can **save space when packing** and make life on the road more convenient. Compact alarm clocks, travel irons, travel wallets, and personal-care kits are among the most common items you'll find. They also carry dual-voltage appliances, currency converters, and foreign-language phrase books. Some catalogs even carry miniature coffeemakers and water purifiers.

U
U.S.
GOVERNMENT

The U.S. government can be an excellent source of travel information. Some of this is free and some is available for a nominal charge. When planning your trip, **find out what government materials are available.** For just a couple of dollars, you can get a variety of publications from the Consumer Information Center in Pueblo, Colorado. Free consumer information also is available from individ-

ual government agencies, such as the Department of Transportation or the U.S. Customs Service. For specific titles, *see* the appropriate sections of Important Contacts A to Z.

W
WHEN TO GO

The Central American climate is marked by a two-season year. The rainy season, called *invierno* (winter), lasts from April through November; the dry season, called *verano* (summer), runs from November through April. Temperatures are virtually the same in both seasons.

During the rainy season, vegetation is at its lushest and most gorgeous, but many roads—especially nonasphalt ones—are washed out. If you have a choice, **visit at the tail end of the rainy season,** when everything is still green, most parts of the region are accessible, and prices are still down. Since most tourists visit during the dry season, that's when hotel and restaurant prices are at their highest and crowds are at their biggest. If you want to escape tourist crowds and prices and don't mind getting very wet, visit during the rainy season. Though some restaurants may close and hotels may offer limited facilities, reservations are easy to get, even at top establishments, and you'll have the Maya ruins and beaches to yourself. Note that Guatemala's busiest time of the year is around Holy Week, from Palm Sunday to

Easter Sunday, and that hotels in Antigua, Panajachel, and Chichicastenango book up months ahead of time.

CLIMATE

Central America's climate varies greatly between the lowlands and the mountains. Guatemala's Caribbean coast, for example, sees sweltering humid weather with soaring temperatures, while the mountains in the northern Western Highlands (as with Belize's peaks) can have downright chilly evenings. Central America's rainy season is marked by sporadic downpours that occur without warning. Generally, rainfall is heavier in the afternoon than in the morning, so you may want to **do the majority of your sightseeing and shopping in the morning hours,** leaving your afternoons flexible. Belize has a particularly heavy rainy season. In the far south, you'll need an umbrella most of the year (as much as 160 inches of rain fall annually) except during a brief respite between February and April. On the cays, the wet season is often accompanied by lashing northerly winds known in Creole as Joe North. In a bad year, Joe North can turn into Hurricane Hattie.

Central America's tropical temperatures generally hover between 70°F and 85°F. The high humidity, however, is the true sweat culprit. Remember to **drink plenty of bottled water to avoid dehydration.**

The following are average daily maximum and minimum temperatures for cities in Belize and Guatemala.

Climate

BELMOPAN, BELIZE

Jan.	81F	27C	May	87F	31C	Sept.	87F	31C
	67	19		75	24		74	23
Feb.	82F	28C	June	87F	31C	Oct.	86F	30C
	69	21		75	24		72	22
Mar.	84F	29C	July	87F	31C	Nov.	83F	28C
	71	22		75	24		68	20
Apr.	86F	30C	Aug.	88F	31C	Dec.	81F	27C
	74	23		75	24		73	23

GUATEMALA CITY, GUATEMALA

Jan.	73F	23C	May	84F	29C	Sept.	79F	26C
	52	11		60	16		60	16
Feb.	77F	25C	June	81F	27C	Oct.	76F	24C
	54	12		61	16		60	16
Mar.	81F	27C	July	78F	26C	Nov.	74F	24C
	57	14		60	16		57	14
Apr.	82F	28C	Aug.	79F	26C	Dec.	72F	22C
	58	14		60	16		55	13

THE GOLD GUIDE / SMART TRAVEL TIPS

1 Destination: Belize and Guatemala

A CONFLUENCE OF INFLUENCE

FOR CENTURIES the tropics have held a unique allure. Something clicks in the mind of Europeans or North Americans—particularly during their respective winters—when the tropics are considered as an ideal vacation spot. Indeed, the tropics are paradise.

Central America has all the attributes needed to fulfill such dreams of equatorial bliss: a languid pace of life; compelling, polychromatic landscapes; and hundreds of miles of coast lined with coconut trees and where jungle foliage spills down nearby mountains. From the volcanic lakes of Guatemala to the offshore cays and islands of Belize, Central America has always been a sensory paradise of color and climate.

Yet it is also a region scarred by violence and upheaval. But there are important exceptions: The only uniforms you will see in Belize are those of the Belizean Defence Force and the crisp white shirts of the Belizean bobby—a kind of Caribbean PC Plod. In Guatemala, however, violence is a fact of life for many; in the 30-plus years of the civil war, an estimated 120,000 lives have been lost. Recent rumors of CIA links with death squads and the murders of several foreigners have painted a very negative picture of what is undoubtedly one of the world's most beautiful nations. But even this is not reason enough to avoid the country. Here, as elsewhere in the world, a certain common-sense caution is in order. If you follow proper procedure and do not venture into the so-called "danger zones," a visit here will leave you with lasting memories of an exciting—and, most importantly, happy—kind.

The Geography of Influence

With a total area of 507,772 square kilometers (196,000 square miles), Central America is about one-fourth the size of Mexico, its northern neighbor. The area is packed with a variety of terrain that rivals the continent of South America: mountain peaks at more than 14,000 feet; jungles in the Darien and the Mosquito Coast that have never been surveyed; deserts, plains, and vast pine barrens; and high-altitude hardwood forests that resemble northern Europe more than the tropics.

The isthmus—in some places as narrow as 80 kilometers (50 miles)—is, in its entirety, smaller than Texas. But its location has opened the area to incredible amounts of foreign influence. It has always stood between things: between the gold and silver of Peru and Spain; between the east and west coasts of the United States when, during the California gold rush, Nicaragua was the preferred route for westward migration; between Mexico and South America; and—at least politically—between the United States and the Soviet Union. The Panama Canal, an added factor, has served to raise the strategic stakes in the region and brought to bear incredible political pressure.

Economically, culturally, and politically, Central America has been washed by repeated waves of foreign influence. Never isolated like Africa or the jungles of the Amazon Basin, its great ancient cultures declined before the European Conquest and were easy prey for the economic and cultural exploitation of Spain. Today it is home to a mélange of various African, Amerindian, and European cultures, with, for the most part, only the Spanish language and the Catholic church to give it a sense of unity. And even Spanish is not universal, as thousands of Central Americans prefer to speak English or indigenous dialects. And while the coasts of Central America and its placement on the globe have exposed it to the outside world, its mountains have hindered communication within.

The Barrier Mountains

The overwhelming geographic fact of life in Central America is the continuous, relentless chain of mountains that dominates nearly every republic. The mountains that run the north–south length of the isthmus are volcanic and young. There are more than 20 active volcanoes in the region. These pressure points of geothermal energy constantly threaten havoc, but ironically it is the rich ash of volcanic eruptions that has given Central America's soil its legendary fertility. Virtually the entire region is an active earthquake zone, and on numerous occasions (as recently as 1976 for Guatemala City), large sections of its capital cities had to be substantially rebuilt.

Over the centuries the mountains have served to divide population groups to the degree that today the cultural landscape of the region is more of a quilt than a melting pot. The terrain of the isthmus, which made roads and communications problematic right into the 1980s, can still be blamed for much of the region's economic underdevelopment. Trade among the Central American republics has always been difficult, and attempts at regional political integration have failed repeatedly. It was only under President Kennedy's Alliance for Progress that a highway linking the republics of Guatemala, Honduras, El Salvador, Nicaragua, Costa Rica, and Panama was constructed. Belize is still cut off from the rest of Central America, with poor mountain roads across to Guatemala and irregular shipping down the coast to Honduras. Even within nations, the mountains and jungles of Central America have kept populations separate: Mountain Indians in Guatemala often speak no Spanish, and the peoples of the Caribbean coasts of Honduras and Nicaragua generally have more relatives in New Orleans or Miami than in Tegucigalpa or Managua.

The ocean has always provided reliable access to the Central American economies, and as a result, Europe and the United States have overwhelmingly influenced the isthmus. Intraregional contact remains a problem. An extractive, agricultural economic system has developed in which most economic activity involves the export of commodities and the import of goods and services from outside the region. Foreign economic powers have brought their cultural and political influences with them, and as a result, Central America today has profound difficulties with regional unity.

The mountains have also stood as a barrier to social equality and to the development of the Central American people. When the riches of the Maya were looted and the gold and silver mines played out,

Spanish conquerors turned to export-oriented agriculture. The indigenous inhabitants of the land were driven to the mountains or barren coasts, where they scratched out whatever subsistence could be had. Even today one finds concentrations of native inhabitants on the coasts and on the highest mountains. The Spanish built their plantations on the richest soil, and the Indians came down to work these fields as day laborers. Indigo, cacao, and then sugar, cotton, coffee, tobacco, and bananas were the primary crops. Few of these products are actually cultivated to feed the people of Central America.

The struggle over land has been at the root of most Central American conflicts throughout the 500 years since the first Europeans arrived, and it remains the principal issue today. Early in its history, Central America divided into two distinct classes of people—those who had the land, and those who worked the land on their behalf.

The Receding Forests

The Caribbean and Pacific coasts, the high-mountain cloud forests, even the supernatural desolation of the volcanoes in Central America, have a transcendent quality. The popular conception of Central America is one of jungle, dense with color and the omnipresent cacophony of insects, reptiles, and multicolored birds.

Despite this fantastic popular view, the hand of man is everywhere apparent; Central America has a dense and rapidly growing population. Beyond the agro-industrial tracts of bananas, cotton, and coffee, most agriculture is of a rudimentary nature: Land is cleared, trees cut down, and the biomass is burned. The soil, often deceptively meager under the canopy of natural growth, rapidly loses nutrients as minerals are leached away. The patch of land is then abandoned for another. Scrub weeds take over and underfed cattle graze where forests once stood. This type of destruction is complicated by the need to cultivate even extremely steep tracts of land to keep up with the demands of a rapidly growing population. The slash-and-burn technique produces alarming erosion and land destruction from which there is little hope of recovery.

For nearly two centuries, Belize was a logging colony that harvested fine hardwoods such as mahogany. As a result, much of the nation was covered by a meager scrub of gnarled trees and undergrowth. Now, however, the land is starting to recover, and forests cover some 60% of the area. In some countries, overcultivation and erosion are complicated by rocketing populations, which further tax the exhausted soil. Water tables are dropping at dangerous rates, and international aid agencies finance digging ever-deeper wells to perform rudimentary irrigation. The rain forests that once characterized the isthmus are, sadly, vanishing. In northern Guatemala and southern Mexico, population pressures are driving subsistence farmers farther into the wilderness in search of new land to slash and burn. The destruction of natural habitats for wildlife in the region is driving many species of animals, notably exotic birds and wildcats, to the brink of extinction.

The struggle over land feeds this Central American conflict, too. Since the best lands are occupied by a tiny minority that controls national economics, it is politically expedient to encourage peasant occupation of unused wilderness lands. Throughout the isthmus, unoccupied lands seem to have great agricultural potential; but on closer inspection, these rain forests and mountains are ill-suited to commercial development. Their occupation merely hastens the ecological crisis.

Central American People

Central America is an ethnic patchwork—a blend of virtually every racial type known to the New World. A foundation of indigenous population built upon by waves of European, Afro-Caribbean, Middle Eastern, and even Asian immigration has created a modern mixture of races known as the mestizo.

The indigenous population of pre-Conquest Central America was in itself a blend of Indians from North and South America. Mezoamerican Indians were the product of highly developed, often urban cultures. The Olmecs, Toltecs, and Aztecs of Mexico and the Maya of Guatemala, Belize, Honduras, and El Salvador are examples of advanced Indian groups living in developed, hierarchical states. Indians migrating north from South America included the Chibcha of Colombia; the Cuna, Chocó, and Guayamí of Panama; and the Rama, Suma, and Miskito of

Nicaragua. These groups lived in less complex societies based on hunting, primitive agriculture, and fishing. Between these two distinct groups were the Lenca, Jicaque, and Paya of Honduras and El Salvador.

The Spanish who settled in Central America soon subdivided into various social strata founded on degrees of racial purity and even place of birth. The Spanish crown dictated that only the *peninsulares* born in Spain could occupy key posts, serving as governors, judges, and administrators, and these Spaniards came to monopolize wealth and power. The Creoles, born in the colonies, were relegated to inferior positions, but eventually had their day when independence destroyed the aristocracy.

Further down the social ladder of colonial Central America were the mestizos, who soon came to represent the majority. The mestizos fell in where the "pure" bloods left off—in small business and small-scale plantation farming. For the most part, they spoke Spanish, embraced European culture, and passed social aggression down the scale to the full-blood Indians, who were held in contempt by all. The Indians served as serfs and slaves, oppressed and put down by every religious, political, and economic institution created by colonialism.

Indians in Central America, even to this day, have had to make a bitter choice—to live in Indian communities and withdraw from advancement along the economic scale or to ignore their cultural heritage by assuming the Spanish language and European dress, abandoning traditional lands and moving to urban areas, and even discarding their indigenous names. This choice between isolation and assimilation is increasingly evident in Central America as Indian communities continue to languish in social and economic poverty.

Africa also lives in Central America—in the thousands of black Central Americans, the vast majority of whom live on the Caribbean coast of the isthmus. Blacks were first brought to the region in the 16th century, when indigenous slave populations working the mines and plantations of the colonies needed to be replenished. Later, groups of blacks from the West Indies were brought to the isthmus for plantation work or, in the case of Panama, for

WHAT'S WHERE

large-scale engineering projects. Many of these black Central Americans speak English as their primary language.

Blacks in the coastal region have intermingled with indigenous groups such as the Miskito, Suma, and Rama Indians of Nicaragua. A smaller subgroup are the Black Caribs of Belize, Honduras, and Nicaragua, the product of a racial mix of Africans and Carib Indians on the island of St. Vincent, who were exported en masse by the British to Central America in the late 18th century.

Various new strains have been added to this mixture. Asians are evident in virtually every Central American city. European-descended Jews are a small but economically dynamic ethnic group, as are the Palestinians sprinkled throughout the region. North Americans of various ethnicities are evident in every Central American nation.

Central America's geography is a mirror of its multiracial history. Guatemala today is overwhelmingly indigenous, with the minority of mestizos and whites concentrated in the cities. Belize is primarily black, with various blends in the principal cities and Maya communities in the south.

Central America is indeed a volatile area, both geographically and politically. Poverty and inequality are an all-embracing fact of life. In an area that has been so ravaged by fickle continental plates and the greed and power of the merciless few—both foreign and home-grown—it seems hard to visualize the beauty and attraction of what it has to offer. Nevertheless, it should not be forgotten that "Central America" is merely a geographic term, and within its boundaries differences—geographic, political, and social—are as blatant as chalk and cheese: the idea of death-squad killings is as alien to most Belizeans as it would be to northern Californians. There is, of course, Guatemala, whose recent history is as troubled as that of Nicaragua or El Salvador, but despite this one may visit the country without knowing that anything is amiss.

— John Mitchem

John Mitchem has covered Latin America for a variety of publications, including the *Philadelphia Inquirer*, the *Denver Post*, and *Américas* magazine.

Belize

Look for a mere geographical sliver wedged between Mexico and Guatemala and you will discover Belize. The country occupies a land mass no larger than the state of Massachussetts, but don't let its diminutive status fool you. Within its borders, Belize probably has the greatest variety of landscapes and peoples, of flora and fauna, of any country of equivalent size in the world. In the Maya Mountains, the central highlands that form the watershed for the thousands of streams and rivers that make their way to the sea, there is dense rain forest. In the north is savanna and sugar cane. One moment you can be in pine savanna; the next, in dense rain forest. Because it has the lowest population density of any country in Central America—El Salvador, the region's only smaller country, has ten times the population—and as Belizeans are by temperament and by tradition town dwellers, most of this green interior remains home to scarlet macaws, tapir, jaguars, kinkajous, mountain lions, and howler monkeys. Even reduced to vapid statistics—300 species of bird, 250 varieties of orchid, dozens of species of butterfly—the sheer variety of Belize's wildlife is breathtaking. The same holds for its nearly 600 Maya ruins, which range from the metropolitan splendor of Caracol to the humble living mounds that you see throughout the country.

Guatemala

Despite its infrastructural problems (including a civil war that has lasted since 1961), Guatemala is one of the most enchanting spots in Central America. Within an area roughly the size of Ohio you will find palm-lined beaches, luxuriant cloud forests, rugged mountain ranges, tumultuous boulder-strewn rivers, a scrubby desert valley, 37 volcanoes, extraordinary Maya ruins, and expansive stretches of rain forest that are home to spider monkeys, toucans, iguanas, and massive mahogany trees draped with mosses, ferns, vines, bromeliads, and rare orchids. Guatemala is home to 9 million people of different ethnic origins—Mayas, but at least 22 different ethnicities; Ladinos, the descendants of Indians and Europeans; Garifunas, a handful of African immigrants; and the European minority, predominantly Hispanic, which has maintained its imported bloodline and colonial lease on power. This diversity creates a kind of multithreaded human tapestry, which makes Guatemala even more colorful than the Indian weavers' most intricate patterns.

PLEASURES AND PASTIMES

Archaeological Ruins

The Maya Empire, which once occupied much of present-day Guatemala and stretched north into Mexico, east into Belize, and south into Honduras and El Salvador, disintegrated in the middle of the 16th century, leaving a cultural and archaeological treasure trove to rival that of any ancient civilization. Only a fraction of the thousands of ruins have been excavated from the jungle that over the centuries has swallowed the once splendid cities, but you don't have to be an archaeology buff to be overwhelmed by those that have. Of the many sites in the northern Guatemalan department of El Petén, Tikal is the most splendid, with majestic temples towering above pristine rain forest; a visit to the top of Temple IV is an experience that you will not soon forget. In Belize, Maya ruins dot the landscape throughout the north and west of the country; the most impressive sites include Altun Ha, 45 kilometers (28 miles) north of Belize City; Lamanai, the oldest Maya site in the country, about 2½ hours west of Belize City; and Caracol, in the Cayo district, a few miles from the border with Guatemala.

Horseback Riding

In Belize's Cayo District, where there's plenty of mountainous terrain but not many roads, the horse has always been the primary mode of transportation. It's still common to see "cattlemen," Belizean cowboys, herding Brahmin cattle on horseback with guns slung over their shoulders (in case of jaguars). These days, riding has begun to catch on with visitors, since it's a great way to explore the mountain landscape. Many hotels and lodges offer hourly as well as daily rates on horse rental, and there are also several specialist operations with fine remudas of horses.

Nature's Bounty

Of the nearly 4.5 million species of animals and plants estimated to exist on earth, nearly two-thirds of them are found in the tropics, making moist tropical forests the most species-rich ecosystems on the planet. As a result, Belize and Guatemala possess between them an almost unfathomable wealth of natural treasures. Both countries have made concerted efforts to preserve their natural heritage, and it has paid off. In Guatemala, the government set up protected areas known as *biotopos* and a national park system, which, despite chronic underfunding, aim to preserve both the country's natural and wildlife resources and its immense archaeological wealth. In Belize, gargantuan efforts have been made to promote ecotourism by establishing well-run national parks, nature reserves, and wildlife sanctuaries. Many of the protected areas in both countries are in remote locations and are often difficult to get to; some are accessible only by all-terrain vehicles and even boat trips through the jungle. If you are well-prepared, however, getting there could well be the most exciting adventure you've ever had.

Scuba Diving

It is no secret that the Barrier Reef, a coral necklace stretching the length of Belize from the Yucatán Peninsula in the north to the Guatemalan border in the south, offers some of the best diving opportunities in the world. Not only is the reef the longest in the Western Hemisphere, but it is also the most spectacular; clear, unpolluted water and a virtual smorgasbord of marine and coral life make diving here an exhilarating experience that few divers will ever forget. Although the diving is excellent almost anywhere along the reef, the very best is around the many coral atolls farther out to sea. Here there are some of the most spectacular wall dives in the world; the water falls away, within sight of the shore, to as much as 3,000 feet. Particularly spectacular is the diving around Turneffe Island and Lighthouse Reef, site of the famous Blue Hole. First dived by Jacques Cousteau in 1970, it has become a place of pilgrimage for divers from all over the world.

Sportfishing

Some of the most exciting sportfishing in the world is to be had in Belize's coastal waters, albeit of the catch-and-release variety, in accordance with the country's strict, ecologically minded laws. Tarpon, snook, bonefish, and permit abound, all of which, when hooked, will make your reel screech and your heart beat faster. Several specialist resorts and fishing camps cater especially to the angler, but most resorts and hotels will be able to organize excellent fishing for you.

NEW AND NOTEWORTHY

More tour companies are offering package trips to Belize's 350-mile **Barrier Reef,** the world's second-largest after Australia's. The reef, which has been proposed as a UNESCO World Heritage Site, is home to a spectacular array of marine life and is still largely unscathed by human impact. Trips feature world-class diving, fishing, and sailing.

Guatemala's **hotel industry** is booming, as new lodgings are under construction in Chichicastenango, Antigua, the Atlantic coast, and Guatemala City, the capital. Big U.S. chains are moving in, and a new $8 million high-tech convention center opened its doors in August 1996. This economic expansion is the result of a more favorable investment image and the recent election of Alvaro Arzu, a civilian president who promises to negotiate an end to the 35-year-old civil war.

A private-sector development foundation called **FUNDESA** has launched a number of initiatives to make Guatemala more tourist-friendly, including sponsorship of a nationwide campaign, called "Let's Keep Guatemala Alive," whose aim is to instill in locals a more welcoming attitude toward tourists. FUNDESA also was instrumental in getting a new board of directors at Guatemala City's airport in order to modernize the terminal's outdated structures. Best of all, the group is behind a campaign to enlist the country's business class in building more roads to hard-to-get-to tourist attractions in the jungles and highlands, while preserving the wildlife and natural beauty of the landscape.

Ecological and adventure tourism is opening Guatemala's wilderness to more visitors every year. Jungle treks, white-water rafting, cave exploration, volcano ascents, river trips, and deep-sea fishing can all be combined with visits to striking Indian villages or ancient ruins.

FODOR'S CHOICE

Archaeological Sites

★**Altun Ha, Belize.** The best-excavated and most accessible Maya ruin in the country is over 2,000 years old; at its height, it was home to 10,000 people.

★**Caracol, Belize.** The most spectacular of the Maya sites in Belize, it contained five plazas and 32 large structures, covered nearly a square mile, and in its heyday was home to as many as 200,000 inhabitants.

★**Lamanai, Belize.** Nearly 60 Maya structures are spread out over this 950-acre reserve, including a massive temple that is the largest pre-Classic building in the country.

★**Quiriquá, Guatemala.** This important Maya trading center is renowned for its massive stelae, the largest in the Maya world.

★**Tikal, Guatemala.** A visit to the country's most famous ruin will leave you in no doubt as to the extraordinary accomplishments of the Maya; this vast array of awe-inspiring temples and intricate acropolises was once a teeming metropolis.

Dining

Note that dining and lodging costs are much higher in Belize than in Guatemala. What's considered expensive in Guatemala might very well be inexpensive or moderate for Belize (☞ individual chapters for definitions of price categories).

BELIZE

★**Elvi's Kitchen, Ambergris Caye.** The banner on the letterhead at this Belizean restaurant states that this is "Di Place for Seafood"; we cannot but agree. $$

★**The Lagoon, Ambergris Caye.** The latest addition to Ambergris's culinary scene, this flashy bistro offers uptown (Manhattan) style in downtown San Pedro. $$

★**GGs, Belize City.** This American-style restaurant serves a wide selection of dishes—from beans and rice to T-bone steaks—in an Italian café atmosphere. $–$$

GUATEMALA

★**Jake's, Guatemala City.** Twenty-five daily specials augment the excellent Italian and international menu at this restaurant in a restored farmhouse. $$$

★**El Bistro, Panajachel.** Come here for the romantic lakeside setting and the delicious, homemade Italian food. $$

Lodging

BELIZE

★**Chaa Creek, Cayo District.** The mixture of jungle seclusion and candlelit conviviality, combined with the excellence of the 40-person staff, the quality of the food and amenities, and Belize's best Natural History Museum make this the queen of the jungle resorts. $$$

★**Rum Point Inn, Placencia.** The feeling you have walking into any of these domelike villas on a pine-dotted beach is of space, light, and air. And hosts George and Coral Bevier couldn't be nicer. $$$

★**Victoria House, Ambergris Caye.** One of the most beautiful properties in the country, this white colonial-style house on a gorgeous beach offers Old World style, excellent food, and a superb dive shop. $$$

GUATEMALA

★**Casa Santo Domingo, Antigua.** Amid the ruins of an ancient monastery, this hotel captures the past without omitting any modern luxuries. $$$$

★**Posada de Santiago, Santiago Atitlán.** Sandwiched between two volcanoes on the shores of a lagoon, this Guatemalan hotel offers American-style comfort in a traditional Indian village environment. $$

Special Moments

★**Night diving at Hol Chan Marine Reserve, Belize.** If you are a strong swimmer, then this will be a special treat; nocturnal animals, including the octopus and the spider crab, unhurriedly go about their business in water lighted by bioluminescence.

★**Sunrise over the New River Lagoon at Lamanai, Belize.** Take a secluded jungle paradise, exotic wildlife, Maya ruins, a romantic lagoon, and you'll only need one thing to make this a picture-perfect view: a sunrise.

★**Good Friday in Antigua, Guatemala.** This religious feast is Guatemala at its most festive and mystical, as processions of costumed disciples weave their way through flower-carpeted streets, leaving behind a trail of incense.

★**Sunset on Lake Atitlán, Guatemala.** At sunset, muted pastels enshroud the looming volcanoes that guard Lake Atitlán, creating an impressionist tableau of water, sky, and mountains.

2 National Parks and Wildlife Reserves

An in-depth look at the region's natural treasures, including Guatemala's biotopos *and Belize's wildlife sanctuaries.*

BELIZE AND GUATEMALA possess an almost unfathomable wealth of natural and archaeological assets. Spread among them are hundreds of important pre-Columbian ruins, more species of plants and animals than scientists have been able to count, and a variety of scenery that ranges from barren mountain peaks to lush forests and vibrant coral reefs. Moreover, the governments of both countries, but especially Belize, have had the foresight to protect a significant portion of their ecological and archaeological wealth as preserves of various kinds. In Guatemala, protected areas created specifically for the conservation of nature are called *biotopos,* and archaeological sites are called national parks (although Tikal National Park is also a very impressive nature reserve). Belize has sanctuaries or reserves.

Though the names may change from country to country, there is one characteristic that all but a few well-developed protected areas have in common—lack of infrastructure. Only a few of the region's parks can be reached by paved roads, many require four-wheel-drive vehicles to visit, and some can only be reached by boat, on horseback, or on foot. Some parks don't have much of a visitor center and trails aren't well marked, but getting in and out of them is half the adventure.

Although the protected areas of Belize and Guatemala contain spectacular scenery and wildlife, don't expect to come face-to-face with a jaguar. Jaguars, tapirs, giant anteaters, and quetzals inhabit many of the region's parks and preserves, but it's unlikely that you will ever see these animals. You are, however, pretty likely to catch glimpses of monkeys, toucans, iguanas, and noisy flocks of parrots and parakeets. Because of the thick foliage and prevalent mist, cloud forests can be tough places to see birds and other wildlife, especially during the rainy season. (For an in-depth discussion of rain forests, cloud forests, and other Central American habitats, read "The Natural Splendor of Central America" *in* Chapter 5.)

Many tour companies offer trips to the national parks and reserves (☞ Tour Operators *in* The Gold Guide's Important Contacts A to Z *and* Guided Tours *in* individual country chapters). Whether you travel on your own or with a tour group, make sure your visit benefits the people who live near the wilderness areas: Use local guides or services, visit local restaurants, and buy local handicrafts or fruits. To ensure these areas will be preserved for future generations, make donations to local conservation groups; tour operators in each country may be able to make suggestions. A few foreign environmental organizations, including Conservation International, World Wildlife Fund, and the Nature Conservancy, are also aiding ecological efforts in the isthmus.

BELIZE

By Richard
Nidever

The backbone of Belize's efforts to promote ecotourism is its marvelous collection of national parks, nature reserves, and wildlife sanctuaries. Since the creation of the first such area, Half Moon Caye National Monument, in 1982, Belize has jumped on the conservation bandwagon with unabashed enthusiasm, putting over 30% of its land under some form of protection. The most interesting and accessible of Belize's many protected areas are described below; for more information about these and others, contact the **Belize Audubon Society** (✉ Box 282, 29 Regent St., Belize City, ☎ 027/7369) or the **Belize Center for Environmental Studies** (✉ Box 666, 55 Eve St., Belize City, ☎ 024/5739).

Belize Zoo

The **Belize Zoo and Tropical Research Education Center** is a good place to learn about the country's conservation efforts and see some native species that you aren't likely to spot in the wild. The Belize Zoo could fit into a small corner of the San Diego Zoo, and it has only a fraction of the animals. So why is it considered by some to be the world's best? Because the natural settings for the animals and the zoo's commitment to wildlife protection make it (and its founder, Sharon Matola) perhaps the single strongest force in Belizean conservation.

Matola originally came to Belize in 1983 to manage a band of local animals for a wildlife film. When the film's budget dried up, she was left with the animals and, knowing that releasing them back into the wild would be a death sentence, decided to start a zoo. From these humble beginnings, Matola slowly built up the zoo while embarking on an ambitious education program aimed especially at children. For the first time, Belizeans were able to see the wild animals who share their country and to learn how valuable the preservation of the animals' habitat could be for a developing nation. Many conservation leaders credit Matola with developing a new appreciation for local wildlife that has been instrumental in the fight to protect and preserve their habitats.

The zoo houses the elusive jaguar, the endangered Baird's tapir (the national animal of Belize and the largest land mammal in Central America), howler monkeys, and many other species. The enclosures replicate as closely as possible the animals' natural environment, which sometimes makes spotting them difficult, so the best time to visit (as well as the coolest) is early morning or late afternoon, when most of the animals are fed.

Getting There

By Bus. Buses from Belize City to San Ignacio stop at the zoo.

By Car. From Belize City, take the Western Highway to Mile 30.

Cockscomb Basin

The mighty jaguar, once the undisputed king of the Central and South American jungles, is now extinct or endangered in most of its original range. But it has found a sanctuary in **Cockscomb Basin Wildlife Sanctuary,** on 102,000 acres of lush rain forest in the Cockscomb range of the Maya Mountains. Because of the jaguar reserve, as this area is commonly called, as well as other protected areas in the country, Belize has the highest concentration of jaguars in the world.

Jaguars are shy, nocturnal animals that prefer to keep their distance from humans, so the possibility of sighting a jaguar in the wild is almost nil. Still, a visit here is rewarding in other ways. The reserve boasts Belize's best-maintained system of jungle and mountain trails, most of which have at least one outstanding swimming hole. The sanctuary also offers spectacular views of the Cockscomb range and Victoria Peak and the chance to see many other endangered flora and fauna, including about 300 bird species. If you plan to do any extensive hiking, pick up a trail map at the visitor center and bring insect repellent, a long-sleeved shirt, and long pants. Keep in mind that the best time to hike anywhere in Belize is early morning or late afternoon/early evening, when temperatures are lower and more wildlife can be seen.

Dining and Lodging

Campsites are available in the park ($5 a night), but most people stay in the area of Dangriga or Placencia (☞ Placencia and the South *in* Chapter 3).

Getting There

By Car. From Dangriga or Placencia, take the Southern Highway to Maya Centre, where you'll find the entrance and a dirt road (four-wheel drive recommended) that leads into the reserve.

Half Moon Caye

Half Moon Caye National Monument, Belize's easternmost island, although difficult to reach and lacking accommodations, offers one of the greatest wildlife encounters in Belize. Part of the Lighthouse Reef system, Half Moon Caye owes its protected status to the presence on the island of the red-footed booby in such stunning profusion that it's hard to believe that the species has only one other nesting colony in the entire Caribbean (on Tobago Island, off the coast of Venezuela). Some 4,000 of these rare seabirds call the island home, along with more than 90 other bird species, iguanas, lizards, and loggerhead turtles. The entire 40-acre island is a nature reserve, and visitors can explore the beaches or head into the bush on the narrow nature trail. Along this trail, above the trees at the center of the island, is a small viewing platform. Climb up, and you're suddenly in a sea of birds; they fill the branches of the surrounding trees so completely that it's hard not to be reminded of a certain Hitchcock movie.

Dining and Lodging

The nearest accommodations are at the Lighthouse Reef Resort, which offers a trip here as part of a weeklong package (☞ The Cays and Atolls *in* Chapter 3).

Getting There

By Boat. Because there are no accommodations and no regular boat service to the island, most people come here on a tour. A visit is usually combined with dives at the Blue Hole and Half Moon Caye Wall, considered by many to be the two best dive sites in Belize. One-day or overnight camping trips can be arranged through several dive operators and resorts (☞ The Cays and Atolls *in* Chapter 3).

Hol Chan

The 13-square-kilometer (5-square-mile) **Hol Chan** (Maya for "little channel") **Marine Reserve** is about 6 kilometers (4 miles) southeast of Ambergris Caye. Because fishing is off limits, divers can see teeming marine life, including green moray eels and spotted eagle rays. A night dive is a special treat: The water lights up with bioluminescence, and many nocturnal animals, such as octopus and spider crabs, can be observed. You need above-average swimming skills; the strong tidal current has caused at least one drowning.

Getting There

By Boat. San Pedro, on Ambergris Caye, is the jumping-off point for trips to the reserve, but before you go, stop in at the Hol Chan office there (⊠ Barrier Reef Dr.) for information on Belize's underwater flora and fauna. All of San Pedro's dive operators offer trips to Hol Chan (☞ The Cays and Atolls *in* Chapter 3), which generally last about two hours and are reasonably priced (about $15 for snorkeling and $30 for a single-tank dive). **Ramon's Dive Shop** (☎ 026/2071) and **Amigos del Mar** (☎ 026/2706) offer glass-bottom-boat tours of the marine reserve—perfect for those who want to see marine life without getting wet.

GUATEMALA

By Jacob
Bernstein

Guatemala's rich natural diversity makes it a fascinating destination
for nature lovers, though the government hasn't invested nearly enough
in protecting the country's natural wonders or in making them accessible. Travel to some areas is nearly impossible. One good way to see
the local flora and fauna is on river trips or other adventure tours. Try
Maya Expeditions (☎ 337–4666) or **Izabal Adventures** (☎ 334–
0323), both of which are experienced and committed to ecotourism.
The friendly and knowledgeable Acuña family arranges custom-designed
adventures throughout Guatemala (☎ FAX 251–1268).

Administered by the San Carlos National University, biotopos were first
established in the late 1970s to protect specific threatened animals or
ecosystems. Today they represent the last stand for many endangered
plants and animals, presenting a window on a marvelous spectrum of
Guatemala's diversity. Although they are chronically underfunded,
biotopos are staffed with friendly, helpful rangers committed to conservation. For more information contact the **Center for Conservation
Studies** (✉ Avenida La Reforma 0–63, Zona 10, ☎ 332–7612). Admission is usually free, but in order to help fund the upkeep of these
magnificent areas, there are donation boxes at the entrances.

Cerro Cahui

Cerro Cahui Wildlife Reserve, with more than 1,500 acres of rain forest, is one of the most accessible biotopos in El Petén, protecting a portion of a mountain that extends into the eastern edge of Lake Petén
Itzá. A hike along either of two easy, well-maintained trails offers the
opportunity to see ocellated turkeys, toucans, parrots, spider monkeys,
and *tepezcuintle* (large rodents hunted for their flavorful meat).
Tzu'unte, a 3-kilometer (2-mile) trail, leads to two lookouts with views
of nearby lakes. The upper lookout, Mirador Moreletii, is known by
locals as Crocodile Hill because from the lake's other side it looks like
the eye of a half-submerged crocodile. Los Ujuxtes, 437 yards long,
offers a panoramic view of three lakes. Both begin at the ranger station, where interpretive guides in English are sporadically available.

Dining and Lodging
Cerro Cahui is close to Camino Real Tikal and El Gringo Perdido. (☞
Tikal and El Petén *in* Chapter 4).

Getting There
By Car. From Guatemala City, head for the Atlantic coast and turn left
after the town of Franceses (there will be a sign for Flores or the Petén;
be prepared for a rough road). Cerro Cahui is after El Remate on the
road to Tikal. Turn left at the sign for Camino Real, and follow the
dirt road to the park entrance.

Chocón Machacas

Chocón Machacas Wildlife Reserve is commonly known as the manatee biotopo, and although manatees are said to inhabit the area, it is
almost impossible to see these shy but endangered marine mammals.
What you can see easily in the 17,790-acre reserve is mangrove swamp,
spectacular rain forest, and varied animal life. The park consists of a
small island surrounded by rivers, and there is only one land trail of
a little less than 1 kilometer (½ mile). It's well maintained, easily
walked, and presents interesting examples of old-growth trees and rain-
forest plants. There is a good chance that Pancho, a harmless but an-

noying spider monkey that rangers brought to the park, will accompany you on your walk and try to hitch a ride on your leg.

The real beauty of the reserve can be seen in a boat ride through the dozens of creeks and lagoons that circle the park, where otters and many bird species can be seen. Most of the major hotels on the Río Dulce rent boats with guides for individual or group tours. Some of the creeks go through thick forest, under giant mahogany, ceiba, and mangrove trees, which overhang the water to form tunnels. There is a visitor center at the park entrance, where interpretive guides in English can be purchased when in stock.

Dining and Lodging
Catamaran Island and Marimonte Inn are the closest accommodations (☞ Atlantic Lowlands *in* Chapter 4).

Getting There
By Boat. The only way to get here is by boat, from the Río Dulce area, Livingston, or Puerto Barrios. It's 45 minutes from Río Dulce, where boat tours can be arranged at most hotels or at the **Río Dulce Travel Warehouse** (✉ Under the concrete bridge, El Relleno, or reached through Izabal Adventures, ☎ 334–0323), which offers tours through the park and along the Polochic and Oscuro, two beautiful rivers teeming with wildlife that flow into Lake Izabal.

Monterrico

Monterrico Natural Reserve, which offers a nice beach and excellent bird-watching, encompasses 6,916 acres of mangrove swamp and tropical dry forest jutting up against the Pacific Ocean. Turtles swim ashore from July to February to lay their eggs; walking along the beach at night, you might encounter them digging their nests. Monterrico has a nice beach, but be careful: The ocean can be rough.

The park has a splendid aquatic trail, which can be followed by boat, and a land trail, which is not worth the effort. The aquatic trail winds its way through swamps with three types of mangrove. A trip here is an excellent opportunity for viewing more than 100 species of migratory and indigenous birds; fisher eagles, pelicans, and herons abound. The best time to go is at dawn or sunset, when enormous flocks of birds flap across a blood-red sky on their way to bed down for the night. From the swamps, there's a magnificent view of four volcanoes, including the active Pacaya. Guided boat tours ($2 per person for two hours) through the swamp trail can be arranged with park guards.

San Carlos University's center inside the reserve is worth a visit. A project to raise animals for locals to sell or eat in lieu of capturing wild ones brings you face-to-face with caimans (relatives of crocodiles), iguanas, and turtles in various stages of development. Also within the reserve is the rustic *aldea* (village) of Monterrico, with about 1,100 people. Here most residents relax in their hammocks in the afternoon, and it's easy to leave civilization behind.

Dining and Lodging
There are several moderately priced hotels along the beach, most of which are little more than concrete rooms with cold showers and beds covered with mosquito netting. They have no addresses but are easy to find along the small beach. **Hotel Baule Beach** (☎ 473–6196 in Guatemala City) has a good restaurant. At the end of the beach is the pleasant **Pez de Oro** (☎ 332–3768 in Antigua for reservations), a series of well-kept, pastel-color bungalows.

$$ ✗ **Divino Maestro.** The best restaurant in the village of Monterrico, this simple establishment has tables under a thatched roof in an open-air room. There is no fixed menu, but you can choose from four types of fresh fish as well as crab, shrimp, meat, or chicken. The *caldo de mariscos* (seafood stew) is delicious. ✉ *Aldea of Monterrico, no phone. No credit cards.*

$$$ 🏨 **Hotel Paradise.** About a 20-minute walk from the town's center, this hotel enjoys a quiet location, a pool, and its own stretch of beach. Although this is Monterrico's best hotel, considering the price, the bungalows are slightly bare and the service can be poor. ☎ *332–0795 or 334–5405 in Guatemala City. Pool, beach. MC, V.*

Getting There
By Bus. Buses depart the main bus station in Guatemala City for Taxisco every half hour. From Taxisco, microbuses depart regularly for La Avellana, where there's a ferry that goes to Monterrico Beach.

By Car. Take the highway to Escuintla from Guatemala City. From Escuintla, take the left to Taxisco and follow the road to the village of La Avellana, where a ferry regularly takes travelers to Monterrico Beach.

Quetzal

The **Quetzal Reserve** offers the chance to see the Guatemalan national bird, the resplendent quetzal, in its natural habitat. The male quetzal is magnificent, with its 2-foot-long train of tail feathers and brilliant, metallic-green body with red and white underparts. You can see its antics between April and June during mating season; the best place to watch, oddly enough, is not in the park itself but in the parking lot of the hotel Ranchito del Quetzal, 1½ kilometers (1 mile) north.

The Quetzal Reserve is also one of the last cloud forests in Guatemala and represents a vital source of water for the region's rivers. A walk along its trails gives the sense of being in a giant sponge. Water, evaporated from Lake Izabal and the Honduran Gulf, comes down in the form of rain and condensed fog, which is then collected by the towering old growth trees and verdant, dense vegetation. The loss of cloud forests such as this one is turning adjacent lowland areas into desert.

Once inside the forest, breathe deep; the air is rich with moisture and oxygen. Epiphytes, lichens, hepaticas, mosses, bromeliads, ferns, and orchids abound. If you're lucky, you can catch howler monkeys swinging above the well-maintained trails.

The biotopo is not large and can be visited in a day, although the best time to see the quetzal is early morning or late afternoon. The park offers two trails: Los Helechos ("the ferns"), which takes about an hour to walk, and Los Musgos ("the moss"), which takes two hours and makes a short detour to a series of beautiful waterfalls. The last part of both trails crosses a river with concrete bathing pools where you can take a swim if you don't mind the cold. An interpretive guide is available at the stand at the trailheads.

Dining and Lodging
Posada Montaña del Quetzal and Ranchito del Quetzal are the closest lodges to the reserve (☞ Verapaces *in* Chapter 4).

Getting There
By Bus. Take any bus to Cobán and ask to be let off at the reserve.

By Car. Take the Carretera Atlantíca (Atlantic Highway) to El Rancho (Km 84); then follow the road to the left, which heads toward Cobán. The reserve is about 75 kilometers (46½ miles) north of El Rancho.

Sierra de las Minas

The **Sierra de las Minas Biosphere Reserve,** said to be named for the Maya jade and obsidian quarries that once were active in the area, represents one of the last truly unexplored places of Central America. Recently declared a biosphere reserve, it is loosely modeled after the Maya Biosphere Reserve (☞ Tikal, *below*). Within its territory—which cuts across four departments in the Atlantic region: Progreso, Baja Verapaz, Zacapa, and Izabal—are at least four types of forest and more than 70% of the species of vertebrates found in Guatemala. Biologists working in the area continue to discover new plant and insect varieties. Unfortunately, there is no tourism infrastructure, and it is almost impossible to arrive without the aid of a four-wheel-drive vehicle or helicopter. If you are undaunted by the challenge, contact **Tamandua** (☎ FAX 332–2690), an environmental group with a special interest in the area, to obtain the most up-to-date information.

Tikal

Tikal National Park is in the Maya Biosphere Reserve, which covers the upper third of El Petén, the department that boasts Guatemala's largest concentration of primary growth forest and its most important archaeological ruins. Surrounded by a multiple-use buffer zone, Tikal National Park is at the biosphere reserve's sacrosanct core and is supposed to be off-limits to human development. Tikal is easily visited and presents excellent opportunities for animal- and bird-watching while one walks among the ruins. There are several nature trails, both within the ruins and outside them. In particular, the short interpretive Benil-Ha Trail is excellent for identifying old-growth trees and rain-forest plants. Outside the park there is a somewhat overgrown trail halfway down the old airplane runway on the left. It leads to the remnants of several old rubber-tappers' camps, and because few people go there, it presents an excellent opportunity to see animals and birds.

Dining and Lodging

The lodges in Tikal are close to the park (☞ Tikal and El Petén *in* Chapter 4).

Getting There

By Bus. Buses depart from the San Juan hotel in Santa Elena at 6:30 AM and 1 PM.

By Car. Tikal National Park is an hour's drive northeast of Flores.

By Taxi. Taxis headed for the park depart from Santa Elena and the airport regularly.

3　Belize

Belize has got it right; from the variety of landscapes and people to the spectacular diving at the Barrier Reef—and, of course, the nearly 600 Maya ruins, which range from the metropolitan splendor of Caracol to the humble living mounds that you see throughout the country—this is a magical place that will thrill most everybody, from the archaeological buff to the diving enthusiast.

By Simon
Worrall

A SLIVER OF LAND wedged between Mexico and Guatemala, 280 kilometers (175 miles) long and 109 kilometers (68 miles) wide at its broadest point, Belize is no larger than the state of Massachusetts. But don't let its diminutive size fool you. Within its borders, Belize probably has the greatest variety of landscapes and peoples, of flora and fauna, of any country of equivalent size in the world.

In the Maya Mountains, the central highlands that form the watershed for the thousands of streams and rivers that make their way to the sea, there is dense rain forest. In the north there is savanna and sugarcane. Because it has the lowest population density of any country in Central America—El Salvador, the region's only smaller country, has 10 times as many people—and as Belizeans are by temperament and tradition town dwellers, most of its green interior remains uninhabited.

Less than an hour's flight from the green heartland is the Barrier Reef, a great wall of coral stretching the length of the coast. Dotting the reef like punctuation marks are the more than 200 cays, and farther out to sea, the atolls—both superb for diving and snorkeling. Some are no more than Robinson Crusoe islets of white coral sand and mangroves, inhabited by frigate birds, pelicans, and the occasional fisherman, who will spend a few days diving for conch and lobster, sleeping under a sheet of canvas strung between trees. Others, like Ambergris Caye, are gradually being developed. Their bars, hotels, dive shops, and discos are a source of pride and wealth for locals.

The name Belize is a conundrum. According to Encyclopedia Britannica, it derives from *belix,* an ancient Maya word meaning "muddy water," and anyone who has seen the Belize River swollen by heavy rains will vouch for its aptness. Others trace the origin to the French word *balise* (beacon), though no one explains why a French word should have caught on in this Spanish-dominated region. Another theory is that it's named for the Maya word *belikin,* but as this is the name of the national beer, perhaps it is a drinker's tale. According to some, Belize is a corruption of Wallace, a Scottish buccaneer who founded a colony in 1620. Others say the pirate wasn't Wallace, but Willis, wasn't Scottish, but English, and that he didn't found a colony in 1620, but in 1638. We'll never know if Wallace and Willis were one and the same or how "w" could become "b," and "a" slip to "e." Perhaps it was too much Belikin. But what's in a name anyway? For centuries, Belize did fine as British Honduras.

There was indeed a pirate called Wallace, a onetime lieutenant of Sir Walter Raleigh who later served as British governor of Tortuga. Perhaps it was liquor or lucre that turned Governor Wallace into pirate Wallace. Sometime between 1638 and 1662 he and 80 fellow renegades washed up on the Viego River, now known as the Belize River, behind St. George's Caye. For years this motley crew managed to live off booty from cloak and dagger raids on passing ships.

The two men on Belize's flag are not pirates, however, but two stout woodcutters, standing in the shade of a logwood tree. Under them is a Latin inscription, *sub umbra floreat:* "In the shade of this tree we flourish." What is remarkable about them is that one is black, the other white—a celebration of the racial mixing emblematic of Belize.

Whites are descendants of the English buccaneers and the settlers that followed them to the Honduran Bay Settlement, as Belize was first known. They came to work under grueling conditions in the jungles and forests of the interior, bringing out logwood for export to England, where it was prized as a valuable textile dye. As the craftsmen of Europe discovered the value of mahogany, they were joined by many more.

Many of today's blacks descended from slaves who were brought from Jamaica to work in the logwood industry, but in Belize the vicious divisions of slave society were loosened and humanized, thanks to its geographical isolation and the residents' innate dislike of authority in any form. Surrounded by hostile nature and subject to attacks by Maya Indians in the interior and Spanish warships on the coast, white and black had only one choice. Domination gave way to codependence, and codependence to cooperation and perhaps even affection.

Not all blacks came as slaves. Some came as free men, others as escapees, still others were shipwrecked on the Mosquito Coast. By the early 18th century the number of people of African descent in Belize already outnumbered those with British origins, and they probably enjoyed greater human rights than much of Central America does today. Surprisingly, slaves were routinely armed, but instead of training their guns on their white masters, they eventually united with them to defeat a common enemy.

That enemy appeared off the coast of Belize early on September 10, 1798, in the form of 31 Spanish naval vessels, manned by 500 seamen, carrying 2,000 well-armed troops, and commanded by the Captain-General of the Yucatán. After more than a century spent trying to uproot the upstart colony from its backyard, the Spanish finally had come to exterminate it.

The Baymen, their slaves, and a few British troops totaled 350, and they had a total of one sloop, some fishing boats, and seven rafts. The battle was over in two hours, with the Baymen triumphant. Many patriotic poems have been written to celebrate the victory; they revel in the gore, as well as the glory, piling images of hideous carnage one on top of the other like so much pastrami. In truth, there were only two casualties, both Spanish, and history became a fable agreed upon. That was the last time the Spanish attempted to forcibly dislodge the settlement, though for nearly a century, bitter wrangles over British Honduras's right to exist continued.

In the 19th century, the early inhabitants—and the original inhabitants, the Maya—were joined by mestizos fleeing the Yucatán during the War of the Castes and a group of Black Caribs, known as the Garifuna, who, after numerous insurrections on the island of St. Vincent, settled in the Stann Creek area. Later came Mennonites fleeing persecution in Europe. All these peoples, like Belize's most recent refugees—the thousands of Salvadorans and Guatemalans who fled their countries' death squads and torture chambers in the '70s—found in this tiny country a tolerant, amiable home. In a country where almost everyone is a foreigner, no one is.

The next wave of immigrants, as many as 50,000 Chinese, is due to arrive after the Communists take over Hong Kong in 1997. Construction sites with signs in Mandarin are springing up all over. Many Belizeans are questioning the visas-for-cash deal struck by the previous government and wondering whether such a large number of immigrants, equivalent to one-quarter of the current population, could upset Belize's complex ethnic balance. Odds are it won't.

The dominant social and ethnic group today is the Creoles. Half African, half Anglo-Saxon, they consider themselves the heirs of the colonial era, and they hold most university, police, and government positions. In Belize City they form approximately 70% of the population. Happily, the races associate harmoniously, and the mixing of the human gene pool has produced exciting variations on the human species. You're likely to see people with all sorts of facial structures and skin colors. There are Chinese-looking women alongside men who could have stepped out of a Goya painting. You'll see blacks with blue eyes and half-Mayan, half-Creole people with green eyes and faces like obsidian masks. Belize is an estimable breath of fresh air in a world filled with ethnic strife.

Having historically maintained strong ties to Britain and the Commonwealth, Belize always belonged far more to the British Caribbean than to Central America, and still has more in common with Trinidad or St. Kitts than with Mexico or El Salvador. The most obvious difference is English—the official language here—which is closely allied to the English of the British Caribbean ("tea" refers to just about any meal, for example, as it does in the West Indies and cockney London). Among themselves, many Belizeans also speak Creole patois, a slang English with its own vocabulary and musical rhythms. Only in a few aspects is Belize like its neighbors: Spanish is widely spoken in the north, central regions, and south, while Maya is heard mainly in the Toledo District in the south. In addition, the population is 62% Roman Catholic and only 12% Anglican.

The British, who at the request of the Belizean government had maintained a small military presence since independence in 1981, finally pulled out in 1994, but relations between the two countries remain close. Belize still has a governor general appointed by the Queen, albeit with the approval of the Belizean parliament; its defense force is still trained by the Brits; and Harrier jump-jets, which used to cause gasps of amazement among arriving tourists by flying backwards over the airport, are still on call should Guatemala try to reassert its claim to what it called its 13th province. At the same time, initiatives like Mundo Maya, an effort by Central American states to coordinate travel to Maya sites, are paving the way for greater regional cooperation.

Meanwhile, more and more tourists are making the journey to this small country of huge contrasts. Luckily, the government has an enlightened attitude toward conservation and the environment. There is little industry—not by default but by choice—and what tourism there is is on a small scale. Some of the resorts can be a bit funky, but the best offer a charm and attention to visitors' needs unmatched elsewhere in the Caribbean. Ecotourism—getting visitors into nature without destroying it—is very big in Belize. And though there are signs that increased traffic is causing minor degradation of the Barrier Reef, the awareness of nature's fragility is prevalent. You'll hear fishermen and schoolchildren earnestly discuss the need to protect the environment.

So if you're looking for Daytona Beach or a golfer's paradise, you'd better look elsewhere. If, on the other hand, you want to take a night dive through a tunnel of living coral, ride a horse through jungle loud with the call of howler monkeys, explore one of the nearly 600 varied Maya ruins, or canoe through the rain forest, the "adventure coast"— as Belize is rightly called—will not disappoint. Experiencing the rich, colorful diversity of birds and animals that still survive here, and showing them to your children, is one of this friendly, easygoing country's richest gifts. Luckily, it will probably remain a nature lovers' haven far into the next century. Clever Belize.

Pleasures and Pastimes

Beaches

Much of the mainland coast is fringed with mangrove swamps and therefore has few beaches. The few that do exist are not spectacular. On the cays, particularly Ambergris, that changes dramatically. Here beaches are not expansive—generally there is a small strip of sand at the water's edge—but with their palm trees and mint-green water, you'll definitely know you're in the Caribbean. The best beach on the mainland is in Placencia, in the south.

Dining

Pig's tails and bread and butter pudding, cow-foot soup, and jam tarts are some of the culinary items left behind by the British, so don't expect gourmet food. Gibnut (often referred to as "the Queen's rat," since she ate it when she visited) is a local specialty, but the staple is rice and beans. When it's well done, it can be delicious. Seafood is as good as any in the Caribbean. Shrimp, lobster, conch, red snapper, and grouper abound, and whether simply cooked in garlic and butter and served with a slice of fresh lime, or smothered in a rich sauce, they are delicious. During spawning season, March 1–June 15, there is no fresh lobster, and conch is off-season July through September. Fresh-squeezed juices, like lime, watermelon, and orange, can be found everywhere and are delicious.

Most of the best restaurants are in the hotels and resorts and bear comparison with good, though not first-class, establishments in North America or Europe. Don't judge a restaurant by the way it looks. Some of the best cooking gets done in the humblest-looking cabanas. Follow your nose. Good cooks don't stay a secret for long.

Belize is a casual place, and little in the way of a dress code exists. The more expensive restaurants prefer, but do not require, a jacket and tie for men. Otherwise, if you have shoes and a shirt, you will probably get served. Reservations are advisable in more expensive eateries.

Prices vary considerably between the interior, Belize City, and the cays. Ambergris Caye, because it's the most developed, is the most expensive. A meal for two at one of the best restaurants costs $40–$60, but you will be able to eat well for much less. Lobster runs $10–$15, depending on the restaurant. A fish like grilled grouper usually costs about $7.50; a substantial American-style breakfast, $5; and a hamburger, $3. As there has been a considerable influx of Hong Kong Chinese in the last few years, Chinese food is plentiful and usually cheap.

CATEGORY	COST*
$$$$	over $50
$$$	$30–$50
$$	$15–$30
$	under $15

per person for a three-course meal, excluding drinks, service, and tax

Fishing

Belize has some of the most exciting sportfishing in the world. Tarpon, snook, bonefish, and permit abound, all of which will make your reel screech and your heart beat faster. Several specialist resorts and fishing camps cater to anglers, but most hotels can organize excellent fishing for you. Note well: In this ecologically minded country, only catch and release is allowed.

Horseback Riding

You can ride horses to the beach or to a Maya ruin. In Belize's interior, particularly in the Cayo, riding is one of the best ways to see the mountainous landscape. Horses tend to be small, tough local breeds (quarter horses often suffer in the climate).

Lodging

Little in the way of standardized, Holiday Inn–style accommodations exists in Belize. Large hotels are the exception rather than the rule. The best places are the small, highly individual resorts that offer personalized service and accommodations. They are strongly shaped by the tastes and interests of their owners—mostly American or British. Most have traveled widely themselves and are excellent hosts, but the quality of the services they provide varies greatly. At the top are those run by professionals, people with some previous training and experience in hotel-keeping. The worst are those opened on a whim by people who came to Belize on a visit, fell in love with the place, and opened a resort to finance their own escape to paradise. Because of the salt and humidity, operating a hotel in the tropics is an art in itself: the closest thing to keeping house on the deck of a ship. Without constant work, things start to rust, the palapa (a frequently used natural building material) leaks, and the charms of paradise quickly fade.

Except for budget properties, most accommodations in Belize contain private bathrooms with showers. Unless otherwise stated in the listings below, you can assume that rooms have private baths.

Hardest to find are good, mid-priced accommodations. Lodgings tend to leap from tropical spartan to luxury Caribbean, and the middle ground is often occupied by either grand hotels that have fallen on hard times or small ones that are overcharging. For budget travelers, a wide selection of accommodations is available, ranging from $12–$15 double rooms to $6–$7 dormitory-style digs.

Generally, accommodations are more expensive than in other Central American countries. Put another way, if you check into a moderately priced room in Belize, you will get the sort of amenities that you had in an inexpensive room in Guatemala. Accommodations are most expensive in Belize City and Ambergris Caye, where prices are usually quoted in U.S. dollars. This is also where you generally get the best value for your money because the infrastructure is more developed, and there is more competition among the hotels.

CATEGORY	COST*
$$$	$90–$195
$$	$45–$90
$	$15–$45

*All prices are for a standard double room, including 6% tax but excluding 10% service charge and 3%–4% credit-card fee charged by many hotels. Off-season (May–October) reductions of 15%–40% are common.

Scuba Diving and Snorkeling

The Barrier Reef, 320 kilometers (200 miles) of coral necklace stretching from the Yucatán Peninsula in the north to the Guatemalan border in the south, is the longest in the Western Hemisphere. If you add to this the three coral atolls farther out to sea—Lighthouse Reef, Glover's Reef, and Turneffe Islands—there are more than 560 kilometers (350 miles) of reef to be dived in Belize, more than in Bonaire, Cozumel, and all the Caymans put together.

One moment you can go around an outcrop of coral in 70 feet of virgin water and come upon an 8-foot, 40-pound, spotted eagle ray, its great wings flapping and its needlelike tail streaming out behind. The next minute you may find the feisty little damselfish, a bolt of blue no bigger than your little finger. Its sides are as smooth as black marble, and its iridescent blue markings glitter like rhinestones.

These are just two of a cast of aquatic characters awaiting you in Belize, one of the finest places for scuba diving and snorkeling in the world. There are bloated blowfish hovering in their holes like nightclub bouncers; lean, mean barracuda patrolling the depths; and queen angelfish that shimmy through the water with the puckered lips and haughty self-assurance of a model. In all, several hundred species of Caribbean tropicals frequent the reef, including 40 kinds of grouper, numerous types of cardinal fish, damselfish and wrasses, squirrel fish, butterfly fish, parrot fish, snappers, jacks, pompanos, and basslets.

Shopping

Belize is a good place to kick the consumer habit. There simply isn't much to buy, and most of the crafts are from Guatemala. Hotel shops sell a few carvings, mostly of wildlife (jaguars and dolphins) or Maya themes, made of zericote wood, a hardwood native to Belize. The best of them are quite good, though nothing compared to African carvings. Other items worth buying are Marie Sharp's famous hot sauces, jams, and jellies and the fine mahogany furniture from the Cayo.

Tours

In recent years, there has been huge growth in the number and variety of tours offered. In addition to standards like visits to Altun Ha and snorkeling trips on the reef, there are now exotic outings like swimming with manatees or flying to Lamanai by seaplane. It used to be that tour operators stayed close to their particular area (Belize City companies offered day trips to the nearby Maya ruins and nature reserves, while those in San Pedro concentrated on diving and snorkeling, for example), but with the increased efficiency of the transportation network, many now run tours to all sorts of destinations.

Water Sports

On the mainland, the cays, and the atolls, getting in or on the water is a very popular pursuit. Many resorts rent Windsurfers, small sailing dinghies, catamarans, Jet Skis, and the newest craze—sea kayaks.

Wildlife Viewing

Even reduced to vapid statistics—300 species of bird, 250 varieties of orchid, dozens of species of butterfly—the sheer variety of Belize's natural world is breathtaking. It is home to scarlet macaws, tapir, and jaguars, kinkajous, mountain lions, and howler monkeys and is one of the best places on earth to give children a sense of the richness and variety of tropical wildlife.

Exploring Belize

Though not the capital, Belize City is still definitely the country's hub. From there you can get to the Maya ruins and nature reserves of the north; the beaches and Barrier Reef of the cays and atolls; the rugged, mountainous, Spanish-accented wilderness that is the Cayo; or the relaxed Afro-Caribbean villages along the coast to the south.

Great Itineraries

Numbers in the text correspond to numbers in the margin and on the maps.

IF YOU HAVE 2–3 DAYS

It's said that Belize is the only country where you can scuba dive before breakfast and hike in the rain forest after lunch, but to do it you have to move fast. If you have only a few days and want a lazier experience, choose the jungle or the cays. If you opt for the latter, fly into

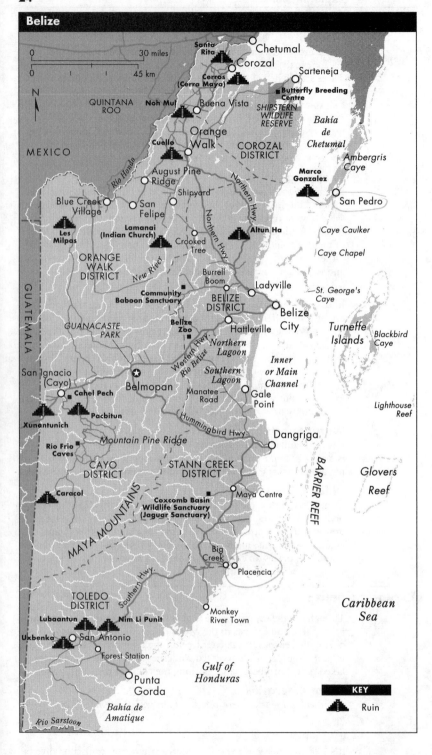

Belize

30 miles
45 km

N

Santa Rita ▲
Chetumal
Corozal
Cerros (Cerra Maya) ▲
Sarteneja
Noh Mul ▲
Buena Vista
Butterfly Breeding Centre ■
QUINTANA ROO
SHIPSTERN WILDLIFE RESERVE
Bahía de Chetumal
Cuello ▲
Orange Walk
COROZAL DISTRICT
MEXICO
Rio Hondo
August Pine Ridge
Shipyard
Ambergris Caye
Marco Gonzalez ▲
San Pedro
Blue Creek Village
San Felipe
Northern Hwy
Lamanai (Indian Church)
Crooked Tree
Altun Ha ▲
Caye Caulker
Les Milpas ▲
ORANGE WALK DISTRICT
New River
Northern Hwy
Caye Chapel
GUATEMALA
Burrell Boom
Ladyville
St. George's Caye
Community Baboon Sanctuary ■
BELIZE DISTRICT
Belize City
Turneffe Islands
GUANACASTE PARK
Belize Zoo ■
Hattieville
Blackbird Caye
Northern Lagoon
Western Hwy
Rio Belize
Southern Lagoon
Inner or Main Channel
San Ignacio (Cayo)
★ Belmopan
Manatee Road
Gale Point
Cahal Pech ■
Lighthouse Reef
Pacbitun ▲
Xunantunich ▲
Mountain Pine Ridge
Hummingbird Hwy
Dangriga
Glovers Reef
Rio Frio Caves ■
CAYO DISTRICT
STANN CREEK DISTRICT
BARRIER REEF
Caracol ▲
Maya Centre
MAYA MOUNTAINS
Coxcomb Basin Wildlife Sanctuary (Jaguar Sanctuary) ■
Big Creek
Placencia
Caribbean Sea
TOLEDO DISTRICT
Southern Hwy
Lubaantun ▲
Nim Li Punit ▲
Monkey River Town
Uxbenka ▲
San Antonio
Forest Station
Punta Gorda
Gulf of Honduras
Bahía de Amatique
Rio Sarstoon

KEY
▲ Ruin

Belize City ①, and take a half day to tour the Maya ruins at **Altun Ha** ⑥, stopping for lunch at Maruba Resort. Continue on to 🖼 **Ambergris Caye** ⑬, where you can spend a few days taking advantage of San Pedro, the cay's main town, and the nearby Barrier Reef, or, if you're looking for a laid-back tropical paradise with fewer tourists and less infrastructure, fly to 🖼 **Placencia** ㉝, in the south. On the other hand, if it's jungle you want, fly or drive from Belize City to the Cayo. If you stop at the **Belize Zoo** ②, drop in for lunch at the Jaguar Paw resort, and continue via **Belmopan** ㉑ to 🖼 **San Ignacio** ㉒. Don't stay right in town, however; head for one of the jungle lodges in the hills. From there you can explore Maya sites at **Xunantunich** ㉓ and **Caracol** ㉗, cross the Guatemalan border to Tikal, tube down the Macal River, or hike through the rain forest.

IF YOU HAVE 5 DAYS
With a bit more time, you can plan a "surf and turf" trip, combining cay and jungle, as described above. If you don't want to move inland or would rather extend your underwater horizons, move on to one of the smaller cays or the atolls, such as the 🖼 **Turneffe Islands** ⑰ or 🖼 **Glover's Reef** ⑳.

IF YOU HAVE 7–10 DAYS
With more than a week, it's worth spending a bit more time around 🖼 **Belize City** ①. For Maya ruins, visit **Altun Ha** ⑥ or **Lamanai** ⑧. If it's nature you want, head for the **Crooked Tree Wildlife Sanctuary** ⑦ and the **Community Baboon Sanctuary** ③. Next, fly to San Pedro, on 🖼 **Ambergris Caye** ⑬, for two or three days of diving and sunbathing; then fly back to Belize City and head for 🖼 **San Ignacio** ㉒, in the Cayo, to see the rain forest animals that make Belize a naturalist's paradise. Finally, head south to 🖼 **Placencia** ㉝ for a delicious last few days of snorkeling and relaxing under palm trees.

When to Tour Belize

Despite popular prejudice, Belize is a year-round destination, though some times are better to go than others. The dry season, from March to May, is the least attractive time for inland trips, with lots of dust and wilting vegetation. The rest of the year, from May to late February, Belize is at its best. True, there is a wet season in June and July, but it varies dramatically between the north and south. In the far south, as much as 160 inches of rain falls annually, but in the rest of the country, where you are likely to travel, there's much less. Besides, the rain is not continuous; it falls Florida-style, in sudden thunderstorms, and then stops. On the cays, however, the wet season can be accompanied by lashing northerly winds, known in Creole as Joe North.

Those interested in scuba can dive all year, but the water is at its absolute glassy clearest from April to June. Between November and February, cold fronts from North America may push southward, producing blustery winds known as "northers," which bring rain and rough weather and tend to churn up the sea, reducing visibility. (Normal visibility is 100–150 feet.) As water temperatures rarely stray from 80°F, many people dive without a wet suit. If you are doing several dives a day, however, you may prefer to use a short suit in winter and a Lycra skin in summer.

Festivals and seasonal events worth noting are:

March 19: **Baron Bliss Day** hears three cheers for Baron Henry Edward Ernest Victor Bliss, a wealthy English sportsman who endowed Belize with an immense estate in return for a holiday devoted to the traditional pursuits of the gentleman: sailing and fishing.

Mid-August: The **San Pedro Sea & Air Festival** is a multicultural bash held on Ambergris Caye. It lasts about four days and features entertainment from Belize and other Central American and Caribbean countries.

September 10: The **Battle of St. George's Caye** celebrates the David-and-Goliath defeat of the Spanish navy by a motley crew of British settlers, buccaneers, and liberated slaves. A week of partying and carnivals keeps the memory alive.

September 21: **National Independence Day,** during Carnival month, honors Belize's independence from the motherland in 1981.

November 19: **Garifuna Settlement Day** marks the arrival of Black Carib settlers, known as Garifuna, from the West Indies in 1823. Processions and traditional dancing abound, above all in Dangriga and the Toledo District.

BELIZE CITY AND ENVIRONS

"Dump" is a word that springs to many visitors' minds when they see Belize City. With its open drains, rusting swing bridge, and dilapidated buildings, it seems to symbolize everything that anthropologist Claude Lévi-Strauss implied in the title of his book *Tristes Tropiques.* From the air, you realize how small it is—more town than city, with a population of about 80,000 and not many buildings higher than the palm trees. After a few miles, the city simply stops. Beyond it is a largely uninhabited country where animals still outnumber people. Belize City is generally a staging post from which to see the natural wonders outside its limits.

Perhaps because of its strange, renegade history, Belize was one of the most neglected colonies of the pax Brittania. The British, who were generally generous in such matters, left little of either great beauty or interest in the capital of their former colony—no parks or gardens, no university or museums. Indeed, one of the clichés about Belize City is that the most exciting thing that happens there is the opening of the swing bridge on Haulover Creek twice a day.

Despite the recent tourist influx, Belize is still a Third World country. The minimum wage is 60¢ per hour, and until recently, crime was significant enough that no one dreamed of strolling about, particularly at night. So bad was Belize City's rap that press accounts of street crime made Belize City sound like south-central Los Angeles or the south Bronx. It never was, and at last, both the government and private sector have taken firm measures to stop the hemorrhaging of visitors, and money, away from the capital.

In 1995, $45 million was set aside to spruce up the city and make it more attractive. More critically, the government has at last cracked down on crime. In April 1995, a Tourism Police Unit was set up, and their black-and-white Jeeps and armed foot patrols are now a familiar sight. A quick trial system and draconian sentences have robbed bag-snatching and pocket-picking of much of their charm. As a result, Belize City is at last off the U.S. State Department's traveler's advisory list. More and more tourists are basing themselves at one of the city's fine hotels—which make arrangements for everything from scuba diving to rain-forest hikes, house most of the city's best restaurants, and often offer very competitive packages—and explore the rest of the country from there. There's still a lot to be done, but gradually Belize City is being reborn.

Numbers in the margin correspond to points of interest on the Belize City and Northern and Central Belize map.

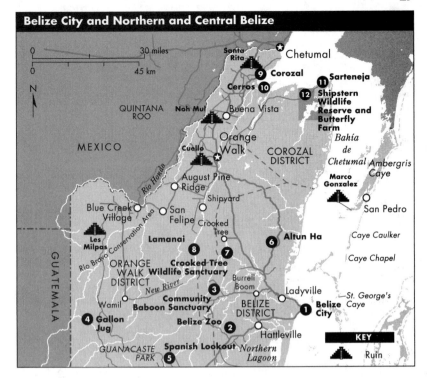

Belize City and Northern and Central Belize

Belize City

❶ If you're prepared to take the time and trouble, Belize City will repay your curiosity. Belizeans are, by temperament, natural city dwellers, and there is an infectious sociability on streets like **Albert and Queen,** the main shopping areas. The best of the fine British colonial–style houses—graceful, white buildings with wraparound verandas, painted shutters, and fussy Victorian woodwork—are on the **North Shore,** near the Radisson Fort George, and this is the most pleasant part of the city to stroll about in.

Government House, the finest colonial structure in the city, is said to have been designed by the illustrious British architect Sir Christopher Wren. Built in 1812, it was formerly the residence of the Queen's representative in Belize, the Governor General. After he and the rest of government moved to Belmopan in the wake of Hurricane Hattie, it became a venue for social functions and a guest house for visiting VIPs. (The Queen stayed here in 1985, Prince Philip in 1988.) In 1995, it was extensively renovated and is now open to the public. Archival records, silver, glassware, and furniture are on display as are the tropical birds that frequent the gardens. ⊠ *Regent St., no phone.* 🗫 *$10, $20 for prearranged bird-watching tours.* ⏲ *Weekdays 8:30–noon and 1–4:30.*

Dining and Lodging

$$ ✕ **El Centro.** Mirrored panels and air-conditioning make this long-established restaurant a cool, pleasant place to eat. Open 11–10, it's a favorite with the local business crowd and one of the few eateries that still serve cow-foot soup, a working-class specialty from Lancashire, England, which died out there long ago but survived in British Honduras. Also available is "reef and beef," a seafood-and-beef kebab. A

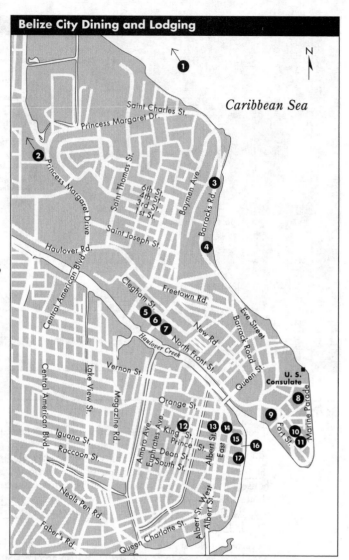

Belize City Dining and Lodging

rather drab hotel is on the premises as well. ⊠ *4 Bishop St.,* ☎ *027/2413,* FAX *027/4553. AE, MC, V. Closed Sun.*

$$ ✕ **The Grill.** Larry Sanford, an American ex-pat, is your host at this much-improved bistro overlooking the water, a half mile past the Radisson. Up a flight of stairs in a handsome white building, the main dining room is decorated with plants and cooled by overhead fans. The staff is attentive and polite. Larry places great emphasis on getting really fresh produce, which shows in the excellent salads, and the seafood is always good, too. Try the shrimp mousse followed by grouper with a creamy coconut and champagne sauce. The specialties, however, are still the steaks and grills. ⊠ *164 Newtown Barracks,* ☎ *023/4201. MC, V. Closed Sun. No lunch Sat.*

$$ ✕ **The Quarterdeck.** Getting here at night is an adventure in itself. A ★ free boat picks you up at Maya Landings, and you head out across the black water with the wind blowing in your hair and the stars shining overhead. After two minutes, you step out at Moho Caye, a sliver of sand and palm trees with the city's best marina behind it. Salty dogs and their molls sit at the bar swapping tall tales of the high seas (and, if the wrong boats are in, getting horribly drunk). The food, prepared by manager Kevin Flynn, a ruddy, blue-eyed Englishman with a string of previous incarnations as salesman, antiques dealer, and caterer, is, by Belize City standards, excellent. The steaks, from finest Cayo beef, are "hung" for 15 days, according to British tradition, to give them maximum tenderness. Seafood includes grouper and, if you're lucky, a sliver of Kevin's private supply of smoked blue marlin. To get the best of both, try the surf and turf combo: a six-ounce fillet steak with lobster. ☒ *Moho Caye,* ☎ *023/5499. AE, MC, V.*

$–$$ ✕ **GG's.** After 20 years in Los Angeles, George Godfrey decided to come
★ home and open an American-style restaurant with first-rate Belizean food. In addition to the best burgers in Belize, he serves T-bone steak, rice and beans with stewed beef or pork, and seafood. The courtyard, with its custard apple tree, traveler's palms, and green-and-white Belikin umbrellas, has an Italian café atmosphere, helping make GG's one of the most popular places in the city for Belizeans to wine and dine. The rest rooms are spotless, and the beer comes in frosted mugs. ☒ *2B King St.,* ☎ *027/4378. No credit cards. Closed Sun.*

$ ✕ **Dit's Saloon.** Dit's is a Belize City institution. More pastry café than restaurant, it's a real local place, with cheery striped tablecloths and a homey feel. (Like many other older Belizean restaurants, it's got the washbasin right in the dining room.) The cakes—try the three-milks cake or the coconut tarts—are sticky and sweet, and breakfasts—toast, eggs, and beans, washed down with ample mugs of tea—are an excellent value. The fresh-squeezed juices are delicious. ☒ *50 King St.,* ☎ *027/3330. No credit cards.*

$ ✕ **Macy's Café.** On the wall of this cozy restaurant is a letter from the
★ bishop of Belize, congratulating the staff on its catering feats, and a photo of Harrison Ford during the making of *The Mosquito Coast* (his was the table by the door). If you're an eco-freak or a vegetarian, Macy's may make you shudder: You've seen the wildlife? Now you can eat it. Wrap your mouth around such game animals as stewed armadillo, brocket deer, "royal" gibnut, and, by request, stewed iguana, known locally as bamboo chicken. Macy, the Jamaican-born proprietor, says it's tough to prepare—it has to be scalded, then washed in lime juice and vinegar—but delicious to eat. Bring your own booze. ☒ *18 Bishop St.,* ☎ *027/3419. No credit cards.*

$$$ ✕🔝 **Bellevue Hotel.** Overlooking the harbor and the bay beyond, this fine old colonial house, built in 1900, has a tradition of excellent hospitality. Personally Speaking, the ground-floor restaurant, is one of the best in the city. Its bread is home-baked, its produce fresh, and the service prompt and attentive. The second-floor Harbor Room, which has white wicker chairs and blue-and-pink decor, is a favorite meeting place for the city's expatriate crowd. There is live music on weekends. ☒ *5 Southern Foreshore, Box 428,* ☎ *027/7052,* 🖷 *027/3253. 35 rooms. Restaurant, bar, pool. AE, D, MC, V.*

$$$ ✕🔝 **Chateau Caribbean.** The rooms in this handsome, white colonial-style building overlooking the water all have phone, air-conditioning, and room service, but the place is best known for its second-floor restaurant. With white tablecloths, gleaming cutlery, abstract art, and great ocean views, it is one of the most elegant places to eat in the city. The menu offers an unusual combination of Chinese and Caribbean dishes. ☒ *6 Marine Parade,* ☎ *023/0800,* 🖷 *023/0900. 29 rooms. Restaurant, bar. AE, MC, V.*

$$$ ✕🔝 **Radisson Fort George.** Though there are no longer porters in pith
★ helmets, there is still a bright red pillar box on the steps for your mail

as well as a breath of British colonialism in the air. The accommodations—72 air-conditioned rooms with phone, cable TV, and minibar—are among the best in the country, especially in the newer six-story wing, which has a tinted-glass frontage and panoramic views of the ocean. The recent addition of the Villa Wing (formerly the Holiday Inn Villa), across the road, makes the Radisson the second-largest hotel in Belize. Completed in December 1995, a $2.4 million refurbishment by Hamptons-based designer Mary McDonald has a British Raj theme. Lush red and ochre fabrics, faux-leopard carpets, and reproduction rattan and hardwood antiques help re-create the ambience of colonial India in the 1880s. A new deck area overlooking the pool, where guests can breakfast or have a drink in the evening, has greatly enhanced what used to be a rather airless bar. And there is even a "quiet room" for reading or playing bridge, though the bizarre portraits of animals dressed as humans are anything but serene. The hotel also offers a full slate of diving excursions and tours. Maxime's, the restaurant, serves decent, though not spectacular, fare, and several meal plans are available. It's worth overnighting in Belize City just to stay here. ⊠ *2 Marine Parade,* ☎ *027/7400 or 800/333–3333 in the U.S.,* ⨍⨯ *027/3820. 72 rooms. Restaurant, bar, pool, shop, laundry service, business services, convention center, travel services. AE, MC, V.*

$$$ ✕⌐⊡ **Ramada Royal Reef.** With 114 deluxe rooms, four suites, a pres-
★ idential suite, and three large meeting rooms, the Ramada is now the biggest hotel in Belize. The rooms are fairly generic, with double beds and rattan furniture, but all have superb ocean views, a private bathroom, cable TV, and air-conditioning. Great emphasis has been placed on landscaping in recent years, and the gardens are some of the most pleasant in the city. Unfortunately, the same cannot be said for the dilapidated tennis courts. At the restaurant, which is not open for lunch, you can count on skillfully concocted international and local cuisine, like lobster and grouper, and fine ocean views. Since 1994, the Ramada has also been home to the best, and safest, night spot in Belize City: Calypso, a high-ceiling dance hall has views to the sea, a bar at one end, a restaurant at the other, and plenty of space to boogie in between. The crowd is a mixture of the local elite and tourists. There are live bands, and on weekends the joint is really jumpin'. Though the hotel does have a small man-made beach, you cannot swim in the ocean here, and the pool is rather small. Like other large resorts in Belize City, the Ramada offers a full raft of dive and tour excursions, and different meal plans are offered. ⊠ *Newtown Barracks, Box 1758,* ☎ *023/2670 or 800/228–9898 in the U.S.,* ⨍⨯ *023/4322. 114 rooms, 5 suites. Restaurant, bar, pool, 2 tennis courts, beach, dock, dance club, laundry service, business services, convention center, meeting rooms, travel services. AE, MC, V.*

$$ ✕⌐⊡ **Fort Street Guest House.** Formerly the private residence of a lead-
★ ing Belizean doctor and his family, this pretty 1920s property with white trim and green and white–striped awnings emanates the warm Southern hospitality of owners Hugh and Teresa Parkey. (As a key member of the Hotel Association, Teresa has been instrumental in getting Belize City's facilities upgraded.) One of the rooms' exotic features is the baldachin-style mosquito net over every bed. The bad news is that there are only shared bathrooms. To make up for it, the downstairs restaurant, cooled by lazy ceiling fans and graced with a full-size poster of Bogart, is one of the liveliest in the city. Belizean chef Ivan Ayuso does a chalk-board menu that's inventive and constantly changing, and the restaurant also serves excellent breakfasts. (A Continental breakfast is included.) Hugh Parkey can arrange just about any tour you want, especially if it is underwater. His company, Belize Dive Connection, is one of the best in the country. ⊠ *4 Fort St.,* ☎ *023/0116,* ⨍⨯ *027/8808.*

6 rooms share baths. Restaurant, bar, shop, laundry service, travel services. AE, D, MC, V.

$$$ ⊞ **Belize Biltmore Plaza.** Why anyone chose to build this hotel in the middle of nowhere, between the airport and the city, is anyone's guess. If you have to come to Belize on business, fly in, and fly out, it is practical, but, for the ordinary traveler, the location is a disaster. Rooms feature all the amenities of a deluxe hotel and open onto verandas overlooking the pool and a tropical garden. The hotel also has excellent conferencing and entertainment facilities (Thursday is karaoke night). ⊠ *Mile 3, Northern Hwy.,* ☎ *023/2302 or 800/396–1153 in the U.S.,* FAX *023/2301. 90 rooms. Restaurant, 2 bars, pool, recreation room, business services, convention center, meeting rooms, travel services, airport shuttle. AE, MC, V.*

$$ ⊞ **Bakadeer Inn.** The surrounding area is drab, but this new Belizean-run hotel has very agreeable rooms built along a quiet, secure courtyard set back from the street. All rooms have a well-stocked minibar, phone, TV, and private bath. There is a cheery breakfast room (Continental plan available) and a reassuringly large night watchman. ⊠ *74 Clegham St.,* ☎ *023/1400,* FAX *023/1963. 12 rooms. Breakfast room, laundry service, business services. No credit cards.*

$$ ⊞ **Colton House.** Good mid-priced accommodations are rare, so this
★ beautiful colonial house with a white wraparound veranda, on the same tree-lined street as the Fort George hotel, is a real find. Inside, there are fine antiques and cool, polished wooden floors. The English family who runs it provides the charm of traditional bed-and-breakfast (unfortunately, without the breakfast). They will also rent you a four-wheel-drive vehicle at a competitive price. As there is only limited space, reservations are essential. ⊠ *9 Cork St.,* ☎ *024/4666. 5 rooms, 2 with bath. Car rental. No credit cards.*

$ ⊞ **Mira Rio Hotel.** This is one of four budget hotels at the junction of Pickstock Street and North Front Street. The outside is bright and cheerful, and though the rooms are spartan, they all have a phone, basin, toilet, and—crucial in muggy Belize City—a fan. The restaurant/bar downstairs (Continental plan available), with its eclectic mix of rastas, fishermen, and backpackers, is funky and fun. ⊠ *59 N. Front St.,* ☎ *024/4970. 6 rooms. Restaurant, bar. No credit cards.*

$ ⊞ **North Front Street Guest House.** The sign on the street calls this weathered, clapboard boardinghouse "world famous," a sobriquet earned from the many backpackers and anglers who have enjoyed its simple but friendly hospitality. The rooms are pretty basic, though the owner recently redid the decor, adding lots of faux-Maya details. "Pure Steinbeck" was how one elderly guest from Georgia described it. ⊠ *124 N. Front St.,* ☎ *027/7595. 8 rooms share baths. No credit cards.*

$ ⊞ **The Seaside Guest House.** Of the budget hotels, this has by far the
★ best location, opposite two of the grandest villas in the city and not far from the water. The accommodations are dormitory style, but the house is a good-looking, two-story colonial-style building, and the owner, Fred Prost, is intent on making your stay an agreeable one. ⊠ *3 Prince St.,* ☎ *027/8339. 6 rooms share baths. No credit cards.*

Scuba Diving

If you're interested in a dive trip out to the reef or the atolls, see the Scuba Diving sections under the Cays and Atolls head, *below.* These sections provide information on what to see as well as tour operators. In addition to the dive shops at the Radisson Fort George and the Ramada Royal Reef, **Belize Dive Connection** (⊠ San Pedro, Ambergris Caye, ☎ 026/2797) provides good service.

Shopping

Try the recently opened **National Handicraft Center** (⌧ Fort St., just past Fort Street Guest House, ☏ 023/3833) for Belizean-made products of all sorts. Both the **Fort Street Guest House** (⌧ 4 Fort St., ☏ 023/0116) and the **Radisson Fort George** (⌧ 2 Marine Parade, ☏ 027/7400) have good gift shops. Belize's beautiful stamps are available from the **Philatelic Society** (⌧ Queen St., behind post office). **Go Tees** (⌧ 23 Regent St., ☏ 027/4082 or 027/5512) has T-shirts for adults and children and a small selection of crafts. A new supermarket, **Save-U** (⌧ Belican Area Plaza), is a good place to browse for bargains.

The Book Centre (⌧ 144 N. Front St., ☏ 027/7457) sells magazines and "the classics." **The Belize Bookshop** (⌧ Regent St., ☏ 027/2054) has magazines, books, and local and U.S. newspapers; it's open a half-day on Wednesday.

Belize Zoo

⟲ ❷ *48 km (30 mi) west of Belize City*

The visitor center at the entrance is named for the famous and very funny British naturalist Gerald Durrell, who was an adviser on the zoo's planning and conception, as well as a mentor for the zoo's staff. Here, you will be able to see all the wildlife that you are very unlikely to see in the wild—April the tapir, a favorite with Belize's schoolchildren; a pair of jaguars; scarlet macaws; crocodiles; gibnut; and the rest of the cast of zoological characters that Belize has rightly become famous for. Unlike most zoos, which are the animal equivalent of Alcatraz, this one was designed with the creatures' welfare, not yours, in mind. What that means is roomy enclosures, tons of vegetation, and lots of places to hide. As a result, you will probably spend most of your time peering into that vegetation playing "Spot That Animal." Don't worry— they're in there somewhere. As the zoo is also the flagship of Belize's conservation policies, great emphasis is placed on education. Green panels next to the cages give short discussions of ecology and the threat posed to their inmates by the bipeds on the other side of the wire. For more information about the zoo, *see* Chapter 2. ⌧ *Mile 30, Western Hwy.*, ☏ *081/3004.* ⌧ *$5.* ☉ *Daily 9:30–4.*

Community Baboon Sanctuary

❸ *50 km (31 mi) west of Belize City; take Northern Highway and turn left on road to Burrell Boom*

This baboon sanctuary (the "baboon" is actually the black howler monkey) is one of the most interesting wildlife conservation projects in Belize. It was established in 1985 by a zoologist from the University of Wisconsin and a group of local farmers, with help from the World Wildlife Fund. Protection of the howler monkey—an agile bundle of black fur with a derriere like a baboon's and a roar that sounds like something between a jaguar and a stuck pig—began after it had already been zealously hunted throughout Central America and was facing extinction. In Belize, it found a refuge. An all-embracing plan, coordinating eight villages, more than 100 landowners, and a 32-kilometer (20-mile) stretch of the Belize River, was drawn up to protect its habitat. Today, there are nearly 1,000 black howler monkeys in the sanctuary, as well as numerous other species of birds and mammals. About 5 kilometers (3 miles) of trails run from the small museum and afford an easily accessible means of exploring the sanctuary. Limited accommodations are available at the visitor center, but early booking is essential. ☏ *024/4405.* ⌧ *Free.* ☉ *Daylight hours.*

Belize City and Environs A to Z

Arriving and Departing

BY BUS

Belize City is the hub of the country's fairly extensive bus network, so you'll find regular service to various regions of Belize and connections to the Guatemalan and Mexican borders (☞ Getting Around By Bus *in* Belize A to Z, *below*).

BY CAR

There are only two highways to Belize City—the Northern Highway, which leads from the Mexican border, 165 kilometers (102 miles) away, and the Western Highway, which runs 131 kilometers (81 miles) from Guatemala. Both roads are paved, though the Northern Highway is frequently potholed.

BY PLANE

Philip Goldson International Airport (⊠ Ladyville) is 14 kilometers (9 miles) north of the city. Cabs to town cost $30 and rising.

Getting Around

BY TAXI

There is no bus service within Belize City, so the only way to get around, if you don't have a car, is by taxi or on foot. Cabs cost $2.50 for one person between any two points in the city and $1 each additional person. Outside the city, the farther you go, the more you'll be charged. Since there are no meters, always be sure to set a price before going. Taxis are available at Market Square, by the swing bridge, or by calling **Cinderella Taxi** (☎ 024/5240) or **Caribbean Taxi** (☎ 027/2888).

Contacts and Resources

EMERGENCIES

Hospital. Belize Medical Associates (⊠ 5791 St. Thomas St., ☎ 023/0303) has a 24-hour emergency room.

Pharmacy. Brodie's Pharmacy (⊠ Regent St. at Market Sq.) is open Monday, Tuesday, Thursday, and Saturday 8:30–7; Wednesday 8:30 AM–12:30 PM; Friday 8:30 AM–9 PM; and Sunday 9 AM–12:30 PM.

VISITOR INFORMATION

The **Belize Tourist Board** (⊠ 8 N. Front St., Box 325, ☎ 027/7213, FAX 027/7490) is open weekdays 8–noon and 1–5.

NORTHERN AND CENTRAL BELIZE

Because of Belize's small size, much of the country is accessible from Belize City. This is especially true of the north, whose Northern Highway is much better for travelers than many of the circuitous routes and bad roads of the south. The landscape is mostly flat—this is sugarcane country—and, although the north has lost out to the Cayo in terms of visitor numbers in recent years, it holds some of Belize's most interesting Maya sites, as well as several first-class resorts.

Numbers in the margin correspond to points of interest on the Belize City and Northern and Central Belize map.

Gallon Jug

❹ *3½ hrs west of Belize City*

What's notable about this town in western Belize is Chan-Chich Lodge and the surrounding 250,000-acre **Río Bravo Conservation Area,** which was created with the help of the Massachusetts Audubon Society and the distinguished British naturalist Gerald Durrell. The extensive nature trails veritably teem with wildlife and, above all, birds. A night walk can be one of the most exciting things you do in Belize.

Dining and Lodging

$$$ ✕▥ **Chan-Chich Lodge.** Whether the spirit of Smoking Shell or some other fierce Maya lord will one day take revenge on Barry Bowen, Chan-Chich Lodge's owner, for erecting a group of cabanas slap in the middle of a Classic Period (AD 300–900) Maya plaza remains to be seen. But since it opened in 1988, this fine jungle resort has established itself as one of the more unusual destinations in Belize. It's a good distance from Belize City, though you can fly, but the abundant wildlife and the particular ambience of the place—it's a bit like camping out in a Roman forum—make it worth it. Barry Bowen is one of the wealthiest, and most powerful, men in Belize (he owns everything from Belikin beer to most of Belize's beef cattle), and, seeing which way the wind was blowing, he decided to join the boom in ecotourism. The result is a magnificent property set in the Río Bravo Conservation Area; guides are excellent and well-informed. Large, handsomely built thatch-covered cabanas have mahogany interiors, private bathrooms, and queen-size beds. President Jimmy Carter is among the many notable guests who have stayed here. Tours include canoe trips along the river and horseback tours to Maya ruins that haven't yet been built on. ✉ *Box 37, Belize City,* ☎ *027/5634 or 800/451–8017 in the U.S.,* ⅎ⅍ *027/5635. 12 rooms. Restaurant, bar, laundry service, travel services. AE, MC, V.*

Spanish Lookout

❺ *19 km (12 mi) north of Western Highway; follow sign at Mile 59*

This small hilltop village is one of the centers of the Mennonite community (another is Blue Creek, to the north). Blonde, blue-eyed, and seemingly out of place in this tropical country, the Mennonites are, in fact, one of its most successful ethnic groups. Belize's carpenters and dairy farmers, they build nearly all the resorts and have a lock on the dairy industry. Most of the eggs and milk you will consume during your stay will have come from Mennonite farms. The women dress in cotton frocks and head scarves, whereas the men wear straw hats, suspenders, and dark trousers. Many still move about in horse-drawn buggies whose wheels, in keeping with tradition, are made of iron. The hardware stores, cafés, and small shops of Spanish Lookout offer a unique opportunity to mingle with these devout and world-wary people, but note that they do not appreciate being gawked at or photographed any more than you do, and probably less.

Altun Ha

❻ *45 km (28 mi) north of Belize City; take Northern Highway to Old Northern Highway to turnoff for ruins*

If you have never visited an ancient Maya city or want to visit one without too much exertion, a trip to Altun Ha is highly recommended. It is not the most dramatic site in Belize—Caracol takes that award—but it is the most thoroughly excavated and the most accessible. Human habitation spans 2,000 years: Its first inhabitants settled here shortly before the crowning of the ancient Egyptian king Sheshonk I, in 945 BC, and their descendants finally abandoned the city the year after King Alfred of England died, in AD 900. At its height, Altun Ha was home to 10,000 people.

The team from the Royal Ontario Museum that first excavated the site in the mid-'60s found 250 structures spread over more than 1,000 square yards. At Plaza B, in the Temple of the Masonry Altars, those archaeologists also found the grandest and most valuable piece of Maya art ever discovered—the head of the sun god Kinich Ahau. Weighing 9¾ pounds, it was carved from a solid block of green jade. In the absence of a national museum, it is kept in a solid steel vault in the central branch of the Bank of Belize. *No phone.* ✉ *BZ$2.* ☉ *Daily 9–5.*

Dining and Lodging

$$$
★ ✕⊞ **Maruba Resort and Jungle Spa.** Everything done here is done with style. Succulent food is served on a palm leaf and decorated with hibiscus flowers, glasses are crystal, and plates are handsome porcelain. A beautiful, small swimming pool with a waterfall and a Jacuzzi (you can steam under the stars at night) graces the property. The resort is the product of many years' work by Nicky Nicholson and his two sisters, Alexandra and Francesca. The land was bought by their father, a physician from the States, in the '70s, and the Nicholsons cleared much of it and did much of the building themselves. Francesca created the fanciful interior design for the cabanas, which are individually furnished with Guatemalan fabrics, local artwork, and such whimsical additions as Coke bottles set into the walls, hand-painted masks, and screens. Nicky functions as majordomo. His rather Waspish sense of humor has been known to irritate some guests, but he is a competent and knowledgeable guide. The convivial center of the resort is the large, circular, thatch-covered restaurant and bar, which produces consistently delicious food, imaginatively prepared and served with excellent salads to the accompaniment of good jazz. (A Maruba favorite is the excellent Ladysmith Black Mombasa, at one time featured with Paul Simon.) Maruba prides itself on its cocktails (served in coconut beakers), and for those with a taste for really exotic drinks, Nicky usually has a bottle of viper rum handy. Be warned: It tastes like old sneakers. Belize's most comprehensive spa program includes everything from seaweed gelée body wraps and full-body massages using oils made on the property to more traditional treatments like manicures, pedicures, and facials. If it's activities you want, there are invigorating tours to Altun Ha and boat trips up the New River to the superb ruins at Lamanai (☞ *below*). The folks at Maruba were the first to do the Lamanai run, and after years of experience, they have it down to a science. In addition to the most informative take on the ruins, they provide hampers of delicious food decorated with the trademark red hibiscus flowers, cold drinks, and tropical fruits, all served on an elegant portable table. ✉ *Mile 40½, Old Northern Hwy., Maskall Village,* ☎ *032/2199; or Box 300703, Houston, TX 77230,* ☎ *713/799–2031. 12 rooms, 1 suite. Restaurant, bar, pool, hot tub, health club, laundry service, travel services. AE, D, MC, V.*

Crooked Tree Wildlife Sanctuary

❼ *53 km (33 mi) northwest of Belize City*

Founded by the Belize Audubon Society in 1984, the sanctuary, one of the most interesting in the country, encompasses a chain of swamps, lagoons, and inland waterways covering 3,000 acres and spanning both sides of the highway. At its center is **Crooked Tree,** one of the oldest inland villages in Belize, with a population of 800. A church and school, and even one of the surest signs of civilization in former British territories—a cricket pitch—are found here.

For bird-watchers, this is paradise. There are snowy egrets, snail kites, ospreys, and black-collared hawks, as well as two types of duck—Muscovy and black-bellied whistling—and all five species of kingfisher native to Belize. The sanctuary's most prestigious visitor, however, is the jabiru stork, a kind of freshwater albatross with a wingspan of up to 8 feet; it's the largest flying bird in the Americas.

The best way to tour the sanctuary is by canoe, and there are a number of excellent local guides in the village. You will be rewarded for your adventurousness: By boat, you are likely to see iguanas, crocodiles, coatis, and turtles. ⊠ *3 km (2 mi) west of Northern Hwy.,* ☎ *027/7745.*

Lodging

$$ ☒ **Crooked Tree Resort.** This small, low-key complex with seven simple, thatched cabanas with hot and cold water is at the edge of one of the lagoons. ⊠ *Box 1453, Belize City,* ☎ *027/7745. 7 rooms share baths. No credit cards.*

Lamanai

★ ❽   *2½ hrs northwest of Belize City via Orange Walk, which is 106 km (66 mi) northwest of Belize City*

Lamanai ("submerged crocodile" in Maya) was the longest-occupied Maya site in Belize, inhabited until well after Columbus arrived in the New World. In fact, archaeologists have found signs of continuous occupation from 1500 BC until the 16th century.

The people of Lamanai carried on a way of life that was passed down for millennia until Spanish missionaries arrived to sunder them from their past and lure them to the faith of the popes. The ruins of the church the missionaries built can still be seen at the nearby village of **Indian Church.** In the same village, there is also an abandoned sugar mill from the 19th century. Its immense drive wheel and steam engine, on which you can still read the name of the manufacturer, Leeds Foundry in New Orleans, is swathed in strangler vines and creepers. It is a haunting sight.

In all, 50 or 60 Maya structures are spread over the 950-acre archaeological reserve. The biggest of them is the largest pre-Classic structure in Belize, a massive stepped temple built around 200 BC into the hillside overlooking the river. A ball court, numerous dwellings, and several other fine temples also grace the grounds. One of the best stelae found in Belize, an elaborately carved depiction of the ruler Smoking Shell, can also be seen here.

Many structures at Lamanai have been only superficially excavated. Trees and vines grow from the tops of the temples, the sides of one pyramid are covered with vegetation, and another rises abruptly out of the forest floor. There are no tour buses and cold-drink stands here—just ruins, forest, and wildlife.

There are several ways to get to Lamanai. A long car ride (four-wheel drive advisable) from Belize City via Orange Walk and the village of San Felipe is possible, except just after heavy rains. Make sure you get good directions before leaving Orange Walk, as the turnoff to San Felipe is not well marked, and then turn again in the tiny village of Indian Church, just before the entrance to the Lamanai Outpost Lodge.

The best way to approach the ruins, however, is by boat. In addition to the Maruba Resort, various Belize City tour operators (☞ Guided Tours *in Belize A to Z, below*) as well as a few local tour guides, including **Mr. Godoy** (⊠ Orange Walk, ☎ 032/2969), run day trips up the New River. The newest way to get here, however, is by seaplane.

For a more in-depth look at Lamanai, *see* "A River Trip to Lamanai" *in Chapter 5.* ☒ *Free.* ☉ *Daily 9–5.*

Dining and Lodging

$$$ ✕⚏ **Lamanai Outpost Lodge.** This fine resort, just a few minutes' walk from the Maya ruins of Lamanai, is rapidly becoming one of Belize's most popular spots. Thatched cabanas have breathtaking views of the huge New River Lagoon, and the hotel offers a variety of wildlife-viewing excursions, including Belize's only nighttime river safari. In 1995 the lodge pulled off a coup by hosting the Camel Trophy, an exacting three-day event combining rally driving (in Land Rover Discovery vehicles), running, rafting, canoeing, and swimming. ✉ *Box 63, Indian Church,* ☎ *023/3578,* 𝖥𝖠𝖷 *023/3578. 7 rooms. Restaurant, bar, boating. AE, MC, V.*

Corozal

❾ *153 km (95 mi) north of Belize City*

The last town before the Río Hondo, the border separating Belize from Mexico, Corozal, like Ambergris Caye, was originally settled by refugees from the Yucatán during the 19th-century caste wars. Though English is still officially spoken here, Spanish is just as common. The town has been largely rebuilt since Hurricane Janet almost destroyed it in 1955, and consequently it is neat and modern. Most houses are clapboard, built on wooden piles. One of the few remaining historic buildings is a portion of the old fort in the center of town, and the town hall, which has a colorful mural depicting local history, is worth a visit. There are only a few restaurants and bars.

Not far from Corozal are several Maya sites. The closest, **Santa Rita,** is just a few minutes' walk from the center of the town. Only a few of its structures have been unearthed, and it requires imagination to picture this settlement, founded in 1500 BC, as one of the major trading centers in the district. *No phone.* ⚏ *Free.* ☉ *Daily 9–5.*

❿ **Cerros,** a late pre-Classic center, is south of Corozal, on the coast. As at Santa Rita, little has been excavated, but the site, which dates from about 2000 BC, includes a ball court, several tombs, and a large temple. The best way to get here is by boat from Corozal. *No phone.* ⚏ *Free.* ☉ *Daily 9–5.*

Dining and Lodging

$$ ✕⚏ **Tony's Inn.** Tony Castillo started this white, two-story hotel 20 years ago and has steadily expanded it. A short distance south of Corozal, overlooking the bay and the Maya site of Cerros beyond, it has one of the prettiest beaches in the north. Tarpon fishing on the New River is an added draw for guests, many of whom come down specially from Cancún. Visit the cool bar for a refreshing cocktail or the restaurant for such piquant specialties as curried lobster. All rooms are fitted with mahogany and tile floors, and all have private bathrooms. The more expensive units have air-conditioning, TVs, and telephones. American plan is available. ✉ *Box 12,* ☎ *042/2055,* 𝖥𝖠𝖷 *042/2829. 29 rooms, including 5 singles. Restaurant, bar, beach, fishing, laundry service. AE, MC, V.*

$–$$ ✕⚏ **Hotel Maya.** This small, friendly, family-run hotel with a restaurant specializing in Mexican and Belizean food is at the southern end of Corozal. Rooms are clean, cheap, and cheerful and have fans and private baths. ✉ *c/o Sylvia and Rosita Mai, Box 112,* ☎ *042/2082,* 𝖥𝖠𝖷 *042/2827. 15 rooms. Restaurant, bar, laundry service. MC, V.*

Sarteneja

⓫ *32 km (20 mi) by boat from Corozal, 97 km (60 mi) by car via Northern Highway south to Orange Walk and northeast on new Sarteneja*

Highway; this drive may take 4 hrs in dry season, 8 hrs in rainy season

This village is a small community of mestizo fishermen and farmers who make a living from lobster fishing and pineapple production. Traditionally, their links were always north, across the Bay of Chetumal to Mexico, rather than south to Belize, but with the building of the roadway, that is beginning to change.

The 81 square kilometers (31 square miles) of tropical forest that is now the **Shipstern Wildlife Reserve and Butterfly Farm** is, like the Crooked Tree Wildlife Sanctuary, a paradise for bird-watchers. Look for egret (there are 13 species here), American coot, keel-billed toucans, flycatchers, warblers, and several species of parrot. A rich tapestry of mammalian life also exists, including deer, peccaries, pumas, jaguars, and raccoons, as well as a dizzying variety of insects and butterflies. In fact, at the butterfly farm adjacent to the reserve's visitor center, pupae are hatched for export, mainly to Britain, where they are used at tourist sites offering a simulated jungle experience. ⊠ *Visitor Center: Sarteneja village. Contact Belize Audubon Society:* ☎ *023/4987,* FAX *023/4985.*

Northern and Central Belize A to Z

Arriving and Departing

BY BUS

Batty Bros. (⊠ 15 Mosul St., Belize City, ☎ 027/2025) and **Venus** (⊠ Magazine Rd., Belize City, ☎ 027/7390 or 027/3354) make the three-hour journey from Belize City to Corozal several times a day. Buses also travel on from there to Chetumal, Mexico.

BY CAR

Corozal is the last stop on the Northern Highway from Belize City before you hit Mexico. Due to the variable state of the roads, the 153-kilometer (95-mile) journey will probably take you a good two to three hours, longer if you stop off at Altun Ha or the Crooked Tree sanctuary on the way.

BY PLANE

Tropic Air (☎ 024/5671, 713/521–9674 or 800/422–3435 in the U.S., FAX 026/2338) has flights to Corozal from both San Pedro, on Ambergris Caye, and Belize City. The journey takes 20 minutes and costs $52 round-trip from Belize City, $95 from San Pedro.

Getting Around

If you haven't got your own wheels, you will have a hard time exploring the north, as no cross-country bus services exist, and little traffic means little hitching potential. Taxis are available in Corozal but are costly. There is a large expatriate community in the town, so if you're stuck, try hooking up with them.

THE CAYS AND ATOLLS

Imagine bouncing over the mint-green water after a day's snorkeling, the white prow of your boat pointing up into the billowing clouds, the base of the sky darkening to a deep lilac, the spray pouring over you like warm rain. To the left, San Pedro's pastel buildings huddle among the palm trees like a detail from a Paul Klee canvas. To the right, the surf breaks in a white seam along the reef. Over the surface of the water, flying fish scamper away like winged, aquatic hares.

That and many other experiences can be had off the coast of Belize, where more than 200 cays (the word comes from the Spanish *cayo* but is pronounced like key in Key Largo) dot the Caribbean like punctuation marks in a long, liquid sentence. Most cays lie inside the barrier reef, which over the centuries has acted as a breakwater, allowing them to take shape, grow, and develop undisturbed by the tides and winds that would otherwise sweep them away. Their names are evocative, and often funny. There is a Deadman's Caye, a Laughing Bird Caye and, don't ask why, a Bread and Butter Caye. Some of their names suggest the sort of company you should expect: Mosquito Caye, Sandfly Caye, and even Crawl Caye, which is infested with boa constrictors. Many, like Cockney Range or Baker's Rendezvous, simply express the whimsy, and nostalgia, of the early British settlers. The vast majority are uninhabited, except by iguana and possum, frigate birds, pelicans, brown and red-footed boobies, and some very lewd-sounding creatures called wish-willies (actually a kind of iguana).

Farther out to sea, between 48 and 96 kilometers (30 and 60 miles) off the coast, are the atolls. From the air they look impossibly beautiful. At their center the water is mint green; the white sandy bottom reflects the light upwards and is flecked with patches of mangrove and rust-color sediments. Around the fringe of the atoll, the surf breaks in a white circle before the color changes abruptly to ultramarine as the water plunges to 3,000 feet.

The origin of Belize's atolls is still something of a mystery, but evidence suggests that unlike the Pacific atolls, which formed by accretion around the rims of submerged volcanoes, these grew from the bottom up, as vast pagodas of coral accumulated over millions of years on top of limestone fault blocks. The Maya were probably the first humans to discover and use the atolls, as stopovers on their trading routes. Piles of seashells and rocks, known as "shell maidens" and thought to have been placed there as markers, have been found on the Turneffe Islands.

The battle of nomenclature fought by the Spanish and English on sea reflected larger frictions over the control of offshore waters. With the rout of the Spanish at the Battle of St. George's Cay in 1798, English names took precedence: Turneffe, for Terre Nef; Lighthouse Reef for Quattro Cayos; Glover's Reef, for Longorif.

Until recently the atolls were sparsely inhabited. Lobster fishing, sponge gathering, and coconut plantations provided a small permanent population with a hard-won living. Recently, however, small dive resorts have begun to open on the atolls, and on more of the cays, bringing economic rejuvenation. Because of logistical realities—power, water supply, transportation (several can only be reached by charter boat)—some are very basic, with no electricity and spartan accommodations. Others are turning increasingly to an exclusive clientele.

Though they cater mostly to divers, these resorts are also marvelous destinations for those who simply want to swing in a hammock, snorkel, and read. If you desire a real castaway experience, this is where to find it. If you like a bit of nightlife and sociability, you might go stir-crazy. Most of the resorts lie in the upper price range. (The five resorts on the atolls, for example, cost $1,200 per week and up.) Because of their isolation, many do only eight-day, seven-night packages, and as all have only limited space, early booking, particularly for the high season (November–April), is essential.

Scuba Diving

Dive destinations can be divided into two broad categories as well—the reef and the atolls. Most of the reef diving is done on the northern section, particularly off Ambergris Caye. Here the reef is close—a few hundred yards from shore—making getting to your dive site extremely easy. The journey time by boat is usually between 10 minutes and half an hour. The farther south you go, the farther apart are coast and coral, and longer boat trips make for greater dependence on weather. On Ambergris, for example, you may be prevented from diving by a morning storm, but you still have a good chance of getting out in the afternoon. Most of the cay dive shops are attached to hotels. The quality of dive masters, equipment, and facilities vary considerably.

Many resorts offer diving courses. A one-day basic familiarization course costs $125. A four-day PADI certification course costs $400. A popular variant is a referral course, in which you do the academic and pool training at home, then complete the diving section here. The cost, for two days, is $250.

If you want to experience something truly dramatic, head to the atolls. They provide some of the greatest diving in the world. The problem is they're awfully far from where you're likely to stay. If you're based on Ambergris Caye, Glover's Reef is out of the question for a day trip by boat, and don't be too optimistic about getting to Lighthouse Reef's Blue Hole. Even when the weather is perfect, which it often isn't in winter, it's a two- to three-hour boat trip. Turneffe is more accessible, but even that is a long and comparatively costly day trip. You're unlikely to reach the southern tip of the atoll, where the best diving is.

If you are determined to dive the atolls, you basically have three choices: stay at one of the atoll resorts, go on a live-aboard dive boat, or do a fly-and-dive trip.

The **Belize Aggressor III** (⊠ Aggressor Fleet, Drawer K, Morgan City, LA 70381, ☎ 504/385−2628 or 800/348−2628, ℻ 504/384−0817 in the U.S.) runs a shipshape, navy-style operation with a khaki-outfitted crew of four. It uses a purpose-built, 120-foot luxury cruiser powered by twin 500-horsepower Detroit Diesels and equipped with the latest communications systems. Weather reports come by fax from Norfolk, Virginia. The schedule—five single-tank dives a day, including one night dive—will leave you begging for mercy. Weeklong tours depart from the dock at the Ramada Royal Reef in Belize City on Saturday night and return from Lighthouse Reef on the following Saturday. Scheduled stops are made at all three atolls, but most diving is on the southeast corner of Lighthouse Reef.

Similar to *Belize Aggressor III*, **Wave Dancer** (⊠ Waterway II, Suite 2213, 1390 S. Dixie Hwy., Coral Gables, FL 33146, ☎ 305/669−9391 or 800/932−6237 in the U.S.) operates from the dock of the Radisson. The 120-foot cruiser has smart accommodations and the latest equipment, and trips are led by well-known diver Peter Hughes.

Expedition Belize (⊠ Oceanwide Sail Expeditions, B.V., Westfalenstrasse 92, D-58636 Iserlohn, Germany, ☎ 800/334−8582 in the U.S.) combines sailing and diving. Guests live aboard the elegant windjammer *Rembrandt Van Rijn,* and most diving is done around the atolls.

As all of the above operations run at about the same price as a week in one of the atoll resorts ($1,200−$1,400), it is not for everyone's pocketbook. An excellent budget alternative is **Out Island Divers** (⊠ Box 7, San Pedro, Ambergris Caye, ☎ 026/2151, 303/586−6020 or 800/258−4653 in the U.S., ℻ 026/2810), run by Ray Bowers, a gangly, Hemingwayesque type originally from New Jersey. On his three 39-foot boats, *Reef Roamer I, II,* and *III,* he offers one-, two-, and three-day trips from San Pedro to the atolls. Accommodations are

simple and often supplemented by a night's cam
operates the only fly-and-dive tour, sort of a sul
skiing. The one-day trip to Lighthouse Reef start
in San Pedro and gets back at sunset.

Numbers in the margin correspond to points o|
Atolls, and Barrier Reef map.

Ambergris Caye

⓭ *56 km (35 mi) northeast of Belize City*

At 40 kilometers (25 miles) long and 7 kilometers (4½ miles) wide at
its widest, its northern tip nuzzled up against the Yucatán Peninsula,
this is the queen of the cays. On early maps it was often referred to as
Costa de Ambar, or the Amber Coast, a name derived from a black-
ish, marbled substance secreted by the sperm whale and often washed
up on the beach. For centuries it was used in perfumery and medicine,
but it wasn't only found here. There is an Ambergris Caye in the Bahamas as well.

Ambergris Caye is sometimes written about as though it is a Belizean
Cancún, which is absurd. It *is* the most developed of the cays—some
would say too developed—and offers the greatest range of accommodations, dining, and diving in Belize. However, **San Pedro,** the main
town, is a hardworking community of fishermen, hoteliers, and trades-
people. With a population of fewer than 2,000 and little stores and
restaurants with names like Lily's, Alice's, Martha's, and Estel's, it is
a small, friendly, and comparatively prosperous Caribbean village.
The town has one of the highest literacy rates in the country and an
admirable level of ecological awareness about the fragility of the reef
from which it now makes its living.

A couple of streets of brightly painted, mostly two-story wooden
houses have the ocean on one side and the lagoon on the other. The
main street—officially Barrier Reef Drive but known by everyone as
Front Street—is a sandy lane running parallel to the sea. It is San
Pedro's commercial center, with the two banks, gift shops, and most
of the town's hotels and restaurants. In sunny yards a few feet behind
it, dogs lie sleeping among a cheerful confusion of fishing boats, laundry, and dismantled outboard motors.

You can walk from one end of town to the other in 10 minutes. At
night it feels like Spain's Costa Brava must have felt 40 years ago. Old
men lean over their balconies to watch the world go by. Teenagers stroll
barefoot up and down Front Street. Every now and again a battered
American station wagon crawls along. Tourists wander back to their
hotels after a meal at one of the many bistros. At their best, these small,
varied restaurants have great food, particularly seafood, but don't expect a five-star dining experience, as decor is often simple. Reservations are advised in high season.

If you like some action at night and don't want to spend too much, a
hotel in San Pedro is ideal. Accommodations are generally simple and
cheap ($10–$100), and though rooms on the main street can be noisy,
it's not so much with cars as with late-night revelers. If, on the other
hand, you want silence and sand, blue water and palm trees, you have
to go out of town, where the larger, resort-style accommodations are
situated. Generally, whether in town or out, hotels offer snorkeling and
fishing tours, and many have their own dive shops.

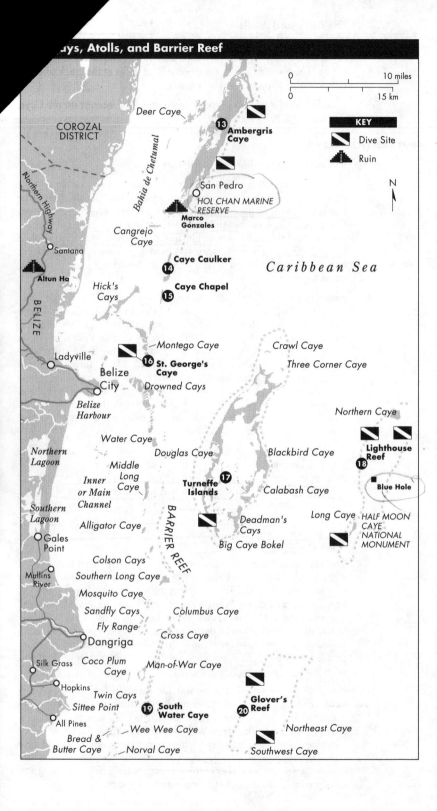

Dining and Lodging

$$ ✕ **Elvi's Kitchen.** When Elvi, a savvy Creole woman from San Pedro,
★ started her restaurant in 1964, she had a few tables on the sidewalk
under a flamboyant tree. Over 30 years later, the tree is still here, al-
beit pollarded to fit inside the roof, and the floor is still sand, but Elvi's
is a long, long way from being a street café. It now has doors of mas-
sive carved mahogany, a staff of 22 in snappy black-and-white outfits,
and a justified reputation for being one of the best seafood restaurants
in Belize. Harrison Ford ate here when he visited, and the restaurant
is immensely popular with tourists for its local color. For old time's
sake, Elvi still has a deli next door, which sells pastries, sandwiches,
and pot pies to the stroll-by crowd. ⌧ *Halfway down Middle St., San
Pedro,* ☏ *026/2176. AE, MC, V.*

$$ ✕ **Jade Garden.** This attractive restaurant, which occupies the top two
floors of a white colonial-style building just outside town, offers the
best Chinese food on Ambergris. Handsome rattan furniture, pastel
tablecloths, and a well-stocked bar also make it one of the more elegant places to eat. In addition to classic Cantonese dishes like fish chow
mein and beef foo yong, there are local variations like conch or surf-
and-turf kebabs—skewers of beef and seafood served with french fries
or baked potato. ⌧ *¼ mi south of airstrip,* ☏ *026/2126. AE, MC, V.*

$$ ✕ **Little Italy.** If you read in the local paper that Umberto Eco will be
reading from his novels here, or Cicciolina will be waitressing topless,
don't believe it. But if you want snapper scaloppine—thin slices of snap-
per, sautéed in olive oil with lime juice, garlic, and herbs—then Mary
Ellen, from Memphis, Tennessee, will serve it with fresh pasta and home-
made garlic bread. Or try the conch seviche. One negative: In recent
years, due to the restaurant's increasing popularity, the prices have
climbed quite steeply and it is no longer the bargain it used to be, al-
though there is an excellent all-you-can-eat lunch for $7. ⌧ *Front St.,
San Pedro,* ☏ *026/2866. AE, MC, V.*

$$ ✕ **Pirate's Landing.** Otherwise known as Vijay's, after the owner, this
simple but cheery Indian restaurant, not far from the Belize Yacht Club,
is a local favorite. Specialties include *gosht vindaloo* (lamb cooked in
cashew and poppy seeds with an extra spicy sauce) or lobster *masala*
(shelled lobster sautéed with fresh tomato, herbs, and spices). There
is also a large selection of vegetarian dishes, such as *darjeeling mirchi*
(sweet peppers stuffed with vegetables) or *sag pannir* (spinach and homemade cheese in a curry sauce). For sports fans, there is a satellite TV.
⌧ *½ mi south of airstrip,* ☏ *026/2146. AE, MC.*

$ ✕ **Estel's.** Estel's father-in-law was a World War II flier with a squadron
★ called "Di Nah Might." (His flying jacket and an old photo are up on
the wall.) So, not surprisingly, this is one of the best places in town to
get an American-style breakfast. She also makes burgers, sandwiches,
and excellent seafood. The little white-and-aqua building with a sand
floor and porthole-style windows is right on the beach. Outside there
is a terrace, where you can sit under an umbrella of palapa leaves and
watch the pelicans splat into the water. ⌧ *Front St., San Pedro,* ☏ *026/
2019. No credit cards.*

$$$ ✕🏠 **Captain Morgan's Retreat.** Getting here—in a speedboat that zips
★ you up the Ambergris coast over impossibly beautiful water—is a plea-
sure in itself. What you'll find when you arrive is a desert island with
first-class American amenities. Handsome thatched cabanas scattered
along 800 feet of golden sand are some of the finest in Belize. They have
high thatched roofs, hardwood fittings, and excellent bathrooms, and
the only sound is the gentle murmur of the breakers on the reef, 500
yards away, and the rustling of palm trees. The efficiency and hard work
of the management ensure that there will be no glitches in paradise. Not

everyone will like the "captain's table" seating arrangements—guests eat together at long mahogany tables—but it is typical of the down-home conviviality in which Captain Morgan's specializes. A splendid new swimming pool surrounded by a hardwood deck offers an alternative to sea bathing, though the palm-dotted beach is a delight. A lookout tower offers panoramic views of the ocean and an excellent perch for bird-watchers. Elmer "Patojo" Paz, the dive master, is one of the best on Ambergris. ⊠ *c/o Magnum Americas, 718 Washington Ave., Box 1560, Detroit Lakes, MN 56502,* ☎ *026/2567, 218/847–3012 or 800/447–2931 in the U.S.,* ⅋ *026/2616. 21 rooms. Restaurant, bar, pool, beach, dive shop, laundry service. AE, D, MC, V.*

$$$ ✕🏨 **Ramon's Village Resort.** It's not quite spring break in Daytona Beach, but the pink-and-blue neon of a Maya warrior's head over the entrance says a lot about what you can expect here. Twentysomethings hang out by the pool, drinking margaritas and playing the dating game. On the pier, big girls in small bikinis and young hunks with surfer glasses pile into multicolored dive boats. Others parasail, Jet Ski, or windsurf. In the evening, there are lots more margaritas and lots more partying. The cabanas, many of them two-story, are thatch to thatch close, but with their mahogany floors and fittings, views of the ocean, and hibiscus plants, they are pleasant enough. But you don't come to Ramon's to cozy up in a cabana. You come to boogie till dawn. If you want peace and quiet, avoid it like the plague. ⊠ *Box 4407, Laurel, MS 39441,* ☎ *026/2071 or 800/624–4315 in the U.S.,* ⅋ *026/2214. 60 rooms. Restaurant, bar, pool, dive shop, dock, windsurfing, jet skiing, parasailing, laundry service. AE, MC, V.*

$$$ ✕🏨 **Sunbreeze Beach Hotel.** This resort, which sits just on the edge of town next to the airstrip, has been extensively refurbished over the last few years. Grouped around a large, plant-filled central courtyard, the rooms all have air-conditioning and TVs; five deluxe units also have whirlpool baths. With accommodations equipped for guests with disabilities, the Sunbreeze has a fine, small beach and a pool, added in 1995. New manager Elton Ross, a Californian with 20 years of Caribbean experience as a chef, has injected new life into the adjacent Coco Palm restaurant, which offers a "we cook your catch" service to guests. Various meal plans are available. ⊠ *Box 14, San Pedro,* ☎ *026/2191,* ⅋ *026/2346. 34 rooms. Restaurant, bar, pool, beach, dive shop, boating, shop, laundry service. AE, MC, V.*

$$$ ✕🏨 **Victoria House.** There is a hammock under a palm tree in the mid-
★ dle of the beach at this beautiful resort 3 kilometers (2 miles) from San Pedro. The white colonial-style house, which is the core of the resort, has the feeling of an old-fashioned diplomatic residence, with airy verandas, flower-filled gardens, and tiled walkways. Various meal plans are available, and the dining room serves excellent buffet meals that combine the best local seafood with imaginative salads and side dishes. It has become a magnet for nonresidents as well, thanks to music, food, and dancing on Tuesday and Friday nights. On Sunday, the hotel serves what is widely regarded as the best brunch in Belize, but it is the excellent accommodations, flower-decked grounds, and general atmosphere of tropical elegance that make visitors return again and again. The original stone-and-thatch cabanas, which are closest to the beach, have private verandas overlooking the sea. To these have been added a newer group of rooms, with gleaming tile, handsome hardwood fittings, and balconies looking into the gardens. All units have telephones, room service, and private bathrooms with showers. The oldest rooms are upstairs in the main house, and though they need a bit of refurbishment, their antique furniture and hardwood floors give them great character. Chris Berlin and Rebecca McDonald run the best dive shop and PADI instruction center on the cay. Sea kayaks, catamarans, and Wind-

surfers are also available as are a full array of sightseeing tours. ✉ *Box 22, San Pedro,* ☎ *026/2067,* FAX *026/2429; or Box 20785, Houston, TX 77225,* ☎ *713/661–4025 or 800/247–5159. 31 rooms. Restaurant, bar, beach, dive shop, windsurfing, laundry service, travel services. AE, MC, V.*

$$–$$$ ✕🏨 **San Pedro Holiday Hotel.** This group of four colonial-style houses,
★ with their cheery pink-and-white trim and seaside ambience, is the closest you will get to a resort in the center of town. It is slightly overpriced, but there is an excellent dive shop with some of the best air in town. Ceili's, on the property, is one of the better restaurants. ✉ *Box 1140, Belize City,* ☎ *026/2014 or 024/2103 in Belize City,* FAX *026/2295. 18 rooms, 2 apartments. Restaurant, bar, beach, dive shop, shop, laundry service. AE, MC, V.*

$$ ✕🏨 **Casablanca Hotel.** Once described as a mixture of Miami Beach and Morocco in the '30s, this new hotel in the heart of San Pedro contains air-conditioned rooms with private bath and high-quality American linens and beds. It shares its distinctive decor—lots of primary colors and African-style fabrics with a sun, moon, and stars theme—with the exceptional Lagoon restaurant. Owners Norman and Deon Gosney have extensive experience in the restaurant and nightclub business in Manhattan, and so they imbued their jazzy eatery with uptown style in downtown San Pedro. Big-band music, waiters in snappy waistcoats, and a choice of seating—at tables ranged across the tile floor or at private banquettes—further enhance the feeling of metropolitan chic. At the center of it all is Deon, a vivacious blonde who bustles about in tight-fitting black outfits, dispensing culinary advice and terse one-liners. She boasts that she can compete with any restaurant in her price range in the world. Certainly the menu is as far from beans and rice as you can get. Shrimp satay from Thailand, Spanish cream of corn soup from Mexico, an excellent vegetarian Indian curry, steak, and seafood, plus mouthwatering desserts like watermelon granita (an ice smothered in blackberry brandy) make it very eclectic. The only thing missing is the yellow cabs. A lounge area offers satellite-TV, books, and CDs. For sunset cocktails, there is a bar on the roof, which can also be used for sunbathing during the day (the hotel does not have its own beach). American plan is available. ✉ *Pescador Dr., San Pedro,* ☎ *026/2327,* FAX *026/2992. 5 rooms. Restaurant (Closed Wed.), bar, room service, laundry service. MC, V.*

$$ ✕🏨 **Spindrift Hotel.** Centrally located, this family-run hotel is something of a meeting place for locals (a hilariously funny game, known as Chicken Drop, is played on the beach outside on Wednesdays) and is a favorite with divers. The rooms, some of which overlook the ocean, are grouped around an inner courtyard and vary considerably in price. ✉ *Front St., San Pedro,* ☎ *026/2174,* FAX *026/2251. 22 rooms, 2 apartments with kitchenettes, 1 large suite. Restaurant, bar, beach, dive shop. AE, MC, V.*

$$$ 🏨 **Belize Yacht Club.** After four years, this property outside of town has begun to have the ambience and facilities that the name implies and is now one of the premier resorts on Ambergris. Accommodations are in attractive, Spanish-style villas grouped around a central area with a swimming pool. All have phone, room service, kitchenettes, and verandas specially angled to face the ocean. For sea dogs, there is a dock with fueling facilities, whereas if you'd rather pump iron, one of the best-equipped gyms in Belize is at your disposal. There is also a new dive shop. Punctuated with bougainvillea and hibiscus everywhere, the landscaping has finally come into its own. An attractive new bar cum restaurant, with awnings made of multicolored sails, offers excellent breakfast, lunch, and cocktails (it's also open to nonguests). The rather small, man-made beach is a slight negative. ⊠ *Box 1, San Pedro,* ☎ *026/2777 or 800/396–1153 in the U.S.,* FAX *026/2768. 44 rooms. Restaurant/bar, room service, pool, exercise room, beach, dive shop, dock, laundry service, travel services. AE, D, MC, V.*

$$$ **★**   🏨 **Caribbean Villas.** Before they decided to build these two graceful white villas on a lovely stretch of beach 3 kilometers (2 miles) south of San Pedro, Wil Lala had been a dentist and his wife, Susan, was an interior decorator. The result of their collaboration is state-of-the-art island architecture, incorporating Caribbean and Spanish styles, in a lush tropical setting. An intelligent and creative design—luggage niches under the built-in sofas and spacious sleeping lofts for six—make these self-catering apartments feel larger than they are. Since opening five years ago, the property has matured, and the Lalas are constantly looking for new ways to improve the facilities. A two-story bird-watching tower has helped make the place a paradise for birders, with as many as 60 species of tropical birds flitting about at any one time. Other new additions include a fleet of bikes, a *Sapo* (a South American coin game) table, and a local couple who will come in and cook breakfast for you, if you wish. The owners also offer wildlife, fishing, and snorkeling tours. ⊠ *3 km (2 mi) south of San Pedro,* ☎ *026/2715 or 913/468–3608 in the U.S,* FAX *026/2885. 10 duplexes. Beach, travel services. AE, MC, V.*

$$$ 🏨 **El Pescador.** Everyone on Ambergris says they offer fishing trips, but if you are seriously into fishing, want the best guides in Belize, the best boats and gear, and don't care too much about your creature comforts, this is the place for you. Owners Juergen Krueger and his Wisconsin-born wife, Kathleen, were the first people to build on the northern part of the cay. Though they refer to El Pescador as a "fishing camp," it is in fact a handsome colonial-style house on a beautiful stretch of beach 5 kilometers (3 miles) north of San Pedro. Accommodations are homey but comfortable. The specialty here is the weeklong fishing package, which includes round-trip airfare from Belize City, three meals a day, and the sole use of a boat and guide for six eight-hour days of fishing. Tours go outside the reef for sailfish, barracuda, wahoo, and tarpon. ⊠ *Box 793, Belize City,* ☎ FAX *026/2398. 12 rooms. Dining room, beach, fishing. AE, MC, V (cash or traveler's checks preferred).*

$$$ 🏨 **Rock's Inn.** Built in an E shape around a pretty central garden, with a little strip of sand in front and a view across the water, this small, modern guest house on three floors offers air-conditioned apartments with well-equipped kitchenettes at reasonable prices. Most rooms have an extra bed, and each additional person costs only $10. Children under 12 are free. ⊠ *Front St., San Pedro,* ☎ *026/2326,* FAX *026/2358. 14 rooms. Bar, baby-sitting, laundry service. AE, MC, V.*

$$–$$$ 🏨 **Alijua Hotel Suites.** A modern block in the center of town, and one of the few three-story buildings in San Pedro, this property offers Florida-style accommodations with air-conditioning, private bath, phone, and cable TV. Rooms are decorated with imitation leather furniture and Guatemalan bedspreads. What they lack in ambience, they make up for in functionality. There are also apartments, with king-size beds, spacious bathrooms, and outfitted kitchens. ⊠ *Barrier Reef Dr. and Buccaneer St., San Pedro,* ☎ *026/2113,* FAX *026/2362. 7 rooms, 3 apartments. Shop, travel services. AE, MC, V.*

$$–$$$ 🏨 **The Palms.** If you want the condominium experience, this is the best place on Ambergris to find it. With four people sharing (each person above two costs $20), you get a lot for your money, too. The one- and two-bedroom units, which are housed in a series of handsome three-story buildings ranged around a pool, all have air-conditioning or ceiling fans, kitchenettes, spacious verandas overlooking the ocean, and custom-made hardwood fittings. There is also an attractive private beach and a pier from which guests can be picked up for dive and snorkeling tours. Maid service is available as are facilities for people with disabilities. The Indian couple who manage the resort are charming and helpful, and San Pedro's restaurants and bars are a five-minute walk away. ⊠ *Coconut Dr., San Pedro,* ☎ *026/3322,* ℻ *026/3601. 12 units. Pool, beach, dock. MC, V.*

$–$$ ⊞ **Martha's.** Backpackers favor this large white house on Middle Street. It's upstairs from a grocery store and two blocks back from the sea. ⊠ *Box 27, San Pedro,* ☎ *026/2053,* ℻ *026/2589. 14 rooms share baths. AE, MC, V.*

$ ⊞ **San Pedrano.** Painted mint green, blue, and white, with crisp linen provided and spotless rooms, this is the cheeriest of the budget hotels in San Pedro. The owners, the Gonzalez family, are friendly and hardworking. They maintain a gift shop downstairs. ⊠ *Front St., San Pedro,* ☎ *026/2054,* ℻ *026/2093. 7 rooms and 1 apartment share baths. Shop. AE, MC, V.*

Outdoor Activities and Sports

HORSEBACK RIDING

For those who want to trot along the beach, a new stable called **Isla Equestrian** (⊠ Barrier Reef Dr., San Pedro, ☎ 026/2895), right by the airstrip, rents horses by the hour.

SCUBA DIVING

The people of Ambergris, sensing that the future lay in tourism rather than fishing, were the quickest at setting up the infrastructure for diving, and in terms of the number of dive shops, the quality of the dive masters, and the range of equipment and facilities, Ambergris Caye remains the most obvious all-around choice as a base for diving. There is even a hyperbaric chamber in San Pedro, paid for by contributions from all the dive shops and through fees attached to diver insurance, which is highly recommended, since emergency services and transport costs could wipe out your savings in a hurry. The dive shops at Captain Morgan's, Holiday Hotel, Ramon's Village, Spindrift Hotel, and Victoria House are some of the better ones.

Diving is generally done out of fast, maneuverable speedboats. There is no bouncing around in Zodiacs here: Transports are hand-built out of solid mahogany. As the boats represent the dive masters' major assets, costing as much as $14,000 each, they are normally lovingly cared for. Power generally comes from two hefty outboards mounted on the back. With the throttle right open, it's an exhilarating ride.

Most of the dive masters are ex-fishermen, locals from San Pedro who started diving as an adjunct to their work as lobstermen and then went on to get certified as dive masters. The best of them are immensely personable and have an intimate knowledge of the reef and a superb eye for coral and marine life. They also have an unusually developed ecological awareness, knowing as they do that the destruction of the reef would not only be a great tragedy in itself, but economic suicide for them. An example is the creation, by a group of dive masters, of a network of buoys fastened to the bedrock to prevent the further destruction of the coral by anchors dropped directly into it. In bad weather, one anchor dragging across the bottom can destroy more coral than a thousand divers.

Dives off Ambergris are usually one-tank dives at depths of 50–80 feet. This gives you approximately 35 minutes of bottom time. The general pattern is two one-tank dives per day—one in the morning at 9 and one in the afternoon at 2—though this can be varied depending on your budget. The following were the prices at press time for diving and snorkeling from Ambergris: snorkeling: $15–$20 for two hours or $40–$50 for a day trip with lunch; diving: $30–$35 for a single-tank dive, $35–$55 for a double-tank dive, $35–$40 for a single-tank night dive, and $125–$200 for day trips with three-tank dives to Turneffe, $65 to the Blue Hole.

With slight variations, diving is similar all along Ambergris Caye. You always dive on the windward side of the reef, and the basic form is canyon-diving. For wall-diving, you have to go out to the atolls.

The highlight of the reef is the **Hol Chan Marine Reserve,** which is 20 minutes from San Pedro, at the southern tip of Ambergris. Basically, it is a break in the reef about 100 feet wide and between 20 and 35 feet deep through which tremendous volumes of water pass with the tides. As well as containing rich marine life and exciting corals, the park has a miniature Blue Hole, a 12-foot-deep cave, the entrance to which is often a favorite spot for such fish as the fairy basslet, an iridescent purple-and-yellow fish frequently seen here. Hol Chan is also home to a large population of the gloomily named *Gymnothorax funebris,* or moray eel.

As with other destinations off Ambergris, canyon-diving is the norm at Hol Chan. The canyons lie between buttresses of coral running perpendicular to the reef, separated by white, sandy channels. They vary in depth from 50 to 100 feet. Some sides are very steep, and others comprise gently rolling undulations. In some spots there are tunnel-like passageways, which you can dive through, leading from one canyon to the next. Not knowing what is going to be in the next "valley" as you come over the hill can be exciting.

Fish are abundant in Hol Chan, as they are everywhere else on the reef. You'll identify large numbers of squirrel fish, butterfly fish, parrot fish, and queen angelfish, as well as Nassau groupers, barracuda, and large shoals of yellowtail snappers. A recent addition to the reef's attractions is **Shark Alley,** a sandbar where you can snorkel with nurse sharks and rays (they gather here to be fed) and even larger numbers of day-trippers from Ramon's resort. With luck, one of them will have a foot bitten off and the place will stop being so crowded.

The fish are generally in the canyons, and as you pass over you have a bird's-eye view of them. Though the rainbow variety of coral you'd find on the Great Barrier Reef in Australia does not exist in Belize— much of it is biscuit-colored here—there is nonetheless plentiful brain, antler, and fan coral. Hol Chan is also one of the best and most popular places to night-dive. As Hol Chan is an open stretch of reef, it does not have opening times as such or admission fees. To learn more about Hol Chan, *see* Chapter 2.

Shopping

The best gift shops in the country are, not surprisingly, where the most tourists go, and that is San Pedro. At **Belizean Arts** (⌧ Middle St., ☎ 026/3019) and its sister shop, **Arts and Crafts of Central America** (⌧ Middle St., ☎ 026/2623), you will find the best selection of works by local painters, plus jewelry and crafts from Central America. These include hand-painted animal figures from Mexico, masks and fabrics from Guatemala, and such local products as brilliantly colored tropical fish made of coconut wood. You may have seen beautiful mahogany furniture during your stay, and you can find a good selection at **Best of Belize** (⌧ Front St., no phone). It has mahogany clam chairs and other furniture, carvings, boxes, salad bowls, and chopping boards. If you want a culinary memento of Belize, head for **Genesis in the Jungle** (⌧ Fido shopping arcade, no phone), which stocks a wide selection of Belizean spices, as well as wines brewed from organic berries and other fruits.

Caye Caulker

14 *8 km (5 mi) south of Ambergris Caye, 29 km (18 mi) northeast of Belize City*

Two signs you often see on this cay—NO SHIRT NO PROBLEM and NO IL-LEGAL DRUGS—pretty much sum up the ambience of Ambergris's little southern brother, which is, after it, the most developed of Belize's cays. In recent years, it has received a reputation as a tropical paradise for tightwad travelers. As a result, it has become immensely popular with the backpack-and-Birkenstock brigade, either young and student or old and poor, and Belize's few Rastafarian clones. Actually, it's a bit of a dump. What the Irish playwright Synge said about his own country—that what most people found beautiful about Ireland was actually its poverty—amply applies to Caye Caulker. The colorful water tubs and flowering shrubs give it the illusion of beauty, but the local people live in dilapidated shacks with no running water. Here, even the pelicans look disheveled.

There are no banks on Caye Caulker, so either come with ready cash or change traveler's checks at your hotel. However, there have been a number of incidences of theft, so you are advised not to leave anything valuable in your room.

Dining and Lodging

$$ ✕ **Marin's Restaurant.** Marin's, the cay's best restaurant, serves good seafood. You can't miss it: Head one block back from Main Street, and you'll see its distinctive black-and-red exterior. ⊠ *1 block west of Tropical Paradise hotel,* ☎ *022/2104. MC, V.*

$-$$ 🏨 **The Tropical Paradise.** Your best bet is these simple but clean rooms
★ in a small cluster of cabanas at the south end of town. All units have ceiling fans, phone, and private bath. The property has both a bar and one of the better restaurants on the cay. ☎ *022/2124,* FAX *022/2225. 15 rooms. Restaurant, bar. No credit cards.*

$ 🏨 **Daisy's Hotel.** This cheerfully painted, two-story house at the south end of town has 12 basic rooms on the first floor, which share showers. ☎ *022/2150. 12 rooms share baths. No credit cards.*

$ 🏨 **Jiminez Huts.** These four simple thatched cabanas, on a small plot of land on the lagoon side of the cay, are set in a pretty garden with flower beds edged with conch shells. Each cabana has one or two double beds and a very basic bathroom (cold water only). Some share a bath. Bring your mosquito repellent as there are lots of the critters breeding in the lagoon. ☎ *022/2175. 4 thatched cabanas (7 rooms; some share baths). No credit cards.*

$ 🏨 **Rainbow Hotel.** You can't miss this two-story, mint-green and blue building at the northern end of the village. Management is friendly, and rooms are spartan but cheerful. All have phone, TV, ceiling fans, and private bathroom with shower. Those overlooking the sea are more expensive. ☎ *022/2123. 17 rooms. Room service, fishing. No credit cards.*

Scuba Diving

A good operator is **Belize Diving Services** (⊠ Box 667, Belize City, ☎ 022/2143, FAX 022/2217).

Caye Chapel

15 *3 km (2 mi) south of Caye Caulker*

This cay, owned by the Pyramid Island Resort, was once an exclusive resort with an airstrip and tennis courts. Recently, however, it has become very run-down and in need of renovation.

St. George's Caye

16 *15 km (9 mi) northeast of Belize City*

This small, relaxed cay a stone's throw from Belize City is steeped in history. The origins of the state of Belize began here, the site of the first capital of the original British settlement and, subsequently, of the decisive sea battle with the Spanish. In more recent times, it was a favorite haunt for Her Majesty's Forces.

Dining and Lodging

$$$ ✕🏨 **Cottage Colony.** The island dependency of the Bellevue Hotel in Belize City, these colonial-style beachfront cottages feature a fine beach and excellent snorkeling. All rooms have telephone and air-conditioning. If you get antsy, Belize City is just a short boat ride away. Dining is on the American Plan. ✉ *c/o Bellevue Hotel, Box 428, Belize City,* ☎ *023/3571,* FAX *027/3253. 13 cottages. Restaurant, bar, beach, dive shop, snorkeling, boating, laundry service. AE, D, MC, V.*

$$$ ✕🏨 **St. George's Lodge.** The original resort has long been a favorite with the British because of its proximity to Belize City. There are 10 rooms in the main building, all constructed of Belizean hardwood (the bar is made of rosewood), and four thatched cottages by the water. Electricity is provided by the lodge's own windmills. Shower water is solar heated. In the restaurant, you can enjoy grilled snapper or grouper. Meals are taken on the American Plan. ✉ *Box 625, Belize City,* ☎ *024/4190 or 800/678–6871 in the U.S.,* FAX *023/1460. 10 rooms, 4 cabanas. Restaurant, bar, beach, dive shop. AE, MC, V.*

Scuba Diving

St. George's Lodge has a good dive shop.

Turneffe Islands

17 *40 km (25 mi) east of Belize City*

This chain of tiny islands and mangrove swamps makes up an atoll the size of Barbados. It's the largest of the three atolls and the most centrally placed. Not surprisingly, the main draw here is the diving.

Dining and Lodging

$$$ ✕🏨 **Blackbird Caye Resort.** Blackbird Caye, a 350-acre sliver of sand
★ and palm trees, was originally a base camp for scientists researching the reef and its wildlife, particularly dolphins. The product of a partnership between a Houston businessman and Belizean Ray Lightburn, the cay still offers total escape (access is by boat only) and some of the best diving and snorkeling in Belize, but in 1995, Paul Hunt, former manager of the Radisson Fort George and one of the best hoteliers in Belize, took over management of the resort and is revamping it to cater to a more discerning clientele. The thatched cabanas have been refurbished and the offerings expanded to include sea kayaking, windsurfing, and nature trails. The heart of the new resort is the dining and lounge area, which is housed in a magnificent circular structure of thatch and poles, supported by a stout mahogany column. The food is Belizean—conch fritters, barracuda steaks, or grilled snapper. Blackbird also offers some superb sport fishing on the nearby Calabash Caye Flats, and at the northern tip of the island is the last breeding ground of the American crocodile. Lodgings are on an all-inclusive basis only. ✉ *1415 Louisiana, Suite 3100, Houston, TX 77002,* ☎ *713/659–5144,* FAX *713/658–0739. 10 cabanas. Restaurant, bar, room service, dive shop, windsurfing, fishing, laundry service. MC, V.*

$$$ ✕🏨 **Turneffe Island Lodge.** Run by Americans Dave and Jill Bennett,
★ the only resort on Caye Borkel is at the atoll's southern edge. Rooms
have water views, and an easygoing atmosphere prevails. For those suf-
fering from castaway syndrome, there are planned evening activities.
Only eight-day packages with meals are offered. Guests must transfer
from Belize City by boat. ✉ *11904 Hidden Hills Dr., Jacksonville, FL
32225,* ☎ *904/641–4468 or 800/338–8149,* 🆕 *904/641–5285. 13
rooms. Restaurant, bar, dive shop, fishing. AE, MC, V.*

Scuba Diving

For diving, Turneffe is second only to Lighthouse Reef, thanks to sev-
eral steep drop-offs in its midst. Only an hour from Lighthouse Reef
and 45 minutes from the northern edge of Glover's Reef, Turneffe is
within day-trip range of Belize's best diving. Blackbird Caye and Turn-
effe Island Lodge both offer good dive services.

The highlight of Turneffe, and probably the most exciting wall-dive in
Belize, is the **Elbow,** situated at the southernmost tip of the atoll. Gen-
erally considered an advanced dive because of the prevailing conditions,
it often has rough seas, even on calm days, and strong currents that
tend to sweep you out toward the deep water beyond the reef. The drop-
off is dramatic. You have the feeling of flying in blue space, your likely
traveling companions large groups of eagle rays who regularly visit this
area. Sometimes as many as 50 flutter together, a rippling herd of rays
that will take your breath away.

Though it is most famous for its spectacular wall-dives, the atoll has
dives for every level, including novice. **Turneffe's western, leeward side,**
where the reef is wide and gently sloping, is good for shallower dives
and snorkeling. There are large concentrations of tube sponges, soft
corals such as forked sea feathers and sea fans, and varied fish, including
plentiful permit. Also on the leeward side is the wreck of the *Sayonara.*
No doubloons to be scooped up here—it was a small passenger and
cargo boat that went down in 1985—but it's a good site for practic-
ing wreck-diving.

Lighthouse Reef

⑱ *80 km (50 mi) east of Belize City*

If Robinson Crusoe had been a man of means, this is where he would
have gone for a break from his desert island. Though it's the farthest
away of Belize's atolls, it's the closest you will get to paradise. It's also
the most accessible atoll, thanks to an airstrip.

Lighthouse Reef is about 29 kilometers (18 miles) long and less than
2 kilometers (1 mile) wide and is surrounded by 67 kilometers (42 miles)
of coral reef. The Lighthouse Reef system—which includes the **Half
Moon Caye National Monument**—has two of the country's five-star
dives: the Blue Hole and the vertiginous walls off Half Moon Caye.
Loggerhead turtles, iguanas, and one of the world's two large colonies
of red-footed boobies are protected at the monument. To learn more
about it, *see* Chapter 2. The atoll's only accommodations are at the
Lighthouse Reef Resort, on Northern Caye.

Dining and Lodging

$$$ ✕🏨 **Lighthouse Reef Resort.** If you want to get blissed out in Belize,
★ this is one of the best places to do it. Once a spartan dive camp for afi-
cionados of the reef, it has gradually been transformed into one of the
most exclusive resorts in Central America. Luckily, small is beautiful
seems to be the guiding principle of the development. No clutter and
no noisy generators here. You always have the feeling that you are the

only person on the island. In addition to the five original brick cabanas, two handsome new British colonial–style villas have just been completed. Each villa is tastefully furnished in Queen Anne style and has a modern, well-equipped kitchenette. Two more villas were under construction at press time. Eight-day, seven-night packages are all that's available, but you have a choice of European or American Plan. The setting—white coral sand, palm trees, mint-green water—is breathtaking, and the diving, under expert and friendly supervision, is as good as any in the world. If you are lucky, you may even meet Peeto, a bottlenose dolphin who lives in the bay. Whatever happens, you'll never want to leave. ✉ *Northern Caye, Box 255, Belize City; or Box 1435, Dundee, FL 33838,* ☎ *813/439–1436 or 800/423–3114,* ℻ *023/1205. 11 rooms. Restaurant, dive shop, fishing. AE.*

Scuba Diving

Less than 2 kilometers (1 mile) from the atoll, the coral reef has precipitous walls that plummet to 3,000 feet, but great depth doesn't always make for the best diving. Many people say that the best is in less than 50 feet of water. Still, the two most famous dives on Lighthouse Reef are the Blue Hole and Half Moon Caye Wall, the Grand Canyon and Matterhorn of Belize's underwater world.

From the air the **Blue Hole,** a breathtaking vertical chute that drops several hundred feet through the reef, looks like a dark-blue eye in the center of the shallow water of the lagoon. Formed in an ice age 15,000 years ago, which exposed the limestone foundations of the reef and created vast subterranean caverns, it was first dived by Jacques Cousteau in 1970 and has since become a divers' place of pilgrimage. Just over 1,000 feet wide at the surface and dropping almost vertically to a depth of 412 feet, the Blue Hole engenders a sensation like swimming down a mine shaft. It is the excitement of that feeling, rather than the marine life (of which you will see far more with a snorkel and flippers at the surface), that has made it a destination worthy of the suitcase sticker: "I dived the Blue Hole."

The best diving on Lighthouse is at **Half Moon Caye,** at the southeastern tip of Lighthouse Reef. The Half Moon Caye Wall is a classic wall-dive, beginning at 35 feet and dropping almost vertically to blue infinity. Floating out over the edge is a bit like free-fall parachuting. Magnificent spurs of coral jut out to the seaward side, looking like small tunnels; they are fascinating to explore and invariably full of fish. Because of the great variety of bottom types, an exceptionally varied marine life exists around the cay. On the gently sloping sand flats behind the coral spurs, a vast colony of garden eels stirs, their heads protruding from the sand like a field of periscopes. Spotted eagle rays, turtles, and other pelagics are frequent visitors by the drop-off. But one of the main reasons this area is so great is the presence of the largest colony of red-footed boobies in Belize. There is nearly as much going on above water as below it.

South Water Caye

🔞 *23 km (14 mi) southeast of Dangriga*

This is the first cay to have been developed for tourism in the south of Belize. The coral is only a few flipper beats away and offers good off-the-beaten-reef diving. A nearby **Smithsonian-run research institute** (✉ Carrie Bow Caye, no phone) welcomes visitors, by appointment. Contact the Blue Marlin Lodge for more information.

Dining and Lodging

$$$ ✕🏠 **Blue Marlin Lodge.** This picturesque resort, accessible from Dangriga, makes an excellent base for fishing excursions and dive trips. The reef is only 50 yards away, and famous sites like the Blue Hole and Glover's Reef are also accessible. Accommodations are in thatched cabanas close enough to the sea to hear it. All have private bath, hot water, electric fans, and phones. A restaurant and bar top off the amenities, and meals are included. ⊠ *Box 21, Dangriga,* ☎ *052/2243,* FAX *052/2296. 14 cabanas. Restaurant, bar, dive shop, fishing. AE, DC, MC, V.*

Glover's Reef

⑳ *113 km (70 mi) southeast of Belize City*

Named after the pirate John Glover, this necklace of coral strung around a 208-square-kilometer (80-square-mile) lagoon is the southernmost of Belize's three atolls. The diving rates as some of the best in Belize, and there is excellent fishing for permit and bonefish. Two resorts now exist here.

Dining and Lodging

$$$ ✕🏠 **Manta Reef Resort.** This fishing and diving resort, on Southwest
★ Caye on the southern tip of Glover's Reef, is the newer and more upscale of the two resorts on the atoll. Accommodations are in mahogany-fitted cabanas, each with a private bath with shower, a small porch, a hammock to swing in, and daily maid service. On a pier overlooking the lagoon, a restaurant and bar offers good home cooking—and even chocolate-chip cookies. The eight-day, seven-night packages include meals and are, as much as possible, tailored to suit individual desires, from diving to fishing to simply lolling in a hammock. Transport to and from the reef is by boat and takes four hours. ⊠ *c/o 102 Laurelwood, San Antonio, TX 78213,* ☎ *023/1895, 305/226–2029 or 800/342–0053 in the U.S.,* FAX *023/2764. 11 rooms. Restaurant, bar, room service, dive shop, fishing, laundry service. AE, MC, V.*

Scuba Diving

Though most of the finest dive sites are along the atoll's southeastern limb, on the windward side, one exception is **Emerald Forest Reef,** named for its mass of huge green elkhorn coral. Because the most exciting part of the reef is only 25 feet down, it's excellent for novices and snorkelers, and it abounds in healthy corals and fish. It also proves an important point: Depth isn't everything.

Southwest Caye Wall, close to the Manta Reef Resort, is a typically dramatic drop-off—an underwater cliff that drops quickly to 130 feet, is briefly interrupted by a narrow shelf, and then continues its near-vertical descent to 350 feet. As with all wall-dives, where it is easy to lose track of depth and time with the exhilaration of flying in blue space, both ascent and descent require careful monitoring.

Long Caye Wall is yet another exciting wall with a dramatic drop-off to hundreds of feet. Overhangs covered in sheet and boulder coral make it a good place to spot turtles, rays, and barracuda.

Glover's Reef Resort (☎ 022/3048) and **Manta Reef Resort** (☎ 023/1895) both provide good dive shops and services.

The Cays and Atolls A to Z

Arriving and Departing

BY BOAT

A variety of boats operate between Belize City and Ambergris. The most dependable are the *Andrea* and *Andrea II*. They depart from the Southern Foreshore, by the Bellevue Hotel, weekdays at 4 PM and Saturday at 1 PM, and return from San Pedro at 7 AM weekdays and 8 AM on Saturday. The journey takes 75 minutes and costs $20 round-trip. Private charter boats also make the round-trip. They leave from the docks around the swing bridge. Rip-offs have been known to happen, so pay the fare only when you reach your destination!

Boats for Caye Caulker leave Belize City from the dock by the Bellevue Hotel and from the dock behind the Texaco station (⊠ N. Front St.), near the swing bridge. The journey takes 45 minutes and costs $7.50 one-way. Departures are every hour between 9 and 3 PM. Finding boats—known locally as skiffs—is no problem; the young kids who hustle for the boat owners will find you. The best-known of these boats is the *Soledad,* captained by a well-known local character called Chocolate. Chocolate also runs trips to Goff's Caye, a small island southeast of Belize City.

The *Thunderbolt* (☎ 026/2217) runs Monday–Saturday to both San Pedro and Caye Caulker, departing from Cesario's Dock in San Pedro at 7 AM and returning from Belize City at approximately 1 PM. On Caye Caulker, the boat docks at the Lagoonside Marina. The fare is $10 round-trip.

To get to the more remote cays, you are basically left to your own devices. Boats can be hired for charter, either in San Pedro or Belize City, but they are not cheap. The resorts on the atolls run their own flights or boats, but these are not services for the public.

For the southern cays, check in Dangriga (☞ Placencia and the South, *below*) for boat availability. The Pelican Beach Hotel has a boat that goes to its resort on South Water Caye, while at the Río Mar Hotel you can find out about boats for Tobacco Reef. Both services are not usually available to the general public, but those not staying at the resorts can sometimes catch a ride if there's room.

BY PLANE

As an increasing number of visitors transfer directly to Ambergris Caye on arrival in Belize City, there are regular flights to San Pedro from both the municipal and international airports. The airstrip—it's not an airport—is right in San Pedro, so much so that when you fly in you feel as though the wing tips are going to drag the washing lines from the surrounding houses with them. You'll always find taxis at the airstrip, and the hotels run courtesy coaches. If you are proceeding on foot, it's two minutes, around the edges of the soccer field, to the main street. There are no buses.

Tropic Air (⊠ Box 20, San Pedro, ☎ 026/2012) and **Maya Airways** (⊠ 6 Fort St., Box 458, Belize City, ☎ 024/4032) both fly to the cay, as does **Island Air** (⊠ San Pedro, Ambergris Caye, ☎ 026/2012 in San Pedro or 023/1140 in Belize City), which runs 10 flights per day, from 7:30 AM to 5 PM. Fares for the 15-minute flight are about $40 (municipal) and $77 (international) round-trip.

Three airlines now fly to Caye Caulker: **Tropic Air** (☎ 024/5671), **Skybird** (☎ 023/2596), and **Island Air** (☎ 026/2012 in San Pedro or 023/1140 in Belize City). Skybird Air Services has a regular service from Municipal Airport. The first flight is at 8:30 AM, the last at 4:30 PM.

Except for flights to these two islands, there are no scheduled plane connections to the cays. Each resort makes its own arrangements for guests to come out. Lighthouse Reef was, at press time, the only atoll with an airstrip.

Getting Around

BY TAXI

In addition to getting a taxi at the San Pedro airstrip, you can also call a cab (☎ 026/2089 or 026/2038).

Contacts and Resources

BANKS

The **Belize Bank** (⊠ 49 Barrier Reef Dr., San Pedro) is open Monday–Thursday 8–1 and Friday 8–1 and 3–6. The **Atlantic Bank** (⊠ Front St., San Pedro) is open Monday, Tuesday, Thursday, and Friday 8–noon and 1–3; Wednesday 8–1; and Saturday 8:30–noon.

EMERGENCIES

On Ambergris: **Ambulance** (☎ 90). **Fire** (☎ 2372). **Police** (☎ 2022).

Hospitals. Lion's Clinic 2073 (⊠ Next to the hyperbaric chamber, near the airstrip, San Pedro, no phone). **Caye Caulker Health Center** (⊠ Opposite Marin Hotel, Caye Caulker, ☎ 022/2166) is open weekdays 8–11:30 and 1–4:30.

Pharmacy. Lopez Drugs (⊠ Front St., San Pedro) is open Monday–Thursday 8–noon and 5:30–9, Friday 8–2, and weekends 7 AM–9 PM.

LAUNDROMATS

J's (⊠ Middle St., San Pedro) and **Belize Laundry & Dry Cleaners** (⊠ Middle St., San Pedro).

POST AND TELEPHONE OFFICES

Ambergris's **post office** (⊠ Barrier Reef Dr., San Pedro) is open weekdays 8–noon and 1–5. Caye Caulker's **telephone office** (⊠ Near the Reef Hotel) is open weekdays 8–noon and 1–4, Saturday 8–noon.

THE CAYO

Comprising more than 5,200 square kilometers (2,000 square miles) of rugged, mountainous land but containing fewer than 15,000 inhabitants, the Cayo—the word originally referred to the peninsula of land between the Macal and Mopan rivers, on which San Ignacio grew up—is both Belize's largest district and one of its least populated. You'll know you are entering the Cayo a few miles west of Belmopan. Having run along the side of the Belize River, the road winds out of the valley and heads into a series of sharp bends. Here you'll see a low, granite wall, probably the first stone wall you will have seen in Belize. It is a safety barrier and confirms the transition from one landscape to another. In a few minutes you'll see cattle grazing on steep hillsides and horses flicking their tails. If it weren't for the Fanta orange sunsets and the palm trees, it could be the Auvergne, in France.

As in all of Belize, the land is never still for long, and the Cayo is full of sudden, surprising contrasts. During a trip to the Mountain Pine Ridge area you can drop, ecologically speaking, from South Carolina to Brazil in the space of a few miles. One minute you're in pine savanna; the next, in lush subtropical rain forest.

Ten years ago, when the first jungle lodges began to open in the Cayo, not many people believed that this wild, western district straddling the Guatemalan border could become an attractive travel destination. It seemed too remote, its roads too bad, and its weather too unpredictable. But today, more than half of Belize's visitors come to the Cayo, making it the country's most popular destination.

Many other things, besides the landscape, change as you enter the Cayo. The heavyset Creoles of the coast give way to light-footed, copper-skinned Mayas and mestizos. Spanish replaces English, and the technology curve shifts. Hurricane lamps replace electric lights, generators and batteries replace main power, telephones give way to two-way radios, and two-wheel drive to four-wheel drive. But the rewards far outweigh the inconveniences. There are majestic, haunting ruins where the lost world of the Maya comes alive even today. And if that wasn't enough for the Indiana Jones in all of us, there are more strenuous pursuits, from wildlife hikes in the jungle to horseback riding to exploring caves.

Most of the wildlife featured on Belize's 20-dollar bill can be found in the Cayo—mountain lions; jaguars; their diminutive cousins, the beautiful, shy ocelot; and the even smaller margay. Birding aficionados carry telescopes, cameras, and tape recorders with microphones the size of Larry King's, but for most people a pair of binoculars and some hiking boots will do. Over 300 species of bird reside in the country, and most of them can be seen in the Cayo. Even if you have never been bird-watching, setting off through the jungle as the sun begins to burn off the early morning mist, in search of Motmots and Masked Tityras, Violaceous Trogons, and Scaly-Throated Leaf-Tossers will soon have you hooked. Most Cayo resorts have birding tours.

When you walk in the bush, you have to keep your eyes on the ground. On horseback, however, you can feast your eyes on the surroundings, and at the end of the day, it's the horses, not you, that feel tired. As a result, riding has become one of the most popular ways of exploring the mountain landscape. Many hotels and lodges offer hourly as well as daily rates on horse rental, and there are also several specialist operations with fine horses, notably Banana Bank Lodge and Mountain Equestrian Trails (☞ *below*).

Recently, National Geographic filmed *Journey to the Underworld* in the Caves Branch River area. Here, amidst lush tropical forest, are interesting limestone caves, many of which have barely been explored. Increasingly, resorts such as Jaguar Paw (☞ *below*) are incorporating cave expeditions into their tours, either by inner tube or boat. Crystal-clear river water and glistening, white columns of stalactites are just some of the highlights. For serious spelunkers, there is the chance to explore with scuba gear. Before trying either, it's worth finding out about hystoplasmosis, a fungal infection of the lungs that can be caught in caves where there are large numbers of bats, as there are here.

As for lodgings, you may be out in the bush, but you won't be roughing it. Indeed, some of the country's most pleasant accommodations are here, from simple cabanas to beautifully landscaped properties. As usual in Belize, each is highly individualized, with a unique ambience created by its owners. All of them, however, place special emphasis on ecotourism, and nearly all are out on what should be christened Safari Strip—the Western Highway heading out of San Ignacio toward the Guatemalan border. All the region's best restaurants are also at the resorts and hotels, and all are open to nonguests.

Numbers in the margin correspond to points of interest on the Cayo, Placencia, and the South map.

Belmopan

㉑ *80 km (50 mi) southwest of Belize City*

The best way to see Belize's capital is through the rearview mirror heading toward the Cayo. The brainchild of Belize's longest-serving prime minister, Vincent Price, it was to be Belize's answer to Brasilia and Canberra—a resplendent, modern capital city in the interior. Instead it is

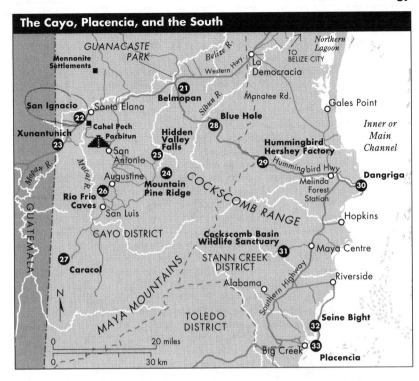

The Cayo, Placencia, and the South

a dreary cluster of concrete office buildings plunked down in the middle of nowhere, proving that cities can't be created overnight but rather must come into being over centuries. It's a great shame, because if the money had been spent on revamping Belize City, that rather sad and grubby place could have been greatly transformed.

The only real reason to come to Belmopan is to see the **Archaeological Vault.** It is, quite literally, a vault, secured by a huge, old-fashioned Chubb lock from England, and it's one of the only hands-on archaeological museums in the world. Not that you will be allowed to touch, but once you have made an appointment, one of the friendly, well-informed staff will be more than happy to hold up priceless Maya vases or jade necklaces for you to see—all over a solid concrete floor. ⊠ *Dept. of Archaeology,* ☎ *082/2106,* 𝔽𝔸𝕏 *082/3345.* ▣ *Free.* ☉ *Wed. 1:30–4:30.*

Worth a quick visit on the way out of Belmopan is the **Guanacaste Park Nature Reserve,** named for the huge guanacaste tree that grows here. There is also a rich population of tropical birds and plants. ▣ *Donations accepted.* ☉ *Daily 9–3:30.*

Dining and Lodging

$$$ ✕▦ **Jaguar Paw.** Owners Cy and Donna Young poured nearly $1 million into this stylish new resort, which opened in February 1996, and
★ it shows. Before coming to Belize, Cy, who bears an uncanny resemblance to Sean Connery in *The Medicine Man,* was in the video and beer business. Donna has extensive experience as a food and beverage manager at U.S. hotels, including the Waldorf Astoria. Though the resort is down 11 kilometers (7 miles) of dirt road on the Cave's Branch River, near Belmopan, it is anything but rustic, and a radical departure from the cabana concept of most resorts. Cresting a hill, you find yourself looking down at a massive, two-story building with a green,

faux-marble entrance. Once inside, you're struck by the 20-foot ceiling and eye-popping Maya murals painted by American Pam Braun. Each room, designed by Donna, has a different theme. There is a Victorian room, with country armoire and French curtains; the Pioneer room, containing a pebble-lined shower and a rough-hewn wooden bed; Serengeti, with African fabrics; a Mennonite room; and even a Chinese room, which has black lacquer furniture, Oriental fabrics, and an intense blue-and-white tile shower. The bar has mirrored panels, a mahogany counter, and a 102-channel satellite TV, and the restaurant offers a variety of seafoods or tenderloin of grain-fed beef flown in from Kansas. Surrounding all this is 215 acres of jungle and river, with numerous turquoise-blue swimming holes and some of Belize's deepest limestone caves. Visitors can inner-tube or row through them. Thirteen kilometers (8 miles) of nature trails are dotted with smaller caves, where the resort's excellent guide, Lazarus, has found numerous Maya artifacts. Imagine clambering into a cave with a flashlight (watch out for bats) and finding a 1,000-year-old clay pot cradled in a crevice. Howler monkeys are frequently heard on the property, and there have been several sightings of jaguars. Donna makes ashtrays from the imprints of their paws. Hence, the name. Baths have showers, and a few meal plans are available. ⊠ *Box 1832, Belize City,* ☎ *081/3023 or 800/335–8645 in the U.S.,* FAX *081/3024. 16 rooms. Restaurant, bar, pool, laundry service, travel services. AE, DC, MC, V.*

$$ ✕▦ **Banana Bank Ranch.** John and Carolyn Carr—she's a painter from ★ Kansas; he's a rancher from Montana—couldn't be nicer hosts. Both came to Belize in the late '70s, love the country, know it extremely well, and are happy to share their knowledge at the communal evening meal. The thatched cabanas, with their curving internal walls, split-level layout, and showers, are simple but pleasant. For horseback enthusiasts, there is a remuda of 25 fine saddle horses who can be used to explore the 5,000-acre estate. The setting, on the bank of the Belize River—Belize's Mississippi—is heavenly. Several domesticated wild animals live on the property: a spider monkey called Simon and the ravishingly beautiful jaguar, Tika (a photo of her graced a World Wildlife Fund calendar). Abandoned as a cub by her mother, she was taken in and reared by the Carrs. Unlike lions, jaguars can never be fully trained or domesticated. In fact, one day, Bill saw something in the big cat's eyes that made him realize that if he went into her cage again, he, not the meat he was carrying, could be Tika's next meal. In recent years, a few ill-informed tourists have unfairly accused the Carrs of cruelty for caging her. Outside the zoo, she is probably the only jaguar you will see in Belize. Various meal plans are available. ⊠ *Box 48,* ☎ *082/2677 or 800/396–1153 in the U.S.,* FAX *082/2366. 9 rooms. Dining room, horseback riding, laundry service. No credit cards.*

San Ignacio

㉒ *37 km (23 mi) southwest of Belmopan*

When you hear a clattering like an express train, you'll know that you've arrived in this, the largest town in, and hub of, the Cayo. The noise is from the Hawkesworth Bridge, built in 1941 by the British and the only suspension bridge in Belize. Even louder is the incredible commotion made by grackles in the trees of the town square at sunset. It's worth standing for a moment to listen to their eerily beautiful sound.

With its well-preserved vernacular architecture, bustling Spanish ambience, and dusty charm, San Ignacio is one of the few Belizean towns where you might wish to linger. Evenings are cool and mosquito-free, there are a few funky and interesting bars and a couple of restaurants, and it's by far the best base for exploring the Cayo. The majority of accommodations are either in or close to town.

The population is typically mixed. Mestizo and Maya dominate, as does the Spanish language (although almost everyone speaks English), but there are also Creoles, Mennonites, Chinese, a few Lebanese, and one charming restaurateur from Sri Lanka. The town was once the center of the chicle and mahogany trades, which flourished in this part of Belize, and it remains an important agricultural center for the district.

An excellent introduction to the Cayo, and a chance to make the acquaintance of the Cayo's two biggest rivers, is the 20-minute walk to **Branch Mouth,** where the Macal and the Mopan join to form the Belize River. A track leads north out of town past a soccer field. Immediately you are in a world of rich tropical vegetation, birds, and butterflies, of which there are clouds everywhere you go in the Cayo. The merging of the waters, with parrots flying overhead and swallows skimming the water for insects, is a fitting prelude to the sights and sounds that await you.

NEED A BREAK?	Not just a bustling café and bar, **Eva's** (⊠ 22 Burns Ave.) is a Cayo institution—a bulletin board, information center, trading post, and meeting place in one. The food is honest-to-goodness Belizean fare, with some bacon and eggs, omelets, and sandwiches thrown in for good measure. Mugs of wickedly strong black tea are always available, and as no one is in much of a hurry, this is an excellent place to write postcards, catch up on your journal, or soak up a bit of authentic Belizean atmosphere. Presiding over the colorful chaos is Bob Jones, a garrulous British ex-serviceman, who can tell you everything from where to hire a canoe, what to do if you get bitten by a fer-de-lance (say your prayers), and where to fix a flat or find a room. Buy him a drink, and he'll tell you a lot about Belize, too.

The **Ix Chel Tropical Research Foundation,** founded by one of Belize's great pioneers, Dr. Rosita Arvigo, is a center for traditional Maya medicine. Adjoining the Chaa Creek jungle lodge property, it has established itself as a very special botanical garden. The Panti Mayan Medicinal Trail offers a splendid self-guided walk through the rain forest and a chance to study the symbiotic complexities of its plant life. Here, you will learn about the healing properties of such indigenous plants as gumbo-limbo and man vine, and you'll see some of the endangered medicinal plants that Dr. Arvigo and her colleagues have rescued and brought to Ix Chel. A shop sells Maya medicinal products like Belly Be Good and Flu Away, as well as Dr. Arvigo's excellent book. If you are lucky, Rosita or one of the other directors, Dr. Michael Balick and Dr. Gregory Shropshire, will be there to talk to you. For those who want an extended conversation, Dr. Arvigo offers a five- to 10-day seminar in natural healing and herbalism for $125 per day.

㉓ The walk up to **Xunantunich** (Shoo-nan-too-nitch) from the Macal River in the village of San José Succotz is a pleasure in itself. Butterflies flit through the air. Maidenhair ferns grow in profusion. Near the top, a magnificent avenue of cahoune palms announces your arrival at an important ceremonial center of the Maya Classic Period. El Castillo, the massive 120-foot-high main pyramid, was built on a leveled hilltop. Though it is not as well excavated as Altun Ha, it furnishes a spectacular 360-degree panorama over Guatemala and the Mopan River valley from its top. On its eastern wall is a reproduction of one of the finest Maya sculptures in Belize, a frieze decorated with jaguar heads, human faces, and abstract geometric patterns. Pan along the frieze with your eyes, then out across the jungle. It's a great sight.

Dining and Lodging

$$$ ✕🗔 **Blancaneux.** This upscale resort, surrounded by the magical
★ Mountain Pine Ridge wildlife reserve, is owned by film director Fran-
cis Ford Coppola, who bought the resort and 10 acres of jungle for a
song in 1981. For many years it was a private getaway for family and
friends, but it opened its doors to the public in 1993. The transition
was a bumpy one, and for the first few years the resort was plagued
by management problems. Designed by Mexican architect Manolo
Mestre, the handsome cabanas were based on local, Belizean structures
and on houses Coppola had seen in the Philippines while shooting *Apoc-
alypse Now* (the fan in the bar came from the set). Laid out on a hill-
side above the Privassion River, the cabanas (there are also three luxury,
family-size villas) have been featured in *Architectural Digest*. They have
soaring, thatch ceilings; spacious living rooms with tiled kitchens; and
screened porches and terraces looking over the river, which, with its
rock pools and swift-running water, is a pleasant place to soak and sun-
bathe. The basic material is Belizean mahogany, the thatch is local fan
palm, and the walls are made of bamboo, palmetto, and stucco. Each
room has a Japanese-style tile bath. For furnishings, Coppola and his
wife, Eleanor, visited antiques stores throughout the Caribbean and Cen-
tral America, bringing back painted masks from Antigua, tiles and rugs
from Mexico, and fabrics from Guatemala. Although you probably won't
see Francis, you can at least enjoy his personal recipes for pizza and
pasta (different meal plans offered). As much of the produce as possi-
ble is grown on the premises (Coppola recently planted coffee trees);
the rest is flown down from Napa where, in addition to producing one
of the best wines in California, Coppola makes his own grappa, olive
oil, and preserves. ✉ *Chiquibul Rd., Box B, Central Farm,* ☎ *092/3878,*
🖷 *092/3919. 7 cabanas, 3 villas. Restaurant, bar, laundry service, travel
services. AE, DC, MC, V.*

$$$ ✕🗔 ◬ **Chaa Creek.** This is the queen of jungle resorts. With nearly
★ 20 years' experience, owners Mick and Lucy Fleming have the place
running like a well-oiled machine. Everything about Chaa Creek, from
the quality of the hardwood furniture to the dedication and friendliness of the staff of 40, is just that much better than anywhere else. The
setting, on 300 acres of rolling hills above the Macal River, is magnificent. The whitewashed stone cottages with their thatched roofs,
Guatemalan decor, and tile floors manage to be both extremely simple and extremely elegant. They have been intentionally left without
phones, electricity, or air-conditioning. In the day, you can canoe down
the river, visit the nearby Maya ruins at Xunantunich, or walk the miles
of well-posted nature trails. Adjacent to the property, but very much
a part of it, is the world-famous Ix Chel Tropical Research Foundation (☞ *above*). In the evening the focus of the resort is the hardwood
deck behind the bar, where guests sit out under the stars and swap traveler's tales. If you're lucky, Mick and Lucy will regale you with stories
of life in Belize. The secret of their success is that they have kept expanding and embellishing. The lawns Mick has just put in will take
another 600 years of rolling before you can have a decent game of cro-
quet, but they add a touch of colonial elegance to the place. Over the
years, Chaa Creek has also greatly expanded its inventory of accommodations: In addition to 19 cottages with showers, there is a honey-
moon suite, a circular thatched building with the best view on the
property; the fine new, self-catering Butterfly House, which sleeps six;
and for the budget traveler, a brand-new jungle camp in a beautiful
clearing above the Macal River, where, for $45, guests can enjoy all
the pleasures of a camping experience with none of its discomforts (except washing their own dishes). State-of-the-art tents are set up on individual wooden platforms under bright orange tarpaulin roofs. The

washrooms and toilets are spotless, and a gas fridge keeps drinks cold. Included in the price are three meals a day prepared by a Belizean chef on a traditional fire hearth, known as a *fogon*. The Boy Scouts it isn't. The most impressive addition at Chaa Creek, though, is its new Natural History Museum. Drawing on a host of contacts made during a lifetime committed to preserving the ecology of Belize (both the Smithsonian and London's Natural History Museum pitched in), the Flemings have created a world-class small museum, where visitors can learn about Belize's flora and fauna from the dedicated and knowledgeable young staff. If that wasn't enough, Chaa Creek's safari-style tours, conducted by dashing ex-British serviceman Dick Strand, are among the best in the land, and particularly good bird tours are led by an exceptionally knowledgeable and skilfull young birder, Gonzalez. Several meal plans are offered. ⊠ *Box 53*, ☎ *092/2037*, ℻ *092/2501. 20 rooms, guest house, tent camp. Restaurant, bar, room service, shop, laundry service, travel services. AE, D, MC, V.*

$$$ ✕▥ **Du Plooys.** By canoe, this ranchlike ensemble of buildings is only a few minutes upstream from Chaa Creek. By road you have to drive for 15 minutes over a bumpy track. The bush feeling, however, stops at the gate. The setting—above a bend of the Macal River known as Big Eddy—is spectacular. From the new deck, suspended on piles 30 feet above the forest, you look straight out to a dramatic sweep of limestone cliffs. Below, there is a sandy beach where you can swim and dive off the rocks into the Macal River. The cottages (with showers) are pleasant and airy, and there are now bed-and-breakfast accommodations for the budget traveler in addition to European, American, and Modified American plans. The gardens are some of the most beautiful in the region and are a popular haunt for numerous species of tropical birds. Originally from Zimbabwe, the owner, an ornithology expert, is glad to share his knowledge with you. He is also one of the most experienced hotel keepers in the country, which, in Belize, counts for an awful lot. ☎ ℻ *092/3301. 13 rooms. Restaurant, bar, room service, beach, laundry service, travel services. MC, V.*

$$$ ✕▥ **Ek Tun.** Owners Ken and Phyllis Dart gave up a life in Boulder, Colorado, to live in a tent while they created this secluded jungle lodge on a lush, green property above the Macal River. Getting here is an adventure in itself. After navigating a thrillingly bumpy road in a Land Rover, you are taken across the river in a skiff. Once on the other side, you step out into a 200-acre property dotted with giant capoc trees and flowering shrubs. There are two cabanas, and though both consist of a large main room plus an airy loft, each is accented slightly differently. One is constructed of thatch and hardwood poles, with a magnificent rough-hewn staircase leading up to the loft, where there is another double and a single bed. The other has stone walls and a flagstone floor, with a stone staircase leading up to the loft. Both have woven floor mats, Guatemalan furnishings, and generous-size bathrooms. Neither has phone, TV, air-conditioning, or electricity. If you want room service and a crowded bar to socialize in, this isn't the place for you. Living at close quarters with the owners, who do everything from taking you on tours to cooking your food, also may not suit all tastes, particularly as there is not yet an infrastructure for wide-ranging tours. But if you want to get away from it all, walk, read, and kick back, this is a perfect place to do it. On the extensive network of loop trails, you can see falcons, spectacled owls, toucans, and howler monkeys. The excellent meals, included in the price, are served in a splendid new stone-and-thatch dining room overlooking the river. Chilled papaya soup and grouper with *santa hoja* (an anise-flavored Belizean spice) are just two of Phyllis's creations. ⊠ *Banque Viejo*, ☎ *091/2002 or 303/442–6150 in the U.S. 2 cabanas. Dining room, bar, laundry service, travel services. MC, V.*

$$–$$$ ✕🍴🏨 **Mountain Equestrian Trails.** If you want a vacation on horse-
★ back, the professionals here can't be beat, but even if you can't ride,
this is a gorgeous place to stay. Two attractive two-room cabanas are
decorated with Guatemalan furnishings and mahogany fittings, and
an excellent camp for budget travelers has Eureka tents, each built on
a wooden platform and outfitted with two high-quality cots. A huge
hexagonal tent some distance away functions as dining room and
kitchen, while meals for regular guests (various plans offered) are
served in a pleasant thatch-covered dining room, with bar, at the other
end of the property. The setting, in the bottom of a lush valley with
views across to the jungle-covered flanks of the Mountain Pine Ridge,
is second to none, but it's the riding that makes MET special. Superbly
trained and conditioned, sure-footed Texas quarter horses pick their
way over the resort's 97 kilometers (60 miles) of jungle trails, some of
which wind up and down quite precipitous slopes. Though they're quite
safe, the horses are no plugs. A flick of the heel and you are off in a
cloud of dust. Owner Jim Bevis, a big, bearded bear of a man with a
chuckling laugh and a white Texan straw hat, couldn't be a better guide.
Not only is he an experienced horseman from California ranching stock,
but he is also a fount of knowledge on Belize's flora and fauna. As you
ride, he describes plants' medicinal and culinary properties. You pass
some Maya caves, but the high point (literally) of any ride is a rocky
bluff where the horses come to a halt and you lean back in the saddle
looking over some of the most majestic land in the Cayo. ⊠ *Mountain Pine Ridge Rd., Central Farm,* ☎ *082/3310,* 𝔽𝔸𝕏 *082/3505. 4
rooms, tent camp. Dining room, bar, horseback riding. MC, V.*

$$ ✕🍴 **Cahel Pech Village.** Perched on a hill above San Ignacio, with spec-
tacular views across the border into Guatemala, this new addition to
the Cayo's hotel roster has already expanded considerably. The thatched
cabanas are all named after a Maya ruin and are constructed entirely
of local materials. Each has a huge veranda with a hammock. Meals
(several plans offered) are taken in the main building, which is fitted
with cedar and mahogany fixtures. A large veranda at the back of the
building has tremendous views, the perfect place for breakfast. The ruins
of Cahel Pech are only five minutes away. For the money, this is one
of the Cayo's best deals. ☎ *092/3740,* 𝔽𝔸𝕏 *092/2225. 14 cabanas.
Restaurant, laundry service, travel services. AE, MC, V.*

$$ ✕🍴 **Maya Mountain Lodge.** Bart and Suzy Mickler have been running
★ this hilltop resort overlooking San Ignacio for 13 years. Though it's
not luxurious, what it does, it does well. The staff is charming. The
grounds, after more than a decade of TLC, are thriving. The tours, everything from horseback riding to mountain biking to visiting Maya
ruins, are extensive. In recent years, the accent has been on family-ori-
ented, educational tourism, and though the regular traveler will enjoy
staying here, it really comes into its own for guests who want an active, learning experience. (The resort also calls itself an Educational
Field Station for Cultural, Archaeological, and Wildlife Studies.) Suzy,
who has a master's degree in curriculum management, is the "head-
mistress." In addition to designing an excellent series of nature trails
(one contains 150 species of edible jungle plants), she has created a
host of courses at different levels, particularly for children: everything
from Belizean history to ornithology, natural history, and ecology. The
whitewashed, thatched cottages have recently been refurbished, and
each now has its own patio, where guests can sit and digest what they
have learned. A large wooden building at the back of the property offers simpler rooms for the budget traveler. Meals are taken in a pleasant, open-sided dining room near the reception area, and the food,
particularly the homemade soups and the salads, is tasty and plentiful. Various meal plans are offered, but alcohol is BYOB. ⊠ *Box 46,*

☎ 092/2164, ℻ 092/2029. 8 cottages with bath
Restaurant, bar, laundry service, travel services.

$$ ✕▦ **Nabitunich.** This ranch and cottage colony i
bit of paradise on the banks of the Mopan Rivei
see the Maya ruins of Xunantunich, which is with
outlined in flame-color light on a hill nearby.
shower) are simple but very pleasant; the atmospher   ⏤ ⏤ ⏤ ved-and-
breakfast. Modified American plan adds to the excellent value. ⊠ San
Lorenzo Farm, ☎ ℻ 093/2096. 8 rooms. Restaurant, laundry service,
travel services. No credit cards.

$$ ✕▦ **San Ignacio Hotel.** The Queen stayed here when she visited the
Cayo, and if you want to stay in the town of San Ignacio itself, this is
the place for you, too. From the outside, it doesn't look like much, but
the rooms are large and comfortable. They all have phones, partial air-
conditioning, large bathrooms, and verandas facing the jungle. There
is also a small swimming pool on the property. European and American plans are offered. ⊠ Box 33, ☎ 092/2034, ℻ 092/2134. 24
rooms. Restaurant/bar, pool, laundry service. AE, DC, MC, V.

$$ ✕▦ **Windy Hill.** When you see the sign that reads GRACELAND over the
entrance, you wonder if you have seen right. You have. The owner, an
ex-marine with impressive arm tattoos, is a devoted Elvis fan. With its
pool, pool table, white plastic chairs, air-conditioned cabanas, and rest
rooms marked cowgirls and cowboys, this is a bit of Memphis trans-
ported south of the Tropic of Cancer. Different meal plans are available.
⊠ Graceland Ranch, ☎ 092/2017, ℻ 092/3080. 19 cabanas. Restau-
rant, bar, pool, billiards, laundry service, travel services. AE, MC, V.

$-$$ ✕▦ **Crystal Paradise.** On the Macal River in the village of Cristo Rey,
not far from Francis Ford Coppola's Blancaneux lodge, this resort, which
opened in 1993, is one of the few locally owned operations in the Cayo.
And what a family this is! The Tuts (pronounced *toots*) have ten children (the tootlets?) and are about an equal mix of all three of Belize's
main cultures: Creole, Maya, and Spanish. Eldest son Jeronie can identify more than 200 bird species and is a medicinal-plant expert; along
with younger brother Evrald, he knows the surrounding jungle of the
beautiful Mountain Pine Ridge area about as well as anyone. The Tuts
offer a variety of very reasonably priced tours, including jungle camping, river excursions, and horseback trips to Caracol. Cabanas have
showers, and Continental breakfast is included. ⊠ Cristo Rey, ☎ 092/
2823, ℻ 092/3075. 8 cabanas. Restaurant, bar. MC, V.

$ ✕▦ **Parrot's Nest.** Fred Prost, creator of the Seaside Guest House in
Belize City, has done it again—this time 5 kilometers (3 miles) outside
San Ignacio amid tropical forest on the banks of the Mopan River. Parrot's Nest consists of four simple thatched-roof cabanas, each with two
single beds, built up into the trees surrounding the main house. At just
$20 a night for two, this is one of the best values in Belize, and good
meals are available at very reasonable prices (though you have to bring
your own liquor). ⊠ Just past village of Bullet Tree Falls; c/o 3 Prince
St., Belize City, ☎ 092/3702. 4 cabanas share baths. Restaurant, travel
services. No credit cards.

Outdoor Activities and Sports
CANOEING
The Cayo's many rivers, above all the Mopan and Macal, make it an
excellent place for canoeing. Most of the larger resorts, like Chaa
Creek and Du Plooys, have canoes. You can also rent them in San Ignacio from **Float Belize** (☎ 092/2188), **Red Rooster Paddle and Ped-
dle Tours** (☎ 092/3016), and **Toni Canoes** (☎ 092/2267).

HORSEBACK RIDING

Though the undisputed local experts are Mountain Equestrian Trails, a new operation, **Blue Ridge Mountain Rider** (✉ San Antonio, ☎ 092/2322), offers equestrian tours of the Maya ruins at Pacbitun and other points of interest in the San Ignacio region.

MOUNTAIN BIKING

If you prefer rubber tires to hooves, head for **B&M Mountain Bike Tours** (✉ Across from Eva's, ☎ 092/2382).

Shopping

The village of **San Antonio** is home to the Garcia sisters, five bright Maya siblings with clever hands and an eye for business who became something of a local legend when they set up their own crafts shop and museum. At the other end of the village, the Magana family has recently opened an arts-and-crafts shop, so you may want to visit both before buying anything.

En Route Heading southeast from San Ignacio, the road winds up from the Macal Valley, through fertile farming country where corn, peanuts, and beans grow in small clearings at the side of the road. Then, a few miles beyond the village of Cristo Rey, the road swings south-southeast away from the river, and the vegetation becomes wilder. Cahoune palms, trumpet trees, wild papayas, and strangler vines grow in a riot, while here and there a crop of banana or corn cuts into the hillside between them. You emerge onto a flat, plateau-like area with fine views of the Maya Mountains shortly before the village of San Antonio. With its sheep, goats, and orange trees, this cluster of brightly painted wooden houses clinging to the side of a hill at 1,000 feet seems like a tropical version of a Greek hilltop village. After San Antonio, the road begins to climb steeply, and the earth grows steadily redder. In the rainy season, it turns into what looks like mango ice cream. You will need four-wheel drive, and even then you may get bogged down.

Mountain Pine Ridge

★ ㉔ *24 km (15 mi) southeast of San Ignacio*

Along with the Cockscomb Basin Wildlife Sanctuary and the ruins at Lamanai, this mountainous, 780-square-kilometer (300-square-mile) nature reserve, a rugged dome of granite and limestone containing some of the most ancient rocks in Central America, is a highlight of any journey to Belize. Getting here is an adventure in itself.

Yellow pines mark the transition from lush tropical forest to pine savanna, and the road follows forest tracks that circle the western slopes of the mountains. Baldy Beacon, at just over 3,000 feet, lies to the east. After the heat and humidity of lowland Belize, the cooler air, the smell of pine resin, and the shady pine woods are both enormously refreshing and totally unexpected. It could be Georgia. It could be the country above Saint-Tropez. It isn't at all what you might have imagined.

The flora changes dramatically. You will see lilac-colored mimosa, St. John's-wort, and occasionally a garish, red flower known as hotlips. There is also a huge variety of ferns, ranging from the tiny maidenhair fern to giants the size of small coconut trees. A fair selection of Belize's 154 species of orchid can also be found in the Mountain Pine Ridge area. Look out, too, for a wild tree called craboo. A brandy-like liqueur believed to have aphrodisiac properties is made from the berries. As birds also love to eat the tree's fruit, any craboo is a good place to look for orioles and woodpeckers.

The roads—and there are about 2,400 kilometers (nearly 1,500 miles) of them, most unexplored—were built by the British army, who still use this area for training in jungle warfare. Some of them have names, but most simply sound algebraic, like A10. The best way to see the area, of course, is not bouncing around in an Isuzu Trooper but with what the Chinese call the Number 11 bus: your own two feet.

25 The **Hidden Valley Falls,** also known as the Thousand Foot Falls (though they are, in fact, nearly 1,600 feet high) are the highest in Central America. A thin plume of spray plummets over the edge of a rock face into a seemingly bottomless gorge below. If it were China, there would be poems carved into the rocks nearby. As there is a shelter and some benches, this is an excellent place to eat a sandwich and soak in the setting. A rest room is available to the public.

At the nearby **Río On,** you will find flat, granite boulders to sunbathe on and a series of crystal-clear pools and waterfalls in which to have a dip. The village of **Augustine** is home to forest reserve headquarters. If you are thinking of camping, this is the only place you can.

Just outside the reserve proper but still part of the Mountain Pine Ridge **26** area are the **Río Frio Caves.** Though it's only a few miles down a steep track to these caves, it's light-years ecologically. In a matter of a few hundred yards, you drop from pine savanna to tropical forest. Nothing in this small country of huge contrasts so clearly shows the extraordinary variety of Belize's landscapes as does this startling transition. Also, nowhere gives you a better sense of where you are than does the interior of this ancient swallow-filled cave, where at night, ocelot and margay pad silently across the cold sand floor in search of their slumbering prey. A river runs right through the center of it, and over the centuries it has carved the rock into fantastic shapes. From the cool, dark interior of the cave, the light-filled world of mosses, birds, and plants outside seems even more intense and beautiful than ever. Bisecting the circle of light and rising vertically through the mouth of the cave, like a spar propping up the whole mountain, is a giant hardwood tree, *Pterocarpus officialis,* its massive paddle-shape roots anchored in the sandy soil of the riverbank and its green crown straining toward the blue sky above.

Caracol

★ **27** *65 km (40 mi) south of San Ignacio, a 3-hr journey by road*

Caracol ("the snail" in Spanish) is the most spectacular of all the Maya sites in Belize and one of the most impressive in Central America. In its heyday, it was home to as many as 200,000 inhabitants, the population of modern-day Belize. It was a Maya Manhattan, a metropolis with five plazas and 32 large structures, covering nearly a square mile. The latest evidence suggests that it gained a crushing victory over the great city of Tikal in the mid-6th century, something that Guatemala has still not quite gotten used to. For centuries, until a group of *chicleros* stumbled on it in 1936, it was buried under the jungle of the remote Vaca Plateau. The great pyramid of Canaa is now officially the tallest structure in Belize. In fact, once Caracol has been fully excavated, it may dwarf even Tikal, which lies only a few dozen miles across the Guatemalan border. The road to Caracol is now officially open, and many Cayo resorts and tour operators are running day and overnight tours there. If you want to drive on your own, be sure to inquire at your hotel about road conditions first.

The Cayo A to Z

Arriving and Departing

Novelo's (⊠ W. Colleti Canal, Belize City, ☎ 093/2954) and **Batty Bros.** (⊠ 15 Mosul St., Belize City, ☎ 027/2025) have frequent service to Belmopan and San Ignacio from Belize City. The journey takes three hours and costs only $2. Batty does the morning run; Novelo's, the afternoon one.

Quite simply, follow the Western Highway from Belize City.

Discovery Expeditions (☎ 023/0748 or 0749, FAX 023/0263), in the capable hands of driver Eddie Rosado, who grew up in Los Angeles, is available for pick-up at all airports and at major hotels in Belize City for all destinations in the Cayo. The cost is $29 one-way, advance reservation required.

Getting Around

There is limited bus service between the main centers in the Cayo, but since this is wild country, the best way to get around is by four-wheel-drive vehicle, which most of the resorts have. Because of the numerous rivers, touring by canoe is another good mode of transportation, as are horses.

Contacts and Resources

Police (☎ 2022).

In the Cayo, the best way to get in contact with local tour operators is to check in at **Eva's** (⊠ 22 Burns Ave., San Ignacio, ☎ 092/2267). Most jungle lodges offer tour-inclusive packages and a full range of day trips. Sharon Burns, of **Jute Expeditions** (⊠ San Ignacio, ☎ 092/2076), conducts excellent guided tours of the region and is used by many of the lodges. **The Divide** (☎ 092/3452) offers three- to seven-day jungle camping trips.

PLACENCIA AND THE SOUTH

The southern portion of Belize is the least commercialized and most remote part of the country. In the area around Punta Gorda, locally known as the Deep South, tourism is still in its infancy, and little in the way of a hotel or restaurant infrastructure exists. In fact, most visitors to "PG" go to catch the ferry to Guatemala. For those who like their traveling rough and adventurous, however, the south is the place to go—though definitely not in the rainy season (as much as 160 inches of rain falls annually), unless you like traveling with galoshes and an umbrella.

The Stann Creek Valley, the broad, flat plain between the Maya Mountains and the sea, is Belize's San Fernando Valley, the place where most of its fruit—mainly bananas, oranges, and grapefruit—is grown. As always in Belize, the transition from one landscape to another is swift and startling. The lush, mountainous scenery to the north gives way to a flat plain bristling with orange trees. Equally startling, if you are coming from the Cayo, is the ethnic contrast: Whereas San Ignacio is strongly Spanish in feeling, this area is strongly Afro-Caribbean. Originally, bananas were produced here, but a blight all but eliminated the crops in 1906. Today, the citrus plantations, which account for 10%

of the nation's production, are touted as one of the country's great success stories, though the fishing community of Dangriga shunned the project with a "bring me the tree and I'll pick it for you" attitude. As a result, the labor force is largely migrant workers from Guatemala.

The most "developed" area is around Placencia. Five years ago, there were only three small resorts north of the town. Now there are nine, stretching up to the village of Seine Bight. None of them is big, but they clearly represent the wave of the future. Construction of a new airstrip has made the area more accessible, though roads are still composed of red dirt and potholes. Much of the rest of the land north of Placencia has been divided up into lots awaiting development. If things continue as they are, the area will one day rival San Pedro, on Ambergris, as a main tourist hub.

Numbers in the margin correspond to points of interest on the Cayo, Placencia, and the South map.

Blue Hole

28 *20 km (12½ mi) south of Belmopan*

This natural turquoise pool surrounded by mosses and lush vegetation is excellent for a cool dip, and after an hour on the Hummingbird Highway from Belmopan, you'll need one. It is, in fact, part of an underground river system. On the other side of the hill is St. Herman's Cave, once inhabited by the Maya. A path leads up from the highway, just by the Blue Hole. It is quite steep and is difficult to pass unless it is dry. To explore the cave, it's best to wear sturdy shoes and bring a flashlight. Some years ago, there were some nasty incidents at the site, with tourists robbed and, in one case, raped. As a result, a full-time attendant was appointed to patrol the area, and the problem has effectively been resolved. ⊠ *Hummingbird Hwy.* ☜ *Free.*

Hummingbird Hershey Factory

29 *48 km (30 mi) southeast of Blue Hole*

The smell of chocolate lets you know you've arrived at Hershey's Belizean outpost. If you want to be Charlie in the Chocolate Factory for an hour or two, the management will be happy to let you walk around. ⊠ *Hummingbird Hwy., no phone.* ☜ *Free.* ⊗ *Weekdays 9–5.*

En Route Traveling through the Stann Creek Valley toward Dangriga, you'll see a study in contrasts. The simple shacks of the migrant Guatemalan workers are visible from the road, as is the resplendent, three-story villa of one of the main plantation owners, Eugene Zabanay, whose brother was involved in a drug-smuggling scandal in Miami. It's on the right just before you arrive in Dangriga.

Dangriga

30 *160 km (100 mi) southeast of Belmopan, 4–5 hrs of driving on bad road*

With a population of 10,000, this is the largest town in the south, home to the Garifuna, or Black Caribs, as they are also known, the most exotic and unusual of the many ethnic groups that have found peace and asylum in this tiny country. Their story is a bizarre and moving one, an odyssey of exile and dispossession in the wake of the confusion wrought on the New World by the Old. They are descendants of a group of black slaves from Nigeria who were shipwrecked on the island of St. Vincent in 1635 en route to slavery in America. At first the Caribs,

St. Vincent's indigenous inhabitants, fiercely resisted their presence, but understanding conquered fear and racial antipathy, and a new Amerindian-African addition to the family of man was born.

In the eyes of the British colonial authorities, the new race was an illegitimate and troublesome presence in one of the Crown's dominions. Worse still, they sided with, and were succored by, the French. After nearly two centuries of guerrilla warfare, the British decided that the best way to solve the problem was to deport them en masse. After a circuitous and tragic journey across the Caribbean during which thousands perished of disease and hunger, the exiles arrived in Belize.

That they have managed to preserve their own cultural identity is one more example of Belize's extraordinary ability to include, and not suppress, diversity. The Garifuna, as they came to be known, have their own belief systems, a potent mixture of ancestor worship and Catholicism; their own language, which, like Carib, has separate male and female dialects; their own music, African-style drumming with a modern disco variant known as punta rock, which you can hear everywhere in Belize; and their own clannish social structure—Garifuna seldom marry outside their own race. In Marcella Lewis, universally known as Auntie Madé, they also had their own poet laureate.

For the visitor, there is not much to see in Dangriga. Imagine the worst bits of Belize City towed down the coast, and you've got it. But on one day of the year, November 19, it is all color and exuberance. It's Garifuna Settlement Day, when these proud people celebrate their arrival in Belize and remember their roots. Then, Dangriga cuts loose with a week of Carnival-style celebrations.

Dining and Lodging

$$ ✕🏨 **Pelican Beach Resort.** This rather lugubrious hotel on the water outside Dangriga might remind you of a tropical version of a Maine boardinghouse in the low season. It's the best in Dangriga, though, and the restaurant is decent. It is also convenient for tours to the Cockscomb jaguar reserve, and the owner is an expert on the flora and fauna of Belize. There are baths in the rooms, not just showers, a rarity for Belize. ✉ *Box 14,* ☎ *052/2044,* FAX *052/2570. 20 rooms. Restaurant, bar, laundry service, travel services. AE, D, MC, V.*

Cockscomb Basin Wildlife Sanctuary

★ ③⓵ *48 km (30 mi) southwest of Dangriga; take the Southern Hwy. to Maya Centre, where there's a road leading into the reserve*

A highlight of any journey to Belize is a trip to this sanctuary known for its jaguars. You have to register in a hut by the entrance before proceeding several miles to the reception center. The road climbs up through dense vegetation—splendid cahoune palms, purple mimosa, orchids, and big-leafed plantains—and as you go higher, the marvelous sound of tropical birdsong, often resembling strange wind-up toys, grows stronger and stronger.

This is definitely four-wheel-drive terrain. You may have to ford several small rivers as well as negotiate deep, muddy ruts. At the top, you will find a very pleasant clearing with hibiscus and bougainvillea bushes, a little office where you can buy maps of the nature trails (notice the marvelous Oripendula nests hanging from the rafters), rest rooms, and several picnic tables. If you do plan to have a picnic, make sure you have some serious bug spray with you—the Cockscomb is alive with no-see-ums (tiny biting flies) and mosquitoes.

In a vain, misguided attempt by an American naturalist to track jaguars' movements in the 1980s, seven were caught and tagged with radio collars. To catch them, special steel cages were built—the animals smashed several wooden ones to pieces—and a live pig was placed behind a grille and used as bait. A jaguar would enter the cage to catch the pig, trip a door behind it, and find itself captive. What followed was a conflagration of fur and fury of almost unbelievable proportions. The captured jaguars were so powerful that in their desperate attempts to escape, they threw the 300-pound cages around like matchboxes. They sheared off most of their teeth as they tried to bite through the steel. Within a year, all seven had died.

Today it is estimated that there are between 25 and 30 jaguars—8 to 10 mature males, 9 to 10 adult females, and the rest, young animals—spread over an area of about 400 square kilometers (152 square miles). It is the largest jaguar population in the world and one of Belize's most significant contributions to conservation (the jaguar was hunted to extinction in the United States by the late 1940s).

Up to 6 feet long and weighing in just below Mike Tyson, *Felis Onca,* or *El Tigre,* as it is known in Spanish, is nature's great loner, a supremely free creature that shuns even the company of its own kind. The term jaguar comes from the Indian word, *Yaguar,* meaning "he who kills with one leap." And that is exactly what a jaguar does, falling on deer, peccaries, or gibnut with a deadly leap and severing the neck vertebrae. Except during a brief mating period, and the six short months the female spends with her cubs before turning them loose, jaguars live alone, roaming the rain forest in splendid isolation. By day, they sun themselves to sleep. By night, they stalk gibnut, armadillo, and curassow, a kind of wild turkey, with the deadly efficiency of a serial killer. To the ancient Maya, the jaguars were intermediaries between this world and the world of the gods.

You will almost certainly not see a jaguar, as they have exceptionally good hearing and sense of smell. If you do, you'll be far too close. But walking along the well-marked nature trails is one of the most pleasant ways to spend a day in Belize. Most of them are loops of 1 to 2 kilometers (½ to 1½ miles), so you can do several in a day. The most strenuous takes you up a steep hill, from the top of which there is a magnificent view of the entire Cockscomb basin.

In addition to the jaguar, the Cockscomb has a wonderful selection of Belize's wildlife, including the other cats—pumas, margays, and ocelots—plus coatis, kinkajous, deer, peccaries, and, last but not least, tapir. Also known as the mountain cow, this shy, curious creature appears to be half horse, half hippo, with a bit of cow and elephant thrown in.

Nearly 300 species of bird have been identified in the Cockscomb, including the keel-billed toucan, the king vulture, several species of hawks, and the scarlet macaw. And everywhere you walk there is the lush, riotous growth of the rain forest. The Cockscomb is an immense botanical garden, heated seemingly to the temperature of a sauna. For more information about the sanctuary, *see* Chapter 2. ⊠ *Outside Maya Centre, no phone.* 🖀 *Free.* ⊘ *Daily 9–6.*

Dining and Lodging

$$$ ✕🏨 **Jaguar Reef Resort.** The setting is magnificent. It's on the coast, just south of the village of Hopkins, and has views over the water in one direction and in the other to the green slopes of the Maya Mountains. The moment you arrive, you sense that a great deal of money has been invested in this resort, which opened in 1995. Unlike most other new resorts, Jaguar Reef has shunned "Mennonite vernacular,"

i.e., palapa and wood cabanas; instead, it has built six solid, two-room cottages of whitewashed stone. Thatch has been kept for the outside, but no spiders will fall on your head here: The high, pitched ceilings are wooden. Rooms are large and airy, with delicious views of the sea, and have been tastefully finished with Mexican tiles and mahogany furniture. The bathrooms have tile baths and mahogany-encased basins. Other fixtures and fittings, like the mahogany-and-canvas beach umbrellas and Pawley Island hammock, are of a similarly high standard. A modest nature trail and some kayaking up the Settee River offer a taste of ecotourism, but the real draw here is the easy access to the Cockscomb jaguar preserve, which is only a few miles away. The food is good, if not spectacular, though a combination of exceptionally low lighting, a towering thatch ceiling, and dreary New Age music gives the dining room a slightly maudlin ambience. It will take a few years for the place to acquire atmosphere, the landscaping to be brought up to par, and the mostly Garifuna staff to be put through their paces. Whether they will win the battle against the sand flies, which are a problem on this part of the coast, remains to be seen. Modified American and American plans are offered. ☒ *Hopkins Village,* ☎ FAX *021/2041 or 800/289–5756 in the U.S. 12 rooms. Restaurant, bar, dive shop, shop, travel services. AE, MC, V.*

Shopping

Near the sanctuary entrance is a small gift shop selling woven baskets and fine embroideries of the Maya calendar.

Seine Bight

③② *44 km (27 mi) south of Dangriga*

Like Placencia, its neighbor to the south, this is a sleepy coastal fishing village that tourism is just discovering. Placencia's resorts are increasingly stretching north to this little hamlet.

Dining and Lodging

$$ ✕ **Seine Bight Hotel.** You can't miss this new restaurant: The red, yel-
★ low, and black trim; drawbridge-style entrance; octagonal towers; and dense thatched roof veritably jump out at you. English owners Pam and Mike Hazeltine (she, a teacher; he, an architect) designed and built it themselves, having arrived in Belize with a couple of tents. Their idea was to get an "outside in" effect, using thatch and poles for the ceiling, and at the same time offer a menu and ambience with a little more style than most restaurants in the area. They have succeeded. Waiters wear bow ties and waistcoats, the cutlery is best Sheffield silver, and the menu is extensive. On any given night, there are as many as 16 entrées, including lobster thermidor, poached red snapper, and the exotic sounding Maison Pie, which turns out to be shepherd's pie. Particular emphasis is also placed on desserts, such as orange bombes and crêpes suzette. The ambience is romantic, courtesy of candlelit tables grouped on two tiers around a central column. Imaginative touches, like paneled screens, palm-frond place mats, and a menu handwritten on a calico scroll, add to this place's charm. Three rooms are under construction. ☎ *062/2491. AE, MC, V.*

$$$ ✕⌂ **Nautical Inn.** The Garifuna fishing town of Seine Bight is a long way from Phoenix, Arizona, and that is how Ben and Janie Ruoti, the owners, like it. Accommodations are in two-tier, octagonal cottages imported from North Carolina. The management prides itself on offering American-style fixtures, like hotel-supplied mattresses from Miami and glass-walled showers. "It's not for campers," is how Ben sums it up, adding that you can even "drink the water from the toilets." All rooms have ceiling fans and air-conditioning. The Oar House restaurant offers good home cooking, and you can take a full meal plan if you choose. There are some sea kayaks as well as a 425-horsepower dive boat to get you to the reef. If you just want to hang out, there is a pretty beach. ☎ 𝐅𝐀𝐗 062/2310. *13 rooms. Restaurant, bar, beach, dive shop, shop. AE, MC, V.*

$$ ✕⊞ **Singing Sands.** Resorts in Belize tend to be strongly shaped by the
★ personalities of their owners, and Bruce Steeds, a talkative Australian, fairly fills this one to the brim with his presence. The cabanas (with showers), by contrast, are small but pleasant, though, as they are turned sideways to the beach, they do not enjoy direct sea views. Bruce claims to have "the coldest beer in the universe," and, even if it isn't, the varnished mahogany bar at the back of the large, open-sided restaurant is a good place to end a day of delicious indolence. The dive shop offers PADI courses. The beach is a treat. ☎ 𝐅𝐀𝐗 062/2243. *6 cabanas. Restaurant, bar, beach, dive shop. MC, V.*

Scuba Diving

Most of the resorts between Placencia and Seine Bight have their own dive shops, but the best are at **Nautical Inn** (☎ 062/2310) and **Singing Sands** (☎ 062/2243).

Shopping

Painter Lolla Delgado moved to Seine Bight from Belize City. At her workshop, **Lolla's Art Gallery,** you will find her well-executed, bright, cheerful acrylic paintings of local scenes, which go for $75 to $500, as well as handicrafts for less. She also sells hand-painted cards, and her husband makes wood carvings. Espresso and pastries are available. The workshop, open 9 AM–10 PM, is up a flight of steps in a tiny wooden house on the main street.

Placencia

㉝ *8 km (5 mi) south of Seine Bight, 52 km (32 mi) south of Dangriga*

This balmy fishing village set in a sheltered half-moon bay, with crystal-clear green water and almost 5 kilometers (3 miles) of palm-dotted white sand, is straight out of a Robert Louis Stevenson novel. Originally founded by pirates, it is today peopled with an extraordinary mélange of races. Everyone looks different, and it is one of the few places in the world where you will find black people with blue eyes. To the west, the Cockscomb Range ruffles the tropical sky with its jagged peaks. To the east, seaward, there is a line of uninhabited cays moored on the horizon. There are tours off into the jungle or to the Maya ruins at Lubantuun, diving, and some of the best sportfishing in the country, but once you get here you will probably just want to lie in a hammock under a palm tree, read, sleep, and swim.

Placencia is so small it doesn't even have a main street. It has a concrete path, just big enough for two walking hand in hand, that sets off purposefully from the south end of town, meanders through everybody's backyard, passes wooden cottages on stilts overrun with bougainvillea and festooned with laundry, and then peters out abruptly in a little clearing of coconut palms and white morning glory as though it had forgotten where it was headed in the first place. That's the sort of place Placencia is. Walk the sidewalk, and you've seen the town.

Along the path are most of the village's guest houses, and little palapa–covered cafés line the beach and serve food of the burgers and rice-and-beans variety. Some of them, like Omar's, also serve fresh-caught seafood, but, with a few exceptions, Placencia is not exactly a gourmet's paradise. Most of the resorts also have restaurants open to nonguests.

Fences don't exist here, so everybody's backyard and, unfortunately, their garbage, is open to public view. In recent years, with more people passing through, this has become something of a problem. The town desperately needs a proper garbage disposal system and a good cleanup. But, if you don't mind that, you will be enchanted by this rustic little village where the palm trees rustle, the waves lap the shore, and nobody is in a hurry.

Dining and Lodging

$$ ✕ **La Petite Maison.** "A private dinner on our balcony" is how owner
★ and chef Bud Edrick and his charming wife, Barbara, describe the experience at their newly opened bistro. With a beautiful Siamese cat guarding the entrance and Barbara's shell and driftwood decorations hanging in the windows, the tiny candlelit dining room feels like something out of Gaugin's South Seas. Gaugin wouldn't have cared about the crisp napkins and tablecloths or the handsome wine glasses, rare in Placencia. Rare, too, is the quality of the French-Belgian food. Bud brings a lifetime of experience to his cooking. Before retiring to Placencia, he was the sous-chef at Le Flamand in New York. The prix-fixe menu, at $22 per person, includes such delicacies as *chou farcis au crevettes* (shrimp-filled cabbage leaves), pork in sauce Robert, poached red snapper, and crème caramel. There is only one sitting per evening, at 7, and guests must bring their own wine. ✉ *Up flight of steps behind acupuncture clinic,* ☎ *062/3172. Reservations essential. No credit cards. Closed Sun., Mon.*

$–$$ ✕ **Tentacles.** The ne plus ultra of Placencia—the town stops here—this dockside restaurant and bar has now become the biggest restaurant and watering hole in town. Guests can dine on the veranda, with views right across the sea, or inside in the mahogany-paneled dining room. The chicken and seafood are well, if simply, done, and the prices are good. It is open daily for breakfast, lunch, and dinner. ☎ *062/3254. No credit cards.*

$ ✕ **BJ's.** From the outside it looks plain enough—a thatched cabana with a cafélike interior—but if you're lucky, you can sample the creations of Betty, a big, smiling Placencian mama. She prepares *serre* (a local dish made with coconut cream, cassava, and lobster) and makes fresh-squeezed juices from the fruit of her own trees. ✉ *About ¼ mi north of town,* ☎ *062/3202. No credit cards.*

$ ✕ **Brenda's.** The life and soul of this cheery little restaurant off Placencia's sidewalk is Brenda, a local woman with a flair for seafood, particularly grouper. There are three outside tables and five more in a charming wooden cottage. The fresh-squeezed juices are divine. *No phone. No credit cards.*

$$$ ✕☷ **Rum Point Inn.** When they first came to Placencia, George and Coral
★ Bevier had to cut their way through the undergrowth to find the old colonial-style house they had purchased. Today the inn, on its own beachfront property, is one of Belize's finest small-scale, highly personalized resorts. The feeling you have walking into any of the domelike villas is of space, light, and air, as though only a thin, tentlike membrane separates you from sea, sky, and palm trees. Each is luxuriously but simply furnished with Guatemalan fabrics and mahogany, and each has a unique arrangement of windows and skylights. Some are portholes; others, geometric patterns cut in the walls. From the inside, they dapple the walls with light by day, providing cutout glimpses of the surroundings. From the outside at night, they make the buildings look like Halloween pumpkins. Conviviality is part of the Rum Point experience, and, in the evening, George and Coral come down to the bar in the main house to join their guests for a drink. At dinner, everyone sits together at long, candlelit tables. As the waves lap below you and the

palm trees rustle, the Beviers preside over lively discussions on every-thing from that day's dive to Maya astronomy to the inside scoop on Belizean politics. Food is cooked by two charming Belizean girls who learned to make such tidbits as lobster and eggplant on English muffins, topped with a layer of grilled Parmesan, from back issues of *Gourmet* magazine. (Modified American and American plans are options.) The library has one of the best collections of books on the Maya in the coun-try, piles of novels and magazines, and, in case you get cultural with-drawal, a raft of CDs and videos. Recent additions to the RPI inventory include a Pro 42 dive boat, complete with carpeted deck and benches; a fleet of sea kayaks; and expanded bar and restaurant areas. For those that want them, there is a full and varied program of tours and activities. If you just want to kick back, there are few more pleasant places in Belize to do it. ⊠ *5 km (3 mi) outside Placencia,* ☎ *062/3239 or 800/747–1381 in the U.S.,* 𝖥𝖠𝖷 *062/3240. 10 rooms. Restaurant, bar, beach, dive shop, laundry service, travel services. AE, D, MC, V.*

$$–$$$ ✕⛱ **Green Parrot.** One of the new resorts on Maya Beach, north of Placencia, this one was built in 1995 by a couple from Saskatoon, Canada, who gave up a life in the fast track for the slow life in Belize. Six two-story buildings, which the owners like to refer to as houses, not cabanas, are solidly built and roomier than many. On the ground floor there is a fold-out bed, dining area, fully equipped kitchenette, and generously apportioned bathroom. Sleeping quarters are upstairs in a loftlike space with a pitched wooden roof. Heat rises, of course, and they may get a little stuffy unless properly ventilated. Each has an attractive double bed with a locally crafted bamboo frame and a hotel-quality mattress imported from Canada. A moving panel in the wall, operated by pulleys, can be opened to give a bed-top view of the ocean. The beachfront restaurant-cum-bar is decorated with high-backed chairs of varnished cane, made by local craftspeople. Various meal plans are offered. ⊠ *No. 1 Maya Beach,* ☎ 𝖥𝖠𝖷 *062/2488. 6 rooms. Restau-rant, bar, beach, dive shop. AE, MC, V.*

$$ ✕⛱ **Kitty's Place.** Kitty's has stood the test of time while gradually ex-panding its amenities and activities. Situated on the same stretch of soft sand as its more upscale neighbor, Rum Point Inn, it offers a mixed bag of accommodations, from single rooms to studio apartments. Some of the nicest rooms are in a spacious, colonial-style house. The upstairs restaurant, with its football penants and Bob Marley posters, is lively and serves good, local-style food. New additions include three cabanas facing the sea. Each has a king-size bed plus two singles, a dining area, coffee machine, and bathroom with shower and tub. There is also a new, large gift shop that sells everything from suntan lotion to Guatemalan crafts. Sea kayaking, diving, and sport fishing are popular activities. For $50 per person, Kitty will pack you off to a remote cay. You bring the camping gear, and Kitty provides the sea kayak and the food. ⊠ *Box 528, Belize City,* ☎ *062/3227,* 𝖥𝖠𝖷 *062/3226. 11 rooms. Restaurant, bar, beach, dive shop, shop, laundry service, travel services. AE, MC, V.*

$$ ✕⛱ **Turtle Inn.** This is the first of the three resorts you reach on Pla-cencia's best beach (Kitty's Place and Rum Point Inn are the others). Owner Skip White, a native of Oklahoma, has been here since 1984 and in that time has built up a faithful clientele of students, divers, and naturalists. Nobody could accuse him of pandering to luxury. The ca-banas are built of rough, unpainted wood and thatched with palapa, and the furnishings are cheerful, though a bit spartan. However, the 650 feet of white sand beach, with its fiddlewood, palm, and cashew trees, is as pleasant as any in the area, and the dive shop is good. Four one-story cabanas face the water, while three more two-story cabanas are ranged along the back of the property. Drinks and meals are taken on a wooden deck overlooking the sea; a full meal plan is an option.

✉ *North end of Placencia,* ☎ *062/3244,* 🗚 *062/3245. 7 rooms. Restaurant, bar, beach, dive shop. MC, V.*

$$ ✕🖬 **Westwind.** If you want to be hosted by a local Belizean, you couldn't do better than George Wesby, the charming, talkative owner of this grey-and-blue, two-story guest house on the beach. His family has lived in Placencia for more than 100 years, though he himself only recently returned with his American wife after a 25-year sojourn in Michigan and Texas. With its U.S. fixtures and fittings (proper screened windows and plate-glass sliding doors), it is now the most substantial structure in the village. Rooms are plain but spotlessly clean and contain double beds, ceiling fans, fridge, and bathroom with shower. The best rooms are in front, looking out over the sea; the others are upstairs, at the back of the house. The downstairs restaurant serves good local fare, particularly fish. The reason for that is that George's cousin is the best fly-fisherman in town (☞ Outdoor Activities and Sports, *below*). Fishing and diving excursions are offered. ☎ *062/3255. 8 rooms. Restaurant, beach, travel services. MC, V.*

$–$$ ✕🖬 **Sonny's.** This local-run resort, a good value, has two kinds of cabanas. The larger ones, directly on the beach, have spacious verandas that look across the water. Smaller ones, set back from the water, are rather cramped, but all cabanas are well-equipped and clean. The restaurant, which has hardwood furniture and cheery tablecloths, serves good local-style food. ☎ *062/3103. 14 rooms. Restaurant, bar, beach. AE, MC, V.*

$$ 🖬 **Ranguana Lodge.** In the center of the village but still on the beach, these five white cabanas, with green shutters and trim and mahogany fittings, are the most pleasant midpriced accommodations in Placencia. The lodge is popular with fishers. ☎ *062/3112. 5 rooms. Beach. D, MC, V.*

$ 🖬 **Paradise Vacation Resort.** At the south end of the sidewalk, just back from Tentacles restaurant, you'll find this large house on stilts. As it has its own compressor, a good dive master, and a dock, it is popular with divers looking for a cheap alternative to Ambergris Caye. As far as lodging goes, basic is the byword. ☎ *062/3179,* 🗚 *062/3260. 16 rooms share baths. Dive shop, travel services. No credit cards.*

Outdoor Activities and Sports

FISHING

The fly-fishing on the flats off the cays east of Placencia is some of the best in Belize. You'll encounter plentiful tarpon—at times, they flurry 10 deep in the water—as well as permit fish, bonefish, and snook. Most of the better hotels can arrange guides; otherwise, try **P&P Enterprise** (☎ 062/3132 or 800/333–5961 in the U.S.). If you want the best local guide, call **Joel Wesby** (☎ 062/3138). Joel has more than 30 years guiding experience and knows where fish are that no one else does.

SCUBA DIVING

By the time you get this far south, the reef is as much as 33 kilometers (20 miles) off coast, necessitating boat rides of 45 minutes to an hour to get to dive sites. As there are not as many cuts and channels through the reef as in the north, it is also more difficult to get out to the seaward side, the best one for diving. As a result, most of the diving is done from the offshore cays, which have minireefs around them, usually with gently sloping drop-offs of about 80–100 feet. If you want spectacular wall dives, this isn't the place. For that, you have to stay in the north or go to the atolls. But there are other boons here. Off Moho Caye, southeast of Placencia, there are brilliant red and yellow corals and sponges that are rarely seen elsewhere in Belize.

In Placencia, the diving costs more. All-day trips, including two-tank dives and lunch, run $65 with a couple of people in the boat, including all the gear. Snorkeling is $40 per day.

Most of the larger resorts, like **Kitty's** (☎ 062/3227), **Turtle Inn** (☎ 062/3244), and **Rum Point Inn** (☎ 062/3239), have good dive shops, though, because of its boat, the operation at Rum Point Inn is a cut above the rest. For been-there-done-that divers, Rum Point has also introduced a new program whereby visitors can take part in R.E.E.F., a marine wildlife survey run out of Key Largo. Divers are asked to fill out survey forms listing the number of bar-fin blennys or mimic triplefin they spot, and the information is forwarded to Florida for cataloging. There are also two dive shops in town itself: **Placencia Dive Shop** (☎ 062/3313) and **Paradise Vacation Resort** (☎ 062/3179).

Placencia and the South A to Z

Arriving and Departing

BY BUS

For routes south to Belmopan, Dangriga, and Punta Gorda, try **Z-Line Bus Service** (✉ Venus Bus Terminal, Magazine Rd., Belize City, ☎ 027/3937).

BY CAR

To get to this region, head southeast from Belmopan on the Hummingbird Highway. Don't be fooled by the name. This is a seriously rough road, and you are best advised to use a four-wheel-drive vehicle even in the dry season. Despite this, the journey is well worth the effort. To the right rise the jungle-clad slopes of the Maya Mountains, mostly free of signs of human habitation except for the occasional clearing of corn and beans.

If you want to go directly from Belize City to Placencia, missing the Blue Hole and St. Herman's Cave, take the turnoff at Mile 30 on the Western Highway for Dangriga and the south.

Contacts and Resources

GUIDED TOURS

Overnight Placencia Déjà Vu Charters (✉ Placencia, ☎ 062/3301) provides assistance in arranging diving, fishing, and jungle excursions.

VISITOR INFORMATION

River Cafe and Tourist Information Centre (✉ Riverfront of Dangriga, ☎ 053/9908). There is a small **information booth** on the main path in the center of Placencia.

BELIZE A TO Z

Arriving and Departing

By Boat

For the adventurous, there is irregular, will-it-or-won't-it **ferry** service from Puerto Barrios, in Guatemala, to Punta Gorda, in Belize. The fare for the three-hour trip is $18. Tickets are available—if the boat, *Indita Maya,* is running—from the **Immigration Office** (✉ 9A Calle, Puerto Barrios). From Punta Gorda, there is bus service on a very rough road to Belize City and several flights a day on Maya Airways or Tropic Air.

By Bus

There is daily bus service from the Guatemalan and Mexican borders, though the route from Guatemala is sometimes impassable in the rainy season. Buses cross from Chetumal, Mexico, and stop in Corozal, Belize, where you can get another bus, or a plane, to Belize City or elsewhere. Buses from Guatemala (via Flores) stop in the border town of Ciudad Melchor de Mencos, at the bridge that separates the two countries. Cross the bridge, and take a bus or a taxi to San Ignacio, 13 kilometers (8 miles) away. As many people commute across the border, you can probably share a ride if you arrive early in the day. Otherwise, it costs $15. From San Ignacio, there is regular service to Belize City.

By Car

It's a three-day drive from Brownsville, Texas, to Chetumal, Mexico, on the border with Belize, and then about another 3½ hours to Belize City. On arrival from Mexico, you will have to hand in your Mexican Tourist Card (and/or car papers, if you have them). On the Belizean side, make sure you get a Temporary Import Permit for your car, or you may be delayed when leaving the country.

By Plane

International flights arrive at **Philip Goldson International Airport** (✉ Ladyville), north of Belize City. It's probably the only airport in the world with a mahogany roof.

The main airlines serving Belize from the United States are **American** (☎ 800/624–6262), with daily flights from Miami; **Continental** (☎ 800/231–0856), which has daily nonstop flights from Houston; and **Taca International** (☎ 800/535–8780), which has flights from New York, Washington, Los Angeles, New Orleans, Miami, and San Francisco. Taca International offers special baggage concessions to divers and has the most modern fleet. The snag is that flights are often late in arriving, which can be a nuisance if you have connections to make. From Miami it is only 2 hours to Belize; from Houston, 2½ hours; from New York, 5 hours; and from San Francisco, 8 hours. There are no direct flights from the United Kingdom; most travelers connect with U.S. flights.

Getting Around

By Bus

Though there is no railway in Belize, there is a fairly extensive bus service, run by franchised private companies. The quality of the buses and of the roads on which they travel vary considerably (Batty's is the best; points south, the worst). However, the buses do run according to reliable schedules, are extremely cheap (about $2 to $4 for all you can take), and remain an excellent way of experiencing Belize as the Belizeans do. Outside the cities you can flag them down like cabs. The driver will let you off whenever you want.

Batty Bros. Bus Services (✉ 15 Mosul St., Belize City, ☎ 027/2025) covers most northern and western bus routes, with stops in Corozal, Belmopan, and San Ignacio. **Novelo's** (✉ W. Colleti Canal, Belize City, ☎ 093/2954) does an afternoon run to San Ignacio. **Venus Bus Service** (✉ Magazine Rd., Belize City, ☎ 027/7390 or 027/3354) heads north to Orange Walk and Corozal, while **Z-Line Bus Service** (✉ Magazine Rd., Belize City, ☎ 027/3937) runs from the same terminal to such southern points as Belmopan, Dangriga, and Punta Gorda.

By Car

Belize is one of the few countries left in the Americas where off-road traveling is still the norm on most roads. Getting somewhere is never a question of simply going from A to B. There is always a bit of adventure involved, and a few detours to Y or Z.

If you're expecting the New Jersey Turnpike, you'll be sorely disappointed. Only the Northern Highway, to Orange Walk and Corozal, and the Western Highway, to Belmopan and San Ignacio, are paved, but even these can be badly potholed after rains. The Hummingbird Highway, to the south, is a difficult road in any season. In the rain it turns to orange slop; when dry, to bumpy concrete. Once you get off the main highways, distances don't mean that much—it's time that counts. You might have only 20 kilometers (12½ miles) to go, but it can take you 90 minutes. If you bring your own car, you will need insurance bought in Belize. Gasoline costs $2.40 per gallon, and note well: It is not unleaded. Fill up whenever you see a gas station.

Most of the major international car-rental companies are now represented in Belize City, as are several local operators. Prices vary from company to company, but all are expensive by U.S. standards ($65–$130 per day). Some of the cars run by the local operators—V8 gas-guzzlers driven down from Mexico—will cost you dearly for gas alone, whereas the international agencies have modern, dependable fleets and prices to match. A four-wheel-drive Suzuki with unlimited mileage from Avis, for instance, costs about $68 per day, though weekly rates are considerably cheaper (about $400). For serious safaris, a four-wheel-drive vehicle (preferably a Land Rover or an Isuzu Trooper) is invaluable, and some companies have clauses that bind you not to go off the main highways without one. All-terrain vehicles with guides are available from most major hotels at a cost of about $200 per day.

By Plane

Like everything good in Belize, flying—in twin-engine island-hoppers—has a bit of adventure attached to it. Most planes flying in-country leave from the **Municipal Airport,** which is only a mile or so from the Belize City center and is therefore more convenient than the international one. The main carriers are **Tropic Air** (☎ 024/5671, 713/521–9674 or 800/422–3435 in the U.S., FAX 026/2338), which flies to Ambergris and Caye Caulker as well as to Placencia and the south, and **Maya Airways** (☎ 024/4032, FAX 023/0585 or 023/0031), flying to San Pedro and to Big Creek, Dangriga, and Punta Gorda in the south. Tropic has the largest and most modern fleet. **Island Air** (☎ 026/2012 in San Pedro or 023/1140 in Belize City) also runs flights to cays as well as to Corozal, while **Skybird** (☎ 023/2596) has a new service to Caye Caulker. **Javier Flying Service** (☎ 023/5360) will take you pretty much anywhere for $170 per hour and has regular flights to Chan-Chich Lodge.

Security

For much of the early '90s, Belize City gained an ugly reputation for street crime. In recent years, however, the government has made strenuous efforts to clean up the problem, and it seems to be working. You should still take the same precautions you would take in any large city—leave valuables in a safe place, don't wear expensive jewelry on the street, and check with your hotel before venturing into any unfamiliar areas, particularly at night. Elsewhere, you will find Belize one of the safest, and friendliest, places you have ever visited.

Contacts and Resources

Car Rentals

International agencies are **Avis** (✉ Radisson Fort George, Marine Parade, Belize City, ☎ 025/2385), **Budget** (✉ 711 Bella Vista, Belize City, ☎ 023/2435), and **National** (✉ Philip Goldson International Airport, ☎ 023/1586). Of the local companies, the following are recommended:

Crystal Auto Rental (✉ Mile 1½, Northern Rd., Belize City, ☎ 023/1600),
Elijah Sutherland (✉ 127 Neal Pen Rd., Belize City, ☎ 027/3582), and
Smith & Sons (✉ 1–8 Central American Blvd., Belize City, ☎ 027/3779).
Safari (✉ Fort St., Belize City, ☎ 023/5395) has an excellent fleet of
new Isuzu Troopers.

Consulates and Embassies

U.S. Embassy (✉ 20 Garbourel La., Belize City, ☎ 027/7161). **Canadian Consulate** (✉ 29 Southern Foreshore, Belize City, ☎ 023/1060).
British High Commission (✉ Embassy Sq., Belmopan, ☎ 082/2146). Note
that there is neither a Guatemalan consulate nor embassy in Belize.

Guided Tours

In addition to companies that offer tours in their local area, there are
several that lead trips outside their region. One of the best is **Discovery Expeditions** (☎ 023/0748, FAX 023/0750), which has an office at
the Ramada Royal Reef. Tours can be arranged virtually anywhere in
the country, and staff members are friendly and well-informed. **Melmish
Mayan Tours** (☎ 024/5221) and **S&L Travel Services** (☎ 027/7594) are
also well-known and reputable. **Amigo Travel** (☎ 026/2180) offers mainland and island tours and snorkeling excursions. The biggest operation on Ambergris is **Hustler Tours** (☎ 026/2538 or 2279); in addition
to leading the standard snorkeling and diving tours, they offer an exciting trip to Lamanai by seaplane. For bonefish and tarpon fishing,
try **Island Tours** (☎ 026/2410) or the **Guerrero brothers** (☎ 026/2043).

4 Guatemala

Guatemala is one of the most enchanting spots in Central America. Within an area roughly the size of Ohio you will find palm-lined beaches, luxuriant cloud forests, rugged mountain ranges, tumultuous boulder-strewn rivers, a scrubby desert valley, 37 volcanoes, extraordinary Maya ruins, and expansive stretches of rain forest that are home to spider monkeys, toucans, iguanas, and massive mahogany trees draped with mosses, ferns, vines, bromeliads, and rare orchids.

By David
Dudenhoefer

Updated by
Patricia Alisau

GUATEMALA HAS BEEN captivating visitors for centuries. From the time of conquistador Pedro Alvarado, who stopped between battles to marvel at the beauty of Lake Atitlán, to that of Aldous Huxley, who waxed poetic on the same lake's shores centuries later, this intricate jewel of a country has inspired its share of foreigners. While its physical beauty is impressive, it is its incredible diversity that makes Guatemala so intriguing to visit. In a matter of days you can stroll the cobblestone streets of an ancient colonial capital, barter with Indians who still speak the tongues of and worship the gods of the ancient Mayas, and explore the exotic web of life that constitutes the tropical rain forest.

Perched at the top of the Central American isthmus and anchored below the Yucatán Peninsula, Guatemala is divided politically into a number of departments or states, and divided topographically into a number of distinct regions: the Pacific Lowlands, the Western Highlands, the Verapaces, the desert of Zacapa, the Caribbean Lowlands, and the jungle region of El Petén. With a territory of 108,900 square kilometers (42,042 square miles), Guatemala is slightly larger than Ohio and is home to more than 10 million people. Within this relatively small and sparsely populated area you can find palm-lined beaches, luxuriant cloud forests, 37 volcanoes (several of which are active), rugged mountain ranges, tumultuous boulder-strewn rivers, a scrubby desert valley, and expansive stretches of rain forest that are home to spider monkeys, toucans, iguanas, and massive mahogany trees draped with mosses, ferns, vines, bromeliads, and rare orchids.

As dramatic as Guatemala's varied landscapes are, its multifaceted human panorama is equally intriguing. Half of the population is indigenous, and though the country's Indians have adopted at least some of the European customs forced upon their ancestors as long as five centuries ago, they remain some of the most dedicated protectors of indigenous culture in the Americas. All of Guatemala's Indians are Maya, but at least 22 different ethnicities, differentiated by language, exist within that group. The other half of the population is divided among Ladinos, the descendants of Europeans and Indians; Garifunas, a handful of African immigrants who live on the Caribbean coast; and the European minority, predominantly Hispanic, which has maintained its imported bloodline and colonial lease on power. Though Spanish is the official language, it's the mother tongue of only about half of Guatemalans. Indians tend to speak one of the many indigenous languages, with Spanish as a second language, and in the area around Livingston, most people speak Garifuna, a mad mixture of African and European languages. This diversity creates a human tapestry even more colorful than the Indian weavers' most intricate patterns.

Guatemala's modern history has been largely the story of a struggle for land and political equality in the face of military rule. In 1944 Jorge Ubico, the last of the old-time strongmen, was deposed in a peaceful revolution. Elected in his place was schoolteacher Juan José Arévalo, who promised to modernize the country through education and agrarian reform. Arévalo was succeeded by Jacobo Arbenz, who accelerated land reform by daring to expropriate a small part of the vast holdings of the U.S.-owned United Fruit Company.

In 1954 the U.S. government, under pressure to protect American interests in Guatemala, sponsored a successful coup that ousted the democratically elected president. The coup effectively closed the door on political participation for the majority for the next 29 years as one right-wing government after another staged fraudulent elections.

In 1961 dissident army officers attempted a coup in response to government corruption. Although the revolt was put down, it set the stage for a prolonged guerrilla war. By the late 1970s the guerrillas had begun to tap into long-held grievances of Guatemala's disenfranchised, landless peasants, most of them Indians. In response to the guerrillas' growing popularity, the government unleashed a violent campaign of genocidal intensity. In the 35 years since the start of the insurgency, as many as 160,000 people have been lost through massacres of entire villages and isolated disappearances on city streets. Thousands fled to Mexico. In 1993 the Guatemalan government announced a repatriation program, promising a safe return to those who wanted to venture back. Although tens of thousands have returned, thouands more remain in refugee camps, unwilling to trust the government.

In 1983, having diminished the threat of a guerrilla victory and burdened by a troubled economy, the military allowed elections. Despite the trappings of an electoral system, however, Guatemala's political situation remains at an uneasy status quo. Elections are marked by an abstention rate of up to 85%, guerrillas continue to operate in isolated mountain villages and jungle regions, and state-sponsored extrajudicial killings continue sporadically. U.N.-moderated peace negotiations between the government and leftist guerrillas will hopefully produce a lasting cease-fire. Currently, though, the country has a strong military presence that may unnerve visitors at first but poses no threat to them. Note: If you enter Guatemala by car, there is *no* entry tax, although border officials may insist that there is. It is also wise to keep an eye on the contents of your vehicle: Soldiers have a reputation for stealing items simply by announcing that they are confiscating them.

The presence of violent bandits is a growing problem, especially along highways after dark or along footpaths to the more remote tourist sights. The need for proper precautions, however, should not dissuade visitors from experiencing a country that, perhaps better than any other, represents the beauty and diversity that is the New World.

Pleasures and Pastimes

Bird-Watching
More species of birds reside in Guatemala than in the United States and Canada combined, and birding easily complements any archaeological tour or beach excursion. The best guidebooks for bird-watching are *Birds of Mexico*, best purchased before your trip, or *Birds of Tikal*, which is available in many Guatemalan bookstores.

Dining
The basis of Guatemalan food is corn, which is usually eaten in the form of a tortilla—a thin pancake hot off the grill—or as a tamale or on the cob. Beans accompany most meals, either whole in a sauce or mashed and refried. In restaurants, these two items often accompany grilled beef or chicken. Turkey is a popular fowl, and in rural areas it's common to see *venado* (venison) and *tepezcuintle* (a large nocturnal rain-forest rodent) on the menu. (Be aware, though, that tepezcuintle is an endangered species; the more it's ordered, the more it'll be hunted down and the harder it'll be to see in the wild.) The most popular fish in fine restaurants is the delicious *robalo,* known as snook in the United States, where it's a favored sport fish. Meats are often served in *caldos* (stews) or cooked in a spicy sauce.

Guatemala has a surprising selection of high-quality, reasonably priced eateries. Though all the expensive hotels and most of the moderate ones have restaurants, you can almost always find better cuisine nearby, often for less money. Guatemala City has the kind of dining variety you might expect from a major city center, with the more expensive restaurants clustering in the new city. Antigua and Panajachel have a remarkable number of fine restaurants, too. Most establishments have international menus or specialize in the traditions of another country or region, but a few specialize in Guatemalan cuisine.

Panajachel may well have more exceptional restaurants than the rest of the Western Highlands. Unfortunately, few are near the beach, so it's difficult to enjoy a good meal with a view of the lake. Dining options are rather limited in Chichicastenango, where the best food is served in the finer hotels. Quezaltenango has a fair selection of good-quality restaurants, all in the inexpensive ($) and moderate ($$) ranges, but the food in the rest of the highlands, though hearty, will elicit little enthusiasm from gourmets.

Most restaurants in El Petén serve beef and chicken dishes. Several Flores restaurants concentrate on rain-forest game, like venado and tepezcuintle. Options are very limited in Tikal National Park. Aside from restaurants in the hotels, there's one next to the big museum and a few simple ones across the street, all inexpensive.

Reservations are recommended at expensive ($$$) restaurants on weekend nights, but dress is informal across the board. Even the more expensive establishments don't require jacket and tie.

CATEGORY	COST*
$$$	over $12
$$	$5–$12
$	under $5

per person for a three-course meal, plus tax and tip. Drinks not included.

Fishing
The Pacific coast offers excellent deep-sea fishing, especially for billfish and mahimahi. The Caribbean coast makes for good snook fishing, and Lake Atitlán is stocked with black bass.

Hiking
Many highland villages can't be reached by car, so hiking is the only way to explore much of this interesting country. Likewise, many archaeological sites in El Petén are best reached on foot, though lowland hiking is much hotter and muddier than its highland equivalent. A number of volcanoes make excellent climbs, some of which can be combined to form multiday trips. Traveling with an adventure-travel company (☞ Guided Tours *in* Guatemala A to Z, *below*) is a good way to avoid getting lost or robbed.

Lodging
The level of comfort and quality of facilities ranges from the luxurious suites of the Camino Real to the stark rooms, tiny beds, and cold showers of the ubiquitous budget hotels. In Guatemala City most of the expensive ($$$) and very expensive ($$$$) hotels are found in the new city, whereas most moderate ($$) and inexpensive ($) hotels are in the old city.

Travel in the Western Highlands tends to be cheaper than in the rest of the country. Panajachel has the widest and best selection of accommodations, and Chichicastenango and Quezaltenango can claim a few creditable establishments. Chichicastenango's hotels tend to fill up on Wednesday and Saturday nights, so it's best to have reservations.

Holy Week is very busy in both Chichicastenango and Santiago Atitlán. Beyond the towns, little exists. Most remote highland villages offer only inexpensive, spartan lodging, if anything at all. There are few official campgrounds, but you may camp anywhere. If you do, and you're near a village, don't leave possessions unguarded.

CATEGORY	COST*
$$$$	over $75
$$$	$45–$75
$$	$20–$45
$	under $20

All prices are for a standard double room, including 10% VAT and 10% tourist tax.

River Trips

Guatemala is filled with countless white-water rivers, most of which have never been run, as well as slow-moving lowland rivers that have been navigated for millennia. Adding to the adventure, most of the popular rivers flow through lush tropical forests that abound with wildlife.

Rivers are rated on a scale of I to VI. Class I signifies no rapids; Class II, small rapids; Class III, difficult rapids with waves; Class IV, very difficult or advanced; and Class V, violent hydrolics for experts only. Class VI rivers are unrunnable. White-water rivers in Guatemala include Chiquibul, Motagua, and Naranjo (Class II–III, year-round) and Cahabón (Class III–IV, year-round). The Candelaria (Class III–IV, March–May) traverses virgin forest and some fascinating caves.

Ruins

The heart of the ancient Maya empire is now the Department of El Petén, much of which remains covered with luxuriant tropical rain forest. Only a fraction of the estimated 1,500 ruins have been excavated, and all remain surrounded, if not covered, by jungle. Aside from Tikal, travel to ruins usually involves boat trips, horseback riding, hiking, or driving a four-wheel-drive vehicle down muddy roads, all of which makes the trip an adventure in its own right.

Shopping

Guatemala offers a mind-boggling selection of traditional handicrafts at remarkably low prices. The work of local artisans and weavers is usually called *típica,* roughly translated as "typical goods." Every tourist town has an overabundance of típica shops, but better deals can usually be found on the street. Bargaining is the modus operandi of street vendors and is also common in the markets and shops. Asking prices are sometimes rather high, so be patient.

Nearly all of Guatemala's handicrafts come from the highlands, and consequently the region is a shoppers' paradise. Most famous are the handwoven fabrics. In every highland village, you'll see women weaving the area's traditional patterns, which go back to pre–Hispanic motifs. But there are countless other kinds of handwork created by Guatemala's indigenous population. Just as each region has its traditional fabrics, so too does it have other specialties, such as baskets, toys, tinwork, statues, bags, or hats. The highland town most famous for shopping is Chichicastenango. However, remember that the lowest prices are usually found in the areas where the handicrafts are made.

Guatemala's Indian markets provide a wonderful glimpse into the everyday lives of the population. Vendors lining a jumble of narrow, warrenlike passages hawk fruits and vegetables, flowers, meat, nuts, candles, incense, toiletries, and gaudy U.S.-made T-shirts. Markets are held on the following days:

Monday: Chimaltenango, Zunil
Tuesday: Comalapa, Sololá
Wednesday: Santiago Sacatepéquez, Santa Lucía Reforma
Thursday: Nahualá, Todos Santos Cuchumatán, Chichicastenango, Nebaj, Santa Cruz del Quiché
Friday: Patzún, San Francisco El Alto
Saturday: Patzicía, Totonicapán
Sunday: Tecpán Guatemala, Chichicastenango, Momostenango, San Cristóbal Verapaz

And if you didn't remember to buy something in the highlands, don't despair; the market in Guatemala City's Zona 1 has a little bit of everything at prices as low as you'll find anywhere else. One final note: Be advised that it's illegal to take pre–Columbian and colonial artifacts or antiques out of Guatemala. Postcolonial works—anything made after 1820—can be exported.

Spelunking

An awesome selection of caves awaits the subterranean adventurer. Aktun Kan, in El Petén, at Santa Elena, is very accessible, and Naj Tunich, near Poptún, has underground lagoons and carbon frescoes painted by the ancient Maya. Lanquín, in Alta Verapaz, is an amazing collection of chambers, and the Candelaria River, also in Verapaz, passes through a series of caverns that are only accessible by water a few months of the year. Many caves remain largely unexplored, however.

Exploring Guatemala

Each of Guatemala's regions has its own peculiar geographic character and tourist attractions. Guatemala City is the capital and political center. To the west lies Antigua, the former colonial seat of government, and, farther west, traditional highland villages where even pre–Hispanic customs are jealously guarded and preserved. The north holds Guatemala's last frontier—the rain-forest lowlands of El Petén, home of one of the Maya's mightiest and most magnificent city-states. Between Guatemala City and El Petén, in the country's central portion, are more exotic Indian villages and Maya ruins, plus protected forest reserves. East of the capital lies the Atlantic, where a colorful Afro-Caribbean culture feels more like Belize than like the rest of Guatemala. Each area is covered in its own section, below.

Great Itineraries

Guatemala is a rugged country where major roads (read: paved) are few and far between and superhighways such as you find in Mexico don't exist. Since there are only two airports—one in Guatemala City, the other in Flores—most travel must be done on roads, such as they are. For this reason, the shortest trip should cover five days, no less, during which you can take in the most popular sites and still get off the beaten path a bit. Eight days provides a bolder look at Tikal and El Petén, while 10 days allows for a trip to the Caribbean coast.

Whatever the length of trip, all but the hardiest travelers will want to base themselves in the country's few cities and tourist towns (where the lodgings are) and explore the region's more remote reaches on day trips. The road system simply doesn't lend itself to touring. Most of the more charming villages are found along roads that end in the mountains, necessitating a lot of doubling back. Also, make sure your trip includes a Thursday or Sunday, market days, in Chichicastenango. Like the rest of your trip, it'll infuse your visit with the vivid colors and living traditions of Guatemala and leave a lasting impression of a place that's moving into the 21st century while respecting its past.

Numbers in the text correspond to numbers in the margin and on the maps.

IF YOU HAVE 5 DAYS

Start by exploring ▦ **Guatemala City** ①–⑭, the country's bustling business and political hub and your overnight base for the duration of your trip. The next day, take in **Antigua** ⑮–㉕, Guatemala's loveliest colonial city. Head out early on the third morning for the mountain village of **Chichicastenango** ㉛ and its exuberant, colorful market (Thursday and Sunday), where the best handicrafts of the region are laid out. You can spend the fourth day driving to Lake Atitlán, a beautiful lake at the foot of three volcanoes. Take time for a boat trip and stop off at some lakeside villages. On day five, take an early morning jet from Guatemala City to **Flores** ㊶, in El Petén, and head straight to the ruins of **Tikal** ㊾. You'll want to get there before the midday heat and sticky humidity settles in. If this is a first visit, you might want to sign up for a day tour out of Guatemala City, since the archaeological site is humongous and having ground trasportation waiting for you in Flores is convenient. After lunch at the ruins, head back to the Flores airport and Guatemala City.

IF YOU HAVE 7 DAYS

As in the shorter itinerary, you'll start sightseeing and spend the first four nights in ▦ **Guatemala City** ①–⑭, a good base for exploring outlying areas. On day two, head for **Antigua** ⑮–㉕, and tour the remarkable ruins of 16th-, 17th-, and 18th-century monasteries and convents. The next day, head for the Indian market in the colonial village of **Chichicastenango** ㉛, in the highlands. After shopping and visiting the churches, take a half-hour hike up the hill behind town to the sacred carved stone image of a Maya deity. Day four can be spent with a visit to the lakeside villages surrounding Lake Atitlán, Guatemala's picture-perfect lake. On the fifth day, take an early morning flight to **Flores** ㊶, in El Petén. Head for the Maya site of **Ceibal** ㊼ via a boat ride from **Sayaxché** ㊷ on the Río de La Pasión (through a tour procured in Guatemala City). Hike through the verdant rain forest to the plaza with temples. Head back on the road toward the Flores airport, but check into a hotel in ▦ **El Remate** ㊸, north of Flores. That night, make arrangements for a taxi to be waiting in front of your hotel at a specified hour the following morning. You'll want to head out before dawn for the breathtaking Maya site of **Tikal** ㊾, once the capital of the ancient Maya empire. Plan to arrive at the park about an hour before sunrise, and bring a flashlight. At the gate, you can hire a guide to lead you through the jungle to Temple IV, the highest. Climb the rustic ladder to the top and sit and watch the dawn unfold over the rain forest that engulfs the ancient city. It's unforgettable. Then tour the rest of the the the site before returning to El Remate. The last day can be spent with a morning hike on the trails of the **Cerro Cahui Wildlife Reserve** ㊿ before returning in late afternoon to the Flores airport and Guatemala City.

IF YOU HAVE 10 DAYS

Follow the seven-day itinerary above, spending nights in ▦ **Guatemala City** ①–⑭ and ▦ **El Remate** ㊸. On day eight, travel by bus or car about 295 kilometers (183 miles) east via Highway CA 9, the Carretera Atlantíca (Atlantic Highway), toward the Atlantic coast. Along the way, stop off at the ruins of **Quiriguá** ㊼ to see the giant Maya stelae. At the ▦ **Río Dulce,** once an important trading river for the Maya, check into a hotel and then sign up for a river cruise to the **Castillo de San Felipe** ㊽. (If you brought a car, you can leave it at your hotel and pick it up on your way back to Guatemala City.) The following day, take an early morning boat ride to the **Chocón Machacas Wildlife Reserve** ㊾

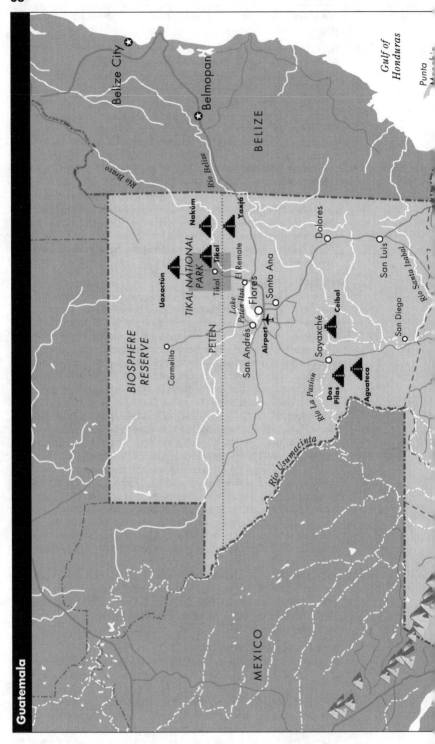

Guatemala

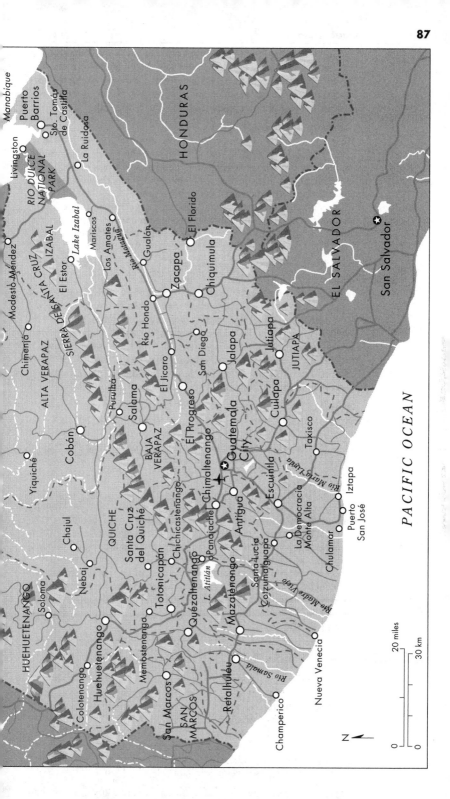

for a tour, and take an afternoon boat ride farther east to the colorful Garifuna community of 🏨 **Livingston** ⑩, where you'll overnight. On the last morning, take a ferry boat to the banana port of **Puerto Barrios** ⑪, where you can swim or take a short waterfront tour. By early afternoon, you'll want to head back to Guatemala City.

When to Tour Guatemala

Most travelers visit Guatemala during the summer (June–August) and winter (January–April) high seasons. The busiest time of year is around Holy Week, from Palm Sunday to Easter Sunday, when hotels in Antigua, Panajachel, and Chichicastenango book up months ahead of time. The rainy season runs from May to November, with a few dry spells in July and August. A typical rainy-season day is sunny in the morning, cloudy at midday, and pouring through the afternoon and evening. Though occasional cold fronts roll south every winter, Guatemala's climate depends more on altitude than season. While the coasts and El Petén are hot and humid, the mountains are drier, with warm days and cool nights. The higher you go, the colder it gets.

The best time of the week to visit any highland village is on its market day, when the streets are packed with families from the surrounding countryside (☞ Shopping *in* Pleasures and Pastimes, *above*). The liveliest time of year for each town, however, is the week or several days of its annual festival, which surrounds the feast day of the town's patron saint. Festivals are an interesting mixture of religious ritual and carnival commotion, with processions, live music, and traditional dancers in costumes that depict animals, gods, and conquistadors.

Important highland festivals occur in Huehuetenango (July 12–17), Santiago Atitlán (July 23–27 and Holy Week), Momostenango (last week in July), Nebaj (August 12–15), Santa Cruz del Quiché (August 14–19), Quezaltenango (September 9–17), Totonicapán (September 24–30), Panajachel (honoring St. Francis, October 1–7), Todos Santos (October 31–November 5), Zunil (November 22–26), and Chichicastenango (December 18–21).

Elsewhere in Guatemala, there are other festivals of note. In Antigua, the Biennial Cultural Festival (February 1997, 1999) includes a variety of artistic events held in the city's ruins and ancient buildings. Antigua also plays host to series of processions, both in the weeks preceding Christmas and during Holy Week, when residents create colorful religious parades and reenactments of Christ's last days in Jerusalem. On All Saints' Day (November 1), huge kites fly from the cemetery of Santiago Sacatepéquez, near Guatemala City, and Independence Day (September 15) is celebrated with traditional music, dances, and costumes throughout the country.

GUATEMALA CITY

The capital is a big, busy, and not-too-pretty city, and it's hardly the reason to visit Guatemala. It's almost unavoidable, however, since traveling to the rest of the country usually means passing through. Though the city as a whole isn't terribly attractive, it has some of the country's best and most varied restaurants and hotels, several excellent museums, occasional cultural events, a healthy nightlife, and all the amenities of the modern world that you might miss while exploring the country's less-developed regions.

A sprawling metropolis divided into 21 zones, this city of more than 2.5 million may seem intimidating when you first examine a map. But travelers have few reasons to stray from four central zones—1, 4, 9,

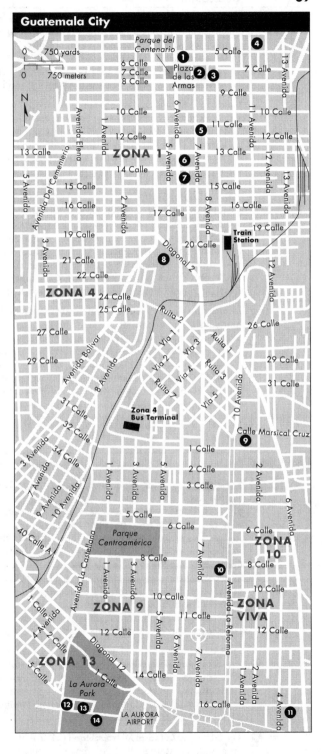

Guatemala City

and 10—which makes Guatemala City, or Guate, as the locals call it, much easier to manage. These areas can be grouped into two basic units: the old city, which is centered on Zona Uno (Zone 1), and the new city, to the south, which comprises Zonas Nueve y Diez (Zones 9 and 10) and stretches up into Zona Cuatro (Zone 4). A sort of transition area between new and old, Zona 4 is dirty, tacky, and best bypassed.

Guatemala City is an easy enough place to find your way around in if you stick to the central zones, where the *avenidas* (avenues) run north and south and the *calles* (streets) run east and west. Zona 4 is a bit of an aberration; streets here run at a 45° angle to the rest of the city. The major arteries of the city are 6 and 10 avenidas: 6 Avenida runs through the center of Zona 1, via Zona 4, into the heart of Zona 9, passing three series of identically numbered calles; 10 Avenida runs through Zonas 1 and 4 and becomes Avenida La Reforma. Most streets and avenues are numbered, and addresses are usually given as a numbered avenida or calle followed by two numbers separated by a dash, the first number being that of a nearby cross street or avenue, the second being that of the specific residence or business. Thus, 9 Avenida 5–22 is on 9 Avenida between 5 and 6 calles, and 9 Avenida 5–74 is on the same block, only closer to 6 Calle. A word of warning: Make sure you're in the right zone; different zones often contain identical addresses.

Ideally, you should spend some time in both old and new cities, though quite a distance separates the two and few attractions appear in between. Luxury-seekers tend to keep to the new city, while deal-seekers frequent the old. As with hotels and restaurants, shopping tends to follow this same pattern, but a good sampling of regional wares, including the country's famous woven and embroidered goods, can be found in both parts of town. With the exception of the big market downtown, shop hours are weekdays 10–1 and 3–7, and Saturday 10–1.

Numbers in the margin correspond to points of interest on the Guatemala City map

The Old City

For a truly "foreign" experience, head to Zona 1. For the most part, the old city is a hot, crowded, slightly gloomy place that closes down pretty early. However, it does have a certain amount of character and is more convenient for those sightseeing by bus or on foot. Those monuments and historic buildings that have survived this century's earthquakes are found here. The heart of the old city is the **Parque del Centenario and Plaza de las Armas** (⊠ Between 6–8 calles and 5–7 avenidas). Dominating the park is a huge band shell, where military bands and musical artists perform. The adjacent plaza is basically an expanse of cement with a parking garage underneath. West of the park is the modern National Library and military offices, while to the south of the plaza is the Portal Comercio, an arcade packed with vendors.

Built by former president Jorge Ubico between 1939 and 1943, the **❶** grandiose **Palacio Nacional** (National Palace) now houses the offices of the president and his ministers. Its ornate stairways, stained glass, fountains, and quiet courtyards provide a pleasant contrast to the city beyond its walls. ⊠ *6 Calle and 7 Avenida, no phone.* ▣ *Free.* ☉ *Weekdays 8–4:30, Sat. 8–noon.*

★ **❷** The intriguing **Catedral Metropolitano** (Metropolitan Cathedral) houses ornate altars, statues, and colonial religious art. Constructed from 1782 to 1868, it stands on the east end of the Plaza de las Armas. ⊠ *8 Calle and 7 Avenida, no phone.* ▣ *Free.* ☉ *Daily 9–6.*

❸ The underground **Mercado Central** (Central Market) comprises a seemingly endless maze of passages where handicrafts from throughout the country are hawked from overstocked stalls. A peep at the colorful and exotic fruit stands on the first floor is a worthwhile cultural and sensory experience. ⊠ *8 Calle and 8 Avenida, no phone.* ⊙ *Mon.–Sat. 9–6, Sun. 9–noon.*

❹ It's worth a walk inside the neoclassical **La Merced** church, consecrated in 1813, to see its baroque interior. Many of the elaborate paintings and sculptures once decorated Antigua's original La Merced. ⊠ *5 Calle and 11 Avenida, no phone.* ☞ *Free.* ⊙ *Daily 6 AM–7 PM.*

❺ One of the city's prettier buildings, the big pink **Edificio de Correos Central** (Main Post Office) deserves a visit even if you've got nothing to drop in the slot. ⊠ *12 Calle between 7 and 8 avenidas, no phone.* ⊙ *Weekdays 8–7, Sat. 8–3.*

❻ The **San Francisco church,** constructed between 1800 and 1851, features an ornate wooden altar and small museum. ⊠ *13 Calle and 6 Avenida, no phone.* ☞ *Free.*

❼ An appropriate metaphor for the Guatemalan justice system, **Cuartel General de la Policía** (Police Headquarters) is a massive, gloomy, medieval-looking structure. ⊠ *14 Calle and 6 Avenida.*

❽ The **Miguel Angel Asturias Culture Center** houses several theaters and a small museum of antique arms. ⊠ *Diagonal 2 and 2 Calle, Civic Center,* ☎ *232–4042.* ☞ *Free.* ⊙ *Weekdays 10–4.*

OFF THE
BEATEN PATH

RELIEF MAP – Constructed in 1904, this cement map depicting Guatemala's precipitous topography is so immense that it must be viewed from observation towers. ⊠ *Minerva Park, at end of Avenida Simon Cañas, Zona 2, no phone.* ☞ *Free.* ⊙ *Daily 8–4.*

KAMINALJUYÚ – From 300 BC to AD 900, an early Maya city that was home to some 50,000 people flourished in what is now the heart of Zona 7. Though most of the city is buried beneath urban sprawl, this impressive site, including several pyramid bases, offers a glimpse of the area's prehistory. Some of the objects found here can be seen at the archaeological and Popol Vuh museums.

Dining and Lodging

$$ ✗ **Altuna.** This popular restaurant in an old house a block off 6
★ Avenida serves a predominantly Spanish menu in a pleasantly hustle-bustle atmosphere. Waiters move briskly about in white jackets and ties in the main dining area—a covered courtyard surrounded by a wooden railing and potted plants—or in several adjacent rooms decorated with Iberian paintings, photographs, and posters. The menu is fairly limited. Consider the calamari, filet mignon with mushroom sauce, or paella. Prices lean toward the low end of moderate. ⊠ *5 Avenida 12–31, Zona 1,* ☎ *232–0669. AE, DC, MC, V. Closed Mon.*

$$ ✗ **Arrin Cuan.** Guatemalan cuisine typical of the Cobán area is served from these two restaurants just half a block apart. The 5 Avenida restaurant is the more pleasant of the two: Its walls are drenched with brightly colored handwoven fabrics, wooden masks, and Guatemalan art. Harp or marimba music plays, and every table is set with flowers in soda-bottle vases. The 4 Calle locale lacks much of the charm of the one around the corner (you'll miss out on the dulcet tones of live music here). Both serve the same extensive menu, with items such as *kak-ik* (a spicy turkey stew) and *gallo en chicha* (chicken in a slightly sweet sauce). ⊠ *5 Avenida 3–27 and 4 Calle 4–79, Zona 1,* ☎ *238–0242. DC, MC, V.*

$$ ✕ **El Gran Pavo.** You can't miss this pink building topped with neon, and you'll soon discover that the inside is just as flashy as the facade. Bright colors bedazzle the innocent initiate; a few mirrors and plants, Mexican hats, and blankets bestow the walls with even more spirited brilliance. The food is authentic Mexican, with the standard *taquitas* (tacos), enchiladas, and moles, but you'll also run across items like *aujas nortenas* (grilled beef strips covered with a red sauce and surrounded by avocado slices) and *camarones siempre joven* (shrimp in a spicy black chili sauce). It's open past midnight and has live music as well as mariachis who often perform private concerts for a small fee. ✉ *13 Calle 4–41, Zona 1,* ☎ *232–9912. AE, DC, MC, V.*

$$ ✕ **Los Cebollines.** A wide selection of delicious Mexican food is the attraction at Los Cebollines, which has, however, a rather banal decor. Two menus are available: a drink menu that includes cocktails, Mexican beers, and sangria; and a food menu that lists traditional tacos, burritos, fajitas, and, less predictably, *caldo tlalpeno de pollo* (a chicken stew with chickpeas and avocado). ✉ *6 Avenida 9–75, Zona 1,* ☎ *232– 7750. AE, DC, MC, V.*

$ ✕ **Café de Imeri.** This elegant establishment in an old house with barrel-tile roof and wooden balcony has seating indoors or in a luxuriantly planted courtyard with a small fountain at one end. The menu is light—mostly sandwiches and soups—but has some wonderful cakes, pies, and coffee for dessert. ✉ *6 Calle 3–34, Zona 1,* ☎ *232–3722. No credit cards. Closed Sun.*

$ ✕ **El Mesón de Don Quijote.** A colorful restaurant in the heart of the old city, Don Quijote serves respectable northern Spanish cuisine—from Asturias to be precise—at reasonable prices. It's a favorite late-night spot (open until 2 AM) of Guatemalan old-timers. The restaurant has a long bar and several adjacent dining rooms, and live music is played at night under a flashy painting of a flamenco dancer. The large menu is filled with such palate pleasers as seafood casserole, cold cuts of Spanish hams, lentils with sausage, baked lamb, and paella (for four people or more). On weekdays, a four-course executive lunch can't be beat. ✉ *11 Calle 5–27, Zona 1,* ☎ *253–4929. DC, MC, V. Closed Sun.*

$ ✕ **Europa Bar and Restaurante.** This second-floor bar has long been a hangout for travelers and members of the American expatriate community. The owner, Oregon native Judy Strong, creates a pleasant and welcoming atmosphere where customers can relax, play backgammon, or watch a sports event on cable TV. There's a functional American menu with mainstays like hamburgers, chili, *pollo migado* (breaded chicken), and mashed potatoes, and a U.S. diner-style breakfast of pancakes or bacon, eggs, and hash browns. ✉ *11 Calle 5–16, Zona 1,* ☎ *253–4929. No credit cards. Closed Sun.*

$ ✕ **Long Wak.** This little hole-in-the-wall serves Chinese food at exceptionally low prices. The decor is simple, but the lunchtime crowds are huge. There is a large menu of typical Chinese favorites, such as chop suey and chicken chow mein, most under $4. ✉ *6 Calle 3–70, Zona 1,* ☎ *232–6611. No credit cards.*

$$$ 🏨 **Hotel Pan American.** Truly the grande dame of downtown hotels, ★   this was the most luxurious lodging house in town about a half century ago. Some people may be put off by the location on busy 6 Avenida, in the heart of Zona 1, but to step into the lobby of this former mansion turned traditional inn is to leave the confusion of the city behind. Hung with attractive wrought-iron chandeliers, the lobby is a spacious covered courtyard. Half of it holds tables from the restaurant, where servers are dressed in traditional highland costumes. Rooms, which were repainted in 1995, are small but attractive, with tile floors and new throw rugs, soft beds covered with highland blankets, cable TVs, and walls decorated with traditional weavings and paintings. ✉ 9 *Calle 5–63, Zona 1, ☎ 232–6807, FAX 232–6402. 56 rooms. Restaurant, concierge, travel services, airport shuttle. AE, DC, MC, V.*

$$ 🔲 **Hotel Chalet Suizo.** This quiet hotel has been a favorite with budget travelers for 40 years, and the property is constantly remodeled and expanded by the Swiss owners to meet the growing demand. Rooms are found on two stories, and most of them face a series of small courtyards. The rooms themselves are pretty basic, with tile floors and small beds with thin mattresses, but the place is clean, the staff is friendly, and the management is willing to store extra baggage for guests while they travel around the country. A small café sits to the right of the entrance, and a little courtyard behind the reception desk has a marble floor, carved wooden pillars, and a few chairs and tables for guests. ✉ *14 Calle 6–82, Zona 1, ☎ 251–3786. 48 rooms, 13 with bath. Restaurant, travel services. No credit cards.*

$$ 🔲 **Hotel Colonial.** Though the rest of this hotel, lodged in a 19th-century town house, doesn't live up to the expectations raised by its outward appearance, it's a pleasant place with a few exceptional rooms. The reception overlooks an enclosed patio full of potted plants, and a small lounge furnished with antique reproductions is to the right of the entrance. Rooms, off wide corridors, have wooden floors and colonial-style decor with tiny, modern baths and optional cable TV. Rooms facing the street have wooden shutters to muffle street noise. Hotel personnel are very friendly, and security is good at night, thanks to a locking front door and guard. A small restaurant in back is open for breakfast only. ✉ *7 Avenida 14–19, Zona 1, ☎ 232–6722 and 229–5542. 35 rooms with bath. Restaurant. No credit cards.*

$$ 🔲 **Hotel Fortuna Royal.** This hotel has succeeded at what few others have: combining American-style comfort and cut-rate prices in the middle of the old city. The marble floors and wood paneling of the lobby give way to wall-to-wall carpeting and floral-pattern wallpaper in the rooms. The immaculately clean rooms are spacious, and all have their own phone and cable TV. Prices are lower if you do not need a receipt. ✉ *12 Calle 8–42, Zona 1, ☎ 251–7887, FAX 251–2215. 20 rooms with bath. Restaurant, room service. AE, DC, MC, V.*

$$ 🔲 **Hotel Sevilla.** Opened in 1994, this hotel in the heart of the old city is a comfortable spot with reasonable rates. The lobby is graced by a small tile fountain, but the predominant decor is modern. Carpeted rooms feature small private baths and cable TV. Not terribly attractive, the hotel is clean, and it has a sauna and a small restaurant and bar. ✉ *9 Avenida 12–29, Zona 1, ☎ 251–2815, FAX 232–8431. 80 rooms with bath. Restaurant, bar, sauna. AE, DC, MC, V.*

$$ 🔲 **Hotel Spring.** This Spanish colonial–style hotel offers inexpensive
★ and moderately priced rooms. The moderate rooms are small and neat, with floral-print bedspreads and cable TV. Most of the other rooms in the two-story building face a large courtyard filled with potted plants and cast-iron tables and chairs, where guests can escape the downtown bustle and soak up the afternoon sun. Rooms have high ceilings, carpeting, and firm beds. There's a small café behind the courtyard, and side-street rooms on the second floor share a balcony that overlooks the avenue. Although this hotel is a good value, note that the shelter attached to the building is a refuge for street children, most of whom are excellent thieves, so hang on to your wallets as you head in and out. ✉ *8 Avenida 12–65, Zona 1, ☎ 232–6637, FAX 232–0107. 43 rooms, 23 with bath. MC, V.*

$$ 🔲 **Posada Belem.** This little bed-and-breakfast on a quiet side street
★ is an exceptional place, thanks to the couple that runs it. The hotel is the family's former residence, built in 1873, and has been renovated just enough to combine traditional charm with modern comfort. Rooms

have tile floors and walls decorated with Guatemalan painting and weaving, handwoven rugs and blankets, and modern private baths. The Posada has a small library and collection of pre–Columbian artifacts, and family-style meals can be cooked to order. The owners are a fount of information and even make travel arrangements for guests. ⊠ *13 Calle "A" 10–30, Zona 1,* ☎ *232–9226,* ⅎⅩ *251–3478. 10 rooms with bath. Dining room, library, travel services. AE, DC, MC, V.*

$ ☷ **Hotel Ajau.** This very basic hotel is built in the Spanish style, with an inside courtyard and three floors of rooms with balconies. The clean rooms have tile floors and a couple of pieces of cheap wood furniture; those with bath also have cable TV. To avoid noise, ask for a room not facing the street. ⊠ *8 Avenida 15–62, Zona 1,* ☎ *232–0488,* ⅎⅩ *251–8097. 38 rooms, 19 with bath. No credit cards.*

$ ☷ **Lessing House.** This small hotel is surprisingly quiet given its central location. The simple rooms are along a hallway decorated with regional weavings. Each has tile floors and wooden furniture. ⊠ *12 Calle 4–35, Zona 1,* ☎ *251–3891. 8 rooms with bath. No credit cards.*

Nightlife and the Arts

For dancing, try the colorful **El Gazabo** (⊠ 6 Calle at 3 Avenida). **La Taberna** (⊠ 6 Avenida "A" 10–73) is a dance spot in the basement of the Hotel Ritz Continental. Poetry readings and concerts are held at **La Bodeguita del Centro** (⊠ 2 Calle 3–55), a popular spot for intellectuals. The late-night **El Mesón de Don Quijote** (⊠ 11 Calle 5–27) has live music that draws a thirtysomething to fiftysomething crowd.

Shopping

The best place for inexpensive handicrafts, including jewelry, leather, and, of course, handwoven fabrics, is the **Mercado Central** (⊠ 8 Calle and 8 Avenida). If the passages of the Central Market make you claustrophobic, try the vendors of the **Portal Comercio** (⊠ South of the Plaza de Las Armas) for cheap jewelry. You'll find mostly handcrafted silver embellished with local stones. Designs range from Maya reproductions to modern. For fine leather products, go to **Arpiel** (⊠ 11 Calle 5–38). Antiques are sold at **El Patio** (⊠ 12 Avenida 3–39).

In Zona 1, try **Mayatex** (⊠ 11 Avenida 4–50), **Yaman Munil** (⊠ 12 Calle "A" 0–10), **La Momosteca** (⊠ 7 Avenida 14–48), **Maya Modern** (⊠ 7 Avenida and 9 Calle), **Lin Canola** (⊠ 5 Calle 9–60), and **Maya Sac** (⊠ 6 Avenida "A" 10–39, 2nd Floor).

Swimming

Swimmers can use Minerva Park's **public pool** (⊠ Zona 2).

The New City

While the old city is the real Guatemala, the new city often feels more like the United States or Canada. It's dominated by big, modern buildings, shopping centers, hidden mansions, and wide avenues like La Reforma (which separates Zonas 9 and 10) and is home to many of the city's museums. Zona 10's "Zona Viva" is packed with fancy restaurants, bars, and discos that are busy until the wee hours, when the old city sleeps. Since the new city's attractions are quite spread out, you'll want to use buses, taxis, or a car to get around.

❾ At the northern end of Zona 10, the small but lovely **Jardines Botánico** (Botanical Gardens) contain an impressive collection of plants and a little Natural History Museum. It's run by the University of San Carlos. ⊠ *Just off the Avenida La Reforma on 0 Calle, Zona 10,* ☎ *331–0904.* ◪ *5¢.* ☉ *Weekdays 8–4.*

★ ⑩ Though smaller than other museums, the **Museo Popol Vuh,** on the sixth floor of the Edificio Galerias Reforma, is very informative. Its collection of Maya artifacts is displayed masterfully. ⊠ *Avenida La Reforma 8–60, Zona 9, no phone.* ☞ *$1.* ⊙ *Mon.–Sat. 9–5.*

NEED A BREAK? You can sip a cappuccino and satisfy your sweet tooth on the porch of **Cafe Zurich** (⊠ 6 Avenida 12–58, Zona 10, ☎ 334–2781), a colonial home. The menu includes specialty coffees, sandwiches, chocolate, and more chocolate.

The **Zona Viva,** the area between La Reforma and Zona 10's 4 Avenida and 10 and 14 calles, is the poshest part of town. Its hotels, shops, restaurants, bars, and dance clubs also make this the liveliest place in the country on weekend nights, but it's fun to visit anytime.

★ ⑪ The city's best museum, **Museo Ixchel** pays homage to Guatemala's Maya past with extensive exhibits on the indigenous population, especially on its weaving and traditional costumes. In addition to an impressive collection of native textiles, the museum contains art exhibits, photos of religious processions, and an anthropology library. An excellent gift shop features many high-quality items. ⊠ *4 Avenida 16–27, Zona 10,* ☎ *331–3622.* ☞ *$2.* ⊙ *Weekdays 8:30–5:30, Sat. 9–1.*

★ ⑫ **Museo Nacional de Arqueología y Etnología** (National Museum of Archaeology and Ethnology) is the most important of the museums skirting La Aurora Park. A large museum dedicated to the ancient and modern Maya, it features an impressive collection of Maya artifacts—pottery, jewelry, and clothing—as well as models of the ancient cities themselves. ⊠ *Edificio 5, La Aurora Park, Zona 13,* ☎ *272–0468.* ☞ *2 quetzals.* ⊙ *Tues.–Sun. 9–4.*

⑬ Surrealism and other styles are represented in the top-notch works of modern Guatemalan artists at the **Museo Nacional de Arte Moderno** (National Museum of Modern Art). ⊠ *Edificio 6, La Aurora Park, Zona 13,* ☎ *331–0703.* ☞ *Small fee.* ⊙ *Tues.–Fri. 9–4.*

⑭ A long-neglected collection of old stuffed animals, plants, and minerals is the main feature of the **Museo Nacional de Historia Natural** (National Museum of Natural History). ⊠ *6 Calle 7–30, La Aurora Park, Zona 13,* ☎ *331–0406.* ☞ *Small fee.* ⊙ *Tues.–Fri. 9–4.*

Dining and Lodging

$$$ ✕ **El Pedregal.** When you step into this premier restaurant, the modern atmosphere of the Zona Viva seems to fade away and you're back in Old Mexico. The main dining room, an enclosed courtyard, has a fig tree at its center and gardens along the edges, softening an atmosphere dominated by stone. Leather chairs add to the elegant hacienda ambience, and a small fountain babbles at one end of the room. Of two smaller dining rooms in back, the one on the left opens onto a garden courtyard with a fountain. Mariachis, strolling trios, and the cuisine—ranging from traditional fajitas to *camarones especiales* (shrimp marinated in cognac, stuffed with cheese, and tied in bacon strips)— are unmistakably Mexican, and service is impeccable. ⊠ *1 Avenida 13– 42, Zona 10,* ☎ *368–0663. AE, DC, MC, V.*

$$$ ✕ **Jake's.** Owner and chef Jake Denburg is a painter who has turned
★ his creative powers to cooking. A converted old farmhouse with hardwood ceilings and tile floors is the setting for his complex, carefully prepared meals. The Italian and international menu is augmented by 25 daily specials, ranging from handmade tortellini filled with smoked chicken and spices to robalo in a green-pepper sauce. Jake has focused much of his artistry on fish; his crowning achievement is the *robalo*

Venecia royal, served in a creamy shrimp sauce over a bed of spinach. All the vegetables are organically grown here—one of the few places in Guatemala where you can enjoy a salad without fear. ✉ *17 Calle 10–40, Zona 10,* ☎ *368–0351. AE, DC, MC, V. Closed Sun., Mon.*

$$$ ✕ **Jean François.** Even without a sign, this restaurant has been full since
★   the day it opened. Inside the main dining room, chairs embroidered with flower patterns, hand-carved wooden cherubs on the walls, and gold stars on the ceiling provide an easy charm. For a more intimate setting, there are candlelit tables on an outside patio. The rich Provençal cuisine features such mouthwatering appetizers as shrimp soufflé in a spinach jacket, and chicken mousse with lemon, blue cheese, and nuts. For a main course, try the ravioli filled with mushrooms and chicken or the *robalo le classique,* a delicate fish fillet sautéed in butter, fresh green herbs, and spices. ✉ *Diagonal 6, 13–63, Zona 10,* ☎ *333–4785. DC, MC, V. Closed Sun. No dinner Sat.–Tues.*

$$$ ✕ **La Cúpula.** The colonial-style building looks a bit out of place in Zona 9, but once inside, you'll forget about what's outside. The *cúpula,* a sort of chimney, rises out of the center of the restaurant where the cooking area would traditionally be but instead is filled with the verdure of potted plants. The white stucco walls parade the work of Guatemalan artists, and antique silver trays and pitchers rest on wooden ledges. Figure on predominantly Italian foods, with items like gnocchi in pepper cream sauce, but you can also eat seafood, such as lobster thermidor and shrimp Veracruz. ✉ *7 Avenida 13–01, Zona 9,* ☎ *331–9346. AE, DC, MC, V. Closed Sun.*

$$$ ✕ **Los Ranchos.** Owned by Managua's business barons, the Lacayo fam-
★   ily, this popular 1995 newcomer near the Camino Real Hotel is a branch of a Nicaraguan chain that also has outposts in Miami. At lunch, the restaurant with the pretty blue colonial facade and big picture windows packs in a clientele of mostly high-powered entrepreneurs. At night, the place turns romantic when candles light the tables. Specialties are succulent steaks and meat entrées, such as the signature dish, *churrasco Los Ranchos,* which hails from Argentina. Most meats, including rib eye and chateaubriand, are U.S. imports, and for non–meat eaters there's grilled lobster and shrimp. Cassava cream soup and fried pork rinds head the list of appetizers, while desserts couldn't be more Guatemalan: *tiramisù* (a spongy, sweet dessert), *tres leches* (cakes filled with yummy whipped cream), and *cajeta* (caramel) crepes. An excellent wine selection represents Chile, France, Argentina, Italy, and Germany, and every Saturday, there's a ceviche lunch buffet with shrimp, clams, black conch, crab, and squid dishes. ✉ *2 Avenida 14–06, Zona 10,* ☎ *363–5028. AE, DC, MC, V.*

$$$ ✕ **Mario's.** Owner and chef Mario Morillo is a Spaniard who moved to Guatemala over a decade ago after quitting his post as head chef at one of Madrid's best clubs. The menu is one of the more varied and original in the country, ranging from appetizers like garlic mushrooms to entrées such as roast suckling pig and a traditional paella. Mario's robalo is a standout—the premier local fish served with a special mushroom sauce. ✉ *13 Calle and 1 Avenida, Zona 10,* ☎ *332–1079. AE, DC, MC, V. Closed Sun.*

$$$ ✕ **Romanello's.** A quiet but popular spot in the heart of the Zona Viva, Romanello's serves a limited but well-prepared selection of the country's best meat and seafood. The restaurant has a simple but elegant decor, with pink stucco walls, wooden floors, arched doorways, and a few antiques. One table at the back overlooks an attractive shopping area with a small garden. There is no menu, but guests usually choose from tenderloin, robalo, lobster, and a pasta dish, all of which can be prepared with a number of sauces. ✉ *1 Avenida 12–70, Zona 10, no phone. AE, DC, MC, V. Closed Sun.*

In case you want to see the world.

At American Express, we're here to make your journey a smooth one. So we have over 1,700 travel service locations in over 120 countries ready to help. What else would you expect from the world's largest travel agency?

do more ®

Travel

In case you want to be welcomed there.

We're here to see that you're always welcomed at establishments everywhere. That's why millions of people carry the American Express® Card – for peace of mind, confidence, and security, around the world or just around the corner.

do more.

Cards

In case you're running low.

We're here to help with more than 118,000 Express Cash locations around the world. In order to enroll, just call American Express before you start your vacation.

do more

Express Cash

And just in case.

We're here with American Express® Travelers Cheques and Cheques *for Two*.® They're the safest way to carry money on your vacation and the surest way to get a refund, practically anywhere, anytime.

Another way we help you...

do more ®

Travelers Cheques

$$$ ✕ **Tre Fratelli.** This smart new place owned by three hip Guatemalan
★ partners caters to the town's young professionals. An outgrowth of the
San Francisco restaurant of the same name, it serves up cuisine and at-
mosphere that are part Italian, part laid-back northern Californian, and
part exotic Guatemalan. Fettucine *frutti di mare* (laced with seafood),
ravioli *alla Bolognese*, manicotti *alla Napolitana,* and the *quattro stag-
gione* pizza are house favorites, and hot, crusty oven-baked bread ac-
companies all meals. Don't miss dessert, if you have room after the
generous portions: scrumptious lemon, strawberry, or chocolate mousse
or *cassatta* (homemade ice cream). Top it off with a cappuccino or
espresso, brewed in Italian coffee urns. Dining can be had under an
awninged outdoor terrace or indoors in a cozy, light, plant-filled room
set with stylish wooden furniture. ⊠ *2 Avenida 13–25, Zona 10,* ☎
331–8985. AE, MC, V. No dinner Sun.

$$ ✕ **Excellent.** One of the city's best Chinese restaurants, this place has
a relatively small but resourceful menu, with items like beef with
mango sauce, green peppers stuffed with shrimp, and conch with
cashews. The decor is nothing to write home about, but the food
makes up for any lack of ambience. ⊠ *13 Calle and 2 Avenida, Zona
10,* ☎ *336–4278. AE, DC, MC, V.*

$$ ✕ **Hacienda de los Sanchez.** This steak house is a Zona Viva favorite
due to its quality cuts of meat, but the atmosphere alone may win over
non–meat eaters. In the canopied interior and cozy yet airy patio,
Guatemala and the Old West meet. The brick floors and abundance
of plants blend well with the picnic tables and old saddles. Although
grilled and barbecued meat dominate the menu, chicken and seafood
are also available. There is a full-service bar and a decent wine list. ⊠
12 Calle 2–25, Zona 10, ☎ *331–6240. AE, DC, MC, V.*

$$ ✕ **Olivadda.** In this ideal lunch spot, tasty Mediterranean cuisine is
served in a tranquil patio setting, with a melodic fountain surrounded
by flowers and hummingbirds. Traditional Middle Eastern appetizers
such as tabuleh, babaghanouj, and falafel can be followed by a chicken-
breast sandwich with cumin dressing or kafta in pita, delicately spiced
beef patties served in pita bread with tahini dressing. For dinner, don't
miss the *linguini à la Cataflana,* linguine with clams simmered in white
wine, Spanish sausage, and tomatoes. Finish your meal with a baked
apple stuffed with almond and cinnamon and baked with orange juice
and honey—a delicious apple pie without the calories. ⊠ *12 Calle 4–
21, Zona 10,* ☎ *331–0421. AE, DC, MC, V.*

$$ ✕ **Pizzeria Vesuvio.** The best pizza in Guatemala City can be found
here, baking in open brick ovens. Vesuvio has three locations in the
city, but this one, in Zona 10, is the most comfortable. In a family liv-
ing-room atmosphere with scenes of Naples on the walls, diners can
choose from a variety of pizza toppings or one of several pasta dishes.
All of the pasta is made in-house. A grand pizza, sufficient for two peo-
ple, ranks as one of the best cheap meals in the city. ⊠ *18 Calle 3–36,
Zona 10,* ☎ *337–1697. DC, MC, V.*

$$ ✕ **Siriacos.** Pasta, seafood, and steak are served in this cheerful bistro.
The decor is vaguely reminiscent of art deco, with tall black chairs, mod-
ern artwork on the walls, and bright primary-color tablecloths. Espe-
cially recommended are the Caesar salad and pasta of the day. ⊠ *1
Avenida 12–12, Zona 10,* ☎ *334–6316. AE, DC, MC, V. Closed Sun.
No lunch Sat.*

$$$$ ▥ **Camino Real.** Affiliated with the prestigious Westin hotel chain, the
★ Camino Real has been luxurious since it opened decades ago. Thanks
to understated elegance, every imaginable service, and a staff who
aims to please, it has wooed many a head of state, the latest being Pope

John Paul II in 1996. Past the hotel's tinker toy–style facade lies a long foyer with a low ceiling and wood-and-mirror walls surrounding over-stuffed leather chairs—all in subdued, dark tones that create a clubby atmosphere. A more spacious reception area has a view of the main swimming pool through tall glass windows. Carpeted rooms are done in dusty rose, green, and brown and furnished with stately carved wooden French provincial pieces. All rooms have electronic locks, tile baths, cable TV, voice mail, room safe, three phone lines, and a minibar. In addition, three executive floors have roomier units, a work area with desk, and double French doors looking out toward the volcanoes. The city's first high-tech convention center—adjacent to the hotel and man-aged by it—opened in 1996. ✉ *14 Calle and Avenida La Reforma, Zona 10,* ☎ *333–4633 or 800/228–3000 in the U.S.,* 📠 *337–4313. 378 rooms. 2 restaurants, bar, 2 pools, massage, sauna, spa, 2 tennis courts, shops, dance club, concierge, business services, convention center, meeting rooms, travel services. AE, DC, MC, V.*

$$$$ 🏨 **El Dorado.** Though its exterior is hardly attractive, El Dorado looks quite different inside. A small lounge to the right of the lobby offers rest to the weary: Guests plop down in the couches and armchairs and order cocktails each evening when jazz is played. Beyond the lobby are the bar, restaurants, shops, offices, and the Cabaña Club, an extensive spa and sports facility open to all guests. Rooms are carpeted, with pink, purple, and green floral patterns on the drapes and bedspreads. All have small balconies, cable TV, and tile baths. ✉ *7 Avenida 15–45, Zona 9,* ☎ *331–7777,* 📠 *332–1877. 259 rooms with bath. 2 restau-rants, bar, pool, hot tub, massage, sauna, spa, tennis, racquetball, squash, shops, travel services. AE, DC, MC, V.*

$$$$ 🏨 **Hotel Las Américas.** This 1993 hotel marketed under the Crowne
  ★   Plaza name is one of the newer posh spots in Guatemala City. Conve-niently located just 3 kilometers (2 miles) from the Aurora Airport, it displays a splendid vista of the surrounding volcanoes. Two giant glass elevators in the middle of the atrium-style lobby ascend to a dizzying view of the city and adjacent residential areas. Rooms on the south side offer the most impressive views of the airport, with Agua and the active Pacaya volcanoes in the background. The bright, modern rooms are decorated with pale-green carpeting and walls of whitewashed wood; all have a minibar and cable TV. The hotel is near several shop-ping centers, bars, and restaurants. ✉ *Avenida Las Americas 9–08, Zona 13,* ☎ *239–0666 or 800/465–4329 in the U.S.,* 📠 *239–0690. 200 rooms with bath. Restaurant, bar, pool, hot tub, sauna, travel ser-vices. AE, DC, MC, V.*

$$$$ 🏨 **Residencia Reforma.** Also known as the Casa Grande, this comfortable hotel in a stately former residence is a wonderful alternative to the mod-ern lodgings that predominate in the new city. You enter the grounds through iron gates: Both the classical statue at the center of the circu-lar driveway and the manicured lawn and gardens enhance the beauty of the white mansion before you. A comfortable lounge with a fire-place is situated just past the reception area, and the restaurant is in the former courtyard. It's decorated with cast-iron chairs surrounded by stout pillars and arches and the greenery of dangling philodendron against white walls. Rooms have tile floors and white walls decorated with Guatemalan art and are furnished with antiques and antique re-productions. In front, units open onto a balcony, but back rooms are quieter. Numbers 13 and 16 are next to a small garden courtyard. ✉ *Avenida La Reforma 7–67, Zona 10,* ☎ 📠 *331–7893. 28 rooms with bath. Restaurant. AE, DC, MC, V.*

$$$$ 🏨 **Stofella.** For those who want a small, quiet, intimate business hotel in the heart of posh Zona 10, this 1994 newcomer oozing with class and discretion is a real find. A small set of stairs at the end of a long walkway leads to a small flower-filled reception area decorated in soothing earth tones. A similar color scheme is carried out in the rooms, which have paisley-patterned bedspreads blanketing double beds and a small alcove/sitting room off the bedroom. For business travelers, a room safe, cellular telephone, fax, and computer can be rented, and secretarial services can be hired. A Jacuzzi, gym, and cozy clubby-looking bar are available for after-business hours. ⊠ *2 Avenida 12–28, Zona 10,* ☎ *334–6191,* ℻ *331–0823. 28 suites. Restaurant, bar, exercise room, laundry service, business services. AE, MC, V.*

$$$$ ⊡ **Viva Clarion Suites.** This new business-oriented hotel opened in business-convenient Zona 10 in October 1995 and touts everything the executive needs, from teleconferencing service to golf and tennis club access. All rooms are two-room suites with two cable TVs, a desk with phone plus laptop and modem jacks, a safe that operates by credit card, minibar, coffeemaker, voice mail, and electronic door lock. The luxurious tiled bathrooms each have a phone, bathtub/shower, hair dryer, and full array of toiletries. Executive floors have even more amenities. Also in the hotel are a sunny, spacious lobby sitting area, an art deco bar, and a restaurant overlooking a pool and an intriguing rock cliff. Service is very amenable, and a complimentary breakfast buffet is included. ⊠ *14 Calle 3–08, Zona 10,* ☎ *363–3333 or 800/221–2222 in the U.S.,* ℻ *363–3303. 171 suites. Restaurant, bar, pool, golf privileges, exercise room, shops, concierge, business services, meeting rooms, travel services, airport shuttle, car rental. AE, DC, MC, V.*

$$$ ⊡ **Cortijo Reforma.** Don't be put off by the pop music playing in the
★ lobby or the worn carpeting in the hallways. This hotel, part of the Dutch Golden Tulip chain, is otherwise very relaxing and comfortable. The T-shaped 12-story high-rise towers over Avenida La Reforma, not far from the U.S. Embassy and museums. It caters to lots of European tour groups, who fill its superspacious suites year-round. Each suite, ideal for families, has a double bed and sofa bed (easily sleeping four), full kitchen, and minibar. Most have 1½ bathrooms. From the upper floors, you can see three volcanoes surrounding the city, a particularly lovely sight in early morning or at sundown. A carpeted restaurant and bar, which resemble a Spanish tavern, are on the lobby level, and shops surround the exterior. The staff is well-seasoned and friendly. ⊠ *Avenida La Reforma 2–18, Zona 9,* ☎ *332–0712, 800/344–1212 in the U.S., or 0800/951–000 in London;* ℻ *331–8876. 50 suites. Restaurant, bar, barbershop, beauty salon, meeting rooms, travel services, airport shuttle, car rental. AE, DC, MC, V.*

$$$ ⊡ **Villa Española.** This popular hotel combines a motel-style design with Spanish architectural elements like barrel-tile roofs, white-stucco walls, and lots of arches. Three stories of rooms face a cobbled parking area, the far side of which is lined by a tile wall, fountain, and small garden. The rooms are fairly small and are furnished with colonial reproductions. Rooms on upper floors open onto wide balconies where you might hear a few parrots competing with the sound of nearby traffic from their perches by the garden. A restaurant is in the basement. ⊠ *2 Calle 7–51, Zona 9,* ☎ *332–3381,* ℻ *332–2515. 63 rooms with bath. Restaurant. AE, DC, MC, V.*

Jogging

The best area for jogging is **La Aurora Park** (⊠ Zona 13).

Nightlife and the Arts

The **Zona Viva** is the liveliest part of town at night, with everything from quiet bars to fashionable discos. **Scalinis** (⊠ 3 Avenida 11–35, Zona 10) is a popular, dark bar with stereo-driven pop music. You'll find young to middle-aged patrons at **New York** (⊠ 3 Avenida 11–65, Zona 10). For live music, try **Casa de Sherlocks** (⊠ Avenida Las Americas 2–14, Zona 13)—the music doesn't blare, much to the relief of a slightly older crowd. Good discos include **Loro's** (⊠ 1 Avenida 13–27, Zona 10), **Status** (⊠ 4 Avenida 3–49, Zona 10), and **Rich and Famous** (⊠ Upstairs at Los Proceres Mall on Avenida La Reforma and Blvd. de los Proceres, Zona 10). **El Establo** (⊠ Avenida La Reforma 14–32, Zona 10) and **Shakespeare's** (⊠ 13 Calle 1–51, Zona 10) are good places to meet foreigners and members of the American expatriate community. There are a number of new bars on Avenida Las Americas between 4 and 9 calles that are hip and youthful without being sophomoric.

Shopping

ANTIQUES

Casa San Antonio (⊠ 2 Avenida 12–75, Zona 10), **Centro Comercial de las Máscaras** (⊠ 13 Calle 2–01, Zona 10), **El Patio** (⊠ 14 Calle 0–25, Zona 10), **San Remo** (⊠ 14 Calle 7–61, Zona 9), and **Collection 21** (⊠ 13 Calle 2–75, Zona 10) are all good bets for antiques.

ART

Plural Galeria de Arte (⊠ Plaza Colonial, 1 Avenida 12–47, Zona 10) carries artwork by contemporary Guatemalan painters.

BOOKS

The **Camino Real hotel bookstore** (⊠ 14 Calle and Avenida La Reforma, Zona 10) has a small selection of English-language books. You can also find some English titles at **Cervantes** (⊠ Avenida La Reforma 13–70, Zona 9). In addition to new books, **La Plazuela** (⊠ 12 Calle 6–14, Zona 9) sells used novels. **Vista Hermosa** (⊠ 2 Calle 18–50, Zona 15) has a good selection of bird guides. The gift shop of the **Popol Vuh Museum** (⊠ Avenida La Reforma 8–60, Zona 9) has some interesting books. A big collection of paperbacks can be bought or borrowed from a bar by the name of **El Establo** (⊠ Avenida La Reforma 14–34, Zona 9). The **IGA** (Instituto Guatemalteco Americano, ⊠ *Ruta 1, 4–05, Zona 4,* ☏ *331–0022)* has an extensive English-language library, which is open to the public.

JEWELRY

As its name suggests, **El Angel Diamantino** (⊠ Geminis Mall, 4 Avenida 3–49, Zona 10) sells diamonds. **Jades S.A.** (⊠ Camino Real Hotel, Zona 10) sells jade. Not surprisingly, **La Esmeralda** (⊠ Camino Real Hotel, Zona 10) specializes in emeralds. **El Sol** (⊠ 13 Calle 2–75, Zona 10) is another of the city's better jewelers. **L'Elegance** (⊠ Camino Real Hotel, Zona 10) sells exquisitely crafted silver trays, jewelry boxes, vases, and place settings by the Italian designing family Camusso.

LEATHER

Shops selling fine leather products include **Arpiel** (⊠ Avenida La Reforma 15–54, Zona 9, and Avenida Las Americas 7–20, Zona 13), **Boutique Mariano Riva** (⊠ 12 Calle 1–28, Zona 9, and Avenida La Reforma 15–54, Zona 9), and **Tata** (⊠ Avenida La Reforma 12–81, Zona 10).

TÍPICA

An above-ground source for típica is the **Handicrafts Market** (⊠ 6 Calle in La Aurora Park, Zona 13). A number of stores in the city sell handicrafts and European styles mixed with traditional weaving. **Sombol** (⊠ 14 Calle and Avenida La Reforma, Zona 9) has an impressive collection of clothing, textiles, and paintings. The smaller **El Gran Jaguar** (⊠ 14 Calle 7–49, Zona 9) is across the street and down a bit; the much bigger and grander **San Remo** is next door (⊠ 14 Calle 7–61, Zona 9). **Típicos Reforma Utatlán** (⊠ 14 Calle 7–77, Zona 13) and **Galerías La Montaña** (⊠ 2 Calle 6–26, Zona 13) are on the same block.

Across Avenida La Reforma, in Zona 10, there are several small típica shops at the corner of 1 Avenida and 13 Calle. One block south is **Bizzarro** (⊠ 14 Calle 0–61, Zona 10). **Galería El Dzunun** (⊠ 1 Avenida 13–29, Zona 10) incorporates traditional weaving into elegant women's clothing, and **Belloto** (⊠ Avenida La Reforma 11–07, Zona 10) has a creditable selection. Also try the elegant **Casa Solares** (⊠ Avenida La Reforma 11–07, Zona 10).

Guatemala City A to Z

Arriving and Departing

BY CAR

All roads lead to Guate, or so it would seem, so if you enter by land it's easy to drive (or hop a bus) to the capital.

BY PLANE

Too close to the city (less than a mile from the heart of Zona 9 or 10), **La Aurora Airport** (☎ 332–6084 to 6087) is where most tourists arrive and depart. A taxi to the airport from downtown runs $6–$8.

Getting Around

BY BUS

The bus system seems chaotic, but the buses, though run-down, are cheap and plentiful. Locals are usually happy to point you to the one you need. The No. 82 and No. 101 are essential routes: They connect the new and old cities by running down La Reforma and through the heart of Zona 1. Other buses also service La Reforma and will say REFORMA on the windshield; likewise, buses that say TERMINAL all pass by the main bus station in Zona 4. Some of the No. 83 buses go to the airport, but only those marked AEROPUERTO. Watch your wallets and purses while on the bus and getting off.

BY TAXI

Taxis park throughout the city, usually near major hotels, parks, or intersections, but they don't cruise the main roads, as in most large cities. Guatemalan taxis—usually beat-up ramshackle cabs of every conceivable size, make, and color—don't have meters, so it's best to negotiate your fare before getting in. To summon a cab by phone, call 232–0342, 232–3236, or 253–3152 in Zona 1 or 331–2867, 331–3716, or 333–5765 in Zonas 9 or 10. Cabs are expensive; a minimum of $4 can be expected even for a ride of a few blocks.

Contacts and Resources

EMERGENCIES

Ambulance (Red Cross, ☎ 125). **Fire** (☎ 122 or 123). **Police** (☎ 120).

Hospitals. Hospital Herrera Llerandi (⊠ 6 Avenida 8–71, Zona 10, ☎ 334–5942 or 334–5959) and **Centro Médico** (⊠ 6 Avenida 3–47, Zona 10, ☎ 332–3555).

Pharmacies. When closed, all pharmacies should have a sign indicating which pharmacy in the area is *en turno* (open all night) that week. The following pharmacies are open 24 hours a day: **Farmacia San José** (⊠ 5 Avenida 16–56, Zona 1, ☎ 232–5314), **Farmacia Siñae Centro** (⊠ 4 Avenida 12–74, Zona 1, ☎ 251–5276), and **El Sauce Las Americas** (⊠ Calle 23 and Avenida Las Americas, Zona 13, ☎ 331–5996). **Farmacia Americana** (⊠ Zonas 9, 10, 13, 14, and 15, ☎ 360–2914) offers free delivery to hotels daily 9–6.

GUIDED TOURS

Many major tour operators offer half- and full-day city tours as well as day trips to nearby sites and towns. The oldest in the country is **Clark Tours** (⊠ Camino Real Hotel, Zona 10, ☎ 368–2056; Hotel Las

Américas, Zona 13, ☎ 339–0676; Zona 1, ☎ 251–4172; ☎ 800/223–6764, FAX 617/581–3714 in the U.S.). Other operators include **Unitours** (✉ Camino Real Hotel, Zona 10, ☎ 337–2858, 337–2861, or 333–4633, ext. 6939, FAX 337–2861; 7 Avenida 7–91, Zona 4, ☎ 331–4199 or 331–4103, FAX 334–2001), **Turansa** (✉ Km 15 Carretera Roosevelt, Zona 11, locale 69, ☎ 595–3575), **Jaguar Tours** (✉ Edificio Topazio Azul, 13 Calle 2–60, Zona 10, locale 1, ☎ 334–0421), and **Tropical Tours** (✉ 4 Calle 2–51, Zona 10, and 6 Avenida "A" 10–52, Zona 1, ☎ 334–5893).

VISITOR INFORMATION

Guatemala's ever-helpful government tourist office, **INGUAT** (✉ 7 Avenida 1–17, Zona 4, ☎ 331–1339 or 331–1333), is open weekdays 8–4 and Saturday 8–1.

ANTIGUA

The most Spanish of Guatemala's towns, Antigua is filled with vestiges of its past—cobblestone streets and vine-covered ruins—offering visitors a glimpse of its former grandeur. Founded in 1543, the city was called Santiago de los Caballeros de Guatemala (Saint James of the Knights of Guatemala), after the patron saint of the Spanish conquistadors. For 200 years, it served as the capital of an area that is now Central America and the Mexican state of Chiapas and, along with Lima and Mexico City, was one of the three great cities of the Americas.

By the late-19th century, Santiago had been destroyed by earthquakes and rebuilt several times and was a major political, religious, intellectual, and economic center. It had 32 churches, 18 convents and monasteries, a university, seven colleges, five hospitals, beautiful private mansions, wide cobblestone boulevards, and many small parks with fountains. However, late in 1773, powerful tremors struck again, reducing much of Santiago's painstakingly restored elegance to rubble. Reluctantly, the government relocated to a safer site in the Ermita Valley, where Guatemala City now stands.

Razed and haggard as it was, Santiago was further violated by the relocation project. Gradually, all that could be stripped and carried—art, furniture, doors, tiles, columns—was moved to the new capital. Even the city's name was lost; renamed Antigua (old) Guatemala, it's commonly referred to simply as Antigua.

Ironically, it is because Antigua was abandoned that it retains so much of its colonial charm. Only its poorest inhabitants stayed put after the capital was moved, but being of limited means, they could only repair the old structures, not build anew. In the 1960s protective laws took effect, and in 1972 the National Council for the Protection of Antigua Guatemala was formed to restore ruins, maintain monuments, and rid the city of such modern intrusions as billboards and neon signage. A quake in 1976 set restoration work back, but the council continues its efforts to rescue the city from centuries of neglect. It's hoped that the new Guatemalan president, a former minister of tourism, will allocate funds for a much-needed paint job.

Today you'll find a mountainside enclave of culture and the creative arts that is even more sophisticated than Guatemala City. The city of 60,000 combines the charmed remnants of its colonial past with both living proof of Guatemala's colorful indigenous culture and amenities of the modern world. Although Indians cannot afford to live here, many travel to the city daily to sell their wares. Another large and visible group is tourists. An ever-increasing influx of visitors has led to increased services, and the city now has some of the country's finest hotels and restaurants, a plethora of shops and galleries, and several dozen language schools that attract students from all over the world. Many foreigners live here permanently, running small lodgings and restaurants.

The most spectacular time to be in Antigua is Semana Santa (Holy Week), which lasts from Palm Sunday to Easter Sunday and features a series of vigils, colorful processions, and reenactments of Christ's last days in Jerusalem. You'll see Roman centurions charging on horseback through the streets, boulevards carpeted with colored sawdust and flowers, and immense hand-carried floats that wend their way through throngs of onlookers. The tourist office has schedules and maps with procession routes; just be aware that Antigua's hotels are booked up months ahead of time for this event.

Downtown Antigua

45 km (28 mi) west of Guatemala City

Even in the center of the metropolis, voices and colors seem subdued and tranquil. Often the splashing water of a nearby fountain is the loudest assault on the ears. As you wander the city's ancient avenues, you will continually be surprised by its restrained pace and by discoveries of tiny, private nooks and sanctuaries, picturesque corners, and views—past the whitewash and barrel tiles—of volcanoes that command the horizons. If you plan to spend much time in Antigua, Elizabeth Bell and Trevor Long's book, *Antigua Guatemala*, is an excellent guide and can be purchased in most of the city's bookstores. Note that some ruins are closed on Monday.

Numbers in the margin correspond to points of interest on the Antigua map.

🔟 A well-tended park with a pretty fountain surrounded by mellow old colonial buildings, **Plaza Mayor** (⊠ Between 4a and 5a calles ponientes and 4a and 5a avenidas surs) is the heart of the city. The place where most public events are staged, it's a favorite hangout of locals and visitors alike.

🔟 **Ayuntamiento** (City Hall) was the seat of the city council in colonial times, and it remains so today. The Ayuntamiento houses two museums: **Museo de Santiago** and **Museo del Libro Antiguo.** The former contains a collection of colonial art and artifacts, as well as the old city jail at the back; the latter displays Central America's first printing press and a collection of ancient manuscripts. ⊠ *4a Calle Poniente, on north side of Plaza Mayor.* 🎟 *Museum: 5¢.* ⊙ *Tues.–Fri. 9–4, weekends 9–noon and 2–4.*

NEED A BREAK?	Wander over to **Cookies, ETC.** (⊠ 4a Calle Oriente and 3a Avenida), a cute little four-table café and pastry shop serving 13 different kinds of homemade cookies filled with nuts, chocolate, coconut, oatmeal, and exotic spices.

🔟 Of the many that once were, only two chapels remain as part of the **Catedral** (cathedral), completed in 1680 and mostly destroyed in 1773. As in most other colonial cities' churches, the cross and altar are to the east so that parishioners face the Holy Land. ⊠ *4a Avenida Sur, on east side of the Plaza Mayor, no phone.* 🎟 *Free.*

🔟 In colonial times, **El Palacio del Capitán General** (Palace of the Captains General) housed royal offices. Today it contains the police department, army barracks, tourist office, and other government

104

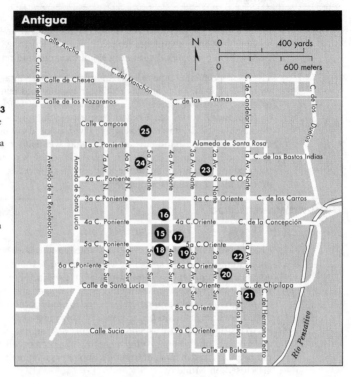

headquarters. Its 26 archways lend a stately appearance to the building, which has not been fully restored. ⊠ *5a Calle Poniente, on south
side of Plaza Mayor.* 🎫 *Free.*

⑲ On the former site of the University of San Carlos, the **Museo de Arte
Colonial** (Museum of Colonial Art) features a collection of mostly
colonial religious paintings and statues and a display on the Holy
Week celebrations. ⊠ *Calle de la Universidad and 4a Avenida Sur, no
phone.* 🎫 *5¢.* ⊙ *Tues.–Fri. 9–4, weekends 9–noon and 2–4.*

⑳ The **Santa Clara Convent** was founded in 1699 and became a large and
elaborate complex that at one time was home to 46 nuns. Destroyed
by an earthquake in 1717, it was rebuilt with the intentions of exceeding
its former glory in terms of size and complexity, only to suffer violent
tremors again in 1773. The convent collapsed and was finally abandoned. Roam the arches and garden courtyards of the ruins first; then
cross the street to a beautiful palm-lined park to the west, where you'll
find an assortment of handicrafts vendors and a public laundry area.
⊠ *6a Calle Oriente and 2a Avenida Sur, no phone.* 🎫 *$2 (valid for
other sites in the area).* ⊙ *Daily 9–5.*

㉑ Containing the most impressive church in the city, the **San Francisco
Monastery** was begun in 1579. Over the centuries, an assembly of structures that contained a college, church, hospital, and monastery grew
to cover four city blocks. The church houses some interesting religious
carvings but is most famous for the tomb of Friar Pedro de San José
de Betancur, who lived in the 17th and 18th centuries and was beati-
fied by Pope John Paul II for his good works. Many miracles are as-
cribed to him, and a sign in Spanish declares that petitioners need only
knock gently on his tomb to have their prayers answered. There's also
a small museum inside the chruch, which contains his letters, monk's

habit, wooden rosary beads, and hundreds of photos of people claiming to have had a miracle performed by the good brother. Also not to be missed is the view of Antigua and its environs from the second story of the ruins. ⊠ *7a Calle Oriente and 1a Avenida Sur, no phone.* 🖃 *5¢.* ☉ *Tues.–Sun. 9–5.*

㉒ **Casa Popenoe** is a beautifully restored colonial mansion. ⊠ *5a Calle Oriente and 1a Avenida Sur, no phone.* 🖃 *Free.* ☉ *Mon.–Sat. 3–5.*

★ ㉓ The former convent of the Capuchin nuns, **Las Capuchinas** was built in the mid-1700s. The ruins include a small museum, a lovely garden, former bathing halls, and a round tower lined with the nuns' cells, two of which have been restored to illustrate the nature of 18th-century cloistered life. Climb to the roof for a memorable view of the surrounding landscape. Although gaudily restored in part by ex-president Jorge Serrano Elias, this is still probably Antigua's finest ruin. ⊠ *2a Calle Oriente and 2a Avenida Norte, no phone.* 🖃 *$2 (also valid for 3 other sites in the area).* ☉ *Daily 9–5.*

㉔ The only remnant of the once enormous **Santa Catalina Convent** is a beautiful yellow arch that spans Calle de Santa Catalina (5a Avenida Norte). It was built to connect the buildings that flanked the road so the sisters could pass from one to the other unseen. ⊠ *Calle Santa Catalina and 2a Calle Poniente, no phone.* 🖃 *Free.*

NEED A BREAK? Near the Santa Catalina arch is the **Posada Don Rodrigo** (⊠ 5a Avenida Norte 17), a colonial mansion that is now a first-class hotel. Even if you don't stay here, it's worthwhile to wander around its courtyards and gardens and visit the restaurant for a snack or drink.

★ ㉕ The ancient church and monastery of the Mercedian fathers, **Nuestra Señora de La Merced** (Our Lady of the Merced) is one of the newer churches in town. Construction began in 1548, the 1717 earthquake destroyed it, and it was finally inaugurated in 1767, six years before the city was devastated by another quake and abandoned. La Merced survived the 1773 quake intact, however, thanks to architect Juan Luis de Dios Estrada. Learning from previous failures, he designed it with a squat appearance, thick walls, and small, high windows. Of particular note are the beautiful interior, stucco facade, and the immense fountain in the monastery, which stands to the left of the church. It is surrounded by a moat and footbridge. This place is particularly beautiful at sundown. ⊠ *1a Calle Poniente and 5a Avenida Norte, no phone.* 🖃 *16¢.* ☉ *Daily 9–6.*

Dining and Lodging

$$$ ✕ **El Sereno.** This exclusive restaurant serves fine food in the elegant atmosphere of a restored colonial house. Ring the bell at the entrance and you'll be led to a table in a small garden courtyard or to one of two rooms with corner fireplaces and walls adorned with paintings by local artists. The menu, which features a variety of dishes leaning toward a French or Italian influence and a few Guatemalan items, changes weekly. Selections include filet mignon with mushroom sauce, 5chicken pesto, fettuccine with a ham and cream sauce, and robalo in various guises. This spot is not suitable for children. You can count on impeccable service. ⊠ *4a Avenida Norte 16,* ☎ *332–0501. AE, MC, V. Closed Mon., Tues.*

$$$ ✕ **La Casarola.** The chef at this restaurant-gallery attempts to create Guatemalan nouvelle cuisine by using local products in original and sophisticated ways. Although the menu changes every 10 days, there are a few standards: Seafood bouillabaisse, which is cooked in a slightly spicy tomato sauce, and steak tenderloin with chiltepe sauce are two

standouts. El Picarón (the gallery) and the restaurant are in a renovated colonial house with fountains and mauve and peach walls lined with rotating exhibitions of photos and paintings. ⌧ *Callejón de la Concepción No. 7,* ☎ *332–0219. DC, MC, V. Closed Mon.*

$$$ ✕ **Welten.** Welten's owner says she wants her customers to feel as if
★   they're guests in her home, and until the bill arrives, you can easily fall under the illusion. Guests have their choice of seating locales: on a plant-filled patio with hammocks and cascading orchids, by a small pool and garden in the back, or in a couple of elegant dining rooms. Homemade pasta, like fettuccine with walnut sauce, and fish and meat dishes complemented by an assortment of sauces are served. Save room for dessert. ⌧ *4a Calle Oriente 21,* ☎ *332–0630. AE, DC, V. Closed Tues.*

$$ ✕ **El Oasis del Peregrino.** This out-of-the-way place, in a comfortable
★   old colonial home, resembles an expensive restaurant in everything but the price. The international menu reflects a strong German influence but serves pasta and vegetarian dishes as well. Guests may sit in the dining rooms decorated with traditional weaving or in a lush outdoor courtyard. ⌧ *7a Avenida Norte 96, no phone. No credit cards. Lunch weekends only; no dinner Wed.*

$$ ✕ **Fonda de la Calle Real.** An old Antigua favorite, this place now has two locations serving the same menu of Guatemalan and Mexican cuisine. The old restaurant is just off the plaza on 5a Avenida Norte and has upstairs seating with pleasant views, but the space is slightly cramped and dingy. The new restaurant, around the corner, is more spacious and attractive, as it's in a large colonial home with both indoor and outdoor seating. The mutual menu includes *queso fundido* (melted cheese with condiments and tortillas) and *caldo real* (a hearty chicken soup). Live music plays on weekends. ⌧ *3a Calle Poniente 7,* ☎ *332–0507; 5a Avenida Norte 5,* ☎ *332–2696. No credit cards.*

$$ ✕ **Katok.** This small corner restaurant has a bar whose picture window looks onto the street. Grilled beef is the mainstay, and service is friendly and efficient. ⌧ *4a Avenida Norte 2,* ☎ *332–0524. AE, MC, V.*

$ ✕ **Café Flor.** This cheerful family-run restaurant with friendly service switched from Mexican cuisine to Thai in 1996 but kept the same low prices. Breakfast is served, too. ⌧ *4a Avenida Sur 1, no phone. No credit cards. Closed Sun.*

$ ✕ **Caffé Opera.** Walking into this restaurant is like stepping into a fanciful pop-art version of an Italian café. The walls are lined with posters of European opera and film stars, the floors covered in large black and white tiles. Nothing on the ample menu of specialty coffees, sandwiches on fresh-baked bread, and exotic desserts (including homemade ice cream) is disappointing. The coffee is the best in Antigua. ⌧ *6a Avenida Norte 17,* ☎ *332–0727. No credit cards.*

$ ✕ **Doña Luisa's.** Named after the adored mistress of Spanish con-
★   quistador Pedro Alvarado, Doña Luisa's is the best breakfast spot in town and a bit of a local institution. A multitude of tables are scattered throughout a dozen rooms and on the balcony and terrace of this former colonial residence, but it's still not easy to get a seat. In addition to early morning specialties like fruit salad, pancakes, and freshly made bread and pies from the in-house bakery, there are plenty of sandwiches and sundry light fare for lunch and dinner patrons. Incidentally, the bulletin board is a great information resource for travelers. After breakfast, visit Doña Luisa's gravesite in town. ⌧ *4a Calle Oriente 11,* ☎ *332–2578. No credit cards.*

$ ✕ **Peregrinos.** A block off the main square, this cozy restaurant serves large portions of Mexican and Italian food at excellent prices. Guests may choose to sit on the raised stone patio or inside, where masks cover the terra-cotta walls. There is a happy hour from 5 to 7. ⌧ *4a Avenida Norte 1,* ☎ *332–0431. No credit cards.*

$ ✕ **Quesos y Vino.** This small Italian restaurant serves homemade
★ pasta, pizzas baked in a wood-burning oven, and a variety of cheeses
and home-baked breads. Choose from an impressive selection of imported wine sold by the bottle. ✕ *5a Avenida Norte 32, no phone. No
credit cards. Closed Tues.*

$ ✕ **Sueños del Quetzal.** This popular vegetarian restaurant is in the court-
yard of Antigua's newest shopping center, La Fuente. Classical music,
hanging plants, and white patio furniture all contribute to the peaceful atmosphere. The menu of international breakfasts, served until 11,
ranges from New York bagels and cream cheese to Mexican tofu
ranchero, beans, wheat tortillas, and avocado. Sueños also has one of
the best desserts in town: pie *de lodo* (mud pie), a decadently rich heated
chocolate brownie topped with coffee ice cream and chocolate syrup.
⊠ *La Fuente, 4a Calle Oriente 14,* ☎ *332–3760. No credit cards.*

$$$$ ✕▦ **Casa Santo Domingo.** In 1992, a truly elegant hostel was built
★ around the ruins of the ancient Santo Domingo Monastery. Long mellow passageways and snug little courtyards and gardens recall a by-
gone era. Dark, carved-wood furniture, yellow stucco walls, and iron
sconces preserve the monastic atmosphere. Fountains, hanging plants,
and colonial furniture decorate the public rooms. And luxury amenities abound, without detracting from the historical setting. Guest
rooms, for example, are the ultimate in comfort, with cable TV, hair
dryers, fireplaces, and deep bathtubs with Jacuzzis. Also within the ruins
is a restaurant of the same name, one of the city's most inspiring eateries. ⊠ *3a Calle Oriente 28,* ☎ *332–0140,* 🗛 *332–0102. 74 rooms
with bath. Restaurant, bar, pool, spa. AE, MC, V.*

$$$ ✕▦ **Posada Don Rodrigo.** A night spent in this restored colonial man-
sion—constructed some 250 years ago—is like stepping back in time.
All the rooms have high ceilings and are furnished with antiques, while
two lovely courtyards and several small gardens enhance the grounds.
The restaurant consists of an ancient dining hall with a tile fountain, fire-
place, and terrace whose garden is lit at night. Marimba music enlivens
every meal. Light sleepers, beware: The festivities here go long and lively
into the night. ⊠ *5a Avenida Norte 17,* ☎ 🗛 *332–0291,* 🗛 *in Guatemala
City 331–6838. 33 rooms with bath. Restaurant. AE, MC, V.*

$$$$ ▦ **Hotel Antigua.** As a tastefully rendered combination of colonial el-
★ egance and modern comfort, this property succeeds where others fail.
Guest rooms are furnished with fireplaces and cable TV and surround
a large lawn and pool. The oldest part of the hotel is a colonial-style
building that houses a restaurant, small bar, and sitting room (with a
view of the ancient San José el Viejo Church). ⊠ *8a Calle Poniente
and 5a Avenida Sur,* ☎ *332–0331,* 🗛 *332–0288. 60 rooms with
bath. Restaurant, bar, pool. AE, DC, MC, V.*

$$$ ▦ **Mesón Panza Verde.** Carpeted with pine needles, the main entrance
of this hotel opens up to a fountain, a garden, and an elegant Italian
restaurant. In back are the rooms, three of which are suites with fireplaces and shared patio; they are furnished with deep bathtubs and down
comforters. Suites sleep up to six with folding beds. ⊠ *5a Avenida Sur
19,* ☎ 🗛 *332–2925. 6 rooms with bath. Restaurant. DC, MC, V.*

$$$ ▦ **Quinta de las Flores.** In Antigua's newest hotel, the colonial and the
★ whimsical have been combined to create a beautiful sanctuary. While
the feel is that of a 19th-century hacienda, the grounds and rooms are
decorated with modern renditions of Guatemalan crafts. The gardens,
easily Antigua's prettiest, boast superb views of all three volcanoes. The
high-ceiling rooms all have chimneys, minibars, and a TV. The bun-
galows, which sleep up to five people, are completely furnished, from
a barbecue patio to toaster oven. A little outside of town, the hotel is

ideal for families or those seeking tranquillity. ⊠ *Calle del Hermano Pedro 6,* ☎ *332–3721,* FAX *332–3726. 8 rooms and 5 bungalows with bath. Restaurant, bar, pool, playground. MC, V.*

$$$ 🏨 **Ramada.** Just outside town on 9a Calle (a short walk will get you here), the Ramada is Antigua's most modern accommodation. Spacious, carpeted rooms furnished adobe-style have balconies or patios that border the handsome grounds. The Ramada has the most extensive facilities in the city—fireplaces, cable TV, spa with sauna and massage, spacious tile bathrooms, two swimming pools, tennis courts, and a bar and disco—but it lacks the colonial charm of other properties. The restaurant is adequate, but you'll find better food in town. Ask about special rates. ⊠ *9a Calle Poniente,* ☎ *332–3002 or 800/228–9898 in the U.S.,* FAX *332–0237. 156 rooms with bath. Restaurant, bar, 2 pools, massage, sauna, spa, tennis courts, dance club. AE, DC, MC, V.*

$$ 🏨 **Hotel Aurora.** This genteel hotel, run by the same family that opened it in 1923, is slightly overpriced but has an unbeatable location in the heart of the city. Comfortable colonial-style rooms with tile floors face a beautiful, huge flower- and plant-filled garden, which is surrounded by a tile portico equipped with plenty of cool rattan chairs for repose. The net effect is a truly quiet oasis in the midst of the hustle and bustle. Rooms have wooden furniture and old-fashioned clothes cupboards, and all have bathtubs and phones. Service is attentive. A small restaurant serves breakfast. ⊠ *4a Calle Oriente 16,* ☎ FAX *332–0217. 16 rooms with bath. Breakfast café. No credit cards.*

$$ 🏨 **Hotel Convento Santa Catalina.** This hotel, aptly named, is built amid
★ the ruins of the old convent. Spacious rooms face a verdant courtyard with an ancient fountain, where a smattering of tables and chairs enable you to sip a drink at leisure in this tranquil setting. ⊠ *5a Avenida Norte 28,* ☎ *332–3080,* FAX *332–3079. 18 rooms with bath. Restaurant. No credit cards.*

$$ 🏨 **Posada San Sebastian.** Here are two pleasant hotels with simple but comfortable rooms. The newly relocated 2a Avenida hotel is more attractive (an older, colonial home with a colorful bar), but the more modern 3A Avenida hotel benefits from its central location. ⊠ *3a Avenida Norte 4,* ☎ *332–2621, 7 rooms with bath; or* ⊠ *2a Avenida Sur 36A,* ☎ *332–3282, 6 rooms with bath. Bar. MC, V.*

$ 🏨 **Hospedaje Santa Lucía.** This lovely, quiet two-story colonial home
★ is the best private lodging of its kind in town. It has attractive whitewashed walls, beamed ceilings, and clean, cozy rooms with bed, table, and reading lamp. It's near the bus station, and you won't wear a hole in your pocket. ⊠ *Calzada de Santa Lucía 7, no phone. 12 rooms with bath. No credit cards.*

$ 🏨 **Posada Asjemenou.** You may not want to hear about yet another charming hotel in a former colonial residence, but the difference here is this one's a true bargain. The rooms are clean and comfortable, the staff friendly and eager. A small café in the hotel serves breakfast and snacks, and if you hanker for more substantial victuals, you can sample the owners' larger restaurant (off the Plaza Mayor), which specializes in pizza. Note: Take caution in leaving your valuables around, as thefts have been reported recently. ⊠ *5a Avenida Norte 31,* ☎ *332–2670. 8 rooms, 4 with bath. Café. MC, V.*

$ 🏨 **Villa San Francisco.** A block east of the Santa Clara ruins, this old hotel is a great value for the money, and there's always something going on. An upstairs walkway has nice views of the San Francisco church and all three volcanoes if the Monday wash is not in the way. A small travel agency in the lobby can provide bookings for mountain-biking and highland hiking tours. The modest rooms are clean, and two of them have TVs. ⊠ *1a Avenida Sur 15,* ☎ FAX *332–3383. 8 rooms, 6 with bath. Travel services. MC, V.*

Nightlife and the Arts
THE ARTS

The **Biennial Cultural Festival,** in February of odd-numbered years, is a relatively new venture but should become an important event. Throughout the year, various **musical and artistic productions,** including opera, are held in the city's ruins, churches, and galleries. Check with the tourist office for current listings.

BARS

You won't have trouble finding a bar in Antigua; many operate out of restaurants. Please note that many bars and clubs do not have telephones. **La Chimenea** (⊠ 4a Calle Poniente and 7a Avenida Sur) is a popular space with a little area for dancing to rock and pop music. An intimate jazz club, **Jazz Gruta** (⊠ Calzada de Santa Lucía Norte 17) has good music Monday–Saturday. **Latinos** (⊠ 7a Avenida Norte 16) features live music but is closed Sunday. The best of a cluster of bars that cater to young tourists is **Picasso's** (⊠ 7a Avenida). **Macondo** (⊠ 5a Avenida Norte, across from the Don Rodrigo) is frequently and festively crowded. If you want to dance the night away, try the Latin and rock rhythms at **Moscas y Miel** (⊠ 5a Calle Poniente 6). With a crowd of gringos and a TV, **Mistral** (⊠ 4a Calle Oriente 7) is Antigua's version of a sports bar.

VIDEO PARLORS

Video parlors, such as **Cinemala** (⊠ 2a Calle Oriente 2, at 4a Avenida Norte) and **Cine Cafe Bistro** (⊠ 5a Calle Oriente 11A), are a popular diversion in Antigua, since the local movie theater tends to run horrendous films. They serve refreshments and alcohol, and weekly schedules are posted on the town's many community bulletin boards.

Outdoor Activities and Sports

The **Ramada** (⊠ 9a Calle Poniente, ☎ 332–3002, ℻ 332–0237) has tennis courts, a spa, and swimming pools that can be used by nonguests for a small fee. Horses can be rented from a **private farm** (⊠ 2a Calle Poniente 31, no phone). **Mayan Mountain Bike Tour** (⊠ 1a Avenida Sur 15, ☎ 332–3383, ℻ 332–3580), run by a Swiss couple, offers a variety of daylong biking and hiking trips and longer rides in Antigua and the highlands. For those interested in touring, there's a **motorcycle rental outfitter** (⊠ 7a Calle Poniente 11, no phone). Expeditions up nearby volcanoes are organized by **Club de Andinismo Chicag** (⊠ 6a Avenida Norte 34, ☎ 332–3343). **Casa Andinista** (⊠ 4a Calle Oriente 5, no phone) rents camping equipment.

Shopping
BOOKS

Due to a sizable expatriate resident population, Antigua has the country's best selection of English-language reading material. **Casa Andinista** (⊠ 4a Calle Oriente 5) sells some hard-to-find titles, note cards, and posters and also rents paperbacks. **Rainbow Reading Room** (⊠ 7a Avenida Sur 8) has a good selection of English titles. **La Gallería** (⊠ 5a Avenida Sur 4) is on the west side of the Plaza Mayor. A smallish shop, **Un Poco de Todo** (⊠ 5a Avenida Sur 10) carries English-language books. A few blocks north of the central plaza, **El Pensativo** (⊠ 5a Avenida 29) carries mostly Spanish-language merchandise.

GALLERIES

El Sitio (⊠ 5a Calle Poniente 15), **Galería de Artes Integradas "Los Nazarenos"** (⊠ 6a Calle Poniente 13), and **Estípite** (⊠ 3 Avenida el Desengaño 22) carry local artists' works, including oils, ceramics, and wood carvings.

HANDICRAFTS

Handicrafts can be purchased from stalls in or near the **main market** (⊠ Off Calzada de Santa Lucía). A permanent outdoor típica market has been created by the **Companía de Jesus Church** (⊠ 4a Calle Poniente and 7a Avenida Norte), along the street and in the church's front courtyard.

Countless shops, scattered throughout the city, offer interesting selections. **Jade S.A.** (⊠ 4a Calle Oriente 34) is a small shopping complex that features jade and silver jewelry, clothing, temple rubbings, and handicrafts. For handpainted pottery, try **Casa Sol** (⊠ 5a Avenida Sur 14). **La Boutique** (⊠ 5a Calle Poniente 13) offers a variety of clothing made from typical weaving patterns and techniques. **Textiles Plus** (⊠ 6a Calle Poniente and Calle de Santa Lucía) has everything from bolts of fabric to pottery. **The Gift Shop** (⊠ 3a Calle Poniente 3b) carries a full range of kitchenware, from ceramics to beautiful hand-blown glassware. Check out the items at **Ojalá** (⊠ 4a Calle Oriente 35). **Ixchel** (⊠ 4a Calle Oriente 20) specializes in hand-spun wool rugs and blankets. For nice embroidery work, try **Colibrí** (⊠ 4a Calle Oriente 3). **The Kashlan Pot** (⊠ La Fuente, 4a Calle Oriente 14) has an excellent selection of *huipiles* (embroidered blouses). A number of foreign-owned shops specialize in taking local fabrics and designs and adapting them to sophisticated North American and European tastes; among them are **Casa de Las Bosas** (⊠ 4a Calle Oriente 22), **Que Barbara** (⊠ 4a Calle Oriente 37), and **IMGUASA** (⊠ 3a Calle Poniente 5). For New Age crystals and mineral rocks, aromatherapy fragrances, and other alternative healing aids, visit the new **Cinco Ajau** (⊠ 4a Avenida Norte 4, locale 3).

JEWELRY

Jade is mined countrywide but worked mostly in Antigua. One outstanding jade shop is **Platería Típica Maya** (⊠ 7a Calle Oriente 9). Smaller jade emporiums include **Casa del Jade** (⊠ 4a Calle Oriente 3), **Jade S.A.** (⊠ 4a Calle Oriente 12 and 4a Calle Oriente 34), and **Jade's J.C.** (⊠ 9a Calle Oriente 2).

Antigua's Outskirts

Cerro de la Cruz, a small park on a hill just north of Antigua, affords an excellent view of town and volcanoes Agua, Fuego, and Acatenango. Tourists have been robbed here in the past, and at press time, the tourist office was dissuading visitors from going here.

San Felipe de Jesús, just north of Antigua, has a small church with a famous Christ figurine and a silver factory. It is also the site of a saint's-day celebration on August 30.

A short drive southwest of Antigua brings you to **San Antonio Aguas Calientes,** a dusty little Indian village built around an ancient church.

San Juan del Obispo, on the slopes of Agua to the south of Antigua, is the site of a mansion built by Bishop Marroquín in the 16th century (only sporadically open to visitors). Consider the stop just for the view of the valley below.

Head a good way up Agua to **Santa Maria de Jesús,** and you'll be privy to a spectacular view.

Shopping

La Antigüeña is a standout jade shop in San Felipe de Jesús. **San Antonio Aguas Calientes** is a good spot to shop for típica.

Spa

Antigua Spa (⊠ 3 Avenida 8–66, Zona 14, Colonia El Campo, ☎ FAX 368–0707), about 3 kilometers (2 miles) from Antigua in the village of San Pedro El Panorama, is a perfect getaway for those in search of pampering. It offers massages and facials, as well as a series of package deals, some of which include an overnight in a suite.

Antigua A to Z

Arriving and Departing

BY BUS

Daily shuttle service (☎ 332–2928 or 332–2664 in Antigua, 595–3574 or 595–3975 in Guatemala City) connects Guatemala City and Antigua. After stopping at Guatemala City's major hotels, vans leave La Aurora Airport for Antigua at around 7:15 AM and 6:15 PM. The Guatemala City–bound shuttle picks up at Antigua's big hotels at about 4:45 AM and 3 PM. Tickets ($10 one-way airport transfer, $7 one-way between downtown hotels) can be purchased on board.

Buses leave Guatemala City (✉ 18 Calle and 4 Avenida or 15 Calle between 3 and 4 avenidas, Zona 1) for Antigua every 15 minutes from 6 AM until about 6 PM. From Antigua, buses depart from the market area (when they're full) on a similar schedule. The trip takes about an hour; in the evening it's slower and the buses more crowded.

To get to the Western Highlands, take one of the hour-long bus rides to Chimaltenango, where buses to most highland destinations can be flagged down on the Interamerican Highway. Buses leave hourly, 6 AM–6 PM, from behind the main market. Shuttles leave Antigua for Panajachel every day at 8 AM, arriving at 10 and returning at noon.

BY CAR

To reach Antigua, drive west out of Guatemala City via the Calzada Roosevelt, which becomes the Interamerican Highway, winding up into pine-covered hills with excellent views. At San Lucas, turn right off the highway and drive south to Antigua. If you're coming from the Western Highlands, turn right just after passing Chimaltenango.

BY TAXI

A taxi between Guatemala City and Antigua should cost about $25. Regular service is available between La Aurora Airport and Antigua. As usual, you'll have to haggle with drivers.

Getting Around

Antigua is not a large city and has no intracity service. People walk or take taxis, which are plentiful, cheap, and easy to flag down or get in the Plaza Mayor or near the bus station, behind the market. Remember to do a bit of haggling before beginning your ride.

To reach Antigua's outlying towns, you can either take any of several buses, which leave regularly from behind the main market and depart whenever the bus is full enough, or haggle with a taxi driver in the Plaza Mayor for a trip to several towns in one day.

Contacts and Resources

CAR RENTALS

Avis (✉ 5a Avenida Norte 22, ☎ 332–2692). **Tabarini** (✉ Ramada, 9a Calle Poniente, ☎ 332–3091).

EMERGENCIES

Police (☎ 332–0251).

Hospital. Pedro de Betancourt (✉ Calle de Los Peregrinos and 4a Avenida Sur, ☎ 332–0301).

Pharmacy. Farmacia Roca (✉ 4a Calle Poniente 11, ☎ 332–0612).

GUIDED TOURS
The tourist office (☞ *below*) can find you a qualified tour guide.

TRAVEL AGENCIES
Turansa (✉ Ramada, 9a Calle Poniente, ☎ FAX 332–2928; 5a Avenida Norte 22, ☎ FAX 332–2664). **Servicios Turisticos Atitlán** (✉ 6a Avenida Sur 7, ☎ 332–3371, FAX 332–0648).

VISITOR INFORMATION
The tourist office, **INGUAT** (✉ East end of El Palacio del Capitán General, 5a Calle Poniente, on south side of Plaza Mayor, ☎ 332–0763), is open daily 8–noon and 2–5.

THE WESTERN HIGHLANDS

The Western Highlands—*Altiplano* in Spanish—are home to the majority of Guatemala's Indians, most of whom live in small villages scattered across the isolated valleys that punctuate this rugged region. The villages themselves are colorful agricultural communities, integrated into a rural economy that functions through a series of weekly markets, and the inhabitants maintain traditions that have dominated the lives of their people for centuries. In addition to being the home of a striking and intriguing people, the highland villages are invariably surrounded by spectacular scenery, composed of volcanic cones, granite peaks, pine-draped hillsides, pastoral plains, and lush tropical valleys.

The highlands are bounded in the south by a chain of volcanoes that begins near Guatemala City and stretches northwest toward Mexico, and in the north by a series of mountain ranges that tower above the rest of the country. Here most villages are accessible only by foot or on horseback, and many of them have rustic hotels for overnights. Though the precipitous terrain and lack of infrastructure make it difficult to visit the majority of highland villages, some are quite easy to reach, and the particular beauty and uniqueness of both the area and its inhabitants are guaranteed to reward any extra effort required to explore the region's farther reaches.

The Cuchumatanes Mountains are an excellent area for hiking, especially in the area of Todos Santos and the Ixil Triangle. Topographical maps can be obtained from the **Instituto Geográfico Militar** (✉ Avenida Las Americas 5–7, Zona 13, Guatemala City, ☎ 332–2611), but the army won't release maps of many areas. If you want to climb volcanoes, it's best to climb with a guide, or consult one before ascending, since some of the country's volcanoes harbor bandits (☞ Security *in* Guatemala A to Z, *below*). Several tour companies arrange volcano trips.

The highland climate is pleasant, with cool nights and warm afternoons, and no doubt inspired a European traveler more than a century ago to dub the country "the land of eternal spring." Temperatures often reach 70°F–80°F (21°C–26°C) in the afternoon, but they can drop to 40°F–50°F (4°C–10°C) at night, so a sweater or warm jacket is essential for the evenings.

Lake Atitlán, which lies at the foot of three volcanoes at the southern end of the highlands, is an awesome sight that has impressed many a visitor over the centuries. The conquistador Pedro Alvarado stopped between battles to marvel at the area's timeless beauty, and since his day the lake has inspired the likes of John L. Stephens and Aldous Huxley. Atitlán means "place of the great waters" in Nahuatl, the language of Alvarado's Mexican troops, and the lake's cool depths are both inviting and impressive: On a moonlit night or early in the morning the water can be as smooth as glass, like an immense liquid mirror reflecting mas-

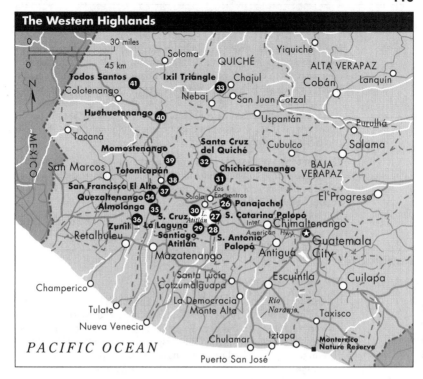

sive volcanic cones. But in the early afternoon, a regular wind known as the *xochomil* blows across the lake, and the surface turns choppy and defiant. The xochomil can turn Atitlán's waters violent in a hurry, creating dangerous currents, so water sports and trips in small boats are advisable only during the morning.

The lake measures about 13 by 17 kilometers (8 by 11 miles), its surface is at some 5,200 feet above sea level, and it is more than 1,000 feet deep, though in some parts its depth has yet to be determined. Its volcanic origin is apparent from the steep ridges that surround it. From the southern shore rise three massive volcanoes. Viewed from the town of Panajachel, San Pedro Volcano (9,920 feet) is on the right, Tolimán (10,340 feet) is on the left, and Atitlán (11,560 feet) is behind Tolimán. Both Tolimán and San Pedro volcanoes are extinct, and Atitlán has been dormant since 1853.

The lake also has its mysteries: Not only was the expedition that attempted to map its bottom unsuccessful in determining the depth at some points, but because the lake is surrounded by hills, it pours into no rivers and instead drains through underground passages. During the 1976 earthquake, the level of the lake dropped 6½ feet, a shift that is still visible on some parts of the shore.

Complementing the natural beauty of the lake are 13 charming villages that stand on its shores. The towns are predominantly quiet agricultural communities, rich in indigenous culture. Most women and many men wear traditional costumes, which vary from town to town, and nearly everybody speaks one of two Maya languages: Tzutujil to the south and Cakchiquel to the north. The inhabitants of the area are a proud, independent, and conservative people whose traditions should be respected. Though the lake is ideal for swimming, bathing should never be done in the nude, and when walking in the villages, make sure you're decently dressed.

In addition to swimming—which, by the way, should always be undertaken upstream of towns to avoid raw sewage—there are other outdoor activites to be enjoyed on the lake. Boating options include ferries, which run regularly between major towns; small motor boats, which can be hired along with drivers; and plastic "kayaks," pedal boats, and Windsurfers, which can be rented at the public beach. Lake Atitlán is stocked with black bass, but no one rents fishing equipment here, so you'll have to bring your own.

The first towns discussed below are those that rim the lake. Those that follow are part of further ventures north into the highlands. Roads are sparse and tend to radiate out from the bigger towns to reach the more remote highland villages.

Numbers in the margin correspond to points of interest on the Western Highlands map.

Panajachel

㉖ *110 km (68 mi) northwest of Antigua*

On the northern shore of Lake Atitlán, Panajachel is a popular base for exploring, since it's easy to reach and has a wide selection of hotels and restaurants. A few decades ago, this was just a quiet Cakchiquel village, but it has since grown into a sprawling tourist town and hippie hangout with little character. The old part of town, up toward the valley, hasn't lost its charm, however, and during Sunday markets it looks much like any other highland village.

Calle Santander, the main drag, has a bank; the Guatel office, where you can make long-distance calls; and a bevy of restaurants, shops, and street vendors along its course to the waterfront.

NEED A
BREAK? **The Deli 2** (⊠ End of Calle Santander) is a great spot for breakfast, lunch, or a snack by the lake. It has good coffee, fresh bagels, pastries, and an unusual menu that includes falafel and hummus.

Some of Panajachel's most popular attractions are the **public beach and docks** (⊠ Calle Rancho Grande).

Dining and Lodging

$$ ✕ **Al Chisme.** This popular restaurant owned by an American woman serves good food in a relaxed atmosphere. Seating is on a covered terrace or in the main dining room, decorated with black-and-white photos of some of Panajachel's more interesting faces. There's usually rock and roll playing on the stereo, and many of the regulars are a testament to the town's reputation as a hippie hangout. As a popular breakfast spot, Al Chisme serves homemade bagels and pastries, but the lunch and dinner menu is even better, with a selection ranging from chicken cordon bleu to shrimp curry crepes to three-cheese lasagna. ⊠ *Avenida de los Arboles, no phone. No credit cards. Closed Wed.*

$$ ✕ **Casablanca.** This restaurant right on the main street has a reputation for serving some of the best food in town. Seating is in a woodtrimmed and white-walled dining room, with windows overlooking the street and artwork by Guatemalan talent enhancing the simple, tasteful decor. Or you may elect to sit upstairs at one of the few tables on the more private upper level. Occasionally the management hires musicians for entertainment. The menu is ample—though more European than Guatemalan—and includes a selection of soups and salads, pasta,

meat dishes, and seafood. ⊠ *Calle Santander, across from Maya Inn,* ☎ *362–1015. DC, MC, V.*

$$ ✕ **El Bistro.** This small Italian restaurant, among the best Panajachel
★ has to offer, is hidden behind a low wall and iron gate where the main
drag hits the lake. A couple of tables are set up in a garden, where hummingbirds dart among flowering vines. Inside are two cozy, intimate
dining rooms. All of the simple but delicious food, from the tasty
bread to the fresh pasta, is homemade. Two standout specialties are
the fettuccine *arrabiata,* with a slightly spicy tomato sauce, and the steak
au poivre, cooked in a wine sauce and served with fresh vegetables. ⊠
End of Calle Santander, no phone. No credit cards. Closed Tues.

$$ ✕ **La Laguna.** On a small street just east of Calle Santander, this comfortable restaurant is set in a former residence surrounded by a large
lawn. Seating is on the porch or in scattered rooms in the old house,
which is decorated with wooden masks and other local handicrafts.
The slightly dark, candlelit interior and mellow jazz or Latin American music on the stereo make it the perfect place for a romantic dinner. Selections range from the traditional *pepian de pollo* (chicken in
a spicy sauce) to black bass from Lake Atitlán. The fixed-price menu
is a good deal. ⊠ *South side of street,* ☎ *362–1231. DC, MC, V.*

$ ✕ **El Patio.** Across the street and north of the Guatel building, this restaurant can be recognized by the patio to which it owes its name. Though
the patio itself is a pleasant spot to sit and watch the world go by, most
of the restaurant's seating is indoors, in a large dining room with little ambience. It's a fairly popular spot for breakfast, but the lunch and
dinner menu offers greater variety, with items like filet mignon, chicken
à la king, roast pork, and a barbecue special on Sundays. ⊠ *Calle Santander,* ☎ *362–2041. DC, MC, V.*

$$$$ ✕🛏 **Hotel Atitlán.** The area's most luxurious and expensive hotel is on
★ a quiet cove about a mile east of town. An older, Spanish-style inn, it
consists of a main building—with reception, bar, restaurant, conference
rooms, and gift shop—flanked by two-story wings that form a semicircle around a pool and gardens. The extensive grounds include a long
stretch of beach and a wooded region traversed by footpaths. Rooms
have a colonial decor, with tile floors, carved wooden furniture, and
handwoven blankets and rugs, and each unit has a balcony or patio with
a view of the lake and tropical gardens. Even if you don't stay here, it's
worth stopping by for a meal or drink, as the view of the water from
both the bar and restaurant is wonderful, especially at sunset. To get
here, take the main road out of town and look for a sign marked HOTEL
at a fork in the road. ⊠ *2 km (1 mi) east of Panajachel,* ☎ FAX *362–
1441 or 337–2557 in Guatemala City. 64 rooms with bath. Restaurant, bar, pool, tennis court, beach, shop, meeting rooms. MC, V.*

$$$ ✕🛏 **Cacique Inn.** This quiet hotel is one block off the main street, and
though it doesn't have a view of the lake, it has an excellent restaurant, a swimming pool, and a lovely garden. Spacious though sparsely
decorated rooms with private baths are in two-story buildings, and large
sliding-glass doors open onto terraces and a garden. The rooms may
seem a bit cool thanks to tile floors and small rugs, but they all have
fireplaces that can warm them up quickly if need be. The hotel grounds
are surrounded by a wall, which makes the terraces and patio by the
pool good private havens for relaxing. The Cacique's restaurant is one
of the best in town, offering an ample selection of international and
Guatemalan cuisine. Cacique's agreeable chefs will sometimes even prepare dishes that aren't on the menu. Room rates include breakfast. ⊠
Calle del Embarcadero, ☎ FAX *362–1205. 33 rooms with bath. Restaurant, bar, pool. MC, V.*

$$$$ ⊞ **Hotel del Lago.** This six-story building behind the public beach is Pana-jachel's biggest and most modern hotel. It may not look like much from the outside, and the colorful contemporary interior is a far cry from those of more traditional hotels, but it is comfortable, conveniently located, and offers first-class services and great lake views. Rooms feature wall-to-wall carpeting, firm double beds, cable TV, large bathrooms, and either balconies or patios (first floor) with Atitlán vistas. There's an airy bar with a verdant backdrop, and the adjacent restaurant that looks onto the pool is huge. ⊠ *Calle Rancho Grande,* ☎ *362–1555 or 334–4545 in Guatemala City,* ℻ *362–1562. 100 rooms with bath. Restaurant, bar, pool, hot tub, massage, sauna, meeting rooms. AE, DC, MC, V.*

$$$ ⊞ **Hotel Vision Azul.** On the road to the Hotel Atitlán, this place is a smaller, cheaper version of that venerable hotel—not as nice but at half the price. Rooms in the main building are decorated in the colonial style, with antique reproductions and traditional weavings, and each one opens onto a small porch or balcony with a distant view of the lake. A series of simple bungalows, with three beds each, sit along the road, and while they're not as attractive as the main rooms, they are very private. The hotel's extensive grounds include a long stretch of waterfront, but all the rooms are set several hundred feet off the lake, on the south side of the road. ⊠ *Less than 2 km (1 mi) east of Pana-jachel,* ☎ ℻ *362–1426. 25 rooms and 8 bungalows with bath. Restaurant, bar, pool, beach. AE, DC, MC, V.*

$$ ⊞ **Hotel Monterrey.** This is the least expensive hotel on the waterfront, and though the two-story cement building isn't attractive by any standards, just wait! Every single unit—clean and with bathroom—has a view of the lake that easily makes up for the lack of decor. There are nice gardens and a deck overlooking Atitlán, as well as a private beach and a restaurant. ⊠ *Waterfront between Calles del Embarcadero and Santander,* ☎ *362–1126. 30 rooms with bath. Restaurant, bar, beach. No credit cards.*

$$ ⊞ **Hotel Regis.** This hotel, conveniently located across from Guatel in the heart of town, isn't quite as attractive or quiet as Rancho Grande, but it's less expensive. A group of bungalows is spread out around not very large but well-tended grounds, where there's a small playground and a Jacuzzi. Room decor is an attempt at the popular colonial motif. Several bungalows have fireplaces, and a couple can sleep six. ⊠ *Calle Santander,* ☎ *362–1149,* ℻ *362–1152. 19 rooms with bath. Hot tub, playground. MC, V (10% surcharge).*

$$ ⊞ **Müllers Guest House.** This simple, tasteful four-room hotel a block from the old town is reminiscent of a European bed-and-breakfast. The rooms are immaculate and very un-típica, with blond hardwood floors and ceilings, and pastel colors. Breakfast in the comfortable, homey sitting room is included in the price. ⊠ *Calle Rancho Grande. Reservations,* ☎ *337–0656 in Guatemala City. 4 rooms with bath. No credit cards.*

$$ ⊞ **Rancho Grande.** About halfway between the beach and old town is Rancho Grande, a series of bungalows that flank the street of the same name. This bed-and-breakfast was opened around 1950 by German immigrant Milly Schleisier, who melded the designs of country houses in her homeland with the colorful culture of her adopted residence. Since 1975 it has belonged to Marlita Hannstein, who has maintained the level of comfort and service established by Schleisier. Every room is unique, but all are spacious, with wood ceilings, white stucco walls, tile floors, and locally woven rugs and bed covers. Some bungalows sleep five, the suite has a fireplace and cable TV, and all units have porches and are separated by lawns and gardens. ⊠ *Calle Rancho Grande,* ☎ *362–1554,* ℻ *362–2247. 12 rooms with bath. Breakfast room. DC, MC, V.*

$ 🏨 **Hotel Galindo.** This hotel is conveniently located in the heart of town behind its own spacious restaurant. Rooms are small and undecorated but surround a lush garden courtyard. Behind the courtyard are several suites, which are considerably larger and have separate sitting rooms and fireplaces. The restaurant is airy and attractive, but better food can be found nearby. Note: The hot water is unreliable. ✉ *Calle Principal,* ☎ *362–1168. 18 rooms with bath. Restaurant. No credit cards.*

$ 🏨 **Hotel Maya Kanek.** On the main street at the edge of the old town, this place is in a quiet area with fewer foreigners than on the tourist side of Panajachel. Arranged like a miniature motel, rooms surround a paved parking area. They're rather small and have little decor to speak of, but they're clean and have firm mattresses. The owner is a friendly fellow, and he has assembled a thorough list of local boat and bus schedules in the lobby. ✉ *Calle Principal,* ☎ *362–1104. 26 rooms with bath. No credit cards.*

Nightlife and the Arts

This resort town probably has the liveliest nightlife in the highlands, which doesn't mean much. The **Circus Bar** (✉ Calle de los Arboles) is a popular night spot that also serves good food. **Chapiteau** (✉ Calle de los Arboles) is a large bar and disco that sometimes offers live music. For a more sedate evening, try the video lounge at the **Zanahoria Chic restaurant** (✉ Avenida de los Arboles). The **Grapevine** (✉ Calle Santander) has both a video lounge and a happy hour, from 7 to 9.

Shopping

Buying and selling is almost as popular in Panajachel as it is on Wall Street, and everywhere you look, someone is hawking típica. Local merchants have assembled an impressive array of goods from around the lake as well as from throughout Guatemala, and prices are competitive. Calle Santander is lined with **vendors,** who hang their wares from fences and makeshift stalls. **Casa Alegri** (✉ East side of Calle Santander), a large boutique, has an interesting selection and good prices. As suggested by its name, **Mayan Relics** (✉ Calle Monte Rey) sells a variety of local and other goods at a bargain. **Mayan Palace** (✉ Calle Santander) has an amazing collection of antiques, although prices are high and the authenticity of some goods may be questionable. **Galeria** (✉ Calle Rancho Grande) features both antique and contemporary art.

Santa Catarina Palopó

㉗ *4 km (2½ mi) east of Panajachel along a dirt road*

Visitors are surrounded by the brilliant blues and greens of traditional native *huipiles* (embroidered blouses) as they walk down the cobblestone streets of this picturesque town. The hotel Villa Santa Catarina, at the lakeside entrance to town, boasts magical views of the water and volcanoes.

Dining and Lodging

$$$ ✕🏨 **Villa Santa Catarina.** This hotel, housed in a long, two-story yellow building with adobe tile roof, offers spectacular views of the lake and volcanoes. Guest rooms are small, with hardwood floors and ceilings, peach walls, and típica bedspreads; each has a private balcony. The restaurant serves typical Guatemalan dishes such as *pepian* (chicken in a spicy gravy) and fresh robalo. Also on site is a large pool. ✉ *Calle de la Playa,* ☎ *362–1291. 31 rooms with bath. Restaurant, bar, pool, windsurfing, waterskiing. MC, V.*

San Antonio Palopó

28 *6½ km (4 mi) east of Santa Catarina Palopó*

Slightly larger than Santa Catarina Palopó, this hill town has the feel of a quiet fishing village. Women dress in white blouses with colored stripes, and men wear headdresses and checked shirts. The main handicraft here is mats woven from water reeds.

Lodging

$$ ⊞ **Terrazas del Lago.** This very basic hotel on the town's public beach is decorated with floral-pattern stone tiles. Guest rooms have stone walls, wood tables, and iron candlesticks; those in front have patios with lake vistas. Breakfast and sandwiches can be prepared for guests in a tiny kitchen in the back. ⊠ *Calle de la Playa,* ☏ *232–8741 in Guatemala City. 14 rooms with bath. No credit cards.*

Santiago Atitlán

★ **29** *21 km (13 mi) west of San Antonio Palopó, 31 km (19 mi) south of Panajachel*

The fascinating Santiago Atitlán, across the lake from Panajachel, is the largest and most traditional of the lake towns and capital of the Tzutuhil Indians, a proud people who have long resisted political domination. The village is famous for the quality of its weaving, and most people still wear the striking traditional costume, including, for women, a headdress resembling a bright red halo. It is also one of the few places where people actively worship Guatemala's cigar-smoking Maximón, a Maya god masquerading as a Catholic saint. Though it is invaded by tourists daily and filled with aggressive hawkers, Santiago Atitlán remains a lovely village.

Dining and Lodging

$$ ✕⊞ **Posada de Santiago.** This fabulous hotel is sandwiched between
★ two volcanoes on the shores of a lagoon. Here in this old-fashioned Indian village, the owners have brought the friendliness of northern California as well as incredible cooking. Bungalows, including one with two suites that was added in 1995, have carved-wood doors, stone walls, fireplaces, and thick wool blankets on the beds. The restaurant serves exquisite specialties, such as smoked chicken píbil in a tangy red sauce and Thai coconut shrimp, and boasts an extensive wine list to boot. Also on the premises is a small store, and canoe and mountain-bike rentals are available. ⊠ *La Orilla de la Laguna, south edge of town,* ☏ FAX *362–7167. 7 bungalows with bath. Restaurant, mountain bikes. No credit cards.*

Santa Cruz La Laguna

30 *40-minute boat ride west of Panajachel*

A highlight of this little village perched on a hill is a small but beautiful **adobe church,** whose walls are lined with carved wooden saints.

Once you've seen Santa Cruz, you can head to nearby towns. A wonderfully scenic four-hour walk west to **San Marcos de La Laguna** guides you past several tiny mud villages where women sit and weave in front of their houses.

Dining and Lodging

$$ ✕⊞ **Arca de Noé.** This rustic lakeside hotel boasts magnificent views, friendly owners, and delicious home cooking. The guest rooms, housed in several attached wood and stone bungalows, are small but neat, with low ceilings. Electricity is solar-powered, and there is no hot water. Meals

are served family-style in the main building, which resembles a New England farmhouse. The menu changes constantly, but each meal comes with fresh vegetables and bread right out of the oven. ⊠ *Main dock,* ☎ FAX *362–1196. 8 rooms, 5 with bath. Restaurant, boating. No credit cards.*

Santo Tomás Chichicastenango

③ *37 km (23 mi) north of Panajachel, 90 km (56 mi) north of Santa Catarina Palopó, 108 km (67 mi) northwest of Antigua*

The main attraction in Chichicastenango, a colorful and accessible highland town, is the **market.** One of the largest in the country, it's held every Thursday (5:30 AM and 1:30 PM) and Sunday (5:30 AM and 3 PM) and, like all other highland markets, was originally the basis of local commerce. Since its fame has grown, however, the local market has been pushed to the periphery. The bulk of today's business is between tourists—arriving en masse twice weekly—and Indian merchants from throughout the highlands, who come to sell their wares to the foreigners. The night before market day is in many ways more intriguing than the event itself, as vendors set up their stalls with pleasant anticipation and the town still belongs to the Indians.

Though the buying and selling may steal the show, Chichicastenango would be well worth visiting if there were no market at all. The quiet town, which stands on a hill surrounded by pine forest, is still tradition-bound in many respects, as Indians proudly worship Christian and pagan deities side by side. This mixing of Catholicism and Maya ritual can be witnessed at **Santo Tomás Church** (⊠ Main plaza), in the heart of the market. Built in the mid-1500s on the site of a Maya altar, Santo Tomás is busy with devotees all day and late into the night. Its steps are usually engulfed in a cloud of copal incense, which worshipers burn while performing rituals before entering the church. You may enter through a door on the right side of the church, and you must refrain from taking photographs while inside.

Capilla de Calvario (Calvary Chapel, ⊠ Across main plaza from Santo Tomás Church) doesn't attract the devotion that its neighbor does but affords a nice view of the market. A little **museum of pre-Columbian artifacts** (⊠ Adjacent to Santo Tomás Church) features the private collection of a local priest.

On a hill a short walk out of town is **Pascual Abaj,** a Maya shrine composed of a waist-high carved stone idol. Each day, the faithful perform prehispanic rituals with incense, candles, and offerings of flowers to the deity. If you don't want to pay a local to take you here, just follow 9 Calle out of town and look for mask-shop signs on the left, which mark the footpath up the hill.

Dining and Lodging

$ ✕ **El Chapincito.** This second-floor restaurant has an enormous dining room that gets packed on market days. It is primarily a steak house, but the menu also features chicken, pork, and pasta. All meals include a bowl of soup. ⊠ *Giron Shopping Arcade, no phone. No credit cards.*

$ ✕ **Las Brasas.** The former chef at the Hotel Santo Tomás opened this breezy steak house overlooking the market, where bright tablecloths and brick walls create a cheery atmosphere. Though the mainstay is steak, there are a fair number of other options, including a vegetarian plate. ⊠ *5 Avenida Gucumatz 6–30, 2nd level,* ☎ *256–1006. MC, V.*

$ ✕ **Tziguan Tinamit.** This corner restaurant is probably the best of Chichicastenango's meager selection of eateries. Both the decor and the menu are pretty basic: You can count on a selection of beef, chicken, or fish served with rice, beans, and a salad. The most interesting item is pizza, which isn't half bad. Breakfast is also served. ⊠ *1 block north of plaza,* ☎ *256–1144. MC, V.*

$$$ ✕⛱ **Hotel Santo Tomás.** A newer hotel built in the Spanish style, this is Chichicastenango's second best. Rooms are spacious and decorated with traditional textiles and antique reproductions, and each one has a fireplace. The back of the hotel is quieter, whereas front rooms overlook the town. Attendants wear traditional costumes, but service is less personalized than it is at the Mayan Inn. To the left of the reception desk is an unmarked room full of masks, statues, and pottery. The large restaurant features a lunch buffet on market days, and on the upper level of the hotel are a heated pool and small spa. The lodging is two blocks east of the plaza. ⊠ *7a Avenida 5–32,* ☎ *256–1316,* 🆇 *256–1306. 43 rooms with bath. Restaurant, bar, pool, hot tub, sauna, exercise room. AE, DC, MC, V.*

$$$ ✕⛱ **Mayan Inn.** Founded, owned, and operated by the Clark family ★ since 1932, the Mayan Inn is still one of the most charming hotels in the country. Rooms, furnished with fireplaces, antiques, and Guatemalan weavings and art, surround a series of beautifully maintained garden courtyards, and newer units look onto the forested hills around town. Highly recommended are the lodgings across the street from the office, in the same compound as the bar and restaurant. They are built into the hillside at different levels; the lower the level, the more likely you'll have a view of the town's cemetery (not as lugubrious as it sounds) and the surrounding pine forests. Service is excellent: An attendant in traditional costume, assigned to each room, does everything from lighting the fire to serving dinner. Meals are taken in stately old dining halls with fireplaces, with a set menu that changes daily. The restaurant is open from 7 to 9 AM, noon to 2 PM, and 7 to 9 PM. ⊠ *1 block west of the plaza, behind Capilla de Calvario,* ☎ *256–1176 or 331–0215 in Guatemala City,* 🆇 *256–1212. 30 rooms with bath. Restaurant, bar. AE, DC, MC, V.*

$$$ ⛱ **Hotel Villa Grande.** This large new luxury hotel at the entrance to town offers the modern amenities absent from most other Chichicastenango hotels but also lacks their charm. The hotel consists of five unattractive buildings, most of which have panoramic views of town. Air-conditioned guest rooms are small, with peach walls and típica bedspreads, while the more spacious suites have fireplaces. ⊠ *Cantón Pachoj Alto,* ☎ 🆇 *256–1053. 67 rooms with bath. 2 restaurants, bar, indoor pool, hot tub, health club. MC, V.*

$$ ⛱ **Hotel Chiuguila.** This pleasant little hotel is in an older building a few blocks north of the plaza. A variety of rooms face a cobblestone courtyard, which is used for parking. The tile portico that most rooms lead off of has some chairs, tables, and potted plants, and there is also a small restaurant with a limited menu. Rooms with shared or private baths are available; the more expensive ones have fireplaces and include a couple of suites with little sitting rooms. ⊠ *5a Avenida 5–24,* ☎ 🆇 *256–1134. 21 rooms, 15 with bath. Restaurant. AE, MC, V.*

$ ⛱ **Hospedaje Salvador.** Sitting in a quiet corner of town, down the hill from the Santo Tomás Church, is this colorful budget hotel. Rooms surround a large cobblestone courtyard decorated with statues and potted plants, and facing the entrance is a small shrine shared by the Virgin Mary and a Maya god. Though rooms are a bit musty, beds are a bit old, and hot water is available only for a couple of hours in the morning, what El Salvador lacks in comfort it compensates for with low rates and character. ⊠ *3 blocks south of plaza,* ☎ *256–1329. 46 rooms, 10 with bath. No credit cards.*

Nightlife and the Arts

Chichicastenango has few nightspots—the hotel bars are as good as it gets. The best entertainment on a Wednesday or Saturday night is to wander around town, visit the church, and watch the vendors set up their stalls.

Shopping

Though the selection of goods from around the country at this town's Thursday and Sunday **markets** is overwhelming, the prices rise the moment the first tour bus rolls into town. If possible, make your purchases the evening before, when the merchants are setting up, or in the early morning or late afternoon of market day, when the big spenders have moved on. The key to getting a deal in Chichicastenango is hard bargaining.

Santa Cruz del Quiché

㉜ *19 km (12 mi) north of Chichicastenango*

Adventurous travelers may want to continue north from Chichicastenango for further glimpses of the department of El Quiché, which offers more fine scenery and traditional villages. A half-hour north of Chichicastenango lies Santa Cruz del Quiché, the provincial capital, which isn't as attractive as Chichicastenango but has inexpensive accommodations, a bank, and several restaurants on the main plaza.

OFF THE
BEATEN PATH

UTATLÁN – Also called K'umarcaaj, which was the ancient capital of the Maya-Quiché kingdom, this once-magnificent site was destroyed by Spanish conquistadors in 1524. The Maya ruins that remain haven't been restored, but they are frequently used for traditional celebrations. Utatlán is 40 kilometers (25 miles) west of Santa Cruz del Quiché, mainly by dirt road. For festival dates, check in at city hall there.

Ixil Triangle

㉝ *95 km (60 mi) north of Santa Cruz del Quiché (5 hours by bus)*

An interesting although somewhat inaccessible part of El Quiché is the Ixil Triangle, which comprises the villages of **Nebaj, San Juan Cotzal,** and **Chajul.** It's a fantastic area for hiking. Nebaj is the most accessible of the three, but Cotzal is serviced by sporadic buses, and Chajul can be hiked or driven to. The Ixil Triangle is the home of the Ixil Indians, a proud and beautiful people who speak a unique language and preserve a rich culture. The area was the scene of intense combat during the early 1980s, when the army razed dozens of villages, and though things are quiet now, a frightening number of widows and orphans populate the area. The friendly nature of the locals here belies the nightmare they lived just a decade ago.

Quezaltenango

㉞ *91 km (56 mi) southwest of Chichicastenango*

Though Quezaltenango is Guatemala's second-largest city, it's little more than an overgrown town. In a valley surrounded by rich farmland, the city has long had an economy based on agriculture, but it is also a significant industrial center known for its textiles. While considered a sprawling minimetropolis with few attractions of its own, it's near some charming highland villages and is thus a good base for exploring the region.

The city received its name, which means "place of the quetzal," from the language of the Mexicans who fought with Alvarado. The conquistador defeated the great Indian warrior Tecún Umán in the area and destroyed the nearby Quiché city of Xelaju. But local Indians have never gotten used to the city's foreign name and instead refer to Quezaltenango as Xela (pronounced *shay*-la), which is the name you'll find on buses.

There are a number of language schools in Xela, as it is a popular alternative to Antigua for studying Spanish. Most tourists stay in Zona 1, in an area near the grandiose Parque Centro América, the city's central plaza, which is surrounded by government buildings and banks (most open 9–7) and the cathedral.

NEED A BREAK?

The inexpensive **Cafe Bavaria** (⊠ 5 Calle and 13 Avenida), just off the plaza, provides an ample selection of excellent coffees as well as a relaxing atmosphere. Treats like fresh pastries, quiches, and hot croissant sandwiches are also served.

Dining and Lodging

$$ ✕ Casa Grande. Though the city has few fine dining options, this restaurant in a hotel and former residence in Zona 3 has certainly filled the
★ void. The "Big House" is an impressive white edifice of modern Spanish design across the street from Benito Juárez Park. Seating is in the foyer and in several simple but elegant rooms decorated with a bit of contemporary art. An interesting array of Continental cuisine is served, ranging from filet mignon to shrimp scampi to cheese fondue. Sit back and enjoy the dinner music on Thursday through Saturday nights; Sunday lunches are enlivened by marimba. A rather plush lounge, paneled in mahogany, is attached to the restaurant. If you're feeling less hungry or fancy, go for the inexpensive café on the second floor, where you can sit outdoors and munch on an afternoon snack. ⊠ *4 Calle and 16 Avenida, Zona 3,* ☎ *361–2601. AE, DC, MC, V.*

$–$$ ✕ Royal Paris. This restaurant caters to the numerous foreigners who are in Xela to study Spanish, so consequently it offers a wide selection of interesting dishes, such as chicken curry and vegetarian sandwiches. It also has a bar, an extensive wine list, and breakfast. The ambience is definitely imported, and the feeling is dark and slightly bohemian, courtesy of Parisian scenes on the walls and jazz on the stereo. ⊠ *Calle 14A–32, Zona 1,* ☎ *361–2149. No credit cards.*

$ ✕ El Kopetin. Aside from the two big hotels, this restaurant serves the best food in Zona 1. It's not large or fancy, but somehow it's comforting, with its wood paneling and long polished bar. The menu has a number of appetizers, like *queso fundido* (melted cheese served with condiments and tortillas), and a selection of meat and seafood dishes, some of which get smothered in rich sauces. Good food and service at reasonable prices have made this place popular with the locals, so it can be tough to get a seat later in the evening. ⊠ *14 Avenida 3–51, Zona 1,* ☎ *361–8381. AE, DC, MC, V.*

$$$ ✕⌂ Hotel Villa Real Plaza. Across the plaza from the Bonifaz is Quezaltenango's other first-class hotel, which was recently remodeled and re-
★ named by new management. The Villa Real surrounds a spacious covered courtyard, topped by skylights. Rooms are large and modern and contain wall-to-wall carpeting, double beds, and fireplaces. The restaurant has an interesting selection that ranges from cordon bleu to a variety of stews and pastas, plus a small sampling of vegetarian dishes. There also is a large bar. ⊠ *4 Calle 12–22, Zona 1,* ☎ *361–6270,* FAX *361–6780. 50 rooms with bath. Restaurant, bar. AE, DC, MC, V.*

$$$ ✕⊡ **Pension Bonifaz.** Don't be fooled by the term "pension" in its name: This is Quezaltenango's most upscale hotel. Inside a stately old yellow edifice by the northeast corner of the central plaza, the Bonifaz isn't quite as grand as its exterior, but it is a comfortable, well-run establishment. Rooms are large and carpeted, have a fairly modern decor, and are equipped with cable TV. The nicest rooms are in the older building—the hotel was expanded years ago—and if you don't mind a little noise, the ones on the street have little balconies that offer some pleasant views of the central plaza. For soaking up the afternoon sun, a quiet spot is the rooftop garden. A small café serving sandwiches and Mexican fare and a sizable restaurant are in the covered courtyard, which is also the lobby. The restaurant offers an extensive menu of Continental cuisine, and it has one of the better kitchens in town. The café and the restaurant share a devilishly tempting pastry cart. ⊠ *4 Calle 10–50, Zona 1,* ☎ *361–4241 or 361–2959,* 𝔽𝔸𝕏 *361–2850. 74 rooms with bath. Restaurant, bar, café, room service. AE, DC, MC, V.*

$$ ⊡ **Hotel Centramericana.** This modern, comfortable hotel is in Zona 3, which, though it's on the periphery of the city, is close to the main bus terminal and several worthy restaurants. The Centramericana resembles a North American motel; its decor is something like '70s Wisconsin, with lots of wood, spacious rooms, new furniture, and ample parking. The key here is comfort, thanks to firm beds and large, modern bathrooms. The hotel does have a large restaurant, but with two excellent restaurants a few blocks away, by Benito Juárez Park, there's no reason to eat anything but breakfast here. ⊠ *4 Calle and 14 Avenida, Zona 3,* ☎ *363–0261. 14 rooms with bath. Restaurant. DC, MC, V.*

$$ ⊡ **Hotel Modelo.** Founded in 1883, the Modelo is a small, family-run establishment that over the years has maintained a distinguished appearance and a tradition of good service. It's situated a few blocks from the plaza, between Avenidas 14 and 15. Rooms face a couple of small courtyards with porticoes leading off the lobby, which also adjoins a fine little colonial-style restaurant. Much of the hotel's furniture is antique, and the rooms have wooden floors and stucco walls decorated with traditional weavings. There's also a nearby annex, which has some newer rooms that rent for less. ⊠ *14 Avenida "A" 2–31, Zona 1,* ☎ 𝔽𝔸𝕏 *363–1376. 24 rooms with bath. Restaurant. AE, MC, V.*

$ ⊡ **Casa del Viajero.** It's a bit of a walk from the plaza, but this clean, comfortable, and safe accommodation is one of Xela's best bets for budget travelers. A small restaurant serves standard Guatemalan fare, and rooms with either private or shared bath are available. There are also a few two-room apartments available, with small kitchens, which cost little more than the hotel rooms. ⊠ *8 Avenida 9–17, Zona 1,* ☎ *361– 4594,* 𝔽𝔸𝕏 *363–0743. 21 rooms, 13 with bath. Restaurant. MC, V.*

$ ⊡ **Casa Kaehler.** This quiet pension a few blocks off the plaza is run by a friendly family of German descent and is a popular spot with travelers on a budget. Rooms are on two floors of a converted residence and face a small, plain courtyard. Though the rooms are simple, they are clean, and the hotel has a separate lounge where guests gather to read, relax, or chat. There's only one room with a private bath and a double bed, but the shared baths are well maintained and have plenty of hot water. ⊠ *13 Avenida 3–33, Zona 1,* ☎ *361–2091. 7 rooms, 1 with bath. No credit cards.*

Nightlife and the Arts

Aside from the lounges in the big hotels, there are only a few nightspots in Xela. A luxurious little bar operates at the **Casa Grande hotel** (⊠ 4 Calle and 16 Avenida, Zona 3), which sometimes has live music on weekends. A restaurant a few blocks from the plaza, the **Royal Paris**

(⊠ Calle 14A–32, Zona 1) also has a quiet bar. If you're in the mood for dancing, try **El Garage Club** (⊠ Blvd. Minerva).

Shopping

Handiwork from most of the villages in the region can be found in the **new market** (⊠ 1 Calle and 15 Avenida, Zona 3), and since there are few shoppers, prices tend to be low. Another **market** (⊠ Near the plaza, Zona 1) has a limited selection of típica. **ADEPH** (⊠ Rodolfo Robles Calle 15–63, Zona 1) is an outlet for a local artisans' association. **AJ Pop** (⊠ 14 Avenida "A" 1–26) is one of many típica shops. At **Salsa Limitada** (⊠ 12 Avenida 1–40, Zona 1), you can have clothes custom-made as well as buy other handicrafts.

Volcano Climbing

The volcanoes of Santa Maria (12,372 feet) and Tajamulco (13,809 feet, Guatemala's highest), near Quezaltenango, are the two best volcanoes for climbing. Both make for strenuous ascents and are best done in two days. When the weather is clear, you can see most of the country's other volcanoes from either summit, including nearby Santiaguito, which erupts frequently.

Almolonga

㉟ *5 km (3 mi) south of Quezaltenango*

The real attraction of Xela is the area that surrounds it. Here, for example, you'll find women wearing bright orange huipiles and beautiful headbands. At the busy Wednesday and Saturday markets, you can buy fruits that are cultivated in the area. A few kilometers beyond town are several hot springs, where private tubs can be rented for a few dollars.

Zunil

★ **㊱** *9 km (5½ mi) south of Quezaltenango*

One of the most picturesque villages in the region, Zunil is set at the end of a valley, above which a river plunges into a massive cascade. The town's colorful presence is accentuated by the purple costumes worn by local women. Market day is Monday, and Zunil is another town where Maximón is actively worshipped—his image is in the basement of a building just down the hill from the church. If you want to visit him, be sure to bear gifts: Money, alcohol, and cigarettes are most welcome.

Lodging

$ 🏨 **Fuentes Georginas.** High in the hills above Zunil, tucked back in a lush valley, are some lovely hot sulfur springs. The local municipality has a dozen bungalows and a restaurant here, and though the cabins are a bit run-down, and in recent years there has been a dearth of water at times, they do have fireplaces and private tubs. The main pool is cleaned on Mondays, and there's a smaller one by the entrance. In addition, the area presents a wonderful example of cloud-forest ecology, there are some nice walks, and the restaurant is decent. Since there's no phone, you're stuck if you arrive and they're full, but the risk is usually confined to weekends. Turn left after passing Zunil, then right on the first dirt road; from there it's about a 20-minute drive into the hills. Or pay a couple of dollars a head for a ride up in one of the pickup taxis that park by the main road. *No phone. 12 bungalows with bath. Restaurant. No credit cards.*

San Francisco El Alto

❸ *14 km (9 mi) northeast of Quezaltenango, 204 kilometers (126½ miles) northwest of Guatemala City*

This town, in the Department of Totonicapán, has one of the country's largest livestock markets, held every Friday. It commands great views of the valley below and the surrounding volcanoes.

San Miguel Totonicapán

★ **❸** *16 km (10 mi) northeast of San Francisco El Alto*

Hop a bus behind the cathedral in Xela to get to this traditional village, famous for its wooden toys, hand-loomed textiles, tinwork, wax figures, and painted and glazed ceramics. Totonicapán's market day is Saturday.

Shopping

All the villages in the Quezaltenango area have weekly markets where típica can be purchased, but Totonicapán is full of **workshops** where a wide variety of handicrafts are actually produced. The tourist office (✉ Casa de Cultura, 8 Avenida 2–17, Zona 1, opposite the Hotel Maya Palace, ☎ 362–1392) produces a brochure about Totonicapán with a map of its more than 60 típica factories and outlets.

Momostenango

❸ *20 km (12½ mi) north of San Francisco El Alto along a dirt road*

An extremely traditional village and the center of an important wool-producing region, Momostenango displays its famous blankets and ponchos woven on foot looms at a Sunday market.

Huehuetenango

❹ *86 km (53 mi) north of San Francisco El Alto, 94 km (58 mi) north of Quezaltenango*

This quiet town at the foot of the massive Cuchumatanes mountain range is the country's highest. Though it doesn't have any real attractions of its own, it is a gateway to these magnificent mountains and the isolated villages scattered across them. The town is centered on a large plaza with a band shell, surrounded by government offices and a few banks. A couple of blocks to the east is the central market, where local handicrafts can be purchased.

OFF THE BEATEN PATH

ZACULEU – About 4½ kilometers (under 3 miles) west of town are some Maya ruins, which, though they hardly constitute one of the country's most spectacular archaeological sites, are well worth a short visit. In the post-Classic period (AD 900–1200), Zaculeu was the capital of the Mam, one of the predominant highland tribes at the time of the conquest but about which little is known. It was conquered by Spanish troops led by Pedro de Alvarado's brother, Gonzalo, and surrendered only after enduring a 45-day siege. The United Fruit Company restored the ruins in the 1940s but did a pretty heavy-handed job and left the site looking rather artificial. Nevertheless, it's a tranquil spot with views of the surrounding pine-draped hills, and a modest museum offers some small insight into the world of the Mam. Minibuses leave for the ruins from the corner of 1 Avenida and 2 Calle in Huehuetenango.

Dining and Lodging

$ ✕ **Jardín Café.** This colorful little corner restaurant serves decent food in a bright, friendly atmosphere, and consequently it's popular with the locals. It opens daily at 6 AM for breakfast (pancakes are excellent), and the lunch and dinner menu includes basic beef and chicken as well as a few Mexican dishes. ⊠ *4 Calle and 6 Avenida, no phone. No credit cards.*

$ ✕ **Las Brasas.** This little steak house is probably Huehuetenango's best restaurant. The decor is unassuming enough, with lots of wood and simple red-and-white tablecloths, but since it's the only restaurant in town that has anything remotely resembling atmosphere, it is a fairly reassuring sight. The house specialty is grilled meat, but the menu is fairly ample and even includes Chinese food, which you sure won't find anywhere else in town. ⊠ *2 Calle and 4 Avenida,* ☎ *364–2339. No credit cards.*

$ ✕ **Pizza Hogareña.** While the ambience is nothing to speak of, you can
★ build your own pizza from a long list of fresh ingredients or opt for spaghetti, grilled meat, or sandwiches. ⊠ *6 Avenida 4–49,* ☎ *364–3072. No credit cards. Closed Mon.*

$$$ ⊞ **Hotel Los Cuchumatanes.** Two kilometers (1½ miles) outside of town, this hotel is ideal for those traveling with a car. On an old plantation, it is clean with a modern, motel-like feel. The hotel has a swimming pool and a terrace that overlooks a garden. Rooms have a frigo bar and color TV, and the owners are constructing tennis courts. ⊠ *Apartado Postal 46, Zona 7,* ☎ *364–1951,* FAX *364–2816. 50 rooms with bath. Restaurant, bar, pool. AE, MC, V.*

$$ ⊞ **Hotel Zaculeu.** This older hotel off the main square has long been Huehuetenango's most charming inn, but recent expansion and remodeling have made it the city's most comfortable one as well. The entrance leads into a lush garden courtyard, which is surrounded by a portico and the hotel's older rooms. A passage on the other end of the courtyard leads to the new rooms, which are built on two levels and surround an enclosed parking area. Take your pick: Older rooms are graced with local weavings and other handicrafts, but the newer ones have wall-to-wall carpeting, modern bathrooms, and TVs; older rooms have more character but can be noisier, especially those along the street, while the newer units are more expensive. ⊠ *5 Avenida 1– 14,* ☎ FAX *364–1575. 38 rooms with bath. No credit cards.*

$ ⊞ **Hotel Mary.** This four-story hotel in the heart of town offers comfortable, clean accommodations at a good price, but not much more. Though not terribly attractive, Hotel Mary is conveniently located across the street from the post and Guatel offices. Several rooms have cable TV. ⊠ *2 Calle 3–52,* ☎ *364–1618. 25 rooms, 11 with bath. No credit cards.*

En Route A short drive north of Huehuetenango, the dirt road begins to wind its way up into the Cuchumatanes Mountains, where traditional villages are set between massive, rocky peaks. There's a *mirador* (scenic view) near the town of Chiantla, 6 kilometers (4 miles) from Huehuetenango. From there it's up, up, up for quite a while.

Todos Santos Cuchumatán

④① *50 km (31 mi) north of Huehuetenango; turn left at the Paquix junction, some 20 km (12½ mi) outside Huehuetenango*

This region offers only budget accommodations and very limited dining options, but if you're willing to rough it a little, you will be well rewarded by your experiences here. Those who aren't can drive to Todos Santos, the most frequently visited mountain village, for the day.

In Todos Santos, traditional male garb—bright red pants and shirts with oversize red collars—is still commonly worn. The best time to come is during the big local festival, October 31 to November 5, which celebrates the Day of the Dead (All Saints and All Souls days) longer than any other village in Guatemala. The high point of the celebration is a horse race done bareback. Market day is Thursday.

Hiking

Todos Santos is a popular base for hiking, which accesses both beautiful mountain scenery and quaint nearby villages, like San Juan Atitán, Santiago Chimaltenango, San Martín, and Jacaltenango. If you're adventurous, head farther north to Soloma, a larger town with markets on Thursdays and Sundays, or on to San Mateo Ixtatán, a small village known for its traditional Chuj Indian inhabitants and a small Maya site. Market days—Thursday and Sunday—are the best time to visit San Mateo. At Barillas, to the east, the mountains begin to drop down toward the rain forests.

The Western Highlands A to Z

Arriving and Departing

BY BUS

To Panajachel, **Transporte Rebuli** (☏ 251–3521) leaves Guatemala City (⊠ 21 Calle 1–34, Zona 1) daily at 5:30 and 6:15 AM, then hourly from 7 AM to 3:30 PM. Buses leave Panajachel at 5, 7, and 8 AM, then hourly from 9:30 AM to 2:30 PM. Count on a four-hour trip.

To Chichicastenango and Santa Cruz del Quiché, **Veloz Quichelense** (no phone) operates hourly buses, departing the capital (⊠ Terminal de Autobuses, Zona 4) on the half hour between 5 AM and 6 PM and returning from Santa Cruz on a similar schedule.

To Quezaltenango, **Galgos** (☏ 232–3661) buses leave Guatemala City (⊠ 7 Avenida 19–44, Zona 1) at 5:30, 8:30, and 11 AM; hourly 12:30–5:30 PM; and then at 7 PM. They depart Quezaltenango (⊠ Off Calzada Indepedencia, Zona 2) five times daily, 3:30 AM–4:30 PM. The trip takes four hours.

To Huehuetenango, you can choose from two bus services for the five-hour run from Guatemala City. **Los Halcones** (⊠ 7 Avenida 15–27, Zona 1, ☏ 238–1979) has departures at 7 AM and 2 PM. **Rapidos Zaculeu** (⊠ 9 Calle 11–42, Zona 1, ☏ 232–2858) runs buses at 6 AM and 3 PM.

From **Antigua,** first take a bus to Chimaltenango, and then wave down a bus on the Interamerican Highway. Anything heading north stops at Los Encuentros, where it's easy to transfer. A shuttle service between Panajachel and Antigua leaves Antigua about 8 AM and Panajachel around noon daily. Tickets can be purchased at the big hotels (☏ 332–2928 in Antigua).

BY CAR

The Interamerican Highway—more country road than highway, really—heads northwest out of Guatemala City, where it is called the Calzada Roosevelt. It passes through Chimaltenango (km 56) before reaching a crossroads called Los Encuentros (km 127), which is marked by a two-story, blue, traffic-police tower. Here the road to El Quiché (Chichicastenango, Santa Cruz del Quiché, and the Ixil Triangle) splits off to the right. Veering left, the Interamerican Highway passes a turnoff to Sololá and Panajachel, 3 kilometers (2 miles) down on the left. The highway skims over some impressive ridges and then descends to a crossroads called Cuatro Caminos, about 200 kilometers (124 miles) from the capital. Here the road to Quezaltenango, 27 kilometers (17 miles) south, heads off to the left. Staying on the highway about 60 kilometers (37 miles) north of Cuatro Caminos, you'll see the short dirt road to Huehuetenango on the right. Roads to the north of Huehuetenango and Santa Cruz del Quiché are unpaved and pretty rough—this is nerve-racking mountain driving relieved intermittently by memorable views.

Getting Around

BY BOAT

A variety of ferries and private boats ply the waters of Lake Atitlán. Daily boats leave Panajachel for Santiago Atitlán at 8:30 AM, 9 AM, 9:30 AM, 10 AM, 4 PM, and 5 PM, returning at 6 AM, 11:45 AM, 12:30 PM, 1 PM, 2 PM, and 5 PM, and for San Pedro La Laguna at 8:20 AM, 10 AM, noon, 2 PM, 4 PM, and 7:30 PM, returning at 4:45 AM, 6 AM, 8 AM, 10 AM, noon, 2 PM, and 5 PM. Several boats per day also travel between Santiago and San Pedro, and a daily excursion leaves Panajachel at 9 AM for San Pedro, Santiago, and San Antonio Palopó, stopping for about an hour at each village and returning around 4 PM. There are also plenty of smaller boats that offer private tours of the lake.

BY BUS

Daily buses leave Panajachel for Chichicastenango at 7, 8, 9, and 10:30 AM, and 1 PM; for Quezaltenango at 5:30 and 11:30 AM, and 2:30 PM; for San Lucas Tolimán at 6:30 AM and 2 PM; and for Santa Catarina and San Antonio Palopó at 9 AM. Hourly buses operate between Quezaltenango and Huehuetenango (a 2½-hour trip), and sporadic service is available between Quezaltenango and Chichicastenango, but it's often quicker to switch buses at Los Encuentros. Service from Quezaltenango to Panajachel runs at 6 AM, noon, and 1. Buses to both San Francisco and Momostenango leave Quezaltenango from the Minerva bus station, in Zona 3, while those to Almolonga and Zunil depart from the area behind the cathedral, in Zona 1. Buses to the Ixil Triangle leave Santa Cruz around 8 and 9 AM and return at 12:30 and 3 AM. There is also early morning bus service between Huehuetenango and Sacapulas. Buses leave Huehuetenango (⊠ 4 Calle and 1 Avenida) for Todos Santos at 11:30 AM and 12:30 PM, returning at 5 and 6 AM, or you can hike down from Todos Santos to the Interamerican Highway via San Juan or Jacaltenango and catch one of the regular buses coming from the Mexican border.

Contacts and Resources

EMERGENCIES

National Police (☎ 2569). **Medical emergencies** (☎ 2471).

Pharmacy. Farmacia Nueva (⊠ 6 Calle and 10 Avenida, Zona 1, Quezaltenango, ☎ 4531).

TRAVEL AGENCY

Guatemala Unlimited Travel Bureau (⊠ 1 Calle and 12 Avenida, Quezaltenango, ☎ 361–6043).

VISITOR INFORMATION

INGUAT offices are in Panajachel (⊠ Edificio Rincón, at beginning of Calle Santander, ☎ 362–1392), open Monday 8–noon and Wednesday–Sunday 8–noon and 2–6; in Quezaltenango (⊠ South end of Parque Centro América, no phone); and in Totonicapán (⊠ Casa de Cultura, 8 Avenida 2–17, Zona 1, opposite Hotel Maya Palace, ☎ 362–1392).

The best places to travel may be the best places to get hepatitis A.

You can pick up hepatitis A when traveling to high-risk areas outside of the United States. From raw shellfish or water you don't think is contaminated. Or from uncooked foods—like salad—prepared by people who don't know they're infected. At even the best places.

Symptoms of hepatitis A include jaundice, abdominal pain, fever, vomiting and diarrhea. And can cause discomfort, time away from work and memories you'd like to forget.

The U.S. Centers for Disease Control and Prevention (CDC) recommends immunization for travelers to high-risk areas. *Havrix*, available in over 45 countries, can protect you from hepatitis A. *Havrix* may cause some soreness in your arm or a slight headache.

Ask your physician about vaccination with *Havrix* at your next visit or at least 2 weeks before you travel. And have a great trip.

Please see important patient information adjacent to this ad.

Havrix®
Hepatitis A Vaccine, Inactivated

The world's first hepatitis A vaccine

For more information on how to protect yourself against hepatitis A, call

1-800-HEP-A-VAX (1-800-437-2829)

Manufactured by
SmithKline Beecham Biologicals
Rixensart, Belgium

Distributed by
SmithKline Beecham Pharmaceuticals
Philadelphia, PA 19101

HA8590   © SmithKline Beecham, 1996

Havrix is a registered trademark of SmithKline Beecham.

Hepatitis A Vaccine, Inactivated
Havrix®

See complete prescribing information in SmithKline Beecham Pharmaceuticals literature. The following is a brief summary.

INDICATIONS AND USAGE: *Havrix* is indicated for active immunization of persons ≥ 2 years of age against disease caused by hepatitis A virus (HAV).

CONTRAINDICATIONS: *Havrix* is contraindicated in people with known hypersensitivity to any component of the vaccine.

WARNINGS: Do not give additional injections to patients experiencing hypersensitivity reactions after a *Havrix* injection. (See CONTRAINDICATIONS.)

Hepatitis A has a relatively long incubation period. Hepatitis A vaccine may not prevent hepatitis A infection in those who have an unrecognized hepatitis A infection at the time of vaccination. Additionally, it may not prevent infection in those who do not achieve protective antibody titers (although the lowest titer needed to confer protection has not been determined).

PRECAUTIONS: As with any parenteral vaccine (1) keep epinephrine available for use in case of anaphylaxis or anaphylactoid reaction; (2) delay administration, if possible, in people with any febrile illness or active infection, except when the physican believes withholding vaccine entails the greater risk; (3) take all known precautions to prevent adverse reactions, including reviewing patients' history for hypersensitivity to this or similar vaccines.

Administer with caution to people with thrombocytopenia or a bleeding disorder, or people taking anticoagulants. Do not inject into a blood vessel. Use a separate, sterile needle or prefilled syringe for every patient. When giving concomitantly with other vaccines or IG, use separate needles and different injection sites.

As with any vaccine, if administered to immunosuppressed persons or persons receiving immunosuppressive therapy, the expected immune response may not be obtained.

Carcinogenesis, Mutagenesis, Impairment of Fertility: *Havrix* has not been evaluated for its carcinogenic potential, mutagenic potential or potential for impairment of fertility.

Pregnancy Category C: Animal reproduction studies have not been conducted with *Havrix*. It is also not known whether *Havrix* can cause fetal harm when administered to a pregnant woman or can affect reproduction capacity. Give *Havrix* to a pregnant woman only if clearly needed. It is not known whether *Havrix* is excreted in human milk. Because many drugs are excreted in human milk, use caution when administering *Havrix* to a nursing woman.

Havrix is well tolerated and highly immunogenic and effective in children.

Fully inform patients, parents or guardians of the benefits and risks of immunization with *Havrix*. For persons traveling to endemic or epidemic areas, consult current CDC advisories regarding specific locales. Travelers should take all necessary precautions to avoid contact with, or ingestion of, contaminated food or water. Duration of immunity following a complete vaccination schedule has not been established.

ADVERSE REACTIONS: *Havrix* has been generally well tolerated. As with all pharmaceuticals, however, it is possible that expanded commercial use of the vaccine could reveal rare adverse events.

The most frequently reported by volunteers in clinical trials was injection-site soreness (56% of adults; 21% of children); headache (14% of adults; less than 9% of children). Other solicited and unsolicited events are listed below:

Incidence 1% to 10% of Injections: Induration, redness, swelling; fatigue, fever (>37.5°C), malaise; anorexia, nausea.

Incidence <1% of Injections: Hematoma; pruritus, rash, urticaria; pharyngitis, other upper respiratory tract infections; abdominal pain, diarrhea, dysgeusia, vomiting; arthralgia, elevation of creatine phosphokinase, myalgia; lymphadenopathy; hypertonic episode, insomnia, photophobia, vertigo.

Additional safety data

Safety data were obtained from two additional sources in which large populations were vaccinated. In an outbreak setting in which 4,930 individuals were immunized with a single dose of either 720 EL.U. or 1440 EL.U. of *Havrix*, the vaccine was well-tolerated and no serious adverse events due to vaccination were reported. Overall, less than 10% of vaccinees reported solicited general adverse events following the vaccine. The most common solicited local adverse event was pain at the injection site, reported in 22.3% of subjects at 24 hours and decreasing to 2.4% by 72 hours.

In a field efficacy trial, 19,037 children received the 360 EL.U. dose of *Havrix*. The most commonly reported adverse events were injection-site pain (9.5%) and tenderness (8.1%), reported following first doses of *Havrix*. Other adverse events were infrequent and comparable to the control vaccine Engerix-B® (Hepatitis B Vaccine, Recombinant).

Postmarketing Reports: Rare voluntary reports of adverse events in people receiving *Havrix* since market introduction include the following: localized edema; anaphylaxis/anaphylactoid reactions, somnolence; syncope; jaundice, hepatitis; erythema multiforme, hyperhydrosis, angioedema; dyspnea; lymphadenopathy; convulsions, encephalopathy, dizziness, neuropathy, myelitis, paresthesia, Guillain-Barré syndrome, multiple sclerosis; congenital abnormality.

The U.S. Department of Health and Human Services has established the Vaccine Adverse Events Reporting System (VAERS) to accept reports of suspected adverse events after the administration of any vaccine, including, but not limited to, the reporting of events required by the National Childhood Vaccine Injury Act of 1986. The toll-free number for VAERS forms and information is 1-800-822-7967.

HOW SUPPLIED: 360 EL.U./0.5 mL: NDC 58160-836-01 Package of 1 single-dose vial.

720 EL.U./0.5 mL: NDC 58160-837-01 Package of 1 single-dose vial; NDC 58160-837-02 Package of 1 prefilled syringe.

1440 EL.U./mL: NDC 58160-835-01 Package of 1 single-dose vial; NDC 58160-835-02 Package of 1 prefilled syringe.

Manufactured by **SmithKline Beecham Biologicals**
Rixensart, Belgium
Distributed by **SmithKline Beecham Pharmaceuticals**
Philadelphia, PA 19101

BRS–HA:L5A

Havrix is a registered trademark of SmithKline Beecham.

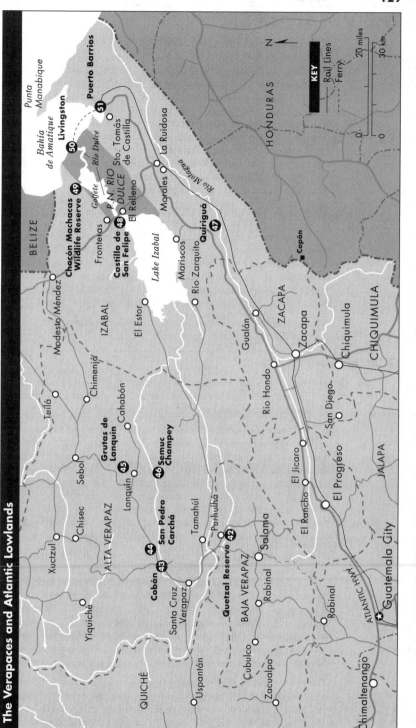

The Verapaces and Atlantic Lowlands

THE VERAPACES

The eastern departments of Alta Verapaz and Baja Verapaz, northeast of Guatemala City, are rich in beauty, culture, and history, but they are missed by the majority of visitors to Guatemala, who spend their entire vacations in the highlands or El Petén. Here you'll find a mountainous region covered with lush forests and coffee plantations, drained by wild rivers, and pierced by deep caverns. The smaller Baja Verapaz is drier than Alta Verapaz, to the north, where deluges are common and mist-covered mountains the norm. The area's humid climate has made it the cradle of Guatemala's cardamon spice and coffee production, but it's also responsible for the lush tropical forests that drape uncultivated hillsides and the crystalline rivers that flow between them, some of which are perfect for white-water rafting.

The region's inhabitants are predominantly Pokomchí and Kekchí Indians, who over the years have lost much of their territory to expanding coffee plantations and have abandoned some of their traditional ways. There is also some lingering remnant of the culture imported by German immigrants, most of whom were expelled years ago but then returned to work the plantations. The region's largest city is Cobán, which doesn't have many attractions of its own but is a good base for exploring surrounding villages and natural wonders.

Numbers in the margin correspond to points of interest on the Verapaces and Atlantic Lowlands map.

Quetzal Reserve

★ ㊷ *164 km (102 mi) northeast of Guatemala City, 75 km (46½ mi) north of El Rancho; from Guatemala City, take the Carretera Atlantíca to El Rancho (km 84), and turn left toward the mountains*

A 2,849-acre tract of cloud forest along the road to Cobán, just south of the village of Purhulhá, the reserve was created to protect Guatemala's national bird, the resplendent quetzal, which is endangered by the indiscriminate destruction of the country's forests. Also called the Mario Dary Reserve, the area was named after the Guatemalan ecologist who fought for its creation and was a victim of the political violence of the early 1980s. Note: The reserve was closed to visitors in November 1995 after an assault on a group of tourists. Check with a travel agency or government tourist office (INGUAT) before planning a trip.

The elusive but beautiful quetzal has been revered since the days of the ancient Maya, who called it the winged serpent. Though the Maya often captured quetzals to remove their tail feathers, which grow back, killing one was a capital offense. The quetzal has long symbolized freedom, since it is said that the bird cannot live in captivity. While the female quetzal is attractive, the male is as spectacular a creature as ever took to the air, with its crimson belly, bright green back, and long-flowing tail feathers. Its unforgettable appearance notwithstanding, the quetzal remains difficult to spot within the mist and lush foliage of the cloud forest.

The reserve has several well-kept trails that wind through the forest, and the 3½-kilometer (2-mile) Los Musgos trail passes a lovely waterfall. Since it is easier to spot quetzals around dawn or dusk, it's worth spending a night in the area. Even if you don't catch a glimpse of the legendary quetzal, there are plenty of other species to be spotted, and the luxuriant greenery of the cloud forest is gorgeous in its own right. For more information about the Quetzal Reserve and other natural areas, *see* Chapter 2. *No phone.* ✉ *Free.*

Dining and Lodging

$$ ✗▦ **Posada Montaña del Quetzal.** This comfortable country lodge near
★ the Quetzal Reserve is the best hotel in the region. Guests may choose
from small rooms within the main building and spacious bungalows,
each with two bedrooms, a sitting room, and a fireplace. The restau-
rant overlooks the swimming pool and serves a limited selection of
Guatemalan and Continental cuisine, and even if you don't spend the
night, this is a good spot for a meal or snack. Wander the trails
nearby—you might catch a glimpse of a quetzal. ⊠ *4 km (2½ mi) south
of the Quetzal Reserve at km 156.5 along the Carretera a Cobán,* ☎
*335–1805 in Guatemala City. 10 bungalows and 8 rooms with bath.
Restaurant, bar, coffee shop, pool, hiking, fishing. No credit cards.*

$ ▦ **Ranchito del Quetzal.** Just north of the Quetzal Reserve is this rus-
tic lodge, a superbudget affair that consists of two cabins packed with
beds and a tiny eatery. You're just a step above camping here, so be
prepared. The food at the restaurant is laughable and the service is spo-
radic at best, but the location is good and the rates are low. ⊠ *1½ km
(1 mi) north of the Quetzal Reserve, no phone. 2 bungalows. Restau-
rant. No credit cards.*

Cobán

❹❸ *50 km (31 mi) north of the Quetzal Reserve*

The principal city of the Verapaces, Cobán is in many ways the city
that coffee built. During the 19th-century coffee boom, Cobán func-
tioned almost independently of Guatemala City, exporting its products
and dealing directly with Germany, whence most of its prominent cit-
izens came. Though German influence declined during World War II,
when the U.S. government pressured Guatemala to expel most of the
region's German residents, traces of their influence remain. The city
has an attractive plaza and cathedral, as well as a selection of hotels
and restaurants.

Dining and Lodging

$$ ✗▦ **Hotel La Posada.** This traditional old inn near Central Park is a
tasteful, comfortable spot—definitely the nicest place to stay in Cobán.
Rooms have wood floors and beamed ceilings, and they are furnished
with antiques and decorated with Guatemalan handicrafts, as are the
porticoes and hallways. The hotel has a beautiful little garden and a
cozy restaurant with a fireplace that serves mostly Guatemalan food.
For entertainment, a TV lounge and Ping-Pong table suffice. ⊠ *1 Calle
4–12, Zona 2,* ☎ ℻ *251–1495. 14 rooms with bath. Restaurant, café.
No credit cards.*

$ ▦ **Casa Acuña.** This delightful hostel is two blocks from the main square
and offers immaculate and comfortable dormitory-style rooms. Light meals
are served in the patio café. The hostel proprietors—the lovely Guatemalan-
American Acuña family—are not only an invaluable resource on Cobán
and the area but take a personal interest in each of their guests. They
also run excellent eco-adventure tours. ⊠ *4 Calle 3–11, Zona 2,* ☎ ℻
251–1547. 7 rooms with shared bath. Café. No credit cards.

San Pedro Carchá

❹❹ *6 km (4 mi) east of Cobán*

An interesting daily market is the highlight of this traditional little town.
Nearby Las Islas, with a waterfall and pool, is a popular spot for pic-
nics and swimming.

Lanquín

63 km (39 mi) northeast of Cobán

This village is on the doorstep of some impressive natural wonders.

45 Stop by the municipal offices and arrange to have someone turn the lights on and let you into the caves called **Grutas de Lanquín,** for which there is a small charge. They have huge subterranean chambers and underground rivers. Only a cave lover would go.

46 A spectacularly beautiful spot, **Semuc Champey** comprises a natural arch topped by a series of emerald pools that are perfect for swimming and are surrounded by dense forest. It's only 10 kilometers (6 miles) south of Lanquín on a dirt road, but you'll need a four-wheel-drive vehicle to reach it. You can get directions at the municipal offices.

Dining and Lodging

$$ ✕▥ **Hotel El Recreo Lanquín Champey.** This large hotel at the mouth of the Lanquín caves is a good place for swimming. Lodgings are in clean, concrete rooms in the main building and in several bungalows out back. The restaurant was built with the expectation of more tourists than usually visit; it serves decent, typical Guatemalan food. ✉ *Across from Lanquín River,* ☎ *251–2160,* ℻ *251–2333. 16 rooms with bath. Restaurant. No credit cards.*

White-Water Rafting

The Cahabón River, which pours into a sinkhole nearby, is popular for white-water rafting farther downstream. Rafting trips on the Cahabón, which last one to three days, can be arranged through **Maya Expeditions** (☎ 337–4666).

The Verapaces A to Z

Arriving and Departing

BY BUS

Transportes Escobar/Monja Blanca runs direct, comfortable, Pullman buses between Guatemala City (✉ 8 Avenida 15–16, Zona 1, ☎ 238–1409) and Cobán (✉ 0 Calle and 4 Avenida, ☎ 251–1536), passing the Quetzal Reserve. Buses depart every hour or so from 4 AM to 4 PM at both ends of the route, and the trip takes four hours. Buses also leave Cobán at 5, 8, and 11 AM for the seven-hour trip to El Estor, on Lake Izabal, which has a budget hotel and ferry service at 5 AM to Mariscos, with bus connections to Puerto Barrios or Guatemala City.

Getting Around

BY BUS

Buses run regularly between Cobán and San Pedro Carchá, where there is sporadic service to Cahabón via Lanquín.

THE ATLANTIC LOWLANDS

Guatemala's small stretch of Caribbean coast and its hinterlands are sparsely inhabited, hot, humid, and comparatively flat, and are covered in many areas with luxuriant tropical forests. Though the indigenous culture is not as striking as what you encounter in the highlands, today's coast has Guatemala's only representation of Afro-Caribbean culture.

In ancient times the region was an important part of the Maya empire, as is attested by the presence of some important archaeological sites. The area's numerous attractions include the impressive ruins of Quiriguá; the ancient Maya city of Copán, just over the border in Honduras; the spectacular and languid Río Dulce; torrid coastal beaches; and the typically Caribbean town of Livingston. Most visitors from Guatemala City arrive and depart here via the Carretera Atlántica (Atlantic Highway), but those who brave the overland route to El Petén will pass through the region on their way.

Numbers in the margin correspond to points of interest on the Veracruz and Atlantic Lowlands map.

Quiriguá

47 *186 km (115 mi) northeast of Guatemala City, and 96 km (60 mi) southwest of Puerto Barrios, on the Carretera Atlántica; turn at km 205 and head south 3 km (2 mi)*

In ancient times the headquarters of an important Maya trading center stood here, on what was then the banks of the Motagua River (the river has since changed its course), and for many years was closely linked to the city of Copán. Quiriguá is famous for its beautiful and intricate carving, similar to that found at Copán, and especially for its massive stelae, which are the largest in the Maya world. The stelae depict Quiriguá's most powerful chiefs, especially Cauac Sky, who was probably the city's most influential leader. Several monuments, covered with interesting zoomorphic figures, still stand, and the remains of an acropolis and other structures have been partially restored. The site is in the heart of banana country, but the ruins are surrounded by a lush stand of rain forest—an island of untouched wilderness in a sea of agricultural production. This is an excellent spot for birding as well as for the area's obvious archaeological assets. *No phone.* ☺ *Daily 8–4.*

OFF THE BEATEN PATH — **COPÁN –** Though it's in Honduras, this ancient Maya city is very close to the Guatemalan border and is actually easy to visit. Comprising a spectacular set of ruins, Copán is famous for its remarkably well-preserved, ornate, free-standing carvings of different rulers, which adorn an expansive central plaza; its group of temples; and its residential area. Stelae are impressive, and a hieroglyphic staircase contains the longest Maya epigraph discovered to date.

The city reached its apex during the eighth century, when it controlled much of the southern realm of the Maya empire and experienced a bloom in artistic development, the remnants of which can be seen today. The 5th-century ruler Yax Kúk Mo began a written history of Copán and was the first of a dynasty of 17 rulers who governed during its golden age. Yax Kúk Mo's tomb, which was discovered beneath a pyramid in 1993 by a University of Pennsylvania research team, will eventually be exhibited to the public. In fact, only a small portion of Copán's estimated 4,000 buildings have as yet been excavated.

The nearby town of Ruinas de Copán offers a variety of accommodations, though limited in luxury. From Guatemala City, take the Carretera Atlántica to Río Hondo; then head south past Chiquimula to Vado Hondo, where a dusty road heads off to the left to the border post of El Florido and on to the nearby ruins. Many Guatemala City travel agencies offer one- or two-day tours to Copán. ⊠ *238 km (147½ mi) northeast of Guatemala City, in Honduras, no phone.* ▣ *Under $1.* ☺ *Daily 9–5.*

Río Dulce

★ *30 km (19 mi) northwest of La Ruidosa, where the road to El Petén leaves the Carretera Atlántica*

Well worthy of an exploration, the short, wide, jungle-lined Río Dulce (Sweet River) drains Lake Izabal, Guatemala's largest, and flows slowly northeast into the Caribbean. Where the road to El Petén crosses the waterway, a massive cement bridge connects the town of Fronteras, on the north bank, with El Relleno, on the south. East of the bridge, the river is lined with an odd mixture of Ladino communities, luxury homes and hotels, and Kekchí Indian villages. The farther you get from the bridge, the fewer fancy homes you'll see. Soon, the river widens into a small lake known as the Golfete, and still farther east, it narrows again and passes through a spectacular forest-draped gorge before pouring into the Caribbean next to the funky town of Livingston. Traffic on the river includes yachts, motorboats, and a variety of dugout canoes called *cayucas*.

The Río Dulce was an important Maya trade route and later became the colony's link with Spain. Because Spanish ships regularly exported Guatemala's products via the river, it was also frequented by pirates, who attacked both the ships and the warehouses on the shore of the lake.

In hopes of curtailing forays by pirates, 17th-century colonists built a series of fortresses on the river's north bank, at the entrance to the lake.
48 Called **Castillo de San Felipe** (no phone), the forts were repeatedly razed by pirates only to be rebuilt bigger and better. In the 1950s the Guatemalan government reconstructed the ruined castle to resemble its last version, and the result is an attractive landmark in a small national park. You can reach it by road or by a short boat ride from El Relleno.

The northern banks of the Golfete are covered by the 17,790-acre
49 **Chocón Machacas Wildlife Reserve.** Included in the reserve are stretches of virgin rain forest and an extensive mangrove swamp that is frequented by manatees—shy marine mammals also known as sea cows. To get here, you can take a 45-minute boat ride from the Río Dulce area. For more information about this wildlife reserve and other natural areas, *see* Chapter 2.

Dining and Lodging

$$ ✕ **Suzanna's Laguna.** This is an excellent restaurant. The catch is that it can only be reached by water, as it's hidden in a cove across from the Castillo de San Felipe, which makes it a good lunch stop if you're taking a boat to the ruins. Boat pilots know how to find it, but it's best to bargain the lunch stop into the price of the river tour before embarking. *No phone. No credit cards.*

$$$$ ✕🏨 **Marimonte Inn.** This large hotel on the river's south bank was recently remodeled and expanded, and now it has the largest variety of accommodations in the area. Though the Marimonte has less character than the competition—sparse grounds and simple rooms—it is easy to reach. Rooms surround a large pool, and a three-story bar-and-restaurant complex overlooks the water. Many new buildings a good distance from the river contain several modern rooms each, but the older bungalows, which are slightly run-down, have much better views of the river. Windsurfers are available for rent, and river trips can be arranged through the management. ⊠ *1½ km (1 mi) east of El Relleno,* ☎ *447–8585,* 🆇 *334–4964 in Guatemala City. 24 rooms with bath. Restaurant, bar, pool, windsurfing, travel services. AE, MC, V.*

$$$ ✕🏨 **Catamaran Island.** On the north bank of the river a few miles east
★ of the bridge, this hotel complex is accessible only by boat. It takes advantage of its waterfront location with a series of one-room bungalows and a restaurant built right over the water. Spacious and

insect-proof, the bungalows make the most of the breezes that blow off the river (when the breeze fails, turn on the fan), but perhaps their nicest feature is their porches, which are perfect for sitting and watching the varied boat traffic that plies the river. Cheaper landlocked rooms aren't nearly as nice. The restaurant and bar are in an immense, open, thatched building with lovely views. A variety of Continental cuisine is served, and among the specialties are steaks and grilled fish, including the delicious robalo, which is common in the river. The hotel arranges boat trips to surrounding attractions and to Livingston. When it's time to cool off, jump in the pool—it's at the center of the grounds— or in the river. ⌧ *5 km (3 mi) east of bridge,* ☎ *447–8361 or* ☎ FAX *336–4450 in Guatemala City. 28 rooms with bath. Restaurant, bar, pool, travel services. MC, V.*

$ 🏨 **Hotel Don Humberto.** This low-budget hotel offers nothing but the basics, but it offers them at an excellent location—at the northern edge of the tiny national park that surrounds Castillo de San Felipe—and with friendly service. Rooms are small cement boxes facing a little courtyard, but they all have private baths and are fairly clean. There's also a small restaurant serving a limited selection of Guatemalan cuisine. ⌧ *Reached via the road to the castle or by a quick boat ride from El Relleno, no phone. 11 rooms with bath. Restaurant. No credit cards.*

River Trips

Trips down the Río Dulce can be arranged through most of the area's hotels or with the **Río Dulce Travel Warehouse** (⌧ Under the concrete bridge, El Relleno, or reached through Izabal Adventures, ☎ 334–0323). The company also offers trips to Finca Paraíso (Paradise Farm) on Lake Izabal. An hour's boat ride takes you to the farm, from which you can walk 45 minutes or hire a tractor to take you to a river with a fabulous hot-springs waterfall secluded in the forest. The owners of the farm charge $1 to visit the site, and they make excellent lunches and have several rustic cabins available for rent.

Livingston

★ ㊿ *37 km (23 mi) northeast of Lake Izabal; take a boat downriver from El Relleno or a ferry from Puerto Barrios*

This charming little beach town that can only be reached via water resembles Belize much more than anything else you'll find in Guatemala. Its main inhabitants are Garifuna, descendants of renegade slaves who migrated here from the island of Roatan, off the coast of Honduras. Their language is a strange mixture of African and European tongues, and their lifestyle is more outdoor-oriented, laid-back, and freewheeling than that of Guatemala's other ethnic groups, which are also represented within the town.

The narrow **beach** that stretches north from the river mouth is lined with shacks for several kilometers and is not very clean near town. A 1½-hour walk or short boat ride to the north takes you to **Siete Altares,** a gorgeous little river with a series of deep pools and rainy-season waterfalls that is ideal for swimming. Nearby are a pleasant beach and restaurant. Don't leave things unguarded at the falls, since the forest sometimes harbors thieves, and avoid walking on the beach late at night.

Boating

Day trips up the Río Dulce to the wildlife reserve or to Punta Manabique can be arranged through the Hotel Tucán Dugú (☞ *below*) and the Río Dulce Travel Warehouse (☞ Río Dulce).

Dining and Lodging

$$$$ ✕🏨 **Hotel Tucán Dugú.** Livingston's only first-class hotel, the Tucán
★ Dugú sits on a hill in the heart of town and consequently has some
great views of the Caribbean. Extensive grounds stretch over the hillside and are largely covered with lush tropical foliage. Units are in a
long, two-story, thatch-roof building, and all of them are spacious and
have views of the gulf. Several suites are available, and some smaller
"bungalows," which are actually just rooms, offer a good value. The
pool, a large bar, a grassy area, and a private beach are down the hill.
The restaurant serves an array of international dishes plus local seafood,
like coconut shrimp and robalo. Trips up the Río Dulce and to spots
around the bay can be arranged. ⌨ *Main St., at top of hill, Barrio San
José,* ☎ *334–5064,* FAX *334–5242;* ☎ *448–1572,* FAX *448–1588 in
Guatemala City. 46 rooms with bath. Restaurant, bar, pool, beach, travel
services. MC, V.*

$ ✕🏨 **African Place.** This mosquelike building houses a restaurant on
the second floor and hotel rooms down below. The rooms face a small
patio that leads to a garden with benches and a shallow pool, and they
are decorated with tile floors and antique reproductions; the restaurant serves the best food in town. Lots of fresh seafood as well as some
more unusual dishes such as Nigerian chicken are the menu's strong
points. ⌨ *West of the school, past the Catholic church, Barrio African
Place, no phone. 11 rooms, 6 with bath. Restaurant. No credit cards.*

Puerto Barrios

⑤ *295 km (183 mi) from Guatemala City at end of Carretera Atlantíca,
or take ferry from Livingston*

Low on attractions but with plenty of hotels and restaurants, this port
town is a good way station if you're headed to or from Belize, Livingston,
or Punta Manabique. You can leave your car at one of the hotels while
you take the ferry to Livingston.

Dining and Lodging

$$$$ ✕🏨 **Cayos del Diablo.** Opened in 1991, this first-class Best Western
hotel on Bahía de Amatique (Amatique Bay) brings luxury accommodations to a spectacular natural setting. Rooms are in a series of
thatched bungalows, with colorful decor, air-conditioning, and cable
TV. The grounds are dotted with tropical gardens and surrounded by
rain forest, and directly in back is a forest-draped hill with a small waterfall. The hotel has a pool, a large restaurant, and private beach, and
trips on the bay and up the Río Dulce can be arranged. ⌨ *13 km (8
mi) west of Puerto Barrios along the Carretera a Livingston, at Las
Pavas, near Santo Tomás de Castilla,* ☎ *448–2361 or 448–0263,* FAX
448–2364; ☎ *333–4633,* FAX *331–5720 in Guatemala City through
the Camino Real Hotel;* ☎ *800/528–1234 in the U.S. 50 rooms with
bath. Restaurant, bar, pool, beach, waterskiing, meeting rooms, travel
services. AE, DC, MC, V.*

$$$ ✕🏨 **Hotel Puerto Libre.** This place stands at a crossroads outside of
town and resembles a U.S. motel, with large, modern, simply fur-
nished rooms built around a parking area and swimming pool. Since
the noise of traffic can rattle the light sleeper, it's worth noting that
units in the far left corner have views of some woods and a small stream
and are quieter. The small restaurant and rooms are air-conditioned.
You can leave your car here if you overnight in Livingston. ⌨ *Cross-
roads for Santo Tomás de Castilla,* ☎ *448–3065,* FAX *448–3513. 30
rooms with bath. Restaurant, pool. AE, MC, V.*

$$ ✕🏨 **Hotel del Norte.** This old waterfront hotel has what the other Puerto
Barrios lodges lack: ambience and a view. A two-story, cream-color,

wooden building with venerable Caribbean character, the hotel has small rooms with high ceilings, soft but small beds, creaky and uneven floors, and porches with wonderful views of the bay. An unattractive cement annex with air-conditioned rooms is available for those who suffer the heat badly. The restaurant downstairs is charming, thanks to old pictures, uniformed waiters, and big windows facing the sea, and it serves some good seafood and local specialties, like *tapado* (a seafood stew). ✉ *7 Calle and 2 Avenida,* ☎ FAX *448–0087. 38 rooms, 20 with bath. Restaurant. No credit cards.*

$$ ✕🛏 **Hotel Henry Berrisford.** A three-story building in town, the Berrisford doesn't look like much, but it offers decent rooms and a pool at a good price. The rooms are rather plain but clean; air-conditioning or a fan keeps units cool, but alas, there is no hot water. A large restaurant is by the swimming pool in back. This hotel has a twin with the same name in Livingston, located right on the waterfront. ✉ *17 Calle and 9 Avenida,* ☎ *448–1557 or 448–1557 in Livingston. 32 rooms with bath. Restaurant, pool. MC, V.*

The Atlantic Lowlands A to Z

Arriving and Departing

BY BUS

Comfortable buses run the route between the capital and Puerto Barrios, with hourly departures from 6 AM to 5 PM, but be sure to ask for the direct bus, **LITEGUA** (✉ 15 Calle 10–40, Zona 1, Guatemala City, ☎ 253–8169). There is sporadic bus or prompt motorcycle-taxi service between the highway and the nearby ruins of Quiriguá. If you're headed for Fronteras, you'll want to get off at La Ruidosa junction and catch a minibus north, but if you're on a late bus (leaving after 1 PM) you'll have to hitch.

All Flores-bound buses pass through Fronteras, but they are slower than the Puerto Barrios buses. Hourly buses leave Guatemala City (✉ 18 Calle and 9 Avenida, Zona 1) for Chiquimula; from Chiquimula, buses regularly leave for El Florido, and a variety of transportation serves the route between the border and Ruinas de Copán.

Izabal Adventures (☎ 334–0323) runs a convenient and comfortable Río Dulce shuttle with door-to-door service to El Relleno on Monday, Wednesday, Friday, Saturday, and Sunday. The van departs Antigua at 5 AM ($37 one way) and Guatemala City at 6 AM ($28), and the ride includes a side trip to Quiriguá. Reservations are required.

BY CAR

The Carretera Atlantíca leaves Guatemala City from the north end of town, at 5 Calle in Zona 2. It heads northeast, first through some mountains, later descending into the desert region of Zacapa, and then through the lush Caribbean lowlands to Puerto Barrios.

Getting Around

BY BOAT

Daily ferry service between Puerto Barrios and Livingston leaves the former at 10:30 AM and 5 PM and the latter at 5 AM and 2 PM. Quicker and slightly more expensive launches also leave regularly between the two cities. The mail boat carries passengers up and down the Río Dulce between El Relleno and Livingston on Tuesday and Friday mornings. There are also plenty of private boats on both ends that will make the trip for a fee. Or you can rent a 46-foot Polynesian catamaran that sleeps 10 people for trips from the Río Dulce to the Belizean cays. Contact **Tivoli Travel** (✉ 5a Avenida Norte 10A, Antigua, ☎ 332–3041).

TIKAL AND EL PETÉN

Both an archaeological and a biological wonderland, what is now the jungle department of El Petén was once the heartland of Maya civilization. For the past millennium, however, it has been a sparsely populated backwater in which ruins dot the landscape and nature reigns. Whatever your primary interest, you'll find plenty to see in this fascinating region, where exploring the remnants of the ancient Maya culture and observing the complexity of the tropical rain forest go hand in hand.

In recent decades the Guatemalan government has attempted to settle this modern-day frontier, but much of the province remains the realm of the monkey and the macaw. Though covering about a third of Guatemala's territory, El Petén is home to less than 3% of the country's 10.3 million inhabitants. Rapid development is costing its wilderness, but the natural and anthropological wonders that remain are ample inspiration for extensive travel.

Rain-forest travel is about as difficult as it gets, however, and reaching many of these sites means driving down muddy roads that require four-wheel drive, along with boating and hiking skills. A growing supply of services makes getting around easier than it used to be, but it still takes a considerable while. Still, the difficulty in getting to some sites can actually enhance the feeling of adventure. Though the ancient ruins are the focus of most expeditions, they often become secondary to the exotic scenery and rare tropical species you'll witness along the way, or to the excitement of the river, horseback, and Jeep trips required to reach them. The only sites that are easy to visit are Tikal and the Cerro Cahui Wildlife Reserve, both of which are connected to the airport by the department's only paved road. Everything else is off the beaten path but well worth the trip.

The hub, and only airport, of this region is in the area around the island town of Flores. The first sites discussed are those south of there, including the second-best ruins in El Petén: Ceibal, on the Río de La Pasión. It should only be visited if you have three or more days in the region because it takes almost four hours to reach from Flores. Following that, sites north of Flores are discussed, including the best: Tikal. The beauty and intrigue of this ancient Maya city, where majestic temples tower above pristine rain forest, warrant at least a two-day visit, though it is possible to see in a day. Your time limitations will dictate what you'll be able to cover, but keep in mind that after exerting so much effort to get here, it's nice to be able to stay a while. If you have the time, consider visiting the ruins at Dos Pilas, Uaxactún, or Yaxjá, or exploring the area around Lake Petén Itzá.

Numbers in the margin correspond to points of interest on the Tikal and El Petén map.

Sayaxché

🛈 *61 km (38 mi) southwest of Flores*

Down a bumpy dirt road from Flores, a muddy frontier town on the southern bank of the Río de La Pasión is a good base for exploring the southern Petén. Sayaxché offers spartan accommodations and services. The La Pasión and nearby Petexbatún rivers lead to a number of important ruins and flow past numerous wonders of tropical nature.

Dining and Lodging

$$ ✕🏠 **La Montaña.** This new arrival on the Petexbatún River is a lodging option that lies somewhere between the jungle luxury of the Posada

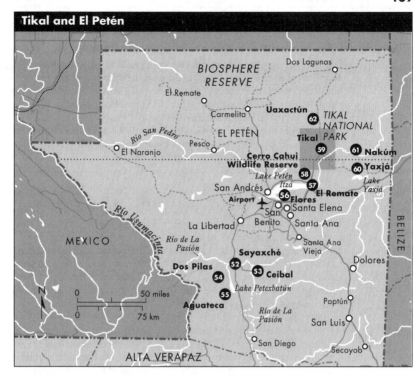

de Matéo and the cheap accommodations in Sayaxché. On a bend in the river, the lodge consists of a series of bungalows built in a clearing hacked out of the rain forest. In each house, you'll find a cement floor, bamboo walls, and a simply appointed private bath. Family-style meals are served in a rustic open-air dining hall. As a guest, you can book a tour of local archaeological sites. ✉ *For reservations, contact Julio Mariona at La Montaña Tours, no phone,* ✆ *250–0622. 8 rooms with bath. Dining room, travel services. No credit cards.*

$ 🏨 **Hotel Guayacan.** A really run-down-looking lodge that stands by the south bank of the Río de La Pasión, the Guayacan offers basic accommodations at a reasonable price. Rooms are on the second floor of this motel-like structure, which is surrounded by mud, and are equipped with decent beds and private or shared baths. There is no decor to speak of, but the establishment is clean and conveniently located. There is a small parking area, and the owner can arrange boat trips to Maya ruins. ✉ *South bank of Río Pasión,* ☎ *250–6111. 10 rooms. Travel services. No credit cards.*

$ 🏨 **La Posada Maya Betal.** On the banks of the Río Usumacinta in the town of Betel, this rustic lodge, basically just hammocks and a thatched roof, is a good jumping-off point for trips to nearby ruins such as Yaxchilán. ✉ *Contact Maya Expeditions,* ☎ *337–4666, or Raphael Sagastume at Villa Maya hotel,* ☎ *331–9872. No credit cards.*

River Trips

The lowland Río de La Pasión flows into the Usumacinta, which winds for countless miles through the rain forest. Both rivers were important trade routes of the ancient Maya and thus pass archaeological sites, like the impressive Yaxchilán, down the Usumacinta on the Mexican side of the river. Both are also easily navigated. As a result, they are popular for expeditions, which can last from a day to more than a week. Along the way, you can catch a glimpse of the area's many animal inhabitants, including turtles, crocodiles, and a vast array of birds.

For river trips out of Sayaxché, talk to Julio Mariona at **La Montaña Tours** (no phone, FAX 250–0622) or **Jorge and Pedro Mendez,** who have an office by the river but are expensive. A day trip to one of the ruins should cost $30–$60, depending on the number of passengers. Bargain before you travel! River trips are also organized by several tour companies in the capital (☞ Guided Tours *in* Tikal and El Petén A to Z, *below*). Trips arranged by **Maya Expeditions** (☎ 337–4666) also include visits to nearby archaeological sites.

Ceibal

★ ⑤ *1 hr from Sayaxché by boat plus a ½-hr climb through the jungle*

Upriver from Sayaxché is an impressive ruin that served as a toll gate for barges plying the river in ancient Maya times. Though its few and far-flung structures don't rival those of Tikal, it is nevertheless beautiful and inspiring in its own right. Ceibal's beauty has much to do with its jungle surroundings, which offer visitors glimpses of the rain forests' seemingly infinite web of life. The site's archaeological attractions include several restored temples, including the only circular one known to date; plazas; and intricately carved stelae. One interesting aspect is the number of anomalies found in monuments, which hint at profound foreign influence, most likely from the Toltecs of central Mexico. Though it can be driven to via a dirt road, which floods during the rainy season, Ceibal is best reached by boat on the Río de La Pasión, followed by a half-hour ascent through the forest. *No phone.* ☐ *Free.*

Lake Petexbatún

2 hrs by boat from Ceibal

This impressive rain-forest lagoon was once an important area for the Maya and is consequently near several significant sites, which once shared trade and cultural ties. A three-hour hike or shorter horseback ride west ⑤ brings you to **Dos Pilas.** Important recent archaeological finds indicate that continual warfare may have caused an ecological imbalance that led to the collapse of Maya civilization. The ancient city's attractions include a staircase covered with hieroglyphics as well as the surrounding forest.

⑤ On the southern shore of the lake lies **Aguateca,** a small site that is beautiful but largely unrestored. It does have a few nice stelae, and the trip here is a wonderful river adventure.

The smaller site of **Punta de Chimino,** on Lake Petexbatún, has little worth seeing but is the location of a wonderful hotel, the Posada de Matéo.

Dining and Lodging

$$$ ✕⌂ **Posada de Matéo.** This luxury nature lodge is spread out over Punta de Chimino, a small peninsula in Lake Petexbatún that archaeologists speculate was once a home for Maya nobility, which makes it the logical location for an exceptional rain-forest retreat. The posada consists of a series of bungalows scattered along the peninsula's edges, each unit set amid the rain-forest foliage, with a private view of the lake and jungle beyond. The bungalows are beautiful, with resin-coated hardwood floors, modern bathrooms, and screened walls that make you feel a part of the jungle while keeping its insect inhabitants at a safe distance. Delicious meals are served in an open-air restaurant, and tours of

nearby archaeological sites are included in the price of the room. ✉ *Punta de Chimino, no phone.* 𝔽𝔸𝕏 *250–0505 in El Petén. 6 rooms with bath. Restaurant, travel services. No credit cards.*

Flores

★ ➄ *61 km (38 mi) northeast of Sayaxché*

This island city, surrounded by the waters of Lake Petén Itzá, was the last outpost of the Maya civilization in Guatemala to be conquered by the Spanish; it didn't fall to the European invaders until 1697. Today the colorful provincial capital is connected to the mainland by a causeway. Though most of the area's population and commerce are in the muddy villages of **San Benito** and **Santa Elena,** Flores is a much more attractive town, a place where you'll likely want to spend more time.

There's a nice view of the countryside from Mirador San Miguel, and there are a bevy of restaurants serving traditional cuisine (with freshwater fish specials) in rustic ambience, all one block off the lake, west of the causeway.

Still, there are things better left to the mainland. Though there are banks in both Santa Elena and Flores, the gas stations are in Santa Elena—don't leave town with less than a full tank. Flores has no sewage-treatment system, so it is inadvisable to swim close to town, though otherwise the lake is acceptable.

Dining and Lodging

$ ✕ **Chal Tun Ha.** This little waterfront restaurant is a pleasant alternative to the rustic eateries that abound on the isle. The restaurant itself is hardly an inspiring structure—a cement building planted on gravel—but its many windows take advantage of the view, and the limited menu offers simple but well-prepared items, like fish from the lake or the standard stuffed peppers. ✉ *Southwest corner of island, no phone. No credit cards.*

$ ✕ **El Tucán.** Turn left off the causeway, take the next two right turns, and you'll find this small lakeside restaurant. A pleasant patio, which serves as a playground for the owner's pet toucans and parrots, looks onto the water. Or you might opt for the small dining room decorated with highland weavings—if you sit by a window, you'll have a good view of one of Flores's colorful cobblestone streets. The menu includes a variety of traditions, though Mexican cuisine is the specialty. Bread is baked inhouse. ✉ *Southeast corner of island,* ☎ *250–1577. MC, V.*

$$$$ ✕▦ **Villa Maya.** Big, bright rooms in a series of bungalows along
★ beautiful Lake Petén Itzá enable guests to bird-watch from their beds (some 50 species of birds populate the lake region). A troupe of seven semitrained spider monkeys roams the grounds. What's more, the hotel owns and protects some 250 acres of rain forest surrounding the lake. Rooms are spacious and tastefully ornamented—mahogany floors and white walls are decorated with colorful weavings and paintings—but the best part of every room is the view of the lake and surrounding jungle, all of which can be explored by following a trail around the lake or renting a rowboat. There is a small zoo on the grounds, a swimming pool, and an open-air restaurant. The hotel also has several vans and offers daily trips to Tikal. ✉ *A short drive north of the paved road, 12 km (7½ mi) east of Santa Elena,* ☎ *334–8136,* 𝔽𝔸𝕏 *334–8023 in Guatemala City. 44 rooms with bath. Restaurant, pool, horseback riding, boating, travel services. AE, DC, MC, V.*

$$$ ✕▦ **Maya International.** This group of thatched bungalows built over Lake Petén Itzá in Santa Elena has some of the best views around. The lake rose several yards in 1979, flooding the bottom floors of the en-

tire hotel, but the top floors are still in good shape and can be reached via a series of pedestrian causeways. The rooms themselves are pretty simple, with twin beds, fans, and private baths, but their private balconies afford some wonderful views, the best ones being units 48 through 54, which are the farthest out. The hotel's pool and grounds having been inundated, the area between bungalows is now covered with water lilies, on which waterfowl forage for dinner. The hotel's moderately priced restaurant, in a round, thatched building with a wooden floor, is built over the water and thus offers a great view of the lake by which to enjoy your meal. Almost every table is near a window. The menu, consisting of a set meal and just a few substitutes, changes daily, since the supply of groceries is rather sporadic in El Petén. ⊠ *A few blocks east of causeway, in Santa Elena,* ☎ *334–8136,* ☎ *334–8134 in Guatemala City;* ☎ *250–1276 for restaurant. 20 rooms with bath. Restaurant. AE, DC, MC, V.*

$$ ✕▥ **Hotel Petén.** This newer place run by friendly Pedro Castellanos
★ is one of the best hotels in Flores. Great views of the lake can be had from the windows and balconies of most rooms and the deck out back. Rooms are simple but clean, with good beds, fans, and private baths with hot water. The staff arranges trips to Tikal or around the lake. ⊠ *West end of island,* ☎ *250–0692,* ☎ *250–0593. 21 rooms with bath. Restaurant, pool, travel services. MC, V (10% surcharge).*

$$$ ▥ **Hotel del Patio-Tikal.** A barrel-tile roof shelters this modern hotel, built in traditional Spanish style. Porticoes, balconies, and rooms face a large, grassy courtyard that contains a small patio with chairs and a central fountain. You'll find red-tile floors, big bathrooms, closets, ceiling fans, and cable TV in the rooms. ⊠ *2 Calle and 8 Avenida, Santa Elena,* ☎ *250–0104,* ☎ *250–1229. 22 rooms with bath. Restaurant. AE, DC, MC, V.*

$$ ▥ **Hotel Yum Kax.** This large building may not be terribly attractive, but it has a good supply of inexpensive rooms. Units are simple, with fans and private baths, but some of the ones on the upper floor face the lake and thus have decent views. The restaurant is best avoided. ⊠ *Southwest corner of island,* ☎ *250–0686. 39 rooms with bath. Restaurant, pool. No credit cards.*

$$ ▥ **Sabana Hotel.** One of the best hotels on the island, the Sabana has a sundeck, a restaurant, and simple rooms with views of Lake Petén Itzá. ▥ *Calle La Union, north side of island,* ☎ *250–1248. 23 rooms. Restaurant. MC, V.*

$$ ▥ **San Juan.** This large hotel a block in from the causeway offers a variety of decent rooms with private or shared baths. In addition, it is a departure point for a lot of early morning buses, so eager-beaver travelers can jump out of bed and hop right on their transport. If you want to sleep late, however, get a back room. ⊠ *2 Calle and 6 Avenida, Santa Elena,* ☎ *250–0041. 60 rooms, 35 with bath. Restaurant, travel services. AE, DC, MC, V.*

Nightlife and the Arts

A light and airy bar-café on a Flores side street, **Las Puertas** (⊠ Across from El Tucán, southeast corner of island) is a place to sit and talk among friends. It has live music at night.

Outdoor Activities and Sports

BOATING

Boat trips on **Lake Petén Itzá** can be arranged through hotels in Flores or by haggling with boat owners found near the causeway.

There are several caves in the hills behind Santa Elena, which have interesting stalactite and stalagmite formations, subterranean rivers, and blindfish. The easiest to visit is **Aktun Kan,** just south of town, but it's strongly advised you go with a guide.

Shopping

Though there are several stores in Flores that sell típica, you can find it just as easily and buy it even cheaper in the rest of the country.

El Remate

57 *30 km (18½ mi) northeast of Flores*

At the eastern end of Lake Petén Itzá, this town has several hotels that make it a good base for exploring the northern parts of the El Petén region.

58 West of town, the **Cerro Cahui Wildlife Reserve** (⊠ On dirt road off road to Tikal) is a good spot for a nature hike or a swim in the lake. The reserve comprises more than 1,500 acres of rain forest and a stretch of lakefront. A hike on the 3-kilometer (2-mile) trail that enters the woods near the ranger station offers a chance to see ocellated turkeys, toucans, parrots, spider monkeys, and a wealth of other tropical critters. For more information about this wildlife reserve and other natural areas, *see* Chapter 2.

Dining and Lodging

$$$$ ✕▥ **Camino Real Tikal.** This is El Petén's premier hotel, and first-class
★ it is. Among its myriad virtues are a top-notch restaurant, a bar, and a swimming pool, and the list goes on. Large, colorful rooms under thatched roofs are equipped with air-conditioning, cable TV, minibar, and balcony or patio, and all have a spectacular view of Lake Petén Itzá, where guests can go canoeing, swimming, fishing, windsurfing, or take a sunset cruise on the hotel's yacht. At the eastern end of the lake, within the Cerro Cahui Wildlife Reserve, the hotel grounds are surrounded by wilderness, and it's just a half-hour drive from the ruins of Tikal. ⊠ *On dirt road to Cerro Cahui Wildlife Reserve, west of El Remate,* ☎ *250–0204 through 209,* FAX *250–0222, or call Camino Real in Guatemala City,* ☎ *333–4633; 800/228–3000 in the U.S. 72 rooms with bath. Restaurant, bar, coffee shop, pool, windsurfing, boating, fishing, shops, recreation room, meeting rooms, travel services, car rental. AE, DC, MC, V.*

$–$$ ✕▥ ⌂ **El Gringo Perdido.** Fortunately for those on tighter budgets, there's a reasonably priced option for staying in the beautiful Cerro Cahui area: a collection of cabins in the forest called the Lost Gringo. Accommodations are dorm-style, with a number of bunk beds packed into each room, but the location compensates for any minor discomfort. The lake, a great spot for swimming, sits at your doorstep, and the forest surrounds you. Trails run through the nearby reserve. Camping is allowed for a few dollars, and a dining hall with a menu that changes daily is on the property. You can get a plan that includes two meals per day or take no meal plan. ⊠ *By the reserve, west of El Remate,* ☎ *334–0135 in Guatemala City. 40 beds. Restaurant. No credit cards.*

Shopping

Whereas other típica here is similar to that found elsewhere in Guatemala, the beautiful **wood carvings** of El Remate are unique to El Petén. More than 70 families in this small town dedicate themselves to this craft, and their wares should not be missed. They are on display on the side of the highway right before the turnoff for the Camino Real hotel on the road to Tikal.

Tikal

★ 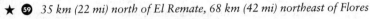 *35 km (22 mi) north of El Remate, 68 km (42 mi) northeast of Flores*

The high point of any trip to El Petén is a visit to the country's most famous and impressive Maya ruins. (In fact, so impressive is Tikal, it's worth saving for last.) Though the forest that surrounds the ruins is today the home of the hummingbird and the jaguar, the area was covered with villages and farms 1,500 years ago, when an estimated 50,000–100,000 people lived here. What remains of that metropolis is an array of well-restored structures, including the tallest pyramid in the western hemisphere; some unrestored but nevertheless fine ruins; and two museums filled with smaller monuments and artifacts that archaeologists have recovered from the jungle—all spread over 585 square kilometers (226 square miles). As it is near the center of the forest-covered, protected Tikal National Park, Tikal is ideal for wildlife observation as well as archaeological exploration. Commonly seen critters include spider monkeys, deer, coatimundis, toucans, parrots, scarlet macaws, and ocellated turkeys. For more information about the national park, *see* Chapter 2.

Though the area had Maya communities by 600 BC, Tikal's civilization didn't reach its height until around AD 600. During the Classic Period (AD 250–900), Tikal was an important religious and administrative center. The great temples that still tower above the jungle were at that time covered with stucco and painted bright colors, and a hierarchy of priests and dynastic rulers used them for elaborate ceremonies meant to please the gods and thus assure prosperity for the city. What makes these structures even more impressive is that the Maya had no beasts of burden, never used the wheel for anything but children's toys, and possessed no metal tools to aid in construction.

The city of Tikal thrived for more than a millennium, trading and warring with city-states both near and far. It probably exerted considerable influence over other cities in the area, only to be heavily influenced itself by the civilization of Teotihuacán, in central Mexico, which dominated the entire region during the latter half of the Classic Period. But by AD 900, Tikal was in a state of chaos as the entire Maya empire began its mysterious decline and the process of depopulation had begun. Though the site may have been sporadically inhabited for centuries thereafter, the civilization of the Maya throughout the region suffered a rapid decline.

As you enter the site, you walk toward the west, and if you keep to the middle trail, you arrive at Tikal's ancient center, with its awe-inspiring temples and intricate acropolises. The pyramid you approach from behind is **Temple I,** or Temple of the Great Jaguar, after the feline represented on one of its carved lintels. It's in what is referred to as the **Gran Plaza,** one of the most beautiful and dramatic plazas in Tikal. Facing Temple I, to the east, is **Temple II,** or Temple of the Masks, dubbed for the decorations on its facade and an exact twin of the Temple of the Jaguar. In fact, construction of twin pyramids distinguishes Tikal from other Maya sites of the ancient realm. The Gran Plaza was built around AD 700 by Ak Cacao, one of the wealthiest rulers of his time. His tomb, comparable in magnitude to that of Pa Cal at Palenque, in southern Mexico, was discovered beneath the Temple of the Great Jaguar in the 1960s. The theory is that his queen is buried beneath the Temple of the Masks.

The **North Acropolis,** to the right of Ak Cacao's temple, is a mind-boggling conglomeration of temples built over layers and layers of previous construction. Excavations have revealed that the base of this

It helps to be pushy in airports.

Introducing the revolutionary new TransPorter™ from American Tourister® It's the first suitcase you can push around without a fight. TransPorter's™ exclusive four-wheel design lets you push it in front of you with almost no effort–the wheels take the weight. Or pull it on two wheels if you choose. You can even stack on other bags and use it like a luggage cart.

Stable 4-wheel design.

TransPorter™ is designed like a dresser, with built-in shelves to organize your belongings. Or collapse the shelves and pack it like a traditional suitcase. Inside, there's a suiter feature to help keep suits and dresses from wrinkling. When push comes to shove, you can't beat a TransPorter™ For more information on how you can be this pushy, call 1-800-542-1300.

Shelves collapse on command.

 American Tourister®

Making travel less primitive®

Your passport around the world.

- Worldwide access
- Operators who speak your language
- Monthly itemized billing

MCI ✦ Calling Card

415 555 1234 2244
J.D. SMITH

Use your MCI Card® and these access numbers for an easy way to call when traveling worldwide.

American Samoa	633-2MCI (633-2624)
Antigua †	#2
(Available from public card phones only)	
Aruba ÷	800-888-8
Argentina ★†	001-800-333-1111
Bahamas (CC)†	1-800-888-8000
Barbados	1-800-888-8000
Belize	815 from pay phones
	557 from hotels
Bermuda ÷†	1-800-888-8000
Bolivia ◆	0-800-2222
Brazil (CC)†	000-8012
British Virgin Islands ÷	1-800-888-8000
Cayman Islands†	1-800-888-8000
Chile (CC)†	
To call using CTC ■	800-207-300
To call using ENTEL ■	123-00316
Colombia (CC)◆†	980-16-0001
Costa Rica ◆†	0800-012-2222
Dominica	1-800-888-8000
Dominican Republic (CC)	1-800-888-8000
Ecuador (CC) ÷†	999-170
El Salvador ◆	800-1767
Grenada ÷	1-800-888-8000

Guatemala ◆	189
Guyana	177
Haiti (CC) ÷	001-800-444-1234
Honduras ÷	122
Jamaica	1-800-888-8000
(From Special Hotels only)	873
Mexico ▲†	95-800-674-7000
Netherlands Antilles (CC) ÷†	
	001-800-950-1022
Nicaragua (CC)	166
(Outside of Managua, dial 02 first)	
Panama†	108
Military Bases	2810-108
Paraguay ÷	008-11-800
Peru	170
Puerto Rico (CC)†	1-800-888-8000
St. Lucia ÷	1-800-888-8000
Trinidad & Tobago ÷	1-800-888-8000
Turks & Caicos ÷	1-800-888-8000
Uruguay	00-412
U.S. Virgin Islands (CC)†	1-800-888-8000
Venezuela ÷◆	800-1114-0

To sign up for the MCI Card, dial the access number of the country you are in and ask to speak with a customer service representative.

MCI

http://www.mci.com

†Automation available from most locations. ÷ Limited availability. ★ Not available from public pay phones. (CC) Country-to-country calling available.
May not be available to/from all international locations. (Canada, Puerto Rico, and U.S. Virgin Islands are considered Domestic Access locations.)
◆ Public phones may require deposit of coin or phone card for dial tone. ■ International communications carrier.
▲ When calling from public phones use phones marked LADATEL.

structure is more than 2,000 years old. Be sure to see the stone mask of the rain god at Temple 33. The **Central Acropolis,** south of the plaza, is an immense series of structures assumed to have been palaces and administrative centers.

If you climb one of the pyramids, you'll see the gray roof combs of other pyramids rising above the green sea of the rain forest's canopy but still trapped within it. Temple V, to the south, and Temple IV, to the west, are both waiting to be restored to some memory of their former grandeur. **Temple IV** is the tallest known structure built by the Maya, and though the climb to the top is difficult and involves some scrambling over roots and rocks, the view is something you will not soon forget. If you can, go at sunrise, when the new light provides fabulous illumination, howler monkeys scream call and response, and toucans fly below.

To the southwest of the plaza lie the **South Acropolis,** which hasn't been reconstructed, and the **Lost World complex,** with its 105-foot-high pyramid, similar to those at Mexico's Teotihuacán. A few trails through the jungle, including the marked interpretative **Trail Benil-Ha,** offer opportunities to see spider monkeys and toucans. Outside the park, a somewhat overgrown trail halfway down the old airplane runway on the left leads to the remnants of old rubber-tappers' camps and is a good bird-watching spot.

The ruins are reached via the only paved road in El Petén. At park headquarters, near the ruins, are the two archaeological museums, three hotels, and a few small restaurants. Tikal deserves more than one day. If you want to see wildlife, it's best to stay in the park and get moving before dawn. For a truly stirring experience, come on a full-moon night, and stay to view the moonrise (bring a flashlight) after all the tour buses are gone; visitors may stay two hours past usual closing time. For more information on the site, William Coe's book *Tikal: A Handbook of the Ancient Maya Ruins* is a good source and can be purchased in the airport, at the area's larger hotels, and sometimes at the park entrance. *No phone.* 🎟 *$5; guides about $10 per person.* ⊙ *Daily 8–6.*

Dining and Lodging

$$$ ✕🏨 **Jungle Lodge.** The largest hotel in the park, the lodge offers rooms
★ with private or shared baths, a restaurant, and a pool, all of which are surrounded by jungle and only a short walk from the ruins. Keep your eyes open for surprises on the grounds, like ocellated turkeys or scarlet macaws. The restaurant is best avoided in favor of the nearby cantinas. ⊠ *Tikal park headquarters,* 🕾 *477–0570; for reservations,* FAX *476–0294 in Guatemala City. 46 rooms, 34 with bath. Restaurant, pool. No credit cards.*

$$$ ✕🏨 **Tikal Inn.** This small hotel near the airstrip consists of a series of comfortably rustic bungalows surrounding a pool. The rooms are much more attractive than the Jungle Lodge's and have thatched roofs, white stucco walls, and traditional fabrics. There is also a small restaurant for guests, with a menu that changes daily. Rates are reasonable and include breakfast and dinner. ⊠ *Tikal park headquarters,* 🕾 *250–0065. 22 rooms with bath. Restaurant, pool. No credit cards.*

Yaxjá

🅿 *10 km (6 mi) east of Tikal, 45 km (28 mi) northeast of El Remate, 80 km (50 mi) northeast of Flores; from the paved road at Tikal National Park, take the dirt road heading toward Belize for 2 hrs and then another dirt road on the left to the ruins of Nakún and Yaxjá*

At the ruins of Yaxjá, which overlook a beautiful lake of the same name, two sections of rectangular structures form plazas and streets, probably inhabited between the pre-Classic and post-Classic periods. Surrounded by virgin rain forest, Lake Yaxjá is also a fine spot for birdwatching. You can only reach it by four-wheel-drive vehicle, on horseback, or by foot, whereas the island ruins of Topoxte can be visited by boat from El Campamento del Sombrero (contact Juan de la Hoz, ☎ 250–0196), a rustic lodge.

Nakúm

61 *26 km (16 mi) east of Tikal*

Nakúm lies deep within the forest connected to Tikal via jungle trails that are sometimes used for horseback expeditions. You cannot visit during the rainy season as you'll wallow in mud up to your ankles. Two building complexes and stelae can be viewed.

Uaxactún

62 *A day trip via four-wheel drive north from Tikal*

This important though unrestored site contains construction that is 4,000 years old, and among the ruins is an observatory. Both the ruins and the road here are surrounded by the natural wonders of the rain forest, so the trip can be an ecological excursion as well. The track to Uaxactún heads out of Tikal between the old museum and the Jungle Lodge, and if current roadwork is successful, it may become possible to make the trip without a four-wheel-drive vehicle in the near future.

Tikal and El Petén A to Z

Arriving and Departing

BY BUS

Bus service to Flores from Guatemala City takes between 10 and 20 hours, and the trip is one of the most uncomfortable in the Western world. It's best to break up the trip with a stop in Poptún, but frankly, unless you're on an incredibly tight budget, you'll want to fly at least one way. Bus companies serving El Petén are **Maya Express** (✉ 17 Calle 9–36, Zona 1, Guatemala City, ☎ 232–1914) and **Petenera** (✉ 16 Calle and 10 Avenida, Zona 1, Guatemala City, ☎ 232–9658). Both offer departures at 4, 6, and 8 PM. Direct buses, which make fewer stops, cost about $10 each way, and reservations are required.

BY PLANE

Flights from Guatemala City to Flores last less than an hour and cost about $75 each way. Several daily flights leave the capital around 7 AM and return around 4 PM, and tickets can be purchased at any travel agency. Airlines that fly to Flores daily include **Aviateca** (☎ 238–1415), **Aerovias** (☎ 331–9663), **Tapsa** (☎ 331–4860), and **Tikal Jets** (☎ 334–5631). The airport is about a mile outside town. Taxis meet every plane and charge about $2 to take you into Flores.

Aerovias has flights from Flores to Belize City at 9:30 AM Monday, Wednesday, Friday, and Sunday. Air service to the Mexican resort of Cancún is offered by **Aviateca** at 5:45 PM on Tuesday and Saturday and by **Aerocaribe** at 5:30 PM on Monday and weekends. Call the **Flores airport** (☎ 250–0042) for information.

Getting Around

BY BUS

The **San Juan hotel** (✉ 2 Calle and 6 Avenida, Santa Elena) is the local bus terminal, with service to the following destinations: Tikal, 6:30 AM and 1 PM (the trip takes 2 hours); Poptún, 5 and 10 AM, 1 and 3:30

PM; Melchor Menos (border with Belize), 5, 8, and 10 AM and 2 and 4 PM. Local buses are inexpensive but very slow.

San Juan Travel (⊠ San Juan hotel, Santa Elena, ☎ 250–0042) runs daily minibus service to Tikal, with departures at 6, 8, and 10 AM and returns at 2, 4, and 5 PM.

BY TAXI

Taxis can be hired at the airport to take you just about anywhere in the region, but tours are often cheaper.

Contacts and Resources

CAR RENTALS

If you're not on a tour, the best way to get around El Petén is by renting a four-wheel-drive vehicle. All the major car-rental companies have offices at the airport, and you can call ahead to reserve from **Budget** (☎ 250–0741) or **Koka** (☎ 250–1232). **Hertz** (☎ 250–0204) also rents Jeeps from an office in the Camino Real Tikal hotel. **San Juan Travel** (⊠ San Juan hotel, Santa Elena, ☎ 250–0042) rents four-wheel-drive Jeeps and vans.

EMERGENCIES

Police (☎ 250–1365).

Hospital. El Petén Hospital (⊠ Flores, ☎ 250–0619). Medical facilities in El Petén are primitive at best. If you are really sick, get on the next plane back to Guatemala City.

Pharmacies. Farmacia Nueva (⊠ Avenida Santa Ana, Flores, ☎ 250–1387) and **Farmacia San Carlos** (⊠ 2 Calle 727, Zona 1, Santa Elena, ☎ 250–0701).

GUIDED TOURS

Toucan Tours (☎ 250–1380), **Maya Expeditions** (☎ 337–4666 in Guatemala City), **Jaguar Tours** (☎ 334–0421), **Intertours** (☎ 331–5421), and **Expedition Panamundo** (☎ 331–7641) operate out of Guatemala City. The El Petén environmental group **ProPetén** (☎ 250–1370), a Nature Conservancy affiliate that seeks economic alternatives for Petén residents to cutting down the rain forest, is planning to offer in-depth adventure trips led by rubber tappers who once worked in the forest.

VISITOR INFORMATION

The **INGUAT** office for both Flores and El Petén is in Flores (☎ 250–0533). An office at the airport is open sporadically.

Arcas (⊠ Calle El Remolino, Flores, ☎ 250–0566), an organization that takes animals captured from poachers and releases them back into the wild, is a great resource on the flora and fauna of El Petén as well as a good source of information on ecotours. It has a tremendous nature library that is open to the public during office hours, daily 9–7.

GUATEMALA A TO Z

Arriving and Departing

By Boat

The Río Usumacinta is a "back-door" route connecting Sayaxché, in El Petén, with Benemerito, Mexico. This boat trip requires several days of jungle travel and is best done with a tour group. You'll have to get your passport stamped in Flores. There are also two routes into Honduras, through Esquipulas, or El Florido, near the ruins of Copán. A boat leaves Puerto Barrios for Punta Gorda, Belize, on Tuesdays and Fridays at 7:30 AM.

By Bus

There is bus service from Guatemala City to both the Mexican and Honduran borders as well as to San Salvador. To La Mesilla, on the Mexican border, **El Condor** (⊠ 19 Calle 2–01, Zona 1, Guatemala City, ☎ 232–8504) runs a seven-hour trip, with departures at 4, 8, 10, 1, and 5. **Fortaleza** (⊠ 19 Calle 8–70, Zona 1, Guatemala City, ☎ 251–7994) has hourly departures, 1 AM–6 PM, to Tecún Umán, on the Mexican border; the journey takes five hours. For service to El Carmen/Talismán, also on the Mexican border, contact **Galgos** (⊠ 7 Avenida 19–44, Zona 1, Guatemala City, ☎ 232–3661). Departures for the five-hour ride are at 5:30 and 10 AM and 1:30 and 5 PM. **Melva International** (⊠ 3 Avenida 1–38, Zona 9, Guatemala City, ☎ 331–0874) has service to San Salvador. Eight buses a day run between 4 AM and 6 PM and take five hours. For service to Esquipulas, on the border of Honduras, try **Rutas Orientales** (⊠ 19 Calle 8–18, Zona 1, Guatemala City, ☎ 253–7282). Buses run almost hourly from 5 AM to 6 PM and take four hours. For El Florido, take the bus to Chiquimula at 7 or 10 AM or 12:30 PM and change there.

On the Caribbean side, **San Juan Travel** (⊠ San Juan hotel, Santa Elena, ☎ 250–0042) runs minibus service to Belize City and Chetumal.

By Car

It is possible to enter Guatemala by land from Mexico, Belize, El Salvador, and Honduras. The Interamerican Highway connects the country with Mexico at La Mesilla and with El Salvador at San Cristobal Frontera, and it passes through most major cities. It's also possible to travel to El Salvador via the coastal highway, crossing at Ciudad Pedro de Alvarado, or via CA 8 to Valle Nuevo. Pacific routes to Mexico pass through Tecún Umán and El Carmen/Talismán. To reach Belize, take the highway east from Flores, passing El Cruce before reaching the border town of Melchor de Mencos. To reach Honduras, take Highway CA 9 east to Río Hondo, where you can take CA 10 south through Esquipulas to Agua Caliente at the border.

By Plane

Guatemala has two international airports: **La Aurora** (☎ 332–6084 to 6087), at the edge of Guatemala City, and the smaller Flores airport near Flores, in El Petén, which is a stop for some flights between the capital and Mexico. The main airport is served by the following airlines: **Aerovias** (☎ 331–9663), **American** (☎ 334–7379), **Aviateca** (☎ 334–7722), **Continental** (☎ 335–3341), **Copa** (☎ 331–6903), **Iberia** (☎ 332–0911), **KLM** (☎ 337–0222 to 0224), **Lacsa** (☎ 334–6905), **Mexicana** (☎ 333–6001), **Sam** (☎ 332–3242), **Taca** (☎ 332–2360), **Tapsa** (☎ 448–1860), **Tikal Jets** (☎ 334–5631), and **United** (☎ 332–2995). There are direct flights to Guatemala from the following U.S. cities: Los Angeles, Dallas, Houston, New York, Washington, Chicago, New Orleans, and Miami. From Miami it is 2½ hours to Guatemala City; from Houston, 4½ hours; from New York or Chicago, 5½ hours; and from San Francisco, 7 hours. Though no direct flights are available from the United Kingdom or Canada, connections can be made through U.S. airports.

By Train

Guatemala is served by a national rail service—**Ferrocarriles de Guatemala** (⊠ 9 Avenida 18–03, Zona 1, Guatemala City, ☎ 238–3030). Service is not extensive, but it does go to the Mexican border town of Tecún Umán. Contact the main office, or go to the government tourist office (INGUAT) for timetables.

Getting Around

By Bus

Buses are the most widely used form of public transportation, with service covering almost every place that has a road. Buses range from comfortable tour bus–style vehicles complete with attendants selling snacks, to run-down converted school buses carrying twice as many people as they were built to hold, plus animals. Most interurban buses leave Guatemala City from private terminals scattered around Zona 1 or from the big terminal in Zona 4.

By Car

A valid driver's license in your home country is all that's needed to drive legally in Guatemala. Roads to larger towns and cities are generally paved; you'll find mostly dirt roads leading to small towns. Four-wheel drive is a necessity in many remote areas, especially at the height of the rainy season. Gas stations are also scarce off the main roads, so be sure to fill up before heading into rural areas. Also, don't count on finding repair shops outside the major towns.

Keep eyes peeled for children or animals entering the road and for branches in the middle of the road, a signal to drivers that there is a stopped car or accident around the next bend (but don't stop for unmanned roadblocks; ☞ Security, *below*). *Alto* (stop) signs or *tumulos* (speed bumps) are often found near military checkpoints; sometimes you may have to stop and let officials check you out. *Frene con motor* (brake with motor) means a steep descent lies ahead.

Breaking into cars is common in the capital, so it's best to park in a guarded lot and avoid leaving anything of value in the car. All expensive and most moderate hotels have protected parking areas.

By Plane

The only commercial domestic air route is the one between Guatemala City and Flores, connecting the capital to the jungle region of El Petén (☞ Arriving and Departing by Plane *in* Tikal and El Petén A to Z, *above*).

By Train

Ferrocarriles de Guatemala (✉ 9 Avenida 18–03, Zona 1, Guatemala City, ☎ 238–3030) does provide rail service to both coasts, but it is sporadic and excruciatingly slow and is not advisable unless you're a fanatical train buff.

Security

Although you are probably safer in Guatemala than in the average U.S. city, crime here is on the upswing.

In early 1994 several women from the United States were attacked as part of a countrywide hysteria fueled by rumors that foreigners were stealing children to sell their organs. A U.S. State Department travel warning is still in effect for rural Guatemala, though it has been somewhat watered down and travelers are unlikely to encounter any problems. However, it is still probably not a good idea to spend time with children in small villages unaccompanied by their parents.

The U.S. State Department's Bureau of Consular Affairs singles out pickpocketing and armed car theft as two major areas of concern. Keep a tight grip on your bags when in crowded areas such as open-air markets, particularly in Chichicastenango. A common ploy used by highway robbers is to construct a roadblock, such as logs strewn across the road, and then hide; when the unsuspecting motorist gets out of the car to remove the obstruction, he or she is assaulted. If you come upon an unmanned roadblock, don't stop; turn around. If you are stopped by thieves with guns, remain calm: Those who offer no resistance are usually not hurt. Visitors should also avoid intercity road travel after sunset and hire taxicabs only from stands at the airport, major hotels, and main intersections. For the latest information on security conditions in the country and advice on the safest routes for traveling to popular sites, call the Citizens' Emergency Center in Washington, DC (☎ 202/647–5225).

Theft remains a problem, especially in the capital. It's not as rough as New York or Miami, but Guatemala City has plenty of hungry people, so be careful with precious articles while strolling in Zona 1, and don't wander that area's streets after midnight. On the other hand, Zona 10 is probably the safest zone in the city. Areas that attract large numbers of tourists usually draw people who prey on them. Antigua can be dangerous late at night, particularly at the Cerro de la Cruz park. In fact, the local tourism office has declared it off-limits for the time being. Both Agua and Pacaya volcanoes have been plagued by robberies and occasional violence, and though most people who ascend them along regular pathways encounter no problems, climbing them is not recommended without a guide and a guard, or on Saturday, when there's a crowd.

Contacts and Resources

Car Rentals

Five international rental-car companies—**Avis** (⊠ 12 Calle 2–73, Zona 9, ☎ 331–6990 or 331–2747), **Budget** (⊠ Avenida La Reforma 15–00, Zona 9, ☎ 331–6546, 332–2591, 331–2788, or 334–3411), **Dollar** (⊠ Avenida La Reforma 6–14, Zona 9, ☎ 334–8285 to 8287), **Hertz** (⊠ 7 Avenida 14–76, Zona 9, ☎ 332–2242 or 334–7421), and **National** (⊠ 14 Calle 1–42, Zona 10, ☎ 368–0175 or 368–3057)—and five local companies—**Ahorrent** (⊠ Boulevard Liberación 4–83, Zona 9, ☎ 332–0544 or 332–7515), **Rentalsa** (⊠ 12 Calle 2–62, Zona 10, ☎ 332–6911), **Tabarini** (⊠ 2 Calle "A" 7–30, Zona 10, ☎ 331–9814, 332–2161, or 331–6108), **Tally** (⊠ 7 Avenida 14–60, Zona 1, ☎ 251–4113 or 232–3327), and **Tikal** (⊠ 2 Calle 6–56, Zona 10, ☎ 232–4721)—have offices in Guatemala City, and most have representatives at both the Guatemala City and El Petén airports. Cars and Jeeps can also be rented in Antigua with **Avis** (⊠ 5a Avenida Norte 22, ☎ 332–2692) and **Tabarini** (⊠ 2a Calle Poniente 19 A, ☎ 332–3091), and in Santa Elena with **Hertz** (⊠ Camino Real Tikal hotel, ☎ 250–0207).

Consulates and Embassies

In Guatemala city: **U.S. Embassy** (⊠ Avenida La Reforma 7–01, Zona 10, ☎ 331–1541), **Canadian Embassy** (⊠ Edificio Edyma Plaza, 8th Floor, 13 Calle 8–44, Zona 10, ☎ 333–6102), **U.K. Embassy** (⊠ Centro Financiero Torre II, 7th Floor, 7 Avenida 5–10, Zona 4, ☎ 332–1604). If you're in Huehuetenango and headed for Mexico, the **Mexican consulate** (⊠ 4 Calle and 5 Avenida) is in the Del Cid pharmacy building.

Guided Tours

Most of the dozens of tour companies that operate out of Guatemala City go to four main destinations—Antigua, Lake Atitlán, Chichicastenango, and Tikal—but some also offer tours off the beaten path, including adventure and natural-history treks. **Izabal Adventures** (☎ 334–0323) probably offers the widest variety of specialized adventure and ecotourism expeditions for independent travelers: These include tours to remote archaeological sites, the Atlantic zone, plus river and sportfishing trips. **Expedición Panamundo** (☎ 331–7641) has an extensive and well-organized system of operations, including camping tours, where participants travel by bus, of the entire Maya region (Guatemala, Belize, and Mexico). **Maya Expeditions** (☎ 337–4666) is the country's premier white-water rafting outfitter. **Intertours** (☎ 331–5421) goes to Copán and Río Dulce and adds interesting excursions to the traditional highland circuit. **Jaguar Tours** (☎ 334–0421) offers a variety of Petén trips. **Viva Tours** (☎ 334–1612) offers fishing and volcano expeditions. **Caribe International** (☎ 250–0145) specializes in journeys to El Petén, the Caribbean, and Alta Verapaz. **Centro de Reservaciones** (☎ 238–0887) has short excursions to Copán, Río Dulce, and the Quetzal Reserve. **Turansa** (☎ 595–3575) runs one-day tours to Mixco Viejo and the Pacific archaeological sites. **Tropical Tours** (☎ 339–3662) concentrates on Alta Verapaz. **Maya Tours** (☎ 335–2797) specializes in adventure and archaeological tours.

In Cobán, **Epiphyte Adventures** (☎ FAX 251–1268), run by Sean Acuña, conducts excellent eco-oriented, personalized trips throughout the Sierra de las Minas and El Petén regions.

5 Portraits of Belize and Guatemala

"The Natural Splendors of Central America," by David Dudenhoefer

"A River Trip to Lamanai," by Simon Worrall

Books

THE NATURAL SPLENDORS OF CENTRAL AMERICA

BANANA REPUBLICS and revolutions. Those are the first things that come to mind when most people think about Central America. It's been the news media's business to familiarize the public with the region's social strife, but not to relate the glory of its ancient ruins, pristine beaches, colorful textiles, and friendly inhabitants. Only recently has a more sophisticated populace begun to associate the inter-American isthmus with its greatest attributes: a treasure trove of tropical nature and an extraordinary variety of scenery.

Comprising an area slightly larger than Spain, and considerably smaller than the state of Texas, the slip of land that connects the North and South American continents claims more species of birds than are found in the United States and Canada combined, and more species of moths and butterflies than exist in the entire continent of Africa. You can find rolling pine forests; rumbling volcanoes; lush cloud forests; serene volcanic lakes; primeval mangrove swamps; stunning palm-lined beaches; sultry lowland rain forests; colorful coral reefs; spectacular cascades; tumultuous white-water rivers; rugged mountain ranges; rare tropical dry forests; scrubby deserts; slow-moving jungle rivers; and stretches of rocky coastline. And because of its compactness, all these diverse landscapes and varied wildlife occur in convenient proximity.

In geological terms, the inter-American land bridge is a rather recent phenomenon. Until a few million years ago, the North and South American continents were separated by a canal the likes of which Teddy Roosevelt—the father of the Panama Canal—couldn't have conjured up in his wildest dreams. In the area that is now occupied by Panama, Costa Rica, and southern Nicaragua, the waters of the Pacific and Atlantic oceans flowed freely together for unfathomable millennia. Geologists have named this former canal the Straits of Bolívar, after the Venezuelan revolutionary who wrested much of South America from Spain.

Beneath the Straits of Bolívar and the continents themselves, the incremental movement of tectonic plates slowly pushed North and South America closer. Geologists speculate that as the continents approached one another, a chain of volcanic islands began to bridge the gap. A combination of volcanic activity and plate movement led to the completion of a land bridge, which closed the interoceanic canal and opened a terrestrial corridor between the Americas about 3 million years ago.

Because several tectonic plates meet beneath Central America, the isthmus has long been a geologically unstable area; earthquakes and volcanic eruptions still hit the headlines occasionally. A curse it may seem, but the fact is there wouldn't be much of a Central America if not for both of these phenomena. Much of the region's best soil was once spewn from the volcanoes, and the upward movement of the Caribbean Plate as the Cocos Plate slipped beneath it pushed many parts of the southern isthmus up out of the sea.

The continental connection 3 million years ago had profound biological consequences, since it both separated the marine flora and fauna of the Pacific and Atlantic oceans and simultaneously created a pathway for interchange between the American continents. Three million years is a long time by biological standards, and the region's plants and animals have changed considerably since the gap was closed. Evolution took slightly different paths in the Atlantic and Pacific waters that flank the isthmus. Organisms that evolved in separate continents made their way into the opposite hemisphere, and the resulting interaction eventually determined what exists in the Americas today. It is important to understand, however, that the plants and animals that live in Central America are more than just the sum of what passed between the continents; the corridor also acts as a filter, so the region is home to many species that couldn't make the journey from one hemisphere to the other. Thus the rain forests of the eastern and southern portions of Central America comprise the most northerly distribution of southern species like the great green macaw and the poison dart frogs, while the dry forests on the western side of the isthmus define the southern limit for northern species like the Virginia opossum and coyote. To top it all off, the many physical barriers and the variety of environments on the isthmus may foster the development of numerous native species.

What all this biological balderdash means for visitors to Central America is that they might be able to spot a South American spider monkey and a North American raccoon sharing the shade of a rain tree, which is native to Central America. On a larger scale, it means that the region is home to a disproportionately high percentage of the planet's plant and animal species. Though Central America covers only one-half of one percent of the earth's land area, about 10% of the world's species live here, so it's no wonder scientists have dubbed it a "biological superpower."

Nearly all of these biological endowments are stored within the region's forests. Though many physical forces combine to determine the characteristics of these forests, the two most important factors are altitude and rainfall. Altitude plays an important role in determining what lives where, and often defines the distribution of different types of forests and the wildlife that inhabits them. Although temperature in the tropics doesn't change much through the course of the year, the highlands stay consistently cooler than the lowlands. This means that you can spend a morning sweating in a sultry coastal forest, then drive a couple of hours up into the mountains, where you will need a warm jacket. In a more temperate area of the world, the cold weather merely hits the mountaintops a month or two before the lowlands, but eventually old man winter gets his icy grip on everything. In the tropics, things are different: The only place it ever freezes is at the top of the highest mountains, so the high-altitude flora tends to be very different from what's found in a nearby valley. Many lowland plants and animals used to a warm climate can't survive the cold-weather journey over tropical mountains, a circumstance that limits the realms of many species and improves the likelihood of new species evolving.

Altitude also plays an important role in determining the humidity of a forest. Clouds tend to accumulate around the highest mountains and volcanoes, providing not only regular precipitation up top but also shade, which slows evaporation. This creates the conditions for the luxuriant cloud forests that cover the upper slopes of many mountains, which spend most of their time enveloped in a thick mist. As you climb higher on either side of a mountain range or volcano, the vegetation becomes more lush; hit the peaks of the highest mountains protruding up from the cloud cover, however, and you'll find fairly arid conditions.

RAINFALL PATTERNS may surprise you: Though people tend to associate the tropics with rain, many areas of Central America receive very little. This, too, is a result of the region's precipitous topography, and a phenomenon called rain shadow, during which one side of a mountain range receives much more rain than the other because clouds heading from one direction lose most of their moisture as they hit the mountains and rise. The Pacific slope of much of Central America experiences a seasonal rain-shadow effect, and the Guatemalan region of Zacapa, a valley almost surrounded by high mountains, is so well shielded from most rainstorms that it has a desert landscape.

Thanks to the relentless nature of the trade winds, the eastern side of Central America receives much more rain than the western half. The trade winds pump a steady supply of moisture-laden clouds southwest over the isthmus, where they encounter warm air and mountains, which makes them rise. The clouds cool as they rise, which leaves them able to hold less moisture and causes them to dump most of their liquid luggage on the Caribbean slope.

During Central America's rainy season, which runs from May to November, regular storms roll off the Pacific Ocean and soak the western side of the isthmus on a near-daily basis. During the rainy season, the entire isthmus gets wet, and the Pacific slope sometimes receives more rain than the Atlantic. But in the dry season, from November to May, the trade winds take over, and hardly a drop falls on the land bridge's western side. The two seasons have a profound effect on the forests of the Pacific lowlands, which receive almost no rainfall from December to May and consequently acquire a desert visage, with many trees dropping their foliage. Those forests quickly regain their verdure when the annual rains return in May, the beginning of a springlike season that is nonetheless referred to as winter by Central Americans.

THE NET RESULT of all this variation in precipitation and altitude is a virtual mosaic of forests studding the isthmus. Biologists have dutifully identified these different forest types and grouped them into categories—rain, cloud, dry, pine, and mangrove—but because conditions often change within a short distance, many forests are considered "transitional," or caught between two categories. Of the major forest types, however, the one that best exemplifies the complexity of tropical nature is the rain forest.

A pristine rain forest is quite an impressive sight, with massive trees towering overhead—most of the leaves and branches are more than 100 feet above the ground—and thick vines and lianas hanging down from the treetops. Most of the foliage in a virgin rain forest is found in the canopy, which is the uppermost spread of the giant trees' leaves and branches plus the many plants that live upon them. Those branches provide platforms for a multitude of epiphytes—plants that grow on other plants but don't draw their nutrients from them—such as ferns, orchids, bromeliads, and vines. This is also where most of the forest's animals spend the majority, if not all, of their time.

Because the canopy foliage filters out most sunlight before it can reach the ground, the forest floor is usually a dim and quiet place, with not nearly as much undergrowth as in those old Tarzan movies. But many of the plants that do grow down below look familiar to northern visitors: Since the light level of the rain-forest floor resembles that of the average North American living room, your basic popular house plant thrives here. The exception to the sparse vegetation rule is found wherever an old tree has fallen over, an event that is invariably followed by a riot of growth, with an excess of plants fighting over the newfound sunlight.

A lack of light characterizes the floor of the rain forest, but a shortage of water is the case up in the canopy. Plants that live here have developed a series of adaptations to cope with the aridity of the canopy environment, such as thick leaves that resist evaporation and spongy roots that soak up large amounts of water in a short period of time. Both traits are common among the thousands of species of colorful orchid that grow in Central America's forests. In the case of tank bromeliads, the plant's funnel shape helps it collect a pool of water at the center of its leaves. As tiny oases of the canopy, they attract plenty of arboreal animals, which drink from, hunt at, or live in the plant's pool. There is even a kind of tree frog whose tadpoles develop in the reservoirs, where they subsist on resident insects and larvae. While the plant provides vital water for an array of animals, the waste and carcasses of many of these animals in turn provide the plants with nutrients, another necessity in short supply up high.

Unfortunately, the great variety of plant and animal life that resides in the rain-forest canopy is difficult to observe from the forest floor, and most animals spend a great deal of their time and energy trying not to be seen. Still, you can catch distant glimpses of many species, such as the very still forms of sloths, furry figures amid the foliage, or the brilliant regalia of parrots, macaws, and toucans. You can't miss the arboreal acrobatics or chatter of monkeys, who leap from tree to tree, hang from branches, or throw fruit and sticks at intruders below. And hikers may occasionally encounter earthbound creatures like the coatimundi, a narrow-nosed relation of the raccoon, or the agouti, a terrier-size rodent that resembles a giant guinea pig. The iridescent blue morpho butterfly, hummingbirds, and the tiny lizards that stand guard on tree trunks or scurry off into the leaf litter are some of the animals one is likely to spot in the rain forest.

An untrained eye can miss the details, however, so a good nature guide is invaluable. You may be standing in front of 100 different species of plants and see only an incomprehensible green mesh. Tropical rain forests are among the richest, most complex, and most productive ecosystems in the world. Their biological diversity is so vast that scientists haven't even named most of the plant and insect species found there, and they have completed thorough studies of only a small fraction of the species that they have identified. Though tropical moist forests cover only 7% of the earth's surface, it has been estimated that they contain about half the planet's plant and animal species, which means a small patch of rain forest can consist of thousands of different kinds of plants and animals.

Aside from the heat and humidity, the rain-forest ecosystem is characterized by intense predation. While animals spend much of their time trying to find their next meal, both plants and animals dedicate a great deal of energy to the goal of not being eaten. Animals tend to accomplish this by hiding or fleeing, but those options aren't available to plants, which have devised a series of defenses such as thorns, leaf hairs, and other substances that make their leaves less than appetizing. Because of the relative toxicity of a large part of the rain-forest foliage, many insects eat only a small portion of any given leaf before moving on to another plant, so as not to ingest a lethal dose of any one poison. The consequence of this can be seen by staring up toward the canopy—almost every leaf is full of little holes that allow the sunlight to shine through the greenery. Some insects develop an immunity to one toxin and eat only the plant that contains it. This is a common strategy of caterpillars, since mobility isn't their strong point.

Popular tactics that animals use to keep from being eaten include staying on the move, keeping quiet and alert, and, of course, hiding. Though they are a chore to spot, the few camouflaged critters that you'll discover are invariably intriguing. Some animals actually advertise: Bright colors help them find a mate amid the mesh of green but can also serve as a warning to potential predators. Take poison dart frogs, for instance: Their skins are so toxically laced with deadly poisons that South American Indians use them to make their darts and arrows more deadly. Another trick for scaring off predators is mimicry. Commonly harmless creatures impersonate venomous ones, but, more rarely, acts of deception reach an amazing level of intrigue.

One caterpillar has a tail that resembles the head of a snake, and a butterfly exists that looks like the head of an owl when it opens its wings.

THE RAIN FOREST is the stage for a constant contest between the eaters and the eaten, as well as for plants' and animals' competition against other species that have similar niches—the biological equivalent of jobs. This competition has fostered cooperation between noncompetitive organisms. Plants need to get their pollen and seeds distributed as far as possible, and every animal requires a steady food supply. Tropical plants are pollinated by everything from fruit flies and hummingbirds to bees and bats, and since they have to feed the animals that deliver their pollen, their flowers are usually designed so nectar is easily available to their pollinators but protected from freeloaders who do nothing for the plant. Some of the more extreme examples of this can be found in the thousands of species of orchids that grow in Central America's forests; many of them are pollinated by only one species of bee or beetle. There is even an orchid that hides its nectar and pollen behind a petal door, which only its pollinator can open.

Competition for limited resources is a predominant force in the rain forest, which keeps trees growing taller, roots reaching farther, and everything mobile working on some way to get more for less. The battle for light has sent most of the rain-forest foliage sky high, whereas the battle for nutrients has caused the process of decay and recycling that follows every death in the forest to take place at breakneck pace. One result of this high-speed decomposition is that most of the nutrients in a rain forest are found within living things, and the soil beneath them retains very little of the essential elements. As a consequence, rain-forest soils tend to be nutrient-poor, and less than ideal sites for farming.

RAIN FORESTS aren't the only types of tropical forests in Central America. The region's rare dry forests are similar to rain forests in many ways, especially during the rainy season. But when the rains stop, the dry forest acquires a seasonal aridity; most of the trees lose their leaves but simultaneously burst into full, colorful flower. Containing many of the plants, animals, and exclusive relationships found in the rain forest, the tropical dry forest is also home to groups associated with the forests and deserts of Mexico and the southern United States, such as cacti, coyotes, white-tailed deer, and diamondback rattlesnakes. Because dry forests are not as dense as rain forests, there is less foliage to hide behind, and you'll find it easier to observe animals here than in the other forest types. This is especially true during the dry season, when the forest's fauna can be found congregating around available water supplies and fruit or flowers.

The upper reaches of many mountains and volcanoes are draped with cloud forest, a more luxuriant, precipitous version of the rain forest. Cloud forests are the epitome of lushness—so lush that it can be difficult to find the bark on a cloud-forest tree for all the growth on its trunk and branches. Plants grow on plants growing on plants: Vines, orchids, ferns, and bromeliads are everywhere, and moss proliferates on the vines and leaves of other epiphytes.

Because cloud forests tend to grow on steep terrain, the trees grow on slightly different levels, which means the canopy forms a less continuous cover than that experienced in a lowland rain forest. Consequently, more pale light reaches the ground, where you'll encounter plenty of undergrowth, like prehistoric-looking tree-ferns and "poor-man's umbrellas," which consist of little more than a few giant leaves.

Cloud forests are home to a multitude of animals, ranging from delicate glass frogs, whose undersides are so transparent that you can see many of their internal organs, to the spectacular quetzal, one of the most beautiful birds in the world. The male quetzal has a bright crimson belly and iridescent green back, with two-foot tail feathers that float behind the bird when it flies, ample inspiration for the name the ancient Mayas gave it—"winged serpent." While the tangle of foliage and almost constant mist can make it difficult to get a good look at much of the cloud forest's wildlife, you should be able to catch a glimpse of plenty of other flying objects, including an array of brightly colored hummingbirds.

Since the cloud forest is almost constantly enveloped in mist, its canopy doesn't suffer the water shortage that plagues other kinds of forests. In fact, the cloud-forest canopy is practically the wettest part of the woods. The upland portions, while receiving few downpours, gain their moisture from a perpetually mobile, moisture-laden mist, which moves through the forest and deposits a condensation on the billions of leaves that make up the mosses, orchids, ferns, vines, bromeliads, and other epiphytes. This condensation results in a sort of secondary precipitation, with droplets forming on the epiphytic foliage and falling regularly down from the branches to the forest floor. Cloud forests thus function like giant sponges, soaking up the humidity from the clouds and sending it slowly downhill to feed the streams and rivers that many regions and cities depend upon for water. And because some of the precipitation that falls on the cloud forests flows west, it usually feeds streams and rivers that run through arid regions, even at the height of the dry season.

Though they may not seem exotic to the visitor from the north, pine forests cover a large part of Central America, especially the highlands of Guatemala and Honduras. The Central American pine forests don't boast the kind of biological diversity found in most other forest types, but they are undeniably beautiful and are home to numerous species of birds and other animals. An interesting aspect of the Guatemalan highlands is that the hilltops and most mountainsides are covered with pine, while secluded valleys that maintain higher average temperatures are draped with luxuriant cloud forests, which contain much more diversity than the adjacent pine forests.

A more exclusively tropical forest is the mangrove, a regularly flooded, primeval-looking profusion that can be found along both of Central America's coasts. Mangrove forests grow in the tidal zone, usually near river mouths, and often surround lagoons or river deltas. Trees in these forests grow propped up on stilt roots, which keeps leaves out of salt water and helps the trees absorb carbon dioxide during high tide. The roots also provide protection for a variety of marine species and serve as props for many kinds of shellfish.

Mangroves are homogenous forests, with stands of one species of tree that often stretch off as far as the eye can see, but they are also productive ecosystems that play an important role in estuaries. Many marine animals—oysters, snapper, and shrimp, for instance—spend particular stages of their lives in mangrove estuaries, while other species are born and die here. This means that mangroves are not only vital to the health of the ocean beyond them, but they are also attractive sites for animals that feed on small fish. You'll find a vast assortment of fish-eating birds, including herons, pelicans, ospreys, kingfishers, and rare creatures like the great jabiru—a massive stork and the largest bird inhabiting the isthmus—or the roseate spoonbill, an elegant pink wader.

IN THE OCEAN beyond the mangroves lie coral reefs, another distinctly tropical phenomenon that supports one of the most diverse ecosystems in the world. Coral reefs occur off both of Central America's coasts, from the crystalline waters that wash against Cocos Island, some 589 kilometers (365 miles) southwest of Costa Rica, to the aquamarine sea along the shore of Ambergris Caye, in northeast Belize. Though the Pacific has some impressive coralline congregations, the most spectacular reef in the region—in the Americas, for that matter—lines the eastern edge of Belize. Here is the second-largest barrier reef in the world (number one is Australia's Great Barrier Reef), an impressive collection of oceanic organisms and a vital ecological organ of the Caribbean Sea's marine body.

On the other geographical extreme—about as far as one could travel from Central America's coastal reefs and still remain in the region—is the *paramo*, a tundralike ecosystem that covers the tops of the Talamanca Mountain Range, in southern Costa Rica. A combination of shrubs and grasses that grow above the tree line, the paramo is common in the heights of South America's Andes, with Costa Rica's patches being the most northerly point in its distribution.

With such remarkable diversity in such a small area of land, one would expect any trip in Central America to pass ever-changing natural panoramas packed with a variety of living things. But it soon becomes clear that the region's predominant landscapes are not cloud forests and rain forests, but the coffee and banana plantations that have replaced them. The ancient Mayas may have revered animals like the jaguar and quetzal, but much of their former realm has become the home of less illustrious beasts: the cow and cattle egret, which are perhaps the two animals that visitors to Central America see more of than any others.

The fact is that more than two-thirds of Central America's original forests have already been destroyed, and most of those trees fell during the past 40 years. It has been estimated that between 3,000 and 3,500 square kilometers (1,158 and 1,351 square miles) of the region's forests were cut every year during the past decade, a rate of deforestation that could leave Central America devoid of pristine forests by the year 2020. Such a fate would not only mean the demise of the jaguars and quetzals, but would have grave consequences for the region's human inhabitants as well. The forests regulate the flow of rivers, by absorbing rains and releasing the water slowly, and deforestation often results in severe soil erosion, which decreases the productive capacity of the land. But the destruction of Central America's forests is a loss for the entire world, since hidden within the flora and fauna are unknown substances, which could eventually be extracted to cure diseases and serve humankind.

Central America's remaining forests face increasing pressure from a growing and impoverished human population. People hunt within them, cut down their valuable hardwoods, and completely destroy many wooded areas in order to establish farms. Forests are cut and burned to make room for banana and coffee plantations, or to become pasture for cattle whose meat is often shipped north. Much of the destruction is the work of small farmers, who fell patches of forest to plant their beans and corn, and after a few years of diminishing harvests, sell their land to cattle ranchers or speculators and move on to cut more forest. The cycle of destruction is fueled by poverty and greed, and though Central American governments have established protected areas and passed laws to limit deforestation, the region's wildlands continue to disappear.

Conservationists point out that the Central American governments don't have the resources to enforce existing laws that protect the environment, or even to effectively manage their national parks and protected areas. Environmentalists are looking for ways to motivate people to protect the forests, and the best way they've found is to teach those responsible for the destruction that conservation pays. Promoting "ecotourism"—increasing the number of tourists who visit a country's natural areas, so the government and rural dwellers will become more interested in protecting them—is a potential means of making conservation profitable.

— David Dudenhoefer

David Dudenhoefer is an environmental and travel writer based in Central America and the author of *The Panama Traveler* (Windham Bay Press).

A RIVER TRIP TO LAMANAI

EVEN THOUGH I spent the entire boat ride huddled under a tarpaulin trying to keep dry, this journey along the New River to Lamanai, the longest-occupied Maya site in Belize, was one of the high points of my visit. We started from just south of Orange Walk, where the Maruba Resort has a boat that takes people up the river.

The town itself is one of the least attractive in Belize—a run-down market town, with six or seven third-rate Chinese restaurants and a lot of bars of dubious renown (Orange Walk has a reputation as being both the drug-distribution center and prostitution capital of Belize). Paradoxically, it is also the center for the Mennonites, and you will often see the lean, fit-looking men running errands in the town—the women are not allowed to "mix"—dressed in the almost standard Mennonite uniform: plaid shirt, suspenders, work boots, and straw hat. With their straw-blond hair, blue eyes, and startlingly Germanic looks, they are the most unusual of the many ethnic groups that have settled in Belize.

Originally a radical splinter group of the Lutheran Reformation in 16th-century Europe, the Mennonites had, metaphorically speaking, many stamps in their passports before they finally got here. From Holland, where their spiritual godfather and namesake, Menno Simons, called the movement into being, they went to Switzerland, and then to Prussia. Like the Amish, whom they resemble in many ways, the Mennonites strongly opposed warfare in any form, and they paid for their treasonable pacificism with banishment. In 1663, a small group traveled to North America. Another group went east, settling in western Russia, until the witch hunts of the 1917 Revolution once again forced them into exile. Many traveled to Canada, and from there, to Mexico. The first settlers to make Belize their home arrived in 1958, and they immediately filled a vacant economic niche as dairymen and farmers. Today, most of Belize's vegetables, milk, and dairy produce are produced by Mennonites. They are also the most skilled carpenters and house-builders in the country.

From Orange Walk, the journey up the river to Lamanai is like a scene from Peter Matthiessen's novel *At Play in the Fields of the Lord*. At first the river is broad and straight, then it contracts to a maze of narrow tributaries that wind in and out of the mangroves. For much of the time, it is no more than a few boat widths across, so you can almost reach out and touch the tangled mass of vegetation on the bank. Many of the trees are covered in a squashy cactus known as "devil's guts" or by huge, black termite nests hanging from the trunks like dollops of Christmas pudding, some of them as much as two or three feet in circumference. As we passed a tree at the water's edge, a colony of bats flew off. Numerous birds took flight as we approached—white herons, diminutive jacana, hawks, and even the rare jabiru stork, the largest bird in the New World, with a wingspan of up to eight feet. Here and there, brilliant, lilac-colored morning glories dotted the dense green undergrowth.

After about an hour, we emerged into a broad lake area the size of the Hudson at Annandale. I could see why the Maya built a settlement here. From the water, the limestone cliffs on which they built their temples would have been impregnable, with a commanding view of the river and the surrounding countryside. As well as providing an abundant supply of fish, turtles, and snails, the New River also served as a trade route, linking Lamanai with most of northwestern Belize, from its source on a line with Belize City, to its estuary near Corozal, and the Yucatán Peninsula beyond.

Lamanai was a miniature Venice, a powerful port-city that lived by river trade and fishing. The river also gave Lamanai its name. In Maya, it means "submerged crocodile," and this densely forested waterway is still home to hundreds of their descendants. To the Maya, the crocodile was a sacred animal, and when archaeologists excavated Lamanai, they found masks depicting a man wearing a crocodile headdress.

Unlike all other sites in Belize, Lamanai was occupied by the Maya until well after

Columbus arrived in the New World. Archaeologists have found signs of continuous occupation from 1500 BC until the 16th century, its people carrying on a way of life that had been passed down for millennia until Spanish missionaries arrived to separate them from their past and lure them to Catholicism. The ruins of the church the Spaniards built can still be seen at the nearby village of Indian Church. In the same village, there is also an abandoned sugar mill from the 19th century. With its immense drive-wheel and steam engine—on which you can still read the name of the manufacturer, Leeds Foundry in New Orleans—swathed in strangler vines and creepers, it is a haunting sight.

In all, 50 or 60 Maya structures were spread over the 950-acre Archaeological Reserve. The most impressive of them is the largest pre-Classic structure in Belize: a massive, stepped temple built into the hillside overlooking the river. A ball court, numerous dwellings, and several other fine temples remain. One of the finest stelae found in Belize, an elaborately carved depiction of the ruler Smoking Shell, can be seen here, as well as the only archaeological museum in Belize, where site caretakers will be glad to show you a 2,500-year progression of pottery, carvings, and small statues.

Archaeologists also found the grave of a seven-year-old child, believed to have been a royal personage. He was buried in an upright sitting position on a bench; at his feet are the bones of five two-year-olds, all with their necks broken. The discovery suggested that the people of Lamanai practiced human sacrifice.

Most of the structures at Lamanai have only been superficially excavated. Trees and vines grow from the top of temples, the sides of one pyramid are covered with vegetation, and another rises abruptly out of the forest floor. At Lamanai, no tour buses, no cold drink stands, intrude: you'll find only ruins, forest, and wildlife.

The path to the ruins leads up through lush forest from the grassy riverbank. We passed huge guanacaste trees, mahogany trees, rubber trees, and even an allspice, with its pungent leaves and fruit. Here and there were magnificent cahoune palms, growing out of the ground like quivers of arrows. After about a 10-minute walk, we reached the first temple, a massive structure of weathered limestone ascending a hill. At the base a moss-covered stone throne is built into the wall, where the ruler would have sat for blood-letting rituals. Remarkably, the throne at Lamanai is embellished with what looks like the Chinese symbol for male and female, the yin-yang, suggesting a possible connection with the Orient. Halfway up is a carving that depicts a man's face inside the mouth of a jaguar. From the top, a spectacular view unfolds through the treetops to the river below and the surrounding countryside.

AS WE STOOD looking down at the throne, a sound, something between a donkey's braying and the roar of a jaguar, shattered the silence. Ahead of us rose the Jaguar Temple, a massive stepped pyramid at the end of a grassy plaza, three of its sides still overgrown with trees and bushes. As we looked over to it, a toucan burst into view and roosted on a giant guanacaste tree. Then we heard the same piercing cry that had moments earlier immobilized us. Another call answered it, then another, until the forest was echoing with the wails of a group of black howler monkeys. Later, we found a group of seven or eight, including a mother and her baby, feeding in a stand of breadnut trees by the ruined foundations of Maya houses. To the Maya, the monkey was a sacred animal—the god of writing—and thanks to the conservation of the land, they are back at Lamanai.

— Simon Worrall

Simon Worral is a British-born writer. He writes regularly for the London Sunday Times Magazine, Geo, and many other European and American publications on travel, technology, culture, and politics. He currently makes his home in East Hampton, New York.

BOOKS

Belize

Two histories stand out: *The Making of Modern Belize*, by C.H. Grant, and *A Profile of the New Nation of Belize*, by W.D. Setzekorn. *Jaguar*, by Alan Rabinowitz, an interesting book about the creation of the Cockscomb Basin Wildlife Sanctuary, unfortunately tells you too much about the man and too little about the cat. Aldous Huxley, who wrote *Beyond the Mexique Bay*, is always hard to beat. If you're interested in the Maya, Ronald Wright's *Time Among the Maya* ties past and present together in one perceptive whole. Classic works on the Maya include *The Maya*, by Michael Coe, a compendious introduction to the world of the Maya, and *The Rise and Fall of the Maya Civilization*, by one of the grand old men of Maya archaeology, J. Eric S. Thompson. For natural history enthusiasts, three books belong in your suitcase: *A Field Guide to the Birds of Mexico*, by E.P. Edwards; *Guide to Corals and Fishes of Florida, the Bahamas and the Caribbean*, by I. Greenberg; and *An Introduction to Tropical Rainforests*, by T.C. Whitmore.

Guatemala

For travel literature, try Ronald Wright's *Time Among the Maya* or Aldous Huxley's *Beyond the Mexique Bay*, which describes his travels in 1934. Nobel laureate Miguel Angel Asturias is the country's most famous author, and his works are full of history and cultural insight, namely *Weekend in Guatemala* and *Men of Maize*. Francisco Goldman's *The Long Night of White Chickens* is a lyrical work of fiction that touches on some contemporary social issues. Michael Coe's *The Maya* is an authoritative book on the lost societies of the region's prehistory, as is Eric S. Thompson's *The Rise and Fall of the Maya Civilization*. For information about the flora and fauna, try John C. Kricher's *A Neotropical Companion*. And for historical and political information, try James Painter's *Guatemala: False Hope, False Freedom*, or Jean-Marie Simon's *Guatemala: Eternal Spring, Eternal Tyranny*, which includes excellent photographs. Victor Perera's *Unfinished Conquest* is a thorough and fascinating account of Guatemala's guerilla war.

SPANISH VOCABULARY

Note: *Mexican Spanish differs from Castilian Spanish.*

English	Spanish	Pronunciation

Basics

English	Spanish	Pronunciation
Yes/no	Sí/no	see/no
Please	Por favor	por fah-*vore*
May I?	¿Me permite?	may pair-*mee*-tay
Thank you (very much)	(Muchas) gracias	(*moo*-chas) *grah*-see-as
You're welcome	De nada	day *nah*-dah
Excuse me	Con permiso	con pair-*mee*-so
Pardon me/what did you say?	¿Como?/Mánde?	pair-*doan*/*mahn*-dey
Could you tell me?	¿Podría decirme?	po-*dree*-ah deh-*seer*-meh
I'm sorry	Lo siento	lo see-*en*-toe
Good morning!	¡Buenos días!	*bway*-nohs *dee*-ahs
Good afternoon!	¡Buenas tardes!	*bway*-nahs *tar*-dess
Good evening!	¡Buenas noches!	*bway*-nahs *no*-chess
Goodbye!	¡Adiós! ¡Hasta luego!	ah-dee-*ohss* *ah*-stah-*lwe*-go
Mr./Mrs.	Señor/Señora	sen-*yor*/sen-*yore*-ah
Miss	Señorita	sen-yo-*ree*-tah
Pleased to meet you	Mucho gusto	*moo*-cho *goose*-to
How are you?	¿Cómo está usted?	*ko*-mo es-*tah* oo-*sted*
Very well, thank you.	Muy bien, gracias.	*moo*-ee bee-*en*, grah-see-as
And you?	¿Y usted?	ee oos-*ted*
Hello (on the telephone)	Bueno	*bwen*-oh

Numbers

1	un, uno	oon, *oo*-no
2	dos	dos
3	tres	trace
4	cuatro	*kwah*-tro
5	cinco	*sink*-oh
6	seis	sace
7	siete	see-*et*-ey
8	ocho	*o*-cho
9	nueve	new-*ev*-ey
10	diez	dee-*es*
11	once	*own*-sey
12	doce	*doe*-sey
13	trece	*tray*-sey
14	catorce	kah-*tor*-sey

15	quince	*keen*-sey
16	dieciséis	dee-es-ee-*sace*
17	diecisiete	dee-*es*-ee-see-*et*-ay
18	dieciocho	dee-*es*-ee-*o*-cho
19	diecinueve	*dee-es*-ee-new-*ev*-ay
20	veinte	*vain*-tay
21	veinte y uno/veintiuno	*vain*-te-oo-no
30	treinta	*train*-tah
32	treinta y dos	train-tay-*dose*
40	cuarenta	kwah-*ren*-tah
43	cuarenta y tres	kwah-*ren*-tay-*trace*
50	cincuenta	seen-*kwen*-tah
54	cincuenta y cuatro	seen-*kwen*-tay *kwah*-tro
60	sesenta	sess-*en*-tah
65	sesenta y cinco	sess-*en*-tay *seen*-ko
70	setenta	set-*en*-tah
76	setenta y seis	set-*en*-tay *sace*
80	ochenta	oh-*chen*-tah
87	ochenta y siete	oh-*chen*-tay see-*yet*-ay
90	noventa	no-*ven*-tah
98	noventa y ocho	no-*ven*-tah *o*-cho
100	cien	see-*en*
101	ciento uno	see-en-toe *oo*-no
200	doscientos	doe-see-*en*-tohss
500	quinientos	keen-*yen*-tohss
700	setecientos	set-eh-see-*en*-tohss
900	novecientos	no-veh-see-*en*-tohss
1,000	mil	meel
2,000	dos mil	dose meel
1,000,000	un millón	oon meel-*yohn*

Colors

black	negro	*neh*-grow
blue	azul	ah-*sool*
brown	café	kah-*feh*
green	verde	*vair*-day
pink	rosa	*ro*-sah
purple	morado	mo-*rah*-doe
orange	naranja	na-*rahn*-hah
red	rojo	*roe*-hoe
white	blanco	*blahn*-koh
yellow	amarillo	ah-mah-*ree*-yoh

Days of the Week

Sunday	domingo	doe-*meen*-goh
Monday	lunes	*loo*-ness
Tuesday	martes	*mahr*-tess
Wednesday	miércoles	me-*air*-koh-less
Thursday	jueves	who-*ev*-ess
Friday	viernes	vee-*air*-ness
Saturday	sábado	*sah*-bah-doe

Months

January	enero	eh-*neh*-ro
February	febrero	feh-*brair*-oh
March	marzo	*mahr*-so
April	abril	ah-*breel*
May	mayo	*my*-oh
June	junio	*hoo*-nee-oh
July	julio	*who*-lee-yoh
August	agosto	ah-*ghost*-toe
September	septiembre	sep-tee-*em*-breh
October	octubre	oak-*too*-breh
November	noviembre	no-vee-*em*-breh
December	diciembre	dee-see-*em*-breh

Useful phrases

Do you speak English?	¿Habla usted inglés?	*ah*-blah oos-*ted* in-*glehs*
I don't speak Spanish	No hablo español	no *ah*-blow es-pahn-*yol*
I don't understand (you)	No entiendo	no en-tee-*en*-doe
I understand (you)	Entiendo	en-tee-*en*-doe
I don't know	No sé	no *say*
I am American/British	Soy americano(a)/inglés(a)	soy ah-meh-ree-*kah*-no(ah)/in-*glace*(ah)
What's your name?	¿Cómo se llama usted?	*koh*-mo say *yah*-mah oos-*ted*
My name is . . .	Me llamo . . .	may *yah*-moh
What time is it?	¿Qué hora es?	keh *o*-rah es
It is one, two, three . . . o'clock.	Es la una; son las dos, tres	es la *oo*-nah/sone lahs dose, trace
Yes, please/No, thank you	Sí, por favor/No, gracias	*see* pore fah-*vor*/no *grah*-see-us
How?	¿Cómo?	*koh*-mo
When?	¿Cuándo?	*kwahn*-doe
This/next week	Esta semana/la semana que entra	*es*-tah seh-*mah*-nah/lah say-*mah*-nah keh *en*-trah
This/next month	Este mes/el próximo mes	*es*-tay mehs/el *proke*-see-mo mehs
This/next year	Este año/el año que viene	*es*-tay *ahn*-yo/el *ahn*-yo keh vee-*yen-ay*
Yesterday/today/tomorrow	Ayer/hoy/mañana	ah-*yair*/oy/mahn-*yah*-nah
This morning/afternoon	Esta mañana/tarde	*es*-tah mahn-*yah*-nah/*tar*-day
Tonight	Esta noche	*es*-tah *no*-cheh
What?	¿Qué?	keh
What is it?	¿Qué es esto?	keh es *es*-toe

Why?	¿Por qué?	pore *keh*
Who?	¿Quién?	kee-*yen*
Where is . . . ?	¿Dónde está . . . ?	*dohn*-day es-*tah*
the train station?	la estación del tren?	la es-tah-see-*on* del *train*
the subway station?	la estación del Metro?	la es-ta-see-*on* del *meh*-tro
the bus stop?	la parada del autobús?	la pah-*rah*-dah del oh-toe-*boos*
the post office?	la oficina de correos?	la oh-fee-*see*-nah day koh-*reh*-os
the bank?	el banco?	el *bahn*-koh
the . . . hotel?	el hotel . . . ?	el oh-*tel*
the store?	la tienda?	la tee-*en*-dah
the cashier?	la caja?	la *kah*-hah
the . . . museum?	el museo . . . ?	el moo-*seh*-oh
the hospital?	el hospital?	el ohss-pea-*tal*
the elevator?	el ascensor?	el ah-*sen*-sore
the bathroom?	el baño?	el *bahn*-yoh
Here/there	Aquí/allá	ah-*key*/ah-*yah*
Open/closed	Abierto/cerrado	ah-be-*er*-toe/ ser-*ah*-doe
Left/right	Izquierda/derecha	iss-key-*er*-dah/ dare-*eh*-chah
Straight ahead	Derecho	der-*eh*-choh
Is it near/far?	¿Está cerca/lejos?	es-*tah sair*-kah/ *leh*-hoss
I'd like . . .	Quisiera . . .	kee-see-air-ah
a room	un cuarto/una habitación	oon *kwahr*-toe/ *oo*-nah ah-bee-tah-see-*on*
the key	la llave	lah *yah*-vay
a newspaper	un periódico	oon pear-ee-*oh*-dee-koh
a stamp	un timbre de correo	oon *team*-bray day koh-*reh*-oh
I'd like to buy . . .	Quisiera comprar . . .	kee-see-*air*-ah kohm-*prahr*
cigarettes	cigarrillo	ce-gar-*reel*-oh
matches	cerillos	ser-*ee*-ohs
a dictionary	un diccionario	oon deek-see-oh-*nah*-ree-oh
soap	jabón	hah-*bone*
a map	un mapa	oon *mah*-pah
a magazine	una revista	*oon*-ah reh-*veess*-tah
paper	papel	pah-*pel*
envelopes	sobres	*so*-brace
a postcard	una tarjeta postal	*oon*-ah tar-*het*-ah post-*ahl*
How much is it?	¿Cuánto cuesta?	*kwahn*-toe *kwes*-tah
It's expensive/ cheap	Está caro/barato	es-*tah kah*-roh/ bah-*rah*-toe

A little/a lot	Un poquito/ mucho . . .	oon poh-*kee*-toe/ *moo*-choh
More/less	Más/menos	mahss/*men*-ohss
Enough/too much/too little	Suficiente/de- masiado/muy poco	soo-fee-see-*en*-tay/ day-mah-see-*ah*- doe/*moo*-ee poh-koh
Telephone	Teléfono	tel-*ef*-oh-no
Telegram	Telegrama	teh-leh-*grah*-mah
I am ill/sick	Estoy enfermo(a)	es-*toy* en-*fair*-moh(ah)
Please call a doctor	Por favor llame un médico	pore fa-*vor ya*-may oon *med*-ee-koh
Help!	¡Auxilio! ¡Ayuda!	owk-*see*-lee-oh ah-*yoo*-dah
Fire!	¡Encendio!	en-*sen*-dee-oo
Caution!/Look out!	¡Cuidado!	kwee-*dah*-doh

On the Road

Highway	Carretera	car-ray-*ter*-ah
Causeway, paved highway	Calzada	cal-*za*-dah
Route	Ruta	*roo*-tah
Road	Camino	cah-*mee*-no
Street	Calle	*cah*-yeh
Avenue	Avenida	ah-ven-*ee*-dah
Broad, tree-lined boulevard	Paseo	pah-*seh*-oh
Waterfront promenade	Malecón	mal-lay-*cone*
Wharf	Embarcadero	em-bar-cah-*day*-ro

In Town

Church	Templo/Iglesia	*tem*-plo/e-*gles*-se-ah
Cathedral	Catedral	cah-tay-*dral*
Neighborhood	Barrio	*bar*-re-o
Foreign Exchange Shop	Casa de Cambio	*cas*-sah day *cam*-be-o
City Hall	Ayuntamiento	ah-yoon-tah-mee *en*-toe
Main Square	Zócalo	*zo*-cal-o
Traffic Circle	Glorieta	glor-e-*ay*-tah
Market	Mercado (Spanish)/ Tianguis (Indian)	mer-*cah*-doe/ tee-*an*-geese
Inn	Posada	pos-*sah*-dah
Group taxi	Colectivo	co-lec-*tee*-vo
Group taxi along fixed route	Pesero	pi-*seh*-ro

Items of Clothing

Embroidered white smock	Huipil	whee-*peel*
Pleated man's shirt worn outside the pants	Guayabera	gwah-ya-*beh*-ra
Leather sandals	Huarache	wah-*ra*-chays
Shawl	Rebozo	ray-*bozh*-o
Pancho or blanket	Serape	seh-*ra*-peh

Dining Out

A bottle of . . .	Una botella de . . .	*oo*-nah bo-*tay*-yah deh
A cup of . . .	Una taza de . . .	*oo*-nah *tah*-sah deh
A glass of . . .	Un vaso de . . .	oon *vah*-so deh
Ashtray	Un cenicero	oon sen-ee-*seh*-roh
Bill/check	La cuenta	lah *kwen*-tah
Bread	El pan	el pahn
Breakfast	El desayuno	el day-sigh-*oon*-oh
Butter	La mantequilla	lah mahn-tay-*key*-yah
Cheers!	¡Salud!	sah-*lood*
Cocktail	Un aperitivo	oon ah-pair-ee-*tee*-voh
Dinner	La cena	lah *seh*-nah
Dish	Un plato	oon *plah*-toe
Dish of the day	El platillo de hoy	el plah-*tee*-yo day oy
Enjoy!	¡Buen provecho!	bwen pro-*veh*-cho
Fixed-price menu	La comida corrida	lah koh-*me*-dah co-*ree*-dah
Fork	El tenedor	el ten-eh-*door*
Is the tip included?	¿Está incluida la propina?	es-*tah* in-clue-*ee*-dah lah pro-*pea*-nah
Knife	El cuchillo	el koo-*chee*-yo
Lunch	La comida	lah koh-*me*-dah
Menu	La carta	lah *cart*-ah
Napkin	La servilleta	lah sair-vee-*yet*-uh
Pepper	La pimienta	lah pea-me-*en*-tah
Please give me	Por favor déme	pore fah-*vor* *day*-may
Salt	La sal	lah sahl
Spoon	Una cuchara	*oo*-nah koo-*chah*-rah
Sugar	El azúcar	el ah-*sue*-car
Waiter!/Waitress!	¡Por favor Señor/Señorita!	pore fah-*vor* sen-*yor*/sen-yor-*ee*-tah

INDEX

NOTES

Fodor's Travel Publications

Available at bookstores everywhere, or call 1–800–533–6478, 24 hours a day.

Gold Guides

U.S.

Alaska	Florida	New Orleans	Santa Fe, Taos, Albuquerque
Arizona	Hawai'i	New York City	
Boston	Las Vegas, Reno, Tahoe	Pacific North Coast	Seattle & Vancouver
California		Philadelphia & the Pennsylvania Dutch Country	The South
Cape Cod, Martha's Vineyard, Nantucket	Los Angeles		U.S. & British Virgin Islands
	Maine, Vermont, New Hampshire		
The Carolinas & the Georgia Coast	Maui & Lāna'i	The Rockies	USA
Chicago	Miami & the Keys	San Diego	Virginia & Maryland
Colorado	New England	San Francisco	Washington, D.C.

Foreign

Australia	Europe	Montréal & Québec City	Scotland
Austria	Florence, Tuscany & Umbria	Moscow, St. Petersburg, Kiev	Singapore
The Bahamas			South Africa
Belize & Guatemala	France	The Netherlands, Belgium & Luxembourg	South America
Bermuda	Germany		Southeast Asia
Canada	Great Britain		Spain
Cancún, Cozumel, Yucatán Peninsula	Greece	New Zealand	Sweden
	Hong Kong	Norway	Switzerland
Caribbean	India	Nova Scotia, New Brunswick, Prince Edward Island	Thailand
China	Ireland		Tokyo
Costa Rica	Israel		Toronto
Cuba	Italy	Paris	Turkey
The Czech Republic & Slovakia	Japan	Portugal	Vienna & the Danube
	London	Provence & the Riviera	
Eastern & Central Europe	Madrid & Barcelona	Scandinavia	
	Mexico		

Fodor's Special-Interest Guides

Caribbean Ports of Call	Halliday's New Orleans Food Explorer	Sunday in New York	Where Should We Take the Kids? Northeast
The Complete Guide to America's National Parks		Sunday in San Francisco	
	Healthy Escapes	Walt Disney World, Universal Studios and Orlando	Worldwide Cruises and Ports of Call
Family Adventures	Kodak Guide to Shooting Great Travel Pictures		
Gay Guide to the USA	Net Travel	Walt Disney World for Adults	
Halliday's New England Food Explorer	Nights to Imagine	Where Should We Take the Kids? California	
	Rock & Roll Traveler USA		

Special Series

Affordables
Caribbean
Europe
Florida
France
Germany
Great Britain
Italy
London
Paris

Fodor's Bed & Breakfasts and Country Inns
America
California
The Mid-Atlantic
New England
The Pacific Northwest
The South
The Southwest
The Upper Great Lakes

The Berkeley Guides
California
Central America
Eastern Europe
Europe
France
Germany & Austria
Great Britain & Ireland
Italy
London
Mexico
New York City
Pacific Northwest & Alaska
Paris
San Francisco

Compass American Guides
Arizona
Canada
Chicago
Colorado
Hawaii
Idaho
Hollywood
Las Vegas

Maine
Manhattan
Montana
New Mexico
New Orleans
Oregon
San Francisco
Santa Fe
South Carolina
South Dakota
Southwest
Texas
Utah
Virginia
Washington
Wine Country
Wisconsin
Wyoming

Fodor's Citypacks
Atlanta
Hong Kong
London
New York City
Paris
Rome
San Francisco
Washington, D.C.

Fodor's Español
California
Caribe Occidental
Caribe Oriental
Gran Bretaña
Londres
Mexico
Nueva York
Paris

Fodor's Exploring Guides
Australia
Boston & New England
Britain
California
Caribbean
China
Egypt
Florence & Tuscany
Florida

France
Germany
Ireland
Israel
Italy
Japan
London
Mexico
Moscow & St. Petersburg
New York City
Paris
Prague
Provence
Rome
San Francisco
Scotland
Singapore & Malaysia
Spain
Thailand
Turkey
Venice

Fodor's Flashmaps
Boston
New York
San Francisco
Washington, D.C.

Fodor's Pocket Guides
Acapulco
Atlanta
Barbados
Jamaica
London
New York City
Paris
Prague
Puerto Rico
Rome
San Francisco
Washington, D.C.

Mobil Travel Guides
America's Best Hotels & Restaurants
California & the West
Frequent Traveler's Guide to Major Cities
Great Lakes
Mid-Atlantic

Northeast
Northwest & Great Plains
Southeast
Southwest & South Central

Rivages Guides
Bed and Breakfasts of Character and Charm in France
Hotels and Country Inns of Character and Charm in France
Hotels and Country Inns of Character and Charm in Italy
Hotels and Country Inns of Character and Charm in Paris
Hotels and Country Inns of Character and Charm in Portugal
Hotels and Country Inns of Character and Charm in Spain

Short Escapes
Britain
France
New England
Near New York City

Fodor's Sports
Golf Digest's Best Places to Play
Skiing USA
USA Today The Complete Four Sport Stadium Guide

Fodor's Vacation Planners
Great American Learning Vacations
Great American Sports & Adventure Vacations
Great American Vacations
Great American Vacations for Travelers with Disabilities
National Parks and Seashores of the East
National Parks of the West

WHEREVER YOU TRAVEL, *H*ELP IS NEVER FAR AWAY.

From planning your trip to providing travel assistance along the way, **American Express®** Travel Service Offices are always there to help.

Belize

Belize Global Travel Services Ltd. (R)
41 Albert Street
Belize City
2/77 185

Guatemala

Banco del Cafe, S.A. (R)
Avenida de la Reforma 9-30, Zona 9
1er Nivel – Torre Del Pais
Guatemala City
2/311 311

Clark Tours (R)
Torre 11, Nivel - 107
Diagonal 6, 10-65, Zona 10
Guatemala City
2/392 877

Travel

http://www.americanexpress.com/travel